RELIGION AND POLITICS
IN PAKISTAN Published Under the
Auspices of *The Near Eastern Center*

University of California

Los Angeles

Religion and politics in pakistan

BY LEONARD BINDER

UNIVERSITY OF CALIFORNIA
PRESS, *Berkeley and Los Angeles*

1963

UNIVERSITY OF CALIFORNIA PRESS
BERKELEY AND LOS ANGELES, CALIFORNIA

CAMBRIDGE UNIVERSITY PRESS
LONDON, ENGLAND

© 1961 BY THE REGENTS OF THE UNIVERSITY OF CALIFORNIA
SECOND PRINTING, 1963
LIBRARY OF CONGRESS CATALOG CARD NUMBER: 61–7537
DESIGNED BY MARION JACKSON SKINNER

To Yona and Naava

Preface

A little over five years ago I left Karachi with a gnawing feeling of unfulfillment. I had spent nearly a year reading and talking about this idea of an Islamic constitution which so many Pakistanis seemed to hold dear, and which seemed so consistently to elude them. The true issues and protagonists were learned only slowly, and by the time I had grasped the nub of the thing, the first Constituent Assembly had been dissolved and the former president, Iskandar Mirza, then minister of interior, was speaking about "guided democracy." It was a strange situation, for the religionists had won a great battle in the draft constitution of 1954 only to find that a genuinely Islamic constitution, in the sense of a legal formula, had no bearing on the critical problems facing Pakistan. That legal formula neither solved them nor resolved them into less critical issues.

At that time, I thought the constitutional controversy an incident, albeit lengthy, not yet completed. Now more than five years later I know that it is not yet ended and perhaps never will be. In a way, these days are similar to those. Parliamentary government has been suppressed and has been blamed for much. A constitution which many thought Islamic has been suspended. In April, 1953, in November, 1954, and in November, 1958, it seemed as though secularism had won the day.

Twice this expectation was denied, but what does the future hold for this third event? Will this third experience be definitive? It seems to me that issues of this kind are not resolved in a generation or two, nor is it given to us to understand and predict from our reading and talking and our prying forth of documents. Our accomplishments are much smaller.

First and deceptively simple in appearance is the task of telling what happened and explaining its circumstances. Explaining its circumstances—this I think is the more formidable, for this book deals with a small group of dependent variables among a multitude of mutually interdependent ones. To explain circumstances is to explain everything. Instead, the setting of federalism in Pakistan has been chosen to frame the issues of Islamic constitutionalism. Other matters are also brought in: the available evidence of Jinnah's and Liaqat Ali Khan's policies was pieced together, some aspects of foreign affairs are considered, and personalities are brought in where relevant.

Among the people I talked to in Pakistan was a clerk at the Public Information Office who edited a religious biweekly in his spare time. He asked me what I was doing in Karachi and I tried, as helplessly as one always does under those circumstances, not to seem to be foolishly wasting time according to his Punjab University standards. Perhaps I failed, but I found myself telling him that of the three major ideas of an Islamic constitution each had been written into one of the three successive drafts of the constitution of Pakistan. Thus was established the form of this study: first to set forth these three theories and then to show how they were written into the constitutional documents. As I worked along on this exercise in the personification of ideas, I realized that some very sincere and religious persons had changed their views during the long and complex constituent process. It was also clear that the causes of this ideological shift were not wholly intellectual.

With this added dimension the study took its final shape in three parts set in a loose chronological framework, in a tighter logical framework for the explication of related ideological elements, and in still a tighter framework for the empirical demonstration of the impact of politics upon Islamic ideology in Pakistan.

This study is primarily concerned with the conflicting theories of the nature of an Islamic state, the manner in which they were stated, and the process by which they were altered. Attention has been concentrated upon the views of those who actually participated, whether directly or indirectly, in drawing up a constitution for Pakistan. The views of the 'ulamā', of the politicians, and of an organization known as the Jamā'at-i-Islāmi were the only ones that have been continually effective from 1947 to the present. The views of the civil service and the military have only recently been brought to bear with some force upon these issues. Popular writers have had no success in calling attention to their ideas of an Islamic state, and ordinary laymen have been completely ignored. Though the overwhelming majority of Pakistanis agree that Pakistan ought to have an Islamic constitution, the difficulty in the communication of ideas has prevented any particular theory from gaining ascendancy with the public. The resultant situation both encouraged and required compromise on the part of the religious interests. The politicians were, however, deeply divided on the issue of the distribution of legislative power among the provinces and on the issue of provincial autonomy. In order to strengthen their own position various groups of politicians were at least willing, if not compelled, to compromise with the 'ulamā'.

The first three chapters deal with the original theoretical orientation of the 'ulamā', the politicians, and the Jamā'at-i-Islāmi. The 'ulamā' tend to equate the political recognition of their own institution with the establishment of Islam. The politicians tend to equate British parliamentarism and Islam by means of a misinterpretation of the doctrine of consensus. The Jamā'at-i-Islāmi wishes to reëstablish something like the orthodox caliphate.

The following four chapters describe the manner in which expression was given to these varying points of view. Basic differences of opinion were glossed over in the equivocal statement of aims and objects resolved upon by the Constituent Assembly. These differences were more clearly revealed in the subsequent work of the constitutional committee. A theoretically inconsistent compromise was then achieved.

The final portion of the work describes the failure of this compromise and the manner in which a more consistent agreement was reached. The core of this agreement was contained in the provision empowering the Supreme Court to invalidate all acts of the legislature which are repugnant to the Qur'ān and Sunnah.

Though political disagreements stimulated the process of a religious compromise, the lack of political agreement continued to affect the religious agreement once achieved. The attempt of a group of East Bengal politicians, who held control over an unrepresentative Constituent Assembly, to force their views into the constitution, brought a strong reaction. Moreover, the excessive play upon religious sentiments by the politicians led to certain disorders which disquieted the civil service, and brought the whole idea of an Islamic constitution into disrepute with this class. The Assembly was dissolved and the draft constitution discarded along with the agreed formula for safeguarding Islamic law in Pakistan.

The events of the years following have been important for Pakistan and for Islamic constitutionalism, but for the latter, 1954 was a watershed. Since that time no really new ideas have come forward and shifts in legal formulations have been more closely related to calculations of expediency. The scene of the drama has changed, too, and the specific provisions of Islamic law rather than its theoretical foundations are now the principal issues. Religion and politics still affect each other in Pakistan, but the constitutional issue has borne all the fruit of which it was capable. That fruit was more than might have been expected, for in no other country were the central issues so well brought out.

The most important of the materials used in this study were the official but unpublished reports of the work of the various constitutional committees. The positions taken by the 'ulamā' were published in the form of amendments and suggestions at various times, but it was found that personal interviews with some of the leading 'ulamā' were indispensable for properly understanding this material. The political differences between the various groups within the Muslim League were elucidated by reference to various party records. In most instances, officials of the League were coöperative in permitting copies to be made or taken, and often enough interviews were granted as well. Officials of the Jamā'at-i-Islāmi were most anxious to make their organization known; and they gave freely of their time to describe its history, its structure, and its goals. Most of the publications of the Jamā'at have appeared in English, Arabic, and Urdu. Since the key to understanding each proposal is to place it in its chronological context and to relate it to a dynamic process, much attention was paid to the daily press and periodical publications.

All Arabic words, except those commonly appearing in English, have been transliterated, as have been the names of authors of classical works. Other names have been retained as they appear in official documents. The titles of books and the names of authors and places of publication have not been changed. Quoted texts have similarly not been changed. A few common Urdu renderings of Arabic have also been retained. Except where otherwise noted, I am responsible for all translation.

In surveying this study I am continuously reminded of the great contributions, both intellectual and informational, that others have made to it. If there is any merit in this work, they are largely responsible for it. In mentioning a very few of them I must absolve them of any responsibility for knowledge of the way in which I have used their teachings, advice, and suggestions. This study was first suggested by Professor L. V. Thomas of Princeton University, whose lectures on Turkish history demonstrated the contemporaneous importance of Islamic constitutional issues for non-Arab Muslims. The research was supported by the Ford Foundation for three years, one at Oxford University, one in Pakistan, and one at Harvard University. For whatever knowledge I have gained of Islamic political thought, I am profoundly indebted to Professor H. A. R. Gibb, formerly Laudian Professor of Arabic at Oxford and now University Professor at Harvard. For encouragement, searching criticism, and many helpful suggestions, I am grateful to Professor Rupert Emerson of Harvard. Professor Gustave E. Von Grunebaum, Director of the Near Eastern Center at UCLA, read the final version of the manuscript and urged that it be published.

I must apologize for not mentioning all of those who helped me in Pakistan. I am astonished even now when I think of how many Pakistanis gave me both their friendship and assistance. I know that some will be disappointed in the opinions expressed in what follows, but I hope they will agree on the facts of the case. For special thanks I would like to single out Professor Abdul Bari, Mr. Yusuf Quraishi, Mufti Muhammad Shafi, Maulana Ihtisham al-Haqq Thanvi, Maulana Abdul

Hamid Badauni, Mssrs. Ghulam Muhammad and Khurshid Ahmad of the Jamā'at-i-Islāmi, Mr. Husain Imam, Mr. Nurul Amin, Khwaja Nazimuddin, Maulana Tamizuddin Khan, and Chaudhri Khaliquzzaman. Above all, I must express my thanks to Maulana Zafar Ahmad Ansari whose house was always open to me and whose knowledge of the problems involved was matched only by his willingness to educate and assist me. He has waited a long time to see the fruit of many hours of discussion and explanation; but he knows that man's true reward is not on this earth, so I hope that he, and others too, will forgive the shortcomings of this work.

Finally I would like to thank my wife who not only encouraged me throughout the long process of research and writing, but also helped with the research, typed the earlier drafts, and criticized them as only one trained in the exact sciences could.

As this preface was written before the final editing of the book, I would like to take the opportunity provided by this second printing to express my gratitude to Mr. James Kubeck of the University of California Press for an outstanding job accomplished largely while I was in the field.

L. B.

Contents

PART TWO: SUBSTANTIATION

PART ONE

Orientation

Abbreviations

BPC	Basic Principles Committee
C.A.P.	Constituent Assembly of Pakistan
NWFP	North-West Frontier Province
PML	Pakistan Muslim League
PRODA	Public and Representative Officers (Disqualification) Act, 1949
UNCIP	United Nations Commission for India and Pakistan

Introduction to Part One

Pakistan came into being as a result of the increasing democratization and Indianization of the government of India in the face of the peculiar geographic distribution of the Muslim population, its cohesiveness, and its fear of Hindu domination. There were three politically significant aspects of the geographical distribution of the Muslim population of India: (1) the majority of the Muslim population was concentrated in two areas, thus making partition feasible; (2) these two areas are separated by about a thousand miles of Indian territory, making their union in a single state all but impractical; and (3) these two areas were among the least developed in all India.

The degree of inner unity among Indian Muslims may be gauged by the fact that a single state was created out of these two widely separated territories, but the cohesiveness of any society is partly a function of external factors. In this case the exclusiveness of Hindu society, its caste system, and its rapid adjustment to British rule were perhaps more important than any theoretical inner unity. The gradual devolution of imperial power to the developing Indian democracy, wherein the numerical superiority of the Hindus was approximately three to one, gave rise to a not unnatural apprehension regarding the status of Muslims and Islam in an Indian nation-state.

Originally, the Aligarh movement and later the Pakistan Muslim League opposed both Indian nationalism and its democratic extension, but with the spread of these ideas in Asia during and after the First World War, Muslims and Hindus joined forces to strive for independence. Separate electorates, the reservation of legislative seats, and the demarcation of new Muslim majority provinces were substituted for reliance upon the imperial power to maintain the political status of the large Muslim minority. The inevitable inadequacy of such constitutional safeguards under a system of majority rule gradually manifested itself with each increase in political autonomy, until absolute Muslim independence was demanded.

To support the demand for independence the Muslims elaborated a two-nation theory. The second Indian nation was simply defined as the Muslims of the subcontinent, a definition that runs contrary to the generally accepted concept of nationality—whereon the right to statehood is supposed to rest. Progressing logically from this difficult position, the Muslim League begged the nationalist question in demanding a separate state so that Indian Muslims might live in accordance with Islam. It was only when the League reached this point, and when full independence was in the offing, that their program had a general appeal to the Muslim masses and to some of the 'ulamā'.

Islamic government, Islamic state, and Islamic constitution were the slogans of the last years of empire and the first of independence; but no one was quite sure what they meant. Sometimes the leaders of the Muslim League admitted that the

Islamic spirit of Pakistan was yet to reveal itself. More often, however, they spoke as if they knew exactly what sort of state was required by the prescripts of Islam. Emphasis upon the evolution of Islamic principles, and the experimental nature of Pakistan as an Islamic state was really an answer to the insistence of the 'ulamā' that the nature of an Islamic state was already known, or knowable, in accordance with the established legal system of traditional Islam. The fact is, though, that neither the politicians nor the 'ulamā' had any definite plan when independence suddenly came upon them.

The intense, emotionally charged expectations of the people of the cities and towns of Pakistan drove both the politicians and the 'ulamā' to improvise, and provided new scope for lay apologists to romanticize the principles of Islamic polity. In the event, all failed to inspire the confidence or to nourish the hopeful courage with which the people of Pakistan originally faced independence. The failure of the intelligentsia of Pakistan is owing in part to various insuperable political and economic problems, but also to the nearly complete lack of expenditure of any intellectual effort on the problem of Islamic government before partition.

The need to provide the country with a constitution forced politicians and 'ulamā' alike to apply themselves to this problem, and the solutions they offered are not without interest, practical as well as academic. The issue at stake was not so much the limited one of providing a constitution for an Islamic state or for Pakistan, as one of uniting the intelligentsia of a Muslim country in their understanding and application to practical circumstances of certain aspects of Islamic legal theory and theology. The practical form that the constitution making process gave to the intellectual controversy between traditionalists and modernists determined that both should state their positions with a clarity not to be found elsewhere. Similar controversies continue in nearly every Muslim country, and a large number of these have had to work out constitutions for themselves in the recent past; but nowhere has the element of democratic nationalism been so weak, the desire for an Islamic constitution so generally admitted, and the cleavage between the Western educated and the 'ulamā' so wide. Over the last fourteen years the interaction of the politicians and the 'ulamā' was continuous. Points of view as well as tactics changed. In the course of time and after some experience, the central issues came to be dealt with as nowhere else in the Muslim world.

These central issues of the nature of an Islamic state and the elaboration of institutions suitable thereto are matters of political theory, religious conscience, and practical wisdom. The resolution of these matters is, however, the subject of politics, properly so taken. It may be a matter of regret to the more devout that the pejorative "politics" should be applied to the constituent process of an Islamic state, but in quite another sense there is no more political an activity than framing a constitution. What is actually deplored in the connotation of the word politics is that there is a serious disagreement among various Pakistanis on the nature of an Islamic state. That the nature of this disagreement was revealed during the constituent process, and that no single view emerged completely victorious testifies to the political character of this process. That most of the groups involved in this political process are willing to abide by its results substantiates its utility.

In analyzing Islamic constitutional developments in Pakistan, we are primarily concerned with the growth and change of a living system of beliefs. The constituent process in Pakistan has been inordinately long (as these things go), but alterations in a variety of conceptions of the Islamic ideal which were necessary to the successful conclusion of this process occurred within an astonishingly brief period (as those things go). Consequently, it is of interest to understand not only the nature of these changes but also the manner in which these changes came about. The latter problem must lead us away from the sublime to the mundane, and demonstrates the organic relationship of law, political theory, and politics.

The political struggle which focused upon the place of Islam in Pakistan did not often manifest itself in terms of conflicts between well-defined interest groups contending for well-defined values or economic benefits. Since we are concerned with a constituent process, there is no doubt of the centrality of such issues as what kind of power would be legitimized by the constitution, or which groups would share that power. However, the major issue was one of *Weltanschauung,* and the most important result was a partial bridging of the gap between the traditional and the Westernized outlooks.

The groups involved in this process are not well defined, yet the persons of influence who participated may be roughly categorized in terms of both outlook and social position. Four important points of view were expressed in the constituent process in Pakistan: a traditional view, a modernist view, a fundamentalist approach, and a secularist orientation. In addition to these four views, and sometimes comprehending aspects of all of them, is a diffuse Islamic romanticism that is widely prevalent in Pakistan, but not so much among influential persons. One might say that nearly all the participants in the constituent process were romantics until they were compelled to choose among specific formulas.

Generally speaking, these points of view are adhered to by four loosely organized social groupings. The traditional view is almost exclusively that of the 'ulamā', who are not only the upholders of tradition but also identify the establishment of Islam with recognition of their own institution. The modernist view is held by most of the politicians, Westernized business-

men, and many professionals in Pakistan. There is an obvious
connection between the modernist and romantic positions.
Both are founded on the assumption that Islam comprehends
all that is good in the West, including democracy, and both
insist that Islam is adaptable to "modern conditions of life";
but the modernist approach insists upon the legal doctrine of
consensus as the basis of both Islamic democracy and adapta-
bility. Hence the modernist would institutionalize the legal
doctrine of consensus in a legislative assembly.

Some objection may be raised against the use of the term
politicians to denote a social grouping, and there are certain
distinctions that may be made among these people. The political leaders of West Pakistan are landowners of substantial
means or princes of various degrees of nobility, those of East
Pakistan are more often lawyers, teachers, or members of other
middle-class professions, and those who migrated from central
India include some of both these categories and a small contingent of industrial and commercial families. Nevertheless,
these three regional elites are remarkably homogeneous in their
education and political socialization, and even their economic
interests are tending to become more rather than less diffused.
In any case, the conflicts among them are not with regard to
the nature of an Islamic state.

There is only one important fundamentalist group in Pakistan, the Jamā'at-i-Islāmi, but its supporters and sympathizers
seem to be drawn from the traditional middle class, the students, and those who have failed to enter into the modern
middle class despite achieving the bachelor's degree. The
bazaar merchants generally support the traditional elites, but
with their intuitive sense for the preservation of their interests
are often in financial support of the Jamā'at.

The secularists are small in number, but extremely powerful
since they are the most highly Westernized and are often found

in important positions in the civil service and the military. The small but growing group of industrialists in Pakistan tend to fall into the latter category.

In Part I of this study the first three of these ideological orientations are described in terms that are as concrete as possible. Each is related to a specific group: tradition to the 'ulamā', ijmā' modernism to the Muslim League leadership, and fundamentalism to the Jamā'at-i-Islāmi. The treatment of the 'ulamā' and tradition is prefaced by a brief discussion of Islamic political thought; the doctrines of the ijmā' modernists are related to the growth of the Pakistan movement in India, and the elaboration of the views of Maududi of the Jamā'at-i-Islāmi are related to the early postpartition religious ferment, so that our preliminary discussion of the major ideological orientations also serves as an historical introduction. The secularist point of view has not been stated in ideological terms but is revealed in the actions of various highly placed persons. The remainder of the study continues the chronological framework, so these actions are discussed where relevant.

1 *Tradition*

Any practical application of the body of social and historical experience known as Islam to the government of a modern society must contend with the accumulated and rationalized expression of that experience as personified by the 'ulamā'. It is sometimes asserted that the conception of Islam held by the 'ulamā' has been unchanged in thirteen hundred years, and that the decline of Muslim power and creativity is owing to such intellectual stagnation. For many the modern age has put Islam to the test. Either it must adapt, or rather be adapted, or lose its hold on the minds and hearts of men.

This is not only the view of the opponents of the 'ulamā', but, in its essence, of the 'ulamā' themselves. Naturally, the 'ulamā' reject the "stagnation thesis," nevertheless they insist that Islam has not and cannot change for it is based on the eternal word of God. If Muslim power has declined, it is because Muslims have not been true to Islam.

By contrast to the conflicting modernist and traditionalist conceptions of Islam as religious and social doctrine, the modernists tend to stress and the 'ulamā' to disregard classical

Islamic political theory. Actually, theory is not so good a term to describe what is in reality a body of expository and polemical literature on the legal attributes of the caliphate. In any case, the 'ulamā' are concerned with law and not theory. The only reason that they may distinguish between classical constitutional law and, say, personal status law, is because the former has not been applied for a millennium. The most significant aspect of the traditional position is that it *has* adapted itself to prevailing circumstances throughout history. The modernist position differs in that it rejects the political adaptation of Islam in the past, and in many instances disagrees with the specific legal and social doctrines preserved thereby.

Three important points are to be kept in mind during the following discussion of the traditionalist position. The first is the unity of religion and politics in Islam; the second is the overwhelmingly legalistic outlook of the 'ulamā'; and the third is the inaccuracy of the "stagnation thesis."

The unity of religion and politics in Islam is neither unique nor unnatural. The invocation of religious sanction in the legitimate exercise of political power has never been absent from Western practice, but the religious functions of government have dwindled as a result of the breakdown of the institutionalization of political power and the growth of its individualization in the medieval feudal nobility. This development was even more marked in the breakdown of the caliphate and the transfer of political power to military adventurers. Although the orthodox theory of the religious character of government was never successfully denied, there gradually developed a distinct division of function and social class between the holders of power and the knowers and interpreters of the law. The separation of religion and government in Muslim states means, in effect, the minimization of the influence of the 'ulamā'.

The legalistic outlook of the 'ulamā' stems from their conception of Islam. The modernists may assert that Islam lays
down only certain general principles of social conduct, but the
'ulamā' insist that God has not left His servants without guidance even in the most minor of their everyday acts. The importance of this emphasis on law, for our present purposes,
depends upon current notions in Pakistan of what a constitution is supposed to be. The whole development of self-government in India, and the impact of direct rule in British India
has tended to develop great respect for the efficacy of positive
law. As is most often true in colonial territories, Pakistani politicians are for the most part holders of degrees in law. Consequently, insofar as this Westernized elite is concerned, a
constitution is a legal document. The 'ulamā', however, have
their own conception of the nature of law. Thus it developed
that the 'ulamā' and the politicians dealt with what each considered to be their own functional sphere, but each started from
entirely different premises.

The inaccuracy of the "stagnation thesis" must be noted in
order to properly understand the preferences and tactics of the
'ulamā'. If we are not aware of the changes that have taken
place in orthodox political theory we shall be unable to differentiate between the traditionalists and the fundamentalists
who would go back to the "original" practices of thirteen centuries ago. This is not the place to enter into a lengthy exposition of the development of Islamic political thought, but a
presentation of some of the broad outlines of the development
of orthodox thought may be useful if only to dispel the influence of the "stagnation thesis."

THE STATE, THE COMMUNITY, AND THE 'ULAMĀ'

Beginning with Muhammad the three principles of unity,
continuity, and divine guidance have remained the basis of

all theological assumptions concerning the community of believers. The principal achievement of the Prophet was the
unification of the tribes of Arabia in a great confederation
under the Quraish. Muhammad claimed no innovation in his
divine guidance; he rather imbued his followers with a strong
sense of prophetic continuity.[1] That the crisis following the
death of the Prophet was solved by the creation of the caliphate
rather than by the transfer of the prophethood to another, must
be ascribed to the common sense of Muhammad's teaching and
to the determination of the Quraish to maintain the leadership
of Arabia. The caliphate was devised by the Companions of
the Prophet to maintain the unity of the Arabs, to retain divine
guidance in their government, and to lend both unity and
guidance a new continuity. Throughout its long and varied
history the caliphate was never separated from these three basic
Islamic principles.

These principles determined the scope of the caliph's activity
and his legitimacy, but the functions of the caliph were at first
defined by the traditional functions of the tribal chief. As the
area of Islamic rule rapidly extended itself, administrative organization and procedure were as rapidly adapted from that
prevailing in Byzantine and Sassanian territories. The caliphate,
then, developed somewhat ahead of Islamic law; while the
insistence upon the continuity of divine guidance determined
that this adaptation of imperial practice should be given theological sanction. In point of fact, it was difficult to reconcile
imperial practice in all its aspects with the slowly developing
comprehensiveness of Islamic law. The result was an intellectual compartmentalization, though not a theological separation, of religion and most aspects of administration and politics.[2]

---

[1] H. A. R. Gibb, *Mohammedanism* (London, 1954), p. 59.
[2] See H. A. R. Gibb, "The Social Significance of the Shu'ūbiya," *Studia
Orientalis Ioanni Pedersen* (Wetteren, 1947), pp. 105–114.

The orthodox Islamic political theory which we have today is primarily the product of the Abbasid period. The Abbasid Caliphate, which lasted over five hundred years, was not only heir to the successors of the Prophet, but also to the universal empire of the Sassanians. In the face of political necessity and cultural fusion, Islamic and Iranian principles blended. Unity came to mean strict political unity under a single caliph; divine guidance came to mean divine right; and historical continuity came to mean the hereditary right of the Abbasids to the caliphal throne.[3]

The Sunni jurists of those days labored long to reconcile the principles that motivated the Companions of the Prophet with the threefold claims of Abbasid government. Allegiance to the caliph at Baghdad became the symbol of membership in the community, and the requisite for salvation.[4] Obedience to the incumbent caliph was made obligatory; and the true Muslim was enjoined by some to flee the territory of a usurper.[5] The unity of all Muslims was taken in a concrete political sense.[6]

The Abbasid Caliphate also came to be the medium of divine guidance. Without the existence of the caliph the Muslims could not order their communal affairs in accordance with the will of God. But the orthodox jurists could not bring themselves to accept the doctrine of divine right. An elaborate system of constitutional principles was devised to camouflage

[3] Ignace Goldziher, *Muhammedanische Studien,* Vol. II, p. 101.

[4] Abu Yūsuf, *Kitāb al-Kharāj* (Cairo, 1352), p. 9, lines 14–16.

[5] This is derived from the original flight of the first Muslims. See al-Bāqillāni, *al-Tamhīd* (Cairo, 1947), p. 181, lines 12–16; W. C. Smith, *Modern Islam in India* (2d ed.; London, 1946), p. 202; W. W. Hunter, *Indian Musulmans* (Calcutta, 1945), p. 62.

[6] Al-Baghdādi would, under certain conditions (i.e., those describing the establishment of the Umayyad Caliphate in Spain), permit the existence of two caliphs *Usūl al-Dīn* (Istanbul, 1928), p. 284, line 11.

the painful truth of hereditary succession, without, however, reducing the Abbasid's claim to legitimacy.[7] The divine guidance of the Muslim community was reaffirmed, but within the framework of a new constitutional system. Succession to the caliphate was legitimized only by the consent of the community. Divine right and hereditary succession were both rejected, and the doctrine of consensus in confirmation of the individual judgment (ijtihād) of the caliph became the legal basis of divine guidance.[8]

The principle of historical continuity was derived by the addition of a time dimension to the principle of divine guidance. This conception of the jurists was complicated by the fact that innovation of the caliphate preceded the organization of a complete code of Islamic law. The parallel development of the institution of the caliphate along with the Sharī'a created a tendency to justify historical fact. The alternative was to deny previous divine guidance and present legitimacy. For the jurists, then, the principle of historical continuity was realized by recognizing the legislative character of history itself. Taken in a strictly political sense, this meant the legitimization of those who had actually ruled as caliphs. The constitutional process which the jurists elaborated came to include all of the actual circumstances by which those caliphs rose to power.

The most comprehensive statement of the legalistic theory of the caliphate was that of al-Māwardi. It is to his work and that of his immediate predecessors that we give the name of classical theory in opposition to the traditional theory devised by the 'ulamā' in the post-'Abbasid period. This classical theory, despite its close dependence upon historical circumstances and contemporary theoretical controversies, is essentially unhistori-

---

[7] Al-Māwardi, *al-Aḥkām al-Sulṭāniya* (Cairo, 1909), p. 7, line 20, *et. seq.*
[8] *Ibid.,* p. 7, lines 18, 19.

cal. Al-Māwardi's work culminates the classical period of Islamic political thought, a period that closely coincided with the century of Būwaihid control over the caliphate. The Būwaihids were Shī'ites and they denied the legitimacy of the Abbasid Caliphate, but tolerated the caliph in order to better control their Sunni subjects. Al-Māwardi's theory was another refutation of Shī'ite claims, but more importantly it insisted that the caliph must be an active ruler, and not a figurehead. He also held the opinion that the caliphate was not valid if the person of the caliph became subject to the physical control of one of his generals if that general acted contrary to Islamic law. In the opinion of some, al-Māwardi went further and advocated encouraging the Sunni Saljuqs to defeat the Būwaihids and undertake the protection of the caliphate. The Saljuqs did take Baghdad, but al-Māwardi's hopes were not fulfilled, for even as the Būwaihids failed to establish a Shī'ite caliphate nor recognize the Fāṭimid Caliphate of Egypt, the Saljuqs refused to allow the Abbasid caliphs any autonomy nor even permit them an effective administrative establishment.

The decline of the Abbasid Caliphate made a mockery of imperial theory, it undermined the legal structure of the 'ulamā', and cast a cloud of doubt over these three foundational principles of Islam. The political unity of the Muslim people was broken under the rule of local war lords. Divine guidance was at best in doubt with the caliph subject to the will of the Saljuq sultans. If the actions of the amirs and the sultans were condemned, the legislative character of history must be denied and the entire orthodox conception of historical continuity collapse in a heap.

Al-Ghazali was the first to attempt a reconstruction of Islamic political theory. He retained the caliphate as the focal point of Islamic government, but he reduced the caliph's function to that of a living symbol of unity, divine guidance, and historical continuity.[9] For the imperial ideal of political unity he substituted the goal of spiritual unity. For the imperial idea of divine right he substituted the goal of government in strict accordance with the Sharī'a. And if these goals were attained, political events might once more be justified, and the principle of historical continuity reaffirmed.

Spiritual unity would be achieved if all the amirs and the sultan recognized the right of the Abbasid caliph, and received from him their investiture. The government of the Muslim community might be in accord with the Sharī'a if the opinion of the 'ulamā' was sought on all legal questions. If the government of the Muslims accorded with the Sharī'a they would be divinely guided. Should the sultan recognize the caliph, and the caliph recognize the 'ulamā', there would be no break with the traditional Islamic political system—and the principle of historical continuity might remain.

With the end of the Abbasid Caliphate, orthodox political theory underwent a grave crisis. Until that time the principles of Islamic government had never been separated from their formal representation in the caliphate. Philosophers, jurists, and statesmen all strove to establish a new basis for legitimacy, and a new symbolism, whereby traditional values might be retained. Ibn Khaldūn, the most original of Muslim thinkers, presented a solution which merits our attention. A philosopher of history, he first seized upon the principle of historical continuity. He found in history a divine order based upon the interrelation of social and physical forces. In the regularity and continuity of history he discovered the divine guidance of the Muslim community. He rejected political unity but admitted the spiritual unity of all Muslims. Finally, though he equated the constitutional and the historical processes, he insisted that

---

[9] L. Binder, "al-Ghazāli's Theory of Islamic Government," *The Muslim World* (July, 1955), pp. 229–241.

good government was only that which accorded with the Sharī'a.[10]

According to Ibn Khaldūn, Islamic society, that is, the entire body of Muslims, has no relation to the government of its various parts. That is to say, that Islamic society, as a whole, is not the specific framework for the establishment of a government. For Ibn Khaldūn, the state-community is delineated by natural phenomena, more or less unrelated to the mission of the Prophet.[11] These are tribal groupings, territorial units, cities and their hinterlands, and so on.

In the classical theory, all relations between the community and its government are determined by Islamic law. Thus, the nature of the community as comprised entirely of Muslims continues operative in its legitimate political organization. Ibn Khaldūn, also, considers the factors constituting the community operative in its political organization, but, as a result, he does not consider Islamic law the determining factor in all society-government relations. Specifically, he rejects the classical theory on the method of appointment of the ruler.[12] In other words, for him Islamic law does not apply to this political sphere at all.

In the classical theory, the sphere of validity of the law of the state, in terms of persons, is conterminous with the number of Muslim believers. Ideally, the law of Islam relates only to persons. Its only important territorial references are to Mecca and Medina. Secondarily, Islamic law, and, therefore, the classical state have a territorial aspect: the territorial sphere of validity of both is limited by the areas within the effective

[10] Ibn Khaldūn, *Muqaddimah* (3d ed.; 1900 Beirut, 1900), p. 190, line 10.
[11] *Ibid.*, Part III, chap. 1, p. 154.
[12] *Ibid.* Though the qualifications of the ruler are discussed in Part III, chapter 26, in familiar classical terms, the entire question of the constitutive process is omitted. The bay'a, or oath of allegiance, indicating consent to the selection of the ruler is dealt with in chapter 29.

control of Muslim arms. As a result the personal and territorial spheres do not necessarily coincide. For Ibn Khaldūn, the constitutive factor of government is force. The successful use of such force depends in large measure upon the nature of the community. The interaction of these two determine the personal and territorial spheres of validity of the law of the state or the commands of the ruler.

The temporal sphere of validity, in the classical view, begins with Muhammad, or at least with the first "state" in Medina. It is to continue on until the end of time. During this time, presumably, this state will be the chosen instrument of God, and its territorial and personal scope continually expand. The determining factors are again functions of the way in which the community was first constituted. Muhammad's mission was the last of a series, and his revelation superseded all others. The Islamic state symbolized the final call to mankind for salvation. Ibn Khaldūn explains that the temporal sphere of validity for his government depends upon the technique of governing. The ruling family and its tribal support are the essential characteristics of the state, since it is the power of this group and their success in its use that determine the other characteristics.[13]

But Ibn Khaldūn's theories did not strike root among the 'ulamā'. Petty dynasties could not be accepted as the partial heirs of the great Abbasid Caliphate, nor was the novel way in which these ideas were put at all satisfying to the 'ulamā'. The 'ulamā' themselves sought about for a way of filling the gap created by the end of the Abbasid Caliphate. Out of their efforts the three primary principles of Islamic political thought took on a new guise. Unity became orthodoxy of which the 'ulamā' were the guardians. Divine guidance was transformed into the requirement that the advice of the 'ulamā' be sought

[13] *Ibid.,* p. 163.

on all legal questions. Divine guidance was further assured by applying the infallibility of consensus to the ijmā' (agreement) of the jurists. Historical continuity became taqlīd,[14] and the symbolization of all three principles by the caliphate was changed to their symbolization by the 'ulamā'.

THE REBIRTH OF CLASSICAL THEORY

The rise of the Ottoman Sultanate allowed the revival of older theories alongside of the new.[15] Principally, the notion of political unity was rejoined to the insistence upon Sunni orthodoxy. Continuity again became dynastic as well as theological. Divine guidance remained the special function of the 'ulamā', except in its political manifestation through the legitimacy accorded the Ottoman rulers. The 'ulamā' themselves were for the first time organized into a vague sort of institution, though they had, under previous dynasties, been recognized at court, appointed to official positions, and been richly rewarded for their services. In return, the 'ulamā' staunchly supported the Ottoman government.

The tacit agreement not to probe too deeply into the religious bases of the Ottoman regime was broken with the rise of the Pan-Islamic movement, and the spurious claim that the Ottomans had received the caliphate from the last of the Egyptian Abbasids back in 1518. The possibility of such a reassertion of the classical theory was always present since the 'ulamā' could never bring themselves to reject the applicability of any authoritative judgment, no matter how outdated. Their own attachment to the idea of the immutability of Islamic law would not permit them to deny the sultan's claim to head the religious

[14] *Taqlīd* is the technical term for the principle whereby the opinions of the founders of legal schools, or later consensi, remain valid for succeeding generations.

[15] H. A. R. Gibb and H. Bowen, *Islamic Society and the West,* Vol. I (London, 1951), pp. 34–35.

institution of Islam, for the caliphate, or a caliph, was an "obligatory" institution.[16]

The confusion in Islamic political thought during the latter part of the Ottoman period was as nothing compared to the intellectual distress that accompanied the abolition of the caliphate by Ataturk. Once again unity, divine guidance, and historical continuity were struck a blow from which they have not yet recovered. Despite its long and varied development the classical view remains the most recent and vital development of Islamic political theory. In India the Khilafat movement was a living expression of this almost incredible phenomenon— a fact that caused most of the 'ulamā' of India to reject the idea of Pakistan until the eve of partition. It was not until later that they thought about embodying their ideas on Islamic government in a modern constitution. The theory from which the idea of Pakistan as an Islamic state might be evolved is that of Ibn Khaldūn; but the traditional storehouse of the 'ulamā' can only supply them with the Abbasid theory of the caliphate and the post-Abbasid idea of the function of the 'ulamā'. Typically, the 'ulamā' sought to utilize both these ideas simultaneously, though the latter had come to replace the former in almost every way.

The unfortunate lack of development from which Ibn Khaldūn's work has always suffered continues. His ideas, to the extent that they differ from the classical tradition, are ignored by the 'ulamā'; the politicians and most lay apologists are unacquainted with them. The apologist, whether a modernist, fundamentalist, or traditionalist, harps upon the "natural laws" of Islam; but Ibn Khaldūn's attempt to give religious sanction to the natural laws of his social science is either ignored or abhorred.[17] As a consequence, the problem of dis-

---

[16] Al-Bāqillāni, *op. cit.*, p. 185; al Baghdādi, *op. cit.*, p. 271; al-Māwardi, *op. cit.*, p. 3; Ibn Khaldūn, *op. cit.*, p. 191.

[17] Smith, *op. cit.*, p. 71.

covering some continuity between the classical Islamic state and Pakistan, or some basis of unity between Pakistan and other Muslim countries, is all but insoluble. It will be found that no real attempt was made to deal with these problems of theory. As unimaginable as it may sound, Pakistan was simply equated with the entire Muslim community, and its government, with the caliphate.

THE 'ULAMĀ' AND THE LAW

The idea of making of Pakistan an Islamic state began with the politicians and not the 'ulamā'. The Westernized leaders of the Muslim League had in mind some mutation of European nationalist theory, but the 'ulamā' were obviously incapable of reconciling nationalism and Islam. One can even yet discern a certain discomfort among the 'ulamā' with the whole conception of Pakistan as an Islamic state. They, nevertheless, threw themselves into the task of providing an Islamic constitution for Pakistan even though the premises upon which they based their ideas on the Islamic state must preclude an Islamic constitution for Pakistan as a theoretical impossibility. Classical theory can give no sanction to either the territorial or personal bases of Pakistan, consequently, Islamic theology can give no sanction at all to whatever system of constitutional law may be devised. At best, it is only the 'ulamā'—as in the aftermath of the Abbasid Caliphate—who can give unity, continuity, and divine guidance to that part of the Islamic community which resides in Pakistan. All that is required of the government is that it recognize the institution and function of the 'ulamā'. As will be shown presently, this was in fact the starting position of the 'ulamā'. The attempt to equate the government of Pakistan with the early caliphate was a result of the inspiration of certain brilliant religious fundamentalists, and of the need to come to some sort of agreement with the politicians. It was this necessity that similarly determined that the principles of unity and continuity be relegated to the background, while the major controversy between the politicians and the 'ulamā' centered on the issue of the divine guidance of the government of Pakistan.

The orthodox notion of divine guidance derived its more concrete political overtones from the early struggle between the Alids and the Umayyads. For this reason the political aspect of divine guidance was primarily negative, in the sense of denying the exclusive legitimacy of various Shī'ite exponents. This denial was accomplished by dissociating legitimacy from either heredity or exceptional religious inspiration.[18] As a result, the Muslim community was divinely guided in its selection of rulers, but not by those rulers themselves. The same means by which rulers might be legitimized was the basis upon which the community might be divinely guided. That means is by strict adherence to the Sharī'a, or the Law of Islam.

Islamic legal theory is based upon the immutability and eternal applicability of the law of the Qur'ān, the inspired perfection of the Prophet's behavior, the limited and orderly nature of all earthly phenomena, and the ultimate validity of human reasoning. Jurisprudence, or Fiqh, was the preëminent Islamic science. All law is preëxisting and eternal. Right and wrong are known by revelation (Qur'ān) and through reports handed down by tradition of the sayings and doings of the Prophet (hadīth). If, indeed, new situations should arise, they will be found upon examination to fit into already known categories so that, by the application of human reason, suitable legal decisions can be made (qiyās). Once a decision has become generally accepted (ijmā'), it is final for all time; for, logically, a thing cannot be both right and wrong; there is no temporal limitation to the validity of the law of God or the

[18] Al-Bāqillāni, *op. cit.,* p, 186, *ult.;* al Baghdādi, *op. cit.,* p. 278, *primo.*

power of human reason. Since the fountainhead of all moral
law is thirteen centuries in the past, it follows that the older
a decision, the more correct it is. The great faith of Islamic
jurists in the power of human reason was limited. To properly
practice the "Science of Right and Wrong" one must first be
trained to understand its sources and rigid methodology.
Reason was not allowed free play but it must conform to a
rigidly logical system of deriving analogous judgments. Without the proper training a man could not aspire to become one
of the 'ulamā', that is, one of those who *know* the law.

The development of schools of law and the granting of a
special status to decisions, based upon the agreement of the
majority of the members of a school, or the agreement of two
or more schools, was not surprising. Such agreements, known
generally as ijmā', or consensus, now form a source of law,
second only to the Qur'ān and Sunnah (i.e., the content of
hadīth). The opinions of acknowledged legal authorities and
the precedents set by the judgments of certain caliphs were
taken as decisive, regarding certain points of law, in a manner
not unlike other legal systems.

It was this highly elaborated system of law that was to be
the mechanism whereby the 'ulamā' could fulfill the function
of the traditional caliphate. So long as the Muslim community
adhered to the law of God, they would be divinely guided;
but that guidance would not be directly related to the actual
governments under which Muslims lived. The legitimacy of the
government of Muslim states would depend upon the guarantee of conditions under which such law could be observed, and
not upon any specific provision of that law itself. Various
theorists differed over the extent to which the government
was subject to Islamic law, but all agreed that it was far more
important to preserve Muslim society and its distinctive way of
life, than to endanger the unity of that community and the
ordered practice of religious duties, by encouraging resistance

against an impious ruler. As knowers of the law, the 'ulamā'
took from the government its responsibility for the moral well-
being of the Muslims. And to the extent that this group is
sprung from the heart of the community itself, a large measure
of individual moral responsibility was returned to ordinary
believers.

THE INSTITUTION OF THE 'ULAMĀ'

The rigidity of the traditional conception of Islamic law,
stemming from the Islamic idea of the purpose of revelation
and the notion of law as an exact science, was counterbalanced
by the lack of a rigid hierarchy in the institution of the
'ulamā'. Anyone who studies the law can be an 'alim. Official
appointments to judgeships (qaḍī) were insisted upon as the
proper method for the establishment of Islam; but the 'ulamā'
so appointed were not necessarily the most influential part of
the institution nor even the most respected. The institution
has its own momentum, its own method of raising and recognizing leaders, and its own system of honors. The mainspring
of the mechanism, based upon the idea that everything was
known and well ordered in a distant period when the Prophet
and his Companions lived, was the idea of discipleship. Human
reason was much respected, but it was, after all, a known and
constant factor in the science of law. It could be made to operate in the correct way only if supplied with the correct data.
The further the individual 'alim was removed from the
Prophet, the less was his knowledge of the intention of Muhammad. The peculiar circumstances surrounding each revealed judgment, or each action of the Prophet, could only be
known from sources closer to the period of revelation. Strict
acceptance of earlier authority, or taqlīd, thus became the
dominant characteristic and the organizational framework of
the institution of the 'ulamā'.

Differing legal tendencies did develop in the form of schools and subschools or regional variants, each with its own chain of authority. Disagreement in minor points of law is not frowned upon in strictly traditional circles so much as is the exercise of individual judgment (ijtihād) to settle controversial points. One should follow his own chosen school or tendency strictly and use his science only for the purpose of applying known principles to new situations by means of discovering legal parallels. Ijtihād was the prerogative of the founders of schools alone; the gate of ijtihād is now closed. To alter the decisions that have been accepted for ages would be to deny the eternal immutability of God's law, and to admit that earlier jurists erred would be to destroy the idea of the continuity of the divine guidance of the Muslim community.

The 'ulamā' of Pakistan are the bearers of the legal and political tradition that has been briefly described. This tradition is still a living tradition; its exponents are both vocal and influential. They are frequently attacked for their conservatism, and as often blamed for the backwardness of Muslim peoples, but their support is continually sought by those who depend upon the votes of the people for their office.

The politicians have not found it easy to manipulate the 'ulamā', for the two groups do not fully understand one another. The politician, with his half-digested Western conceptions and his romantic belief in the superiority of an Islam of which he is ignorant, does not know where he is heading, he knows only that he does not want to remain where he is. Progress, experiment, development—even revolution—are the stock words of the politician, but the 'alim, with his static view of the universe, has not even the sense of time to understand what these mean.

The 'ulamā' are unappreciative of change, their function after all is to preserve, to maintain, and to renew the unity, the continuity, and the divine guidance of the Muslim community.

Circumstances during the past several years have forced them to accept changes and to do so in an unequivocal manner (this is important because it goes contrary to the tendency of never rejecting any generally accepted earlier decision) through such unheard of time-saving devices as conferences, conventions, and committees. Decisions by representatives of nearly all schools have been made in days rather than generations. The 'ulamā' are proud of the unanimity they have thus demonstrated, but one has the feeling that they have been somewhat ruffled by the unprecedented necessity of setting dates and learning the rudiments of parliamentary procedure.

The 'ulamā' are, however, human; and many do enjoy a sense of power or public recognition. Because they are disorganized, and because no school will fully accept the leadership of an exponent of a differing tendency, the number of potential leaders is legion. There is, furthermore, a traditional tendency among them to confuse the establishment of Islam with patronizing the 'ulamā', but lacking a hierarchy the choice of 'ulamā' to represent the institution remains with the politicians. The chosen group will always have its rivals, but for the bulk of the institution as for the mass of Muslims they must be the focal point of all religious pressure.

Religious pressure is focused upon the 'ulamā' who have been recognized by the politicians because they are, collectively, the point of contact between the 'ulamā' and the government. In every other way the 'ulamā' see themselves as standing between the government and the community. They are, of course, primarily concerned with the religious well-being of the community, and in their activity the government may either help or hinder. When the government is to be persuaded in some policy, it is only through the 'ulamā' of its choice that this may be accomplished. As a rule, the 'ulamā' will not appeal to the people "over the heads" of the government. The reasons for their predilection for "lobbying" tactics are deeply rooted in a tradition that accepts government as given, that does not fully recognize the moral responsibility of the individual, dreads civil disorder, and is reluctant, at best, in its attitude toward democracy.

A fairly recent phenomenon arising out of the intensely political atmosphere of Imperial India was the organization of the 'ulamā'. The only important organization of this type before partition was the Jamī'at-al-'Ulamā'-i-Hind, comprised mostly of Deobandi [19] 'ulamā'. This group was imbued with a heritage of opposition to British rule. It coöperated closely with the Indian National Congress which helped in its organization at the time of the Khilafat agitation,[20] and it opposed the Muslim League right up to partition.

In view of the extreme difference in outlook between the 'ulamā' and Muslim politicians it is not at all surprising that the Muslim League failed to win the confidence of the religious institution. What is surprising is that they did manage to get the support of a group of 'ulamā'. Until the political reforms of 1935, that is, until a fairly large measure of popular electoral support was needed, the League made little or no attempt to win over the 'ulamā'. At that time the League could do no more than recognize the authority of the Jamī'at-al-'Ulamā'-i-Hind in "matters of a purely religious character."[21] Unilateral efforts such as this by the Muslim League Parliamentary Board in 1936 brought no results. Of course, the League did have a few supporters among the 'ulamā' but they were neither influential among their own number nor among the Muslim

---

[19] Deoband is the location of the most famous Indian Academy of theology and Islamic jurisprudence. For further information see Smith, *op. cit.,* pp. 293 ff.

[20] Smith, *op. cit.,* p. 199.

[21] Raghib Ahsan, "Mechanism of Aiwan and Diwan for an Iqbalian State," *Islamic Literature* (Jan.-Feb., 1955), p. 7.

masses. Some of this support was found among the Bareilly [22] group of 'ulamā', if anything, a more conservative group than the Deobandis with whom they have strong doctrinal and personal differences.

The claim of the Muslim League to be the sole representative of the entire Muslim community in India was gravely weakened by the opposition of the most important group of Indian 'ulamā'. After the elections of 1936 even greater efforts were made to win over the 'ulamā', this time on the Pakistan platform and the slogan of an Islamic state. Moderate success attended these efforts in the sense that the idea of self-determination for the Muslims of India was accepted by the 'ulamā', though they did not accept the League itself.[23] The prospect of new elections at the end of the war was the signal for an even greater effort on the part of the League on the now-wavering 'ulamā'. The League and the idea of Pakistan had increased greatly in popularity by 1945 so that the conditions for success were in fact greater than ever before.

Contact with certain of the more prominent 'ulamā' and religious leaders, such 'as Maulana Maududi of the Jamā'at-i-Islāmi, was made through Maulana Zafar Ahmad Ansari who served as office secretary of the All-Indian Muslim League, secretary of the Parliamentary Board, and of the Committee of Action.[24] Ansari's main target was Maulana Madani, the head of the Deoband Academy, and the president of Jamī'at-al-'Ulamā'-i-Hind, but he could not win him over. The first important 'alim who was successfully persuaded to accept at face value the League's "two-nation" theory and its idea of an Islamic state was Maulana Shabbir Ahmad Usmani, one of the

[22] Bareilly is the site of a school with an older tradition than that of Deoband. *Barelvi* is the Urdu adjective. See Smith, *op. cit.*, pp. 293 ff.
[23] Smith, *op. cit.*, p. 270.
[24] Interviews.

senior teachers at Deoband.[25] The Pir of Manki Sharif in North-West Frontier Province, a much respected divine, was won over in connection with the referendum in that province, and had much to do with the victory of the Muslim League at the polls.[26] To make up for the lack of support from eminent religious figures in the Punjab, ordinary politicians were given important religious titles,[27] but in East Bengal, Usmani's influence was extemely effective in winning over the 'ulamā' to the support of the Muslim League. In November, 1945, the League's proselytization among the 'ulamā' had proceeded well enough to permit the calling of a convention in Calcutta.[28] At this convention the Jamī'at-al-'Ulamā'-i-Islām was founded, and Maulana Shabbir Ahmad Usmani was elected as its first president though he was himself absent from the meeting.

Most of the 'ulamā' who attended the Calcutta meeting were Deobandis, and the leadership there chosen was similarly oriented. The 'Ulamā'-i-Islām was therefore a dissident group of the pro-Congress 'Ulamā'-i-Hind. The outcome of the meeting was distinctly favorable to the Muslim League, though the few Bareilly 'ulamā' from whom the League had received a sort of tentative support in the past were dissatisfied. Maulana Abdul Hamid Badauni attempted to establish yet a third organization of 'ulamā' at a meeting in Banaras early in 1946, but he was not successful.

Partition had the same effect upon the organization of the 'ulamā' as it had upon numerous other communal groups. The

[25] For some particulars of Usmani's career see *C.A.P. Debates,* Vol. VI, no. 1 (Dec. 22, 1949), pp. 1–4.

[26] See A. Campbell-Johnson, *Mission with Mountbatten* (London, 1951), pp. 77, 80; M. S. W. Sharma, *Peeps into Pakistan* (Patna, 1954), p. 125, for non-Muslim points of view.

[27] *Report to the Court of Inquiry Constituted Under Punjab Act II of 1954 to Enquire into the Punjab Disturbances of 1953* (2d ed.; Lahore, 1954), p. 255 (hereafter cited as *Punjab Disturbances*).

[28] Interviews.

leadership of the pro-Pakistan 'ulamā' found themselves forced
to leave their homes and their sources of income, and to migrate
from central India to the less advanced areas that fell to
Pakistan. Many of their followers stayed behind while the
organizational machinery of the Jamī'at fell apart. Maulana
Usmani went to Karachi, and stayed with a locally influential
politician. Usmani summoned Mufti Muhammad Shafi, a close
associate of his at Deoband, to Karachi, while other 'ulamā'
who had already settled in the area, notably Maulana Ihtishamul Haqq Thanvi, gathered around him. Zafar Ahmad Ansari
remained in close association with this group.

Maulana Badauni and other Barelvi 'ulamā' also came to
Pakistan shortly after partition. Within a few months after his
arrival, Badauni found conditions suitable for organizing the
Barelvi group which seemed to have been somewhat more
numerous in the less advanced parts of India. In any case, the
Jamī'at-al'Ulamā'-i-Pākistān was founded in the first part of
1948 in Karachi. These two groups, the 'Ulamā'-i-Islām and the
'Ulamā'-i-Pākistān, remain the only organizations of genuine
'ulamā' in Pakistan. The 'Ulamā'-i-Islām were the recipients of
official patronage from the government, and Usmani was even
given a seat in the Constituent Assembly by the Muslim League
Parliamentary Board. Badauni's group was not exactly ignored,
but it certainly received no official recognition.

There are important differences in the "Islamic" political outlook of the Deobandi and Barelvi 'ulamā' in Pakistan, but it
must not be forgotten that the 'Ulamā'-i-Islām were the allies
of the Muslim League while the 'Ulamā'-i-Pākistān remained
outside struggling for recognition. The doctrinal basis of the
differences between the two groups goes back at least two
centuries to the beginning of the orthodox reform movement.
Deoband stands in the forefront of the movement to discard
Sūfī (mystic) and Hindu accretions to Islam. The reform has,

over two centuries, been largely successful, but the changes that have taken place in the intervening period have left the movement with comparatively unimportant social and political significance. The goal of the Deoband 'ulamā' remains the Islamic orthodoxy of the Abbasid period. The "modernism" and fundamentalism which have sprung from this transcendentalist reform are both unwanted developments. On the other hand, certain aspects of these more recent lay movements in Islam have helped at least to preserve orthopraxy while they have discouraged irrationalism, mysticism, and saint worship. To this extent the Deoband 'ulamā' have passed silently over the doctrinal errors of the modernists.

The mere founding of the state brought with it such a wave of religious enthusiasm as to immediately enhance the prestige of the 'ulamā', but to maintain this prestige new arguments were needed. Without changing their ultimate goal, often even without considering theoretical implications of what they were saying, the Deoband 'ulamā' began to borrow from the new historical and literary approach of Nadwat al-'Ulamā',[29] especially their emphasis on akhlāq (ethics) as opposed to fiqh (jurisprudence). They also borrowed to some extent from the theology of Iqbal. But above all, they borrowed the new scholasticism of Maududi, his violent anti-Westernism, and some of his political theory. The shift from the lecturers's chair to the soap box has not suited the 'ulamā' who have a traditional tendency to change what they say but not what they mean. Their purposes are definitely opposed to those of the modernists and the politicians, and though both groups often now use the same words, they mean different things. Their statements have been used again and again by the politicians to support ideas that the 'ulamā' in fact oppose. The real test of what the 'ulamā' mean by an "Islamic Constitution" lies in their concrete

[29] Smith, *op. cit.,* pp. 293 ff.

suggestions, not in their vague statements of general principles.

It was in the summer of 1948, several months after the controversy over an Islamic constitution had suddenly broken over the heads of the politicians, that several 'ulamā' met at the residence of Maulana Shabbir Ahmad Usmani and worked out a plan for a semi-independent ministry of religious affairs.[30] The plan has never been published but it is said to have been complete and detailed even to the names of the secretaries and under-secretaries. According to some reports, the Minister of Religious Affairs would be under the Head of the State and not subject to ordinary votes of confidence in the legislature. The Ministry would not only control and supervise religious institutions, mosques, endowments and qaḍī courts, but it would act as general censor of all government activities, and exercise general supervision over the behavior of all government servants. The aim of the 'ulamā' was to preserve not to change; their method was through political recognition of their institution.

As for the Barelvi 'ulamā', they are practically oblivious of the new changes and pressures in Islam. They are not at all interested in new and modern statements of the orthodox position. They are opposed to modernism but they are not much troubled by it. If the Deoband 'ulamā' seek to reëstablish the Islamic state of al-Māwardi, the Bareilly 'ulamā' will be satisfied with that of ibn-Jamā'a.[31] They have so completely identified themselves with the unity, the historical continuity, and the divine guidance of the Muslim community that they equate their own political recognition with the establishment of Islam. They are willing to compromise with the existing government; they desire recognition rather than power.

[30] Interviews.
[31] Gibb and Bowen, *op. cit.,* p. 32 (see esp. the quotation).

2 Ijmā' Modernism

NATIONALISM AND THE PIOUS SULTAN

Pakistan was brought into existence through the efforts of the Westernized Muslim middle class of India. It was they who said that Pakistan would be an Islamic state, though it has no basis in the classical exposition of the Sharī'a. It was they who claimed that the Muslims of India were a nation, though there is no justification for this claim in any objective theory of modern nationalism.[1] Both Islamic law and nationalist theory were to be satisfied by the fructiferous middle-class mind, and the Islamic nationalist theory which was the result was to provide the constitutional orientation of the Muslim League government of Pakistan.[2]

[1] For a fairly detailed discussion of Pakistan in terms of objective theory, see Ambedkar, *Pakistan* (Bombay, 1946), pp. 11–21, and Prasad, *India Divided* (Bombay, 1946), pp. 7 ff.

[2] The theory which it is the purpose of this essay to explain is not the product of a single pen. It is the result of the agglomeration of a number of ideas, and only emerged as a rational whole after partition.

Classical Islamic political theory cannot recognize the existence of an Islamic nation that is not identical with the entire community of believing Muslims. The unity of all believers has always been a part of Islamic theory, but classical theory alone insisted upon political unity.[3]

The traditional Islam which is espoused by the 'ulamā' to this day is an outgrowth of the situation brought about by the end of the Abbasid Caliphate. From 1258 onward the legitimacy of Islamic government could no longer be based upon its form, but only upon its performance. The 'ulamā' are practical idealists, for centuries they have accepted various forms of government and varying political divisions within the Islamic community.[4] On the other hand, none of these forms or divisions was ever endowed with Islamic justification. The 'ulamā' ignored Ibn Khaldūn's view that behind the proliferation of petty Muslim kingdoms was the hand of God rather than the sin of man. They ignored somewhat less the Platonic "community of utility" expounded by al-Farabi and the "Philosophers," but that was vague enough to be comparatively harmless.[5] "Community of utility" is a phrase that may be applied to any existing state without giving it theological sanction. It could be applied to Pakistan once it is in existence—or it may not if Pakistan were found to be economically, politically, or geographically unworkable.

Defining a state as a "community of utility" lends it no special Islamic character.[6] It merely becomes a potential political support for the Islamic way of life. To receive religious sanction, such a government must uphold the Sharī'a as interpreted by

[3] See above, p. 17.
[4] H. A. R. Gibb and H. Bowen, *Islamic Society and the West,* Vol. I (London, 1951), p. 34.
[5] Al-Farabi, *Ara Ahl al-Madīna al-Fādhila,* p. 77.
[6] Naṣīr al-Dīn al-Tūsi, *Akhlāqi Naṣīri,* Third Treatise, Chapter Three: "Classification of Societies and Description of Cities."

the 'ulamā'.[7] The determining factor in the question of whether a government will be "Islamic" is not its constitution but the "piety," that is, lawful administration, of the ruler.[8] This theory may be loosely referred to as the "pious-sultan theory." An appropriate historical example of the application of this theory to an actual ruler is the general approval by the 'ulamā' of the government of Aurangzeb-i-Alamgir, the last great Mughal ruler.[9]

Apparently there is nothing in this theory which prevents its application to a Muslim nation-state in anticipation of its good behavior, nor is there anything that prevents its being appropriated by the Westernized middle classes to justify their own nationalism. Why did this not happen? Our answers to this question will explain the elements that eventually did go into the Islamic nationalist theory of the modernists.

The attitudes and behavior of the 'Ulamā' and the modernists are partly interdependent, but there are aspects of the traditional orientation of the 'ulamā' which created an inner momentum antagonistic to nationalism. It was not merely the universality and egalitarianism of Islam which militated against nationalism, but also certain traditional ways of thinking about Islamic polity which made their way into the more realistic political philosophies from Byzantine and Sassanian origins. These ways of thinking existed alongside of classical theory, and persisted through the breakup of the Islamic empire to take on some practical aspect under the Ottoman and Mughal empires. The common element in classical and Ottoman or Mughal thought was the stubborn conception of a centralized, and really universal, empire ruling over the entire civilized

[7] Henri Laoust, *Essai sur les Doctrines Sociales et Politiques de Taki-D-Din ibn Taimiya* (Le Caire, 1939), pp. 282, 307, 294, 315.

[8] Ibn Khaldūn, *Muqaddimah* (Beirut, 1900), p. 191; Gibb and Bowen, *op. cit.*, p. 33.

[9] Gibb and Bowen, *op. cit.*, p. 35.

world in coöperation with a well-organized religious institution.[10] The population of this empire is divided and organized into a host of unified interest, kinship, and functional groups each knowing and fulfilling its proper place in the worldly scheme of things. Within this static framework of order and stability, so much desired after centuries of disorder, invasion, and war, the 'ulamā' would minister to the spiritual needs of the Muslims. It is true that this universal empire was not truly universal, but to the extent that heterodox Persia was interposed between the Ottoman and Mughal empires they were as universal as practicable.[11] No conflict between the two empires could arise to dispel the notion of orthodox unity. Even before the Mughal dynasty was brought to a close the number of contacts between India and the Ottoman empire had increased to the point where it was not difficult to fix the locus of Islamic unity in Constantinople. As a consequence of the existence of this conception of the universal Islamic empire, and particularly as a result of the association of this conception with practical rather than theoretical Islamic politics, we can denote a glide of tradition toward the classical theory of the caliphate. The effect of this tendency was apparent in the part the 'ulamā' played in the Khilafat movement.

On the other side, the Westernized middle classes did not avail themselves of the versatility of the "pious-sultan theory" because they did not know of its existence, because of their preference for classical over traditional Islam, and because they no longer needed it when the time for a nationalist theory arrived.

[10] Nizām al-Mulk, *Siassat-Nameh;* See L. Binder "The Political Theory of Nizām-Mulk," *Iqbal* (Jan., 1956), pp. 27–59; see also Gibb and Bowen, *op. cit.,* p. 29.

[11] For an interesting discussion of the significance of the division of the "Iranic" world, see A. J. Toynbee, *A Study of History* (2d ed.; London, 1935), Vol. I, Ci (b) Annex 1, esp. pp. 388–402.

The average educated middle-class Muslim was totally ignorant of the legal works in which might be found some odd references to the caliphate interspersed between discussions of the nature of prophecy and the timing of prayers.[12] Religion and Islamic law were the private preserve of the 'ulamā', and even the Aligarh graduate learned little more than a few points about prayer, marriage, and inheritance law.[13] They certainly never learned about the caliphate of the "pious sultan."

Their ignorance was not owing to their English education, for they would have remained ignorant of Islamic law in any case. But their English education did open a path for a different notion of the caliphate. This was the classical caliphate as presented by a few outstanding Muslim apologists from the works of Western orientalists.[14] They could not know, nor hardly appreciate, the complex legal tradition the 'ulamā' had built up to protect Islam from political depredation.

REFORM

The degraded state of Muslims was a point on which the 'ulamā' and the apologists agreed, but their explanations were different. As might be expected, the 'ulamā' found the decline in piety and the growth of un-Islamic behavior the reason for the material decline of the Muslims.[15] The apologists found the reason in the refusal of the Muslims to accept Western ways and Western education. The apologists blamed the 'ulamā' for their opposition to the study of English, to the acceptance of civil-service positions under the British, and for their insistence

---

[12] Maulana Muhammad Ali, *My Life; A Fragment,* ed. Afzal Iqbal (Lahore, 1942), p. 3.

[13] *Ibid.,* p. 23.

[14] For example: al-Māwardi's exposition of the caliphate; edited by Enger 1854; utilized by von Kremer in his *Kulturgeschichte des Orients,* which was translated by Khuda Bakhsh as *The Orient under the Caliphs* (Calcutta, 1920).

[15] W. C. Smith, *Modern Islam in India* (2d ed.; London, 1946), p. 295.

upon nonfraternization with the British.[16] As a consequence
of these views, the modernist movement in Indian Islam began
and continued in opposition to the 'ulamā'. Even had they
known of the existence of the "pious-sultan theory," they would
have considered it a devious subterfuge to gloss over the decline
of Muslim political institutions from the ideal.

Wilfred Smith has shown that one of the principal contributions of the modernist movement was its idealization of the
early history of Islam, and he emphasized this view by calling
it the "Movement in Favor of Islamic Culture of the Past." [17]
Now a common historical tradition is acknowledged to be one
of the primary elements in forming a nation, or in rationalizing a nationalist claim, and this was certainly the beginning of
such a structure in Muslim India. We must, however, note a
general tendency to avoid discussion of the Mughal heritage,
and a contrary emphasis upon the earliest period of Islamic
history which is the heritage of all Muslims.[18] The concentration upon the earliest period came to explain the present low
state of Muslims by reason of the failure to uphold the high
ideals of the first Muslims.[19] The plea for reform which is at
least implicit in the writings of the romantics was to be similarly implicit in Islamic nationalist theory.

From the demand for the reform of Muslim education to
Islamic nationalism was a long and devious way. In the meantime, the reform movement itself was to provide the basic
elements, Islamic and Western, for the full elaboration of nationalist theory without reference to traditional Islam.

The demand for social reform within the Muslim commun-

[16] G. F. I. Graham, *Syed Ahmed Khan* (London, 1885), pp. 246 ff.

[17] Smith, *op. cit.,* p. 47.

[18] "Being pioneers in the field of reconstructing our history we have a won-
derful opportunity." *Presidential Address,* I. H. Qureshi, Pakistan History
Conference, 1954.

[19] Amir Ali, *The Spirit of Islam* (London, 1946), p. 292.

ity of India arose out of the apologetic movement and its accompanying approval of Westernization. The continuing goal
of Sir Saiyid Ahmad was to make the Muslims better liked and
better favored by the British.[20] Sir Saiyid Ahmad's beginnings
were romanticized in the works of Saiyid Amir Ali and Muhammad Ali and their followers.[21] It was soon apparent that
the idealized Islam of the romantics differed greatly in fact
from that practiced in India, and even more in spirit from that
preached by the 'ulamā'. Sir Saiyid made great efforts to show
the 'ulamā' that his views were not contrary to Islamic tenets,
but to no avail.[22] The romantics were even more estranged
from the 'ulamā', and soon accused them of obscurantism and
the perversion of Islam.[23] For their part the 'ulamā' decided
that "modernism" was the most dangerous heresy of the day,
and they fought it vigorously.

In this struggle the 'ulamā' used all of their power and prestige as the knowers and qualified interpreters of the law. Indeed, the essential function of the 'ulamā' is to find out and
apply the God-given law of Islam. In the course of history, and
throughout a long succession of impious sultans, this function
was largely diverted to preserving Islamic law and thereby
maintaining the Islamic way of life of the Muslim community.
The romantics not only threatened to alter the Islamic way of
life, but even presumed so far as to interpret the law of Islam
themselves.[24]

It must be remembered that the romantic movement was
an extension of the apologetic movement, and as such it was

[20] Graham, *op. cit.*, p. 188, pp. 237 f.
[21] Smith, *op. cit.*, pp. 49 f., and p. 300.
[22] *Ibid.*, p. 19.
[23] Amir Ali, *op. cit.*, p. 231.
[24] *Ibid.*, p. 186, "The reformation of Islam will begin when once it is
recognized that divine words rendered into any language retain their divine
character . . ." (on the question of translating the Qur'ān).

primarily oriented toward the criticisms of Islam made by Western observers. Principal among these criticisms was the accusation that "Islam imposes a code, hard, fast and imperative in every detail, which however well it may have suited Arabia thirteen centuries ago, is quite unfitted for the varying requirements of other times and places." [25] If this criticism were correct and the views of the 'ulamā' and the "corrupted" practice of Indian Muslims really representative of Islam, then the whole structure of the social and ethical principles of Islam built by the apologists must collapse.

Saiyid Ahmad's answer was to ask the 'ulamā' to "change not their dogmas, but their policy, so that independence of mind and political liberation should no longer be counted as symptoms of heterodoxy." [26] The word "symptoms" is putting it mildly, for he was damned to perdition by the 'ulamā' for his pains. The romantics, led by Saiyid Amir Ali, openly blamed the 'ulamā' for Muslim stagnation. To do this they had to go behind the rulings of the 'ulamā' and attack them upon their own ground, that is, upon the ground of legal theory.

The doctrine of taqlīd [27] was singled out by Amir Ali for particular attack: ". . . it is the common belief that since the four Imams no doctor has arisen qualified to interpret the laws of the Prophet. No account is taken of the altered circumstances in which Moslems are now placed. . . . They mixed up the temporary with the permanent, and the universal with

[25] W. Muir, *Mahomet and Islam* (3d ed.; London, 1895), p. 246. See also von Kremer, *Orient under the Caliphs* tr. Bakhsh (Calcutta, 1920), p. 211; where substantially the same sentiment is expressed concerning a situation obtaining in the year 100 A.H.

[26] Graham, *op. cit.*, p. 201.

[27] ". . . a want or a deficiency, on the part of a Mohammedan, which is called Takleed (a blind belief in the opinion of others) and which, when exhibited in that of foreigners is known by the name of partiality, bias, prejudice, or bigotry." Sir Saiyid Ahmad Khan, *A Series of Essays on the Life of Mohammad,* preface, p. xi.

the particular . . . not a few were the servants of sovereigns and despots." [28] Amir Ali went on to urge that the spirit be regarded above the letter, and this was to be rediscovered in the Qur'ān and not the law books that flooded the Islamic world in later centuries.[29]

The effect of taqlīd is to restrict the exercise of independent judgment in the interpretation of the sources of Islamic law. The exercise of such judgment is called ijtihād, and this was defended by the Ahmadi, Muhammad Ali, who pointed out that even the founders of the four orthodox schools of law did not lay down the restriction of ijtihād.[30] He went on to say that decisions based upon reasoning in one generation may be rejected in the next.[31] And he concluded that Muslim communities may not only make laws for themselves but they *must* apply their own judgment to changed conditions.[32]

The emphasis on ijtihād is an example of the way in which Western individualism, perhaps bourgeois individualism, was being assimilated into modern Islam. Its absence was attributed to ignorance, its proper exercise was to be based on understanding the "spirit" of the Qur'ān and the traditions of the Prophet. But can a religious system continue to exist with no fixed doctrine, and where every individual may interpret its spirit as he likes? Is this the way in which religious reform ought to take place? How are the new interpretations to be fixed?

The answer to these questions lies in the legal doctrine of ijmā'. Ijmā' means agreement, and, in its traditional usage in legal theory, a consensus of opinion on a specific interpretation of the Sharī'a which is so narrowly short of unanimity as to invoke the authority of the tradition of the Prophet: "My peo-

[28] Amir Ali, *op. cit.,* p. 184.
[29] *Ibid.,* p. 185.
[30] Mohammed Ali, *The Religion of Islam* (Lahore, 1950), p. 112.
[31] *Ibid.,* p. 104.
[32] *Ibid.,* p. 115.

ple will never agree in error"; and at the same time eliminate the working of the contrary tradition: "Disagreement among my people is a blessing." The persons whose opinions are constitutive of an ijmāʿ are variously the Companions of the Prophet, all the jurists of a particular age, all the jurists of a particular school of law, or the four schools of law collectively taken. Taqlīd may be applied only to the ijtihād of the decisions of the founder of a school, and these decisions are binding only upon that school. An ijmāʿ if universal settles a question of law for all schools, and restricts the exercise of ijtihād on the question so settled. The restriction of ijmāʿ to that of the Companions of the Prophet, and thereby reducing the number of questions so settled, was actually a device to permit the ijtihād of reforming ʿulamā'.[33] For the modernists the problem was to abrogate previous ijmāʿ and yet permit the same process of fixation to function in the modern age. This was done by applying the notion of the need to adapt Islamic practice to changing times. It was consequently held that an ijmāʿ could be abrogated by a later one, which then becomes valid in terms of its own time and place. Ijmāʿ was similarly considered to be the product of the views of all Muslims and not merely those with special legal qualifications.[34]

This is in broad outline the new legal theory that the modernists brought forward. No part of this theory is really new or revolutionary. What was new was the spirit in which it was intended that Islam be reinterpreted. In point of fact, little in the way of concrete reinterpretation was offered; the important point was that there should be no restriction upon the manifestation of the true spirit of Islam in the modern age.

The individualism of ijtihād was to be used as the Islamic

[33] Sir Muhammad Iqbal, *The Reconstruction of Religious Thought in Islam* (London, 1934), p. 144.
[34] *Ibid.*, p. 165.

basis of democracy. The doctrine of ijmā' demonstrated the existence of an Islamic basis for majority rule. The combined operation of these two would bring into reality the true spirit of Islam, a spirit in complete accord with the requirements and the values of the twentieth century, a spirit that would be reflected in the achievements of the Muslims themselves. Here, unknowingly, were laid down the basic elements of Islamic nationalism.

HINDU NATIONALISM

The second factor that encouraged and gave direction to Islamic nationalism was the increasing Hindu-ization of the nationalism of the Congress. The origins of this tendency may be traced back into pre-British India to the time of Kabir and Nanak.[35] Out of these, and similar deliberate attempts to establish a common religious ground between Islam and Hinduism we find a new emphasis on orthodoxy arising. Such an emphasis is, of course, the prelude to reform in the sense that the orthodox position must be restated in terms of the new circumstances and the new dangers. One of the principal features in Islam was the emphasis on the unity of interest of all Muslims;[36] whereas on the Hindu side it was in part represented by a new emphasis upon the restrictions of caste.[37] The British arrived on the scene while both these movements were in progress.

[35] Tara Chand, *Influence of Islam on Indian Culture* (Allahabad, 1954 [written in 1922, see preface]), p. 148, on Kabir: "His teaching was of so independent a character that both Hindus and Muslims . . . tried to suppress him . . ."; J. C. Archer, *The Sikhs* (Princeton, 1946), pp. 42, 54, 56 (where Archer indicates the degree to which Nanak's movement was dependent upon Kabir), 84.

[36] Qadari, *A Moslem's Inner Voice* (Lahore, n.d.), reverse of flyleaf, quotation from the Mujaddid Alf-i-Thani: "He who claims to believe in Islam . . . but allies himself with the unbelievers . . . is a cursed man. . . ."

[37] L. S. S. O'Malley, *India's Social Heritage* (Oxford, 1934), p. 21.

The Muslim response to British imperialism was generally negative and that of many Hindus was positive, and this single fact is the dominant feature of the entire development of two rival nationalisms in India.[38] The response of the Hindus seems the more natural in the light of almost universal colonial experience, whereas the subsequent alteration of the Muslim attitude seems to have been artificially delayed by the anomaly of the continued existence of the Mughal Sultanate despite actual British government through the East India Company. The result of this arbitrary sequence was, perhaps, inevitably, that Westernizing Muslims should copy Westernizing Hindus. A further result was that the orthodox revival in Islam should continue longer and stronger than that in Hinduism.[39] Among the Hindus the movement continued powerful only in the Maratha strongholds where it was the Hindus and not the Muslims who delivered their authority over to the British.[40] As Poona was to the Hindus, so was Delhi the center of the orthodox revival of Islam.

The nature of the "positive" response to British imperialism was, as we have mentioned, the same for both Muslims and Hindus. The first phase is the defense of the Eastern religion against the attacks of Christian missionaries. This is done by a rerationalization of the basic tenets of the religion in terms of values acceptable to the West—in a word, by a partial Christianization of Hinduism or Islam. In Hinduism with its more flexible doctrinal system there was perhaps a more conscious attempt to "assimilate" Christian principles.[41] The result of this modern apologetic tendency is the alienation of the powerful forces of the orthodox revival. New religious organizations

[38] W. W. Hunter, *The Indian Musulmans* (Calcutta, 1945), pp. 138 ff.
[39] *Ibid.*, passim.
[40] Yusuf Ali, *The Making of India* (London, 1925), p. 174.
[41] Moreland and Chatterjee, *op. cit.*, pp. 342, 397.

are formed, and they have their parallel in other nonreligious organizations of the middle classes.[42] At this point Western scholarship comes to the aid of the modernizing apologists by uncovering and often translating basic religious works that had hitherto been the private heritage of the Brahman or the 'alim.[43] English education is then sufficient to permit a reading of the "original sources," and the intelligence of, say, an official of the government of India is sufficient to permit their sensible interpretation. By the time these religious positions were well formulated among the Hindus, the Hindu middle classes had become conscious of their interests.[44] Democracy and nationalism as expressed by eminent Britons of the nineteenth century began to take on real meaning in terms of the divergence of Hindu and British interests. This stage is best exemplified by the founding of the Indian National Congress in 1885.[45] Despite the political uneasiness that this represents, the outward form of "positive" response is maintained. Loyalty to Britain is asserted and reasserted; gratitude for all the British have done for India is profuse and not much less genuine for being much more formal. The break came with the partition of Bengal.

When this first real conflict with Britain arose the Congress was suddenly found to be split between moderates and extremists. The extremists were mainly from Bengal, but they found support among the orthodox revivalists of Poona and Deccan.[46] The historical tradition of the south was adopted by the extremists, modified by the modernizers, and developed into an unrelenting theory of Indian nationalism by the politi-

[42] B. P. Sitaramayya, *The History of the Indian National Congress* (Madras, 1935), pp. 13, 16.
[43] Hunter, *op. cit.,* pp. 188, 189.
[44] Moreland and Chatterjee, *op. cit.,* p. 401.
[45] Sitaramayya, *op. cit.,* p. 22.
[46] T. K. Shahani, *Gopal Krishna Gokhale* (Bombay, 1929), p. 187.

cal activists.[47] Some emphasis must here be placed upon the fact that the partition of Bengal was one on which Hindu and Muslim interests were definitely divided.[48]

The combination of the Bengal nationalists and the orthodox revivalists of the Deccan was vigorous enough to win its points in the Congress of 1906, but not strong enough to wrest the leadership of the Congress from the moderates.[49] The struggle between the two factions continued throughout the second decade of the twentieth century, and the results of this struggle produced a profound change in the nationalist attitude of the Indian Congress. Nor should it be forgotten that it was during this same decade the "right of self-determination" for nations was admitted as a principle of international politics.

The most striking change in a fundamental attitude of the Congress was in regard to the Hindu religion. This change is not so evident from explicit statements of policy as from the methods used and the explanations given for the implementation of that policy. The coalition between religious conservatives and political extremists, whose religious knowledge was both meager and at the same time greatly influenced by Western values, led to yet newer attempts at a restatement of Hindu religion. In this, apologetic became aggressive, and Western values were in many instances rejected.[50] The need for social

[47] See B. C. Pal, *Swadeshi and Swaraj* (Calcutta, 1954), p. 73: "The Sivaji celebrations were first started in Calcutta!" The irony of this admission stems from the fact that Sivaji was a Maratha hero, and not a Bengali. Some further details of the nationalist symbolism of Sivaji are given below.

[48] Maulana Muhammad Ali, *My Life: A Fragment,* ed. Afzal Iqbal (Lahore, 1942), p. 37.

[49] R. P. Masani, *Dadabhai Naoroji* (London, 1939), pp. 495–497; Shahani, *op. cit.,* p. 180.

[50] Jawaharlal Nehru, *Autobiography* (London, 1953), p. 157. It should be mentioned that neither religious conservatives nor political extremists comprise mutually exclusive classes. In general, the extremists referred to were Bengalis and the religious conservatives were from Maharashtra. B. G. Tilak

reform was minimized,[51] and the glory of past achievements exaggerated. As the orthodox revival became more useful in terms of the political aspirations of the extremists, so did their ideas become more highly valued. However, one could not expect of these Westernized Bengalis, these "extremists," the religious spirit born of conservative traditionalism. Their Hinduism was almost as new as their attempt at orthodoxy. Their product was a neo-orthodoxy akin to fundamentalism.

The Hinduism which the (Bengali) Congress extremists supported was not that of India in the twentieth century, for they had rejected that as backward and superstitious in their school days.[52] Their Hinduism was a reconstruction of an imaginary past ideal that had been corrupted.[53] And so the religious and the nationalist urge combined in a new interest in history. Out of this interest there arose the gradual popularization of the national historical myth of Hindu India. In broad outline this nationalist historical tradition stressed the high civilization and relative prosperity of Ancient India.[54] More striking than this expected feature was the tremendous emphasis placed upon the assimilative capacity of the Hindus.[55] The Muslim invasions were taken as a challenge to this assimilative capacity, characterized as they were by destruction and murder or proselytization.[56] The struggle between Hindu

may be mentioned as an example of one who was both a religious conservative of great knowledge and a political extremist. It must be left to others more familiar with Indian ideologies to decide whether or not Tilak was really a fundamentalist, and hence more akin to Maududi.

[51] Reform was still a watchword of the nationalist movement, but only in the sense of going back to romanticized original practices.

[52] B. Prasad, *India's Hindu-Muslim Questions* (London, 1946), p. 23.

[53] B. C. Pal, *op. cit.,* p. 75.

[54] E.g., A. Besant, *India: A Nation* (Madras, 1930), pp. 21–24.

[55] E.g., Ishwar Nath Topa, *Growth and Development of National Thought in India* (published Ph.D. dissertation, n.p., n.d.), p. 23.

[56] B. Prasad, *op. cit.,* p. 14; Besant, *op. cit.,* pp. 24–25.

and Muslim ends with the Mughals, who are appropriated for Hindu purposes for their tolerance and association of certain caste-Hindus with their government.[57] The contributions of the Mughals to the Indian nation was a wide political and territorial unity, administrative uniformity, the development of a common vernacular, the encouragement of common arts, literature and social manners, the *revival* of monotheism and mysticism, and improvements in the "arts of war and civilization."[58] It is of course Akbar who is most praised for these worthy accomplishments.[59] One has the feeling that this is at least as much due to his attempt to establish a common religion for all his subjects as for his very real political and military accomplishments.[60] In any case, the Mughals are credited with a degree of religious tolerance permitting a "religious rapprochement"[61] or in less careful, if more popular, terminology, the Hindu-ization of Islam. With the accession of Aurangzeb all of this changed. Aurangzeb was intolerant, he reinstituted the subject tax upon the Hindus, he stressed the Islamic nature of his government, he encouraged the ʿulamāʾ, and he destroyed temples. Mrs. Besant calls him "Aurangzeb, the destroyer."[62] Perhaps Aurangzeb's greatest sin was in attempting to strengthen his direct control of the Deccan principalities. In this he was opposed by Sivaji, a Maratha noble. Sivaji's purpose was "the building of a nation."[63] The tradition goes on to claim that the Maratha Confederacy wrested the control of most of India from the Mughals, and so it was from the Hindus

[57] B. Prasad, *op. cit.,* p. 19.

[58] Sochin Sen, *Political Philosophy of Rabindranath* (Tagore) (Calcutta, 1929), p. 88, n.1.

[59] Besant, *op. cit.,* p. 28, described as the greatest Muslim emperor.

[60] Moreland and Chatterjee, *op. cit.,* p. 214.

[61] B. Prasad, *op. cit.,* pp. 17, 18.

[62] Besant, *op. cit.,* p. 29.

[63] *Ibid.,* p. 34.

and not the Muslims that the British took over control of
India.[64]

These two tendencies toward fundamentalism in religion
and the Hindu-ization of the national historical myth were
made possible in large measure by the historical and religious
work of Europeans. The role of Europeans in the popularization of non-European nationalist histories is rather well known,
but somewhat less well known is their part in the development
of non-Christian fundamentalist movements through their
translations and loving expositions of the ancient sources of
exotic doctrines in a context of modern Christian values. Mrs.
Besant, president of the Theosophical Society, went further
and took the lead of a political movement based on these two
tendencies, and aimed at securing home rule for India.[65] The
Home Rule Movement was not to be opposed to the Congress,[66]
but its radicalism did keep the Congress from becoming too
moderate, until Gandhi arrived on the scene and carried these
twin tendencies to their logical extreme in the method of nonviolent noncoöperation.[67]

The use of these methods, and the heightened religio-spiritual
atmosphere that Gandhi brought to the Indian Congress, were
his greatest political achievements and the guarantee of continued success for the Congress. More striking than his ability
to lead the Congress in this direction was his ability to pledge
the 'ulamā' to the use of nonviolent noncoöperation rather than
jihād in the attempt to achieve the ends of the Khilafat movement.[68] We need not wonder, then, that some Muslims at least,
after the failure of the Khilafat movement, felt that they had
been seduced religiously into performing some sort of Hindu

[64] *Ibid.*, p. 35.
[65] Sitaramayya, *op. cit.*, p. 126.
[66] Massani, *op. cit.*
[67] Ambedkar, *op. cit.*, pp. 8–9.
[68] Nehru, *op. cit.*, pp. 45–46.

rite, and politically into alienating the British guarantors of their political rights.[69]

On the Muslim side, the categories and tendencies were basically the same, but modified in their development by the different position of the Muslims at the time of the British conquest and later by their numerical inferiority to the Hindus and, as will be discussed below, the apparent relentlessness of the democratic advance of India. The dominant feature for the superficial observer remains that the Hindus were copied by the Muslims.

The orthodox revival of Islam met no organized resistance until the time of the Aligarh movement. Originally it was related to the Mughal political breakdown after Aurangzeb, and after the British conquest it received added strength from a mutation of the original Arabian Wahhabi movement. In India, this movement, identified by the same name, is better understood in relation to the orthodox revival and the decline of Muslim political power rather than as a genuine fundamentalist movement.[70] One of the outstanding features of this Indian Wahhabi movement was its emphasis on jihād.[71]

The "positive" response of the Muslims was delayed until after the Mutiny of 1857 and the end of nominal Muslim rule in India. Sir Saiyid Ahmad set out to reconcile Muslim and Briton, and although he was partly successful he became the target of orthodox attack. Out of his loyalist Aligarh movement there developed a more radical tendency which sought the political rights of Muslims, and began to assert the superiority of Muslim culture. The historical bases for these assertions were found in the early history of Islam, whereas the Mughal period in India, already appropriated by the Hindus, was

[69] Gandhi, *Young India, 1924–1926* (New York, 1927), p. 23.

[70] Muhammad Abd-al-Bari (Ph.D. dissertation, Oxford, 1954); a comparison of the two Wahhabi movements.

[71] W. W. Hunter, *The Indian Musalmans* (Calcutta, 1945), p. 6, *et passim*.

largely ignored. The ending of the partition of Bengal in 1911 was a political issue that had within it the possibility of uniting political radicals and the orthodox revivalists, but because the Indian Congress since 1905 had almost a monopoly of opposition to the British, and had a great deal more power than the 'ulamā', there was instead a coalition between the Muslim League and the Congress in the Lucknow Pact (1916).[72] These same circumstances determined that the Congress act as midwife at the birth of Islamic fundamentalism in the Khilafat movement.[73]

The Khilafat movement in India had as its goal the maintenance of the territorial integrity of the Ottoman empire. Its origins may be traced back to the Pan-Islamic preaching of Jamal-al-Dīn al-Afghani, but more immediately to the sympathetic attitude of India's Muslims during the Ottoman trials of the Balkan war.[74] To some extent the movement was a sublimation of the educated repressions that resulted from the knowledge that Muslims would no longer rule in India.[75] A further need was supplied by the provision of a supraterritorial justification of the distinctive organization and cohesiveness of Islamic society in India. The movement was essentially antinationalist as regards Islam,[76] but permissive of nationalism in India. In the context of Hindu-Muslim relations, the movement was "nonpolitical," though not as regards Indo-British

[72] Lal Bahadur, *The Muslim League* (Agra, n.d.), pp. 87 f., and p. 95. The agreement was based upon an agreed program of constitutional reforms, the lack of which had delayed coöperation from 1912 to 1916.

[73] Sitaramayya, *op. cit.*, p. 274: "The same doubt was expressed in 1920 when the Punjab tragedy and the Khilaphat [*sic*] wrong were made by him [Gandhi] the issue on which to inaugurate the noncooperation movement— not Swaraj."

[74] Muhammad Ali, *op. cit.*, pp. 37–40.

[75] *Ibid.*, p. 6.

[76] The movement strongly opposed Arab nationalism, and many persons in Pakistan retain these feelings today; Khaliquzzaman, *Conception of a Quranic or Islamic State*, pp. 7–8.

relations. One of its possible results was the depoliticization of the Muslims of India. And this may be one of the reasons that Gandhi and the Congress encouraged the movement,[77] while Jinnah and the Muslim League refused to go along with it.[78] That the 'ulamā' joined this movement is somewhat surprising, and bears explanation.

The 'ulamā' did support the Khilafat movement, primarily because they feared that the holy places were to be placed under Christian political influence. They also understood that many Muslims would come under a similar influence, and they knew from their own experience what that had meant in India. These practical considerations determined the tendency of the 'ulamā'; the doctrinal aspects of the issue followed closely along. The necessity of a sympathetic political power to ensure the proper religious organization of the community is a recurring feature of traditional theory.[79] It also lies at the basis of the classical theory that finds this organization legitimized by the existence of the caliphate.[80] Traditional theory turned this system upside down and would have had the 'ulamā' legitimize the "caliphate" of a good sultan if he ruled in accordance with the Sharī'a. The consequence of this post-Abbasid development of Islamic political theory was the authorization of the use of the term Khalīfa for almost any Muslim ruler, including the Mughals.[81] If the 'ulamā' identified the Ottoman sultan with the caliph of classical theory, it was not because there had been no change in Islamic thought, but rather because Islamic legal theory cannot admit change. The

---

[77] *Congress and the Problem of Minorities,* All-India Congress Committee, Allahbad, pp. 50–51, 66, 67.

[78] Lal Bahadur, *op. cit.,* p. 166.

[79] E.g., al-Ghazzali, *al-Iqtisād fi-l-l'tiqād* (Cairo, n.d.), p. 105, line 12.

[80] L. Binder, "Al-Ghazzāli's Theory of Islamic Government," *The Muslim World* (July, 1955), p. 235.

[81] Gibb and Bowen, *op. cit.,* pp. 34, 35.

dissolution of the Mughal Sultanate left a gap to be filled; the simultaneous revival of the classical theory after its rediscovery by Western scholars gave the appearance of being the established Islamic theory. When confronted by the romantics with al-Māwardi's doctrines the 'ulamā' were bound to regard the sultan of Turkey as the caliph of all Islam.

The failure of the Khilafat movement was not only a tremendous disappointment to the romantics and the 'ulamā', but it also seriously undermined the theoretical, and hence the rational, basis of their political activity. The result was confusion, inefficiency, and even inactivity. After a period of quiet the 'ulamā' again supported the Congress against the British and the Westernized Muslim middle class.[82] The romantics, too, lapsed into comparative inactivity, and then burst forth in a new aggressive movement bordering on nationalism. The Khilafat movement had succeeded in arousing the Muslim population to some extent, and although Gandhi was pleased with this development,[83] it seems to have prepared them for even more irrational attempts to cure the intellectual malaise of the Muslim middle class of India.

To sum up the results of the Khilafat movement which concern us here, we may say that it well nigh destroyed the strongest antinationalist Islamic theory; but it also discredited the "pious-sultan theory" of the caliphate; and finally it caused romantic notions of Islam to become more widespread among Indian Muslims. In a sense, then, it prepared the way for a local Islamic nationalism, although the sense in which it did so was negative. The need was not yet for a theory of nationalism, though forces were already at work which would make it a necessity.

The two outstanding immediate results of the failure of the

[82] Smith, *op. cit.*, p. 297.
[83] Gandhi, *op. cit.*, pp. 22–23.

Khilafat and the noncoöperation movements were the revival of the Muslim League in 1924, and a noteworthy increase in violent communal clashes.[84]

The Muslim League, despite the agreement of various of its leaders, had remained aloof from the noncoöperation movement.[85] It had also remained aloof from too close contact with either the romantic Khilafatists or their temporary allies, the 'ulamā'. The outlook of the League continued to be strictly legalistic. Their goals remained the acquisition of a maximum guarantee for Muslim interests, within a context of increasing democratization. Their platform was the continuation of separate electorates, increased weightage to minorities, and greater provincial autonomy.[86] The League was, in fact, so consistent with the ideals of its aristocratic and "loyal" (to the British) founders that it was almost wholly out of sympathetic touch with the urban Muslim population.

The recrudescence of communal violence is not so easy to explain. The types of incidents that produce riots have been enumerated, and though the potential causes are manifold and almost daily occurrences, they cannot fully explain the variation in frequency of such incidents.[87] There is virtual unanimity in suggesting that various economic factors had much to do with the heightening communal tensions,[88] though these factors cannot be classified easily as variants of either simple competition or more complex rivalries between peasant and landowner, debtor and creditor, worker and capitalist, or unemployed graduate and employed professional. All of these factors were present, and we have ample testimony to permit a loose classification of certain economic functions on the basis

[84] Moreland and Chatterjee, *op. cit.,* p. 479.
[85] Nehru, *op. cit.,* pp. 46, 47.
[86] Moreland and Chatterjee, *op. cit.,* p. 480.
[87] R. Coupland, *The Indian Problem 1833–1935* (London, 1945), pp. 29, 30.
[88] Nehru, *op. cit.,* p. 140; Smith, *op. cit.,* p. 164.

of religious differences and geographical distribution. Yet, these differences existed previously, and in some measure they may be traced back to pre-British times.[89] Nor, despite a steady and not inconsiderable absolute increase in urban population, can we find a statistical change of sufficient magnitude to explain the qualitative change in communal awareness.[90] The answer must be sought in the kind and not the amount of social mobilization that resulted from the war effort, the discharge of numbers of soldiers who remained in the towns, the provincial elections under the new constitution of 1919, and finally the appeal of the Congress and Khilafat movement directly to the masses on a highly emotional level.

Hindus and Muslims alike suffered some revulsion of feeling after the Khilafat fiasco.[91] On the Hindu side this is represented by the organization of the Hindu Mahasabha, a fundamentalist organization with strong traditional sentiments.[92] There was to be no similar Muslim organization for nearly a decade, but the same feelings were undoubtedly present. However, there was no one to lead the movement, for the most competent leadership was already intellectually committed in other directions. The respectable leadership of the Muslim League simply took up where they had left off, whereas the romantic fundamentalists were too deeply involved with the Congress. Maulana Abul Kalam Azad stayed on as the leading Congress Muslim to become the minister of education in the Indian government, while Muhammad Ali split with the Congress, and doggedly kept the Khilafat movement gasping. The Khilafatists continued to support the Turk-

[89] Smith, *op. cit.*

[90] Kingsley Davis, *The Population of India and Pakistan* (Princeton, 1951), pp. 127, 132; K. W. Deutsch, *Nationalism and Social Communication* (New York and Cambridge, 1953), p. 200.

[91] See n. 83.

[92] Moreland and Chatterjee, *op. cit.,* p. 480.

ish government even after it had abolished the caliphate, and Iqbal went a long way toward justifying Kemal's "ijtihād." [93] The 'ulamā' were left somewhere between, grieving over the end of the caliphate which they had been maneuvered into supporting, and continuing the orthodox revival. About a decade was to pass before some direction was given to this increasing intensity of popular feeling.

The dominant tendency among the less articulate urban classes was one of aggressive self-differentiation, but this tendency was further characterized by geographic and linguistic sectionalism. Sectionalism or regionalism among lower middle-class Muslims was naturally limited to those areas in which the Muslims comprised an overwhelming majority of the rural population, and an embattled minority in the cities. It was under these circumstances that a few hitherto unknown persons could appeal to the peasants and tribesmen, eliciting from them a powerful response.[94] As far as the lower classes were concerned their response was at once regional, communal, and economic; but because the Muslims were in the majority in these areas their leaders could remain loyal to the broad national democratic *official* ideal of the Congress.

In the Hindu majority areas the Muslims thought in terms of constitutional guarantees whether they gave their allegiance to the League or the Congress or to neither. The League did add provincial autonomy to its political platform, but this did not alter the wholly negative character of its program. It failed to take up Iqbal's suggestion for the formation of a Muslim state in northwestern India,[95] nor did Rahmat Ali seem to be expressing anyone's opinion but his own in publish-

---

[93] Iqbal, *op. cit.*, p. 145.
[94] Smith, *op. cit.*, pp. 220 f., and pp. 229, 230, 231.
[95] Presidential Address to Allahabad Session of All-India Muslim League, 1930, quoted in S. Hyder, *Progress in Pakistan* (Lahore, 1947), pp. 34, 35.

ing a book entitled *Pakistan*.[96] In the event it was to be only through the League's acceptance of regionalism as an all-India goal that the unification of the Muslims was to come about. Although provincial autonomy, even "sovereignty," was to be the constitutional basis of communal unity, its real basis was the earnest desire of many of the Muslims of India to realize in fact the romantic dream they had for decades been assuring one another was the true Islam.

DEMOCRATIZATION

The third factor which both encouraged and in large measure determined the nature of Islamic nationalism was the gradual democratization of the government of India. The dominant features of this erratic process were the broadening of the electorate and the Indianization of various legislative bodies and of the civil service. A third noteworthy feature of the growth of self-government was the continued emphasis on minority guarantees that grew into a complex structure of constitutional provisions, political convention, and interparty understanding. There were many complaints of bad faith regarding the implementation of extraconstitutional arrangements; consequently, the Muslims emphasized legal guarantees and the contractual rather than the moral association of majority and minority.

These elements of the process by which self-government developed determined the major theoretical problem facing the Muslim middle class. This problem was essentially concerned with the relationship of nationalism and democracy. The Congress assumption that there existed a single Indian nation led

[96] Choudhary Rahmat Ali, *Pakistan: The Fatherland of the Pak Nation* (1st and 2d ed. cyclostyled, 3d ed. published in Cambridge, England, as Pakistan Literature Series no. 1 [first published in 1935]).

them to the radical conclusion that the constitutional order of their future government should be that of unlimited democracy. This conception of a single people with a single will and a single interest was reluctantly modified only to take account of the pattern of provincial autonomy fostered under British rule. This single concession of the Indian National Congress to the constitutional limitation of democracy might satisfy the Muslim majority provinces that afterward comprised Pakistan, but it could not dispel the apprehensions of the major part of the Muslim middle class which was resident in the Hindu majority provinces of central India and Bombay. This important segment of the Muslim middle class, which dominated the Muslim League, required some constitutional recognition of the special character of the Muslim community. Such recognition required, on the theoretical level, some derogation from either the principle of democracy or from the comprehensive claims of Indian nationalism. Democracy was not to be denied; the denial of the nationalist doctrine of the Congress could result in effective minority guarantees only if accepted by the Hindu majority.

Although the fear of Hindu domination developed as gradually as did the Indianization of the government, it had long before been expressed by Sir Saiyid Ahmad in 1883.[97] The dual ideal of democratic nationalism had been well implanted in the Indian middle-class mind in the early twentieth century through the British educational system. The Congress insisted that the Indian nation was defined by the territorial extent of British paramountcy, and it only reluctantly and for a short period agreed to electoral guarantees for Muslims.[98] Gandhi, Nehru, and a host of other Congress leaders resisted the legal-

[97] Coupland, *op. cit.,* Appendix II, pp. 154 f.
[98] Sitaramayya, *op. cit.,* p. 529.

istic notion that constitutional guarantees were needed, and they preached instead the purification of hearts.[99] Hindus and Muslims alike were asked to avoid making "deals," but urged to freely concede the other's request out of the goodness of their hearts.[100] This attitude was small consolation for the Muslim middle class which found itself gradually being ousted from its important position in the cities of northern India, and unable to gain a foothold in the urban centers of what is now Pakistan against the entrenched financial and professional position of the Hindus. Two years of Congress rule in the Muslim minority provinces, where the largest part of the Muslim middle class resided, was enough to convince them that independence meant an unsympathetic Hindu raj. Democratic nationalism, however, could not be rejected by the Muslim middle class, for it was their heritage, too; and they had already included it in their idealization of Islam.

Democracy was one of the Western virtues that Islam learned to comprehend. It was, in fact, not difficult to defend this contention on the basis of the universality of Islam and the equality of all believers. The special treatment, guarantees, and civic limitations upon nonbelievers was not to be stressed until the period after partition. Democracy by ballot could not, of course, be claimed for early Islam, but the genuine character of the democratic spirit could be demonstrated by reference to a kind of "legislative" body, the institution of the shūra.[101] The shūra referred to was not a legally constituted body, but an advisory or "consultative" council with a floating membership of the important members of the Arab aristocracy resident at Medina. The importance of this institution was heightened by reference to the verse of the Qur'ān "determining" that the

[99] *Ibid.;* Gandhi, *op. cit.,* pp. 21 ff.
[100] Gandhi, *op. cit.,* p. 75.
[101] Maulana Muhammad Ali, *The Early Caliphate* (Lahore, 1932), pp. 177 f.

affairs of the Muslims be settled by consultation among themselves.[102] Not much emphasis was given to the tradition that all decisions taken in shūra were unanimous, and the Western-educated Muslim may be forgiven if he confused consultation with democracy.

If democracy could not be denied by the Muslim modernists, there remained the sole alternative of rejecting the Congress conception of Indian nationalism. The political consequences of such rejection are two: either India must become a binational state or its territory must be partitioned. The first alternative requires constitutional limitations of democracy in the form of minority safeguards, whereas the second permits adherence to a pure doctrine of unrestricted democracy. The first alternative appealed to the Muslim League leaders of northern and central India because they were a regional minority. Moreover, partition of the Hindu majority provinces was impractical because there were few districts in which Muslims were in a local majority and these were widely separated. The Congress was unwilling to concede separate Muslim electorates and was even disinclined to permit a wide measure of regional autonomy. Consequently the second alternative appealed more to the leaders of the Muslim majority provinces, if only as a bargaining demand to achieve maximum provincial autonomy.

In 1936 the Muslim League, under the leadership of Muhammad Ali Jinnah, fought the provincial elections on the platform of the sweet reasonableness of the contractual approach and failed. The real and fancied expressions of Hindu nationalism and communal favoritism by the Congress governments of 1937–1939 crushed all possibility of a contractual solution short of the right of secession. The day the Congress governments quit was celebrated by the Muslim League as a "day of deliverance," and this demonstration was followed in less than six

[102] *Qur'ān*, Surah 42, verse 38.

months by the famous Lahore resolution of the Muslim
League:

> Resolved that it is the considered view of this session of the
> All-India Muslim League that no constitutional plan would be
> workable in this country or acceptable to the Muslims unless
> it is designated on the following basic principle, viz. that geo-
> graphically continguous units are demarcated into regions
> which should be so constituted with such territorial adjustments
> as may be necessary, that the areas in which the Muslims are
> numerically in a majority as in the Northwestern and Eastern
> zones of India should be grouped to constitute "Independent
> States" in which the Constituent Units shall be antonomous and
> sovereign.[103]

The Lahore resolution contemplated neither a unified Indian
Muslim nation nor the nationalist ideology which accrued to
the Muslim League program in the years following. The resolution was, in fact, neither nationalist nor Islamic. It was in the
tradition of the contractual limitation of Indian nationalism.
As every writer on Pakistan is sure to record, the Lahore resolution is a restatement of part of Muhammad Iqbal's presidential
address to the 1930 meeting of the Council of the Muslim
League. The context in which he made his suggestion for an
autonomous Muslim state is unequivocally antinationalist as
was its restatement ten years later.[104] Even the argument from
omission has here great weight, for seven years earlier Rahmat
Ali had published his *Pakistan* containing a fully elaborated
national myth; but the word Pakistan finds no place in the
resolution.

The resolution was not Islamic because the religion of Islam
was not taken as the basis of political organization, nor as

[103] Ambedkar, *op. cit.,* p. 3.
[104] F. K. Khan Durrani, *The Meaning of Pakistan* (Lahore, 1946), appendix, pp. 149 ff.

defining its goals. The Sharī'a says nothing about Muslim minorities or majorities. All that might be argued is that the resolution is not un-Islamic, and that would not hold for all Muslim viewpoints unless it is conceded that it is not nationalist either.[105] At any rate, the resolution, as has been shown, can be perfectly well explained without reference to Islam, though not without reference to Muslims.[106]

As the key phrase of the resolution shows, the first official acceptance of the Pakistan idea by the Muslim League was an outgrowth of its earlier policy. It was a logical development of the negative character of contractually limited democracy; for constitutional guarantees can only be counted upon to safeguard and not to promote the interests of minorities. In fact the word "nation" nowhere appears in the resolution, and despite the reference to "Independent States" it is the autonomous Muslim majority provinces that are to be sovereign. The whole of the constitutional development of India under Britain is not denied. The right of secession is rather insisted upon as the next step in that development. However confused this statement may be, it was sufficient to give a tangible goal and a political rationale to the myriad of aggressively self-differentiating organizations and clubs of Muslims which had arisen over the preceding fifteen years in India.

Within a very short time the term "Muslim India" was largely dropped for "Muslim nation." For the logic of consti-

---

[105] Abu-l-Ala Maududi, *Nationalism and India* (Pathankot, 1947), p. 25: "These satanic principles [of nationalism] have stood as formidable obstacles and powerful adversaries against the moral and spiritual teachings embodied in the heavenly books and against the law of God."

[106] It is true that traditional Islam is rather flexible on the question of the form of government, but fundamentalist Islam is not. Even in traditional Islam one ought not assume an indifference toward means as contrasted with ends. To seek the lesser of two evils is not necessarily to compromise all principle. In any case, the 'ulamā' have consistently attempted to Islamize governmental practice.

tutional history (though by no means entirely forgotten) there
was substituted the nationalist logic of the West, and its ultima
ratio—self-determination. The new tendency was enhanced by
the indignant Hindu insistence that the Muslims of India did
not constitute a nation. From this point the argument from
minority guarantees was dropped, and great efforts were concentrated upon demonstrating that the Muslims of India were
a nation.[107]

The conceits and categories of Western nationalist theory
were not at all new to India in 1940. Moreover, the material
for filling its various conceptual rubrics had already been supplied in large measure by the self-differentiating romantic
movement. Perhaps the single basis of nationality which was
not equally treated by Muslim proponents and Hindu opponents was precisely that evidenced by the continuing self-
differentiation. The Muslims gave primary emphasis to the
subjective character of nationalism, while the Hindus insisted
upon reasoning from objective characteristics. Subjective attitudes were the most impressive part of the Muslim claim, even
if they were supported by objective arguments. By the mid-
'forties we have not only large numbers of local clubs and
organizations for discussing, propagating, and purifying Islam,
but also a fascist organization of lower-middle-class Muslims,
Muslim labor organizations, a Muslim peasant association, a
Muslim student organization, and even Muslim chambers of
commerce. The Muslim League itself, after it had won over
many independent Assembly members, may be looked upon as
a self-differentiating group dedicated to the promotion of the
interests of Muslim politicians, in particular those from the
Muslim minority provinces.

[107] Durrani, *op. cit.;* Hyder, *op. cit.;* Jamal ud-Din Ahmad, *Through Pakistan to Freedom* (Lahore, 1946); Rahmat Ali, *op. cit.,* see also Pakistan Literature Series; Bashir Ahmad Dar, *Why Pakistan?* (Lahore, 1946).

A recurring feature of the belated Muslim "awakening" is its contradiction of what had been assumed to be accepted fact. Akbar's policy was found to have led to competition not co-operation between Hindus and Muslims.[108] Sivaji revolted against duly constituted authority. Aurangzeb was the greatest of all Muslim rulers.[109] The British took over India from the Muslims and not the Hindus. It was the Muslims and not the Hindus who were a resurgent power after Ahmad Shah Abdalli defeated the Marathas at Panipat in 1761. The Congress is not a "national" but a communal organization. There are three parties struggling for control of India, not two: the British, the Congress, and the Muslim League. There are two nations in India, not one.

The objective arguments ran down the list of territory, language, culture, and history. The territoriality of Muslim nationalism was based on the contiguous Muslim majority areas, though India as a whole was taken as the "country" in which the nation was formed. The Arabic and Persian elements in Hindustani, as well as those languages themselves, were the linguistic basis. The all-inclusive character of Islam was the cultural basis. And it was particularly during this period that the idea of a national mission was popularized.

The political exigencies of the time permitted two rather conflicting conceptions of the Muslim nation of India to persist side by side once the Lahore resolution had elicited the idea of nationalism. The first that was given most prominence in Hindu-Muslim polemic was that the Muslim nation already existed,[110] while the second arising from the compensatory aspect of romanticism was that the Muslim nation in India had to be built.[111] The two views were not taken as contradictory,

[108] Durrani, *op. cit.*, p. 32.
[109] Rahmat Ali, *op. cit.*, p. 195.
[110] Hyder, *op. cit.*, p. 2.
[111] *Ibid.*, pp. 24, 135.

for they appear side by side in the words of the same man. The second view does not mitigate the "metaphysical" right of the nation-in-becoming to statehood, though it may weaken its "political" right. About the first view, statehood is an end in itself, but about the second view, all sorts of questions regarding means and ends may be raised.

Perhaps the reason that no attempt was made to reconcile these two views before partition was that they are so easily reconciled in either Western or fundamentalist Islamic theory.[112] The first assumption of Western theory is that there must be sufficient "basic agreement" among the members of the nation. This was specifically assumed.[113] The next step is to assert that the true spirit of the nation will be evolved in history through the unhampered working of the democratic system.[114] In fundamentalist theory they are reconciled on the basis of the assumption that both means and ends are already laid down by Islam. Obviously it was preferable to use both views and not to reconcile them, for it is the reconciliations and not the views that are incompatible.

Of course the romantic fundamentalists were extremely indefinite, and often held conflicting opinions about the nature of Islam in regard to the form and goals of an Islamic state. Those few who were not so indefinite we shall divide into two groups: (1) those oriented toward Islamic tradition, and (2) those oriented toward modern Western conceptions. The largest group still tends to be swayed by the two smaller sections simultaneously; so we shall call them merely romantics, and fun-

---

[112] But not in the traditional theory; the 'ulamā' would have nothing to do with nationalism.

[113] Jamal ud-Din Ahmad, *op. cit.,* pp. 5 ff.

[114] This theory has been set forth for the "secularists" by Wilfred Smith in his *Pakistan as an Islamic State* (Lahore, 1951), p. 69: "An Islamic State in sense (1) is a state which its people are trying to make an Islamic State in sense (2). *An Islamic state in sense* (2) *is a state which Muslims consider to be good."*

damentalists no longer. The traditionally oriented alone shall retain the title "fundamentalists," and the smallest group of all shall be called the modernists.

The religious outlook of the old line Leaguers has been aptly described by Smith as ending with communalism.[115] After the establishment of Pakistan, secularism, in a political sense at least, best describes their point of view.

The fundamentalists opposed the Pakistan movement, and still oppose nationalism as a form of polytheism. They were ineffective only in their opposition to Pakistan, though their views on many other issues have had a great deal of influence on the Muslims of India. Their aggressive support of all things Islamic merely strengthened the mass of romantics in their support of the League before partition; but since then they have been a thorn in the side of a predominantly Westernized, if not secular, government. They are extremely important in themselves, but the more so for compelling the modernists to make their views more explicit.

As might be expected, the modernist theory is legislative, legalistic, nationalist, and democratic. It is based upon Iqbal's idea of the limitation of ijtihād by time and place, the renewability of ijmāʿ, and his suggestion that ijmāʿ be institutionalized in a legislative assembly.[116] All the Islamic legal heritage is not to be done away with. On the contrary, for no Islamic legislature may be permitted to agree on legislation that is contrary to the Qurʾān and the traditions reporting what the Prophet said or did.[117] Of course, the Islamic parliament would have the constitutional power to interpret the "principles" contained in these sources. By this theory ijmāʿ ceases to be a "source" of law and becomes a dynamic process for discovering the law. Logi-

---

[115] Smith, *Modern Islam in India,* p. 182.

[116] Iqbal, *op. cit.,* p. 165.

[117] I. H. Qureshi, *The Future Development of Islamic Polity,* Pakistan Literature Series no. 8 (Lahore, 1946), esp. p. 15.

cally ijmā' has always been a process, but since in fact the existence of an ijmā' could only be determined retrospectively, its dynamism was hardly perceptible.

Islamic tradition also insists upon certain qualifications in those who may exercise ijtihād or participate in an authoritative ijmā'.[118] This problem troubled Iqbal a great deal, but he had no solution for it.[119] Others were not as troubled by such fundamentalist qualms, and were more convinced by the romanticization of early Islamic democracy. They said that all Muslims had the right to interpret the law. Islam, they said, recognizes no priesthood. They found a verse in the Qur'ān to support their views: "I have placed you as vice-gerents on earth." [120] The caliphate, they said, must be the government of the people.[121]

This theory may justify the existence of a parliament in an Islamic state, but how can it reconcile Islam and nationalism? The answer lies in the limitation of the efficacy of an existing ijmā' by the circumstances obtaining at its formation. The circumstances qualifying the new ijmā' must naturally be the special territorial, linguistic, economic, historical, and cultural realities of Muslim India.

The modernist theory has within it the great virtue of attempting to reconcile the teleological nationalist and the fundamentalist Islamic views. It insists that the true spirit of Islam will reveal itself in the working of the machinery of ijmā'; and at the same time it recognizes that both means and ends are laid down by Islam. This theory may even be considered to be in conformity with the *modus operandi* of Islamic tradition, as an

[118] See "Idjma," "Idjtihad": *Encyclopedia of Islam*.

[119] Iqbal, *op. cit.;* he also did not believe that legislative ijmā' could work in India because non-Muslims would be represented in the legislature by their coreligionists. There were, however, later attempts to solve this problem.

[120] *Qur'ān*, Surah 6, verse 165. Ibn Khaldūn cites Abu Bakr, the first caliph, as specifically denying the "general caliphate" since a caliph can only represent someone who is absent and God is never absent. *Muqaddima*, p. 191.

[121] Durrani, *op. cit.*, p. 118.

attempt to Islamize social reform, parliamentarism, constitutionalism, and nationalism, though it is actually in opposition to the substance of Islamic tradition itself.

One cannot blame the 'ulamā' for being unresponsive to the intellectual symmetry of the ijmā' modernist theory of Islamic nationalism. In the first place it deprives the 'ulamā' of their exclusive right to interpret the law and in the second place it vests the right of interpretation in the politicians who are largely ignorant of Islamic tradition. There are, indeed, grave potential dangers to Islam inherent in a system that permits the rapid change and rechange of basic Islamic doctrines, giving democracy an excess of power and permitting the wholesale violation of religious conscience. Ijmā' modernism would Islamize democratic parliamentarism, even nationalism; but it could secularize Islam.

3 *The Catalyst*

FUNDAMENTALISM

The diffuse romanticism that permeated the middle-class Muslim mind gave rise to ijmā' modernism, but it also gave rise to a new fundamentalist movement. It is not difficult to see where the connection between romanticizing the past and going back to fundamental religious sources lies. Nor from a comparison of fundamentalist and romantic writings may one be immediately impressed with the difference of orientation. The major difference arises from the very diffuseness of the original romanticism. Professor H. A. R. Gibb has noted that the romantics are very vigorous in their defense of Islam, but they do not know what they are defending.[1] The fundamentalists do know what they are defending. In a sense the difference rests on the fact that the fundamentalists, having been first convinced of the validity of the romantic argument have gone back to read various early Islamic sources, and so have applied that argument to as much of traditional Islam as it could possibly comprehend.

[1] H. A. R. Gibb, *Modern Trends in Islam* (Chicago, 1950), p. 71.

One of the reasons that makes it difficult to ascribe distinct economic, or (initially) political, motives to the fundamentalists as opposed to the romantics arises from the general impression that they have merely carried romanticism to its logical conclusion. Logic is important in this instance not merely because it is a central element of Islamic legal theory, but also because of the manifest illogic of the romantic approach. To illustrate this point reference need only be made to the difficulty in reconciling various of the writings of Sir Muhammad Iqbal, who is now the prophet of romanticism, now of ijmā' modernism, and now of fundamentalism.[2] The key to the appeal of fundamentalism lies in this logic, to which students of law, Islamic and Western, and students of nonpractical "Western" science are both partial.

The logic of the fundamentalist argument, however, does not immediately come into play; for it follows two preliminary elements. The first of these is the general romantic argument that Islam is a complete, an all-embracing or perfect, religion. It is a natural religion, in the sense that the laws of God order all nature. Following Islamic precepts leads to happiness in this world as well as the next. The second element is the actual citation of various of these precepts from the Qur'ān and Sunnah. It must strike the reader that here there is an attempt to reconcile the modern and traditional points of view—though not necessarily "modernists" and "traditionalists" themselves. Ijmā' modernists and the traditionalists (the 'ulamā') have already solidified their ideas, but not so the general run of romantics. It should be clear, however, that romanticism itself provides a fertile field in which fundamentalism can work. The most effective means by which fundamentalism is superimposed on romanticism is the very traditionalist notion that decisions as to

[2] See W. C. Smith, *Modern Islam in India* (2d ed.; London, 1946), chaps. 3 and 4.

proper Islamic practice must be derived in accordance with a logical system from an accredited text. The Ijmā' modernists have tended to treat these texts as statements of general principles only, while they have concentrated their attention upon the nonrevealed legal system itself.[3] The consequence of these two tendencies upon romantic thinking has produced its dominant characteristic: that of citing passages from the Qur'ān to support rather modern, often crackpot ideas,[4] not in the sense of a specific application of a general principle, but as rigorous requirements of straightforward exegesis. When we come to the political theory of fundamentalists we shall find that in regard to the institutions of the Islamic state they revert to the status of romantics themselves. The reason for this intellectual retrogression is based upon the success of the modernists in proving the Islamic nature of consultative government and of popular franchise. The necessity of accommodating these ideas to traditional theory, while maintaining the framework of a rigid and comprehensive law, brought about a shifting and unsatisfactory result.

The new Islamic fundamentalism was not influenced solely by modernism. It is true that its first statements were aimed against modernism and at the Western educated, but this would merely associate it with extreme traditionalist opposition. Though such opposition exists, the reader will subsequently find the 'ulamā' to be rather accommodating to the facts of life and Western influence. The reader will also find that the 'ulamā' do not feel that such accommodation compels them to make any intellectual concession to modernism, as the fundamentalists have done. The real connection between fundamentalism

[3] E.g., Khalifa Abd al-Hakim, *Islamic Ideology* (Lahore, 1951), esp. pp. 212 ff.; and I. H. Qureshi, *The Future Development of Islamic Polity,* Pakistan Literature Series no. 8 (Lahore, 1946), esp. p. 9.

[4] For a good collection see *The Islamic Literature,* "Islamic State" (Special Number, Jan.-Feb., 1955).

and Islamic tradition lies not in the main stream of tradition, but in its revivalist tendency to which we have referred previously.[5] Fundamentalism, therefore, comprehends as great a desire for reform as does modernism.

The idea of reform is inherent in the term fundamentalism, if only in the sense of going back to some purer original religious practice. But it follows, too, that the reform contemplated is a reform of traditional religion and not merely of what are considered antireligious tendencies. Antireligious tendencies are vigorously opposed, but their manifestation is explained by the failings of traditional religion. In a way, this explanation is not an unreasonable starting position, since it rejects all earlier compromises of the 'ulamā' with their social and political environment, and thus preserves the "essence" of Islam while preparing for a new compromise. Of course, the stand of the fundamentalist is singularly uncompromising—except for the fact that their interpretation of religious fundamentals, obscure in themselves, must be conditioned by their own, that is, "modern," experience.

Although the relation of fundamentalists to modernists is characterized by outright hostility, that between fundamentalists and 'ulamā' is not free of friction. There is a significant doctrinal basis to this friction arising out of the reforming tendency of fundamentalism. The principal feature of this doctrinal difference is the rejection of taqlīd, and of the traditional view of ijmā'. Taqlīd is the essence of tradition, for by the operation of this principle every wise adjustment or application of the law to circumstances is fastened to the body of Islamic legal wisdom. Taqlīd is the product of, as well as the generator of, discipleship, which, as we have seen, is the *modus operandi* of tradition itself. The denial of taqlīd and the extension of the application of reason to the Qur'ān and Sunnah is the very definition of funda-

5 See above, p. 46.

mentalism. The denial of taqlīd is also the denial of the historical continuity of the Muslim community in the only sense in
which it is comprehensible to the 'ulamā'. An ijmā', or consensus, once it is found to exist, is also subject to taqlīd.
The main difference between ijmā' and other decisions so
treated being that an ijmā' may comprehend more than one
school of law. Ijmā' is, nevertheless, a broad enough concept
to permit cognizance to be taken of the practice of the community, so that there is a dynamic aspect which may, after an extended period, override taqlīd. Reforming movements have
opposed this aspect of ijmā', though the existence of the principle of consensus could not be denied, for it exists in the Sunnah itself.[6] The problem is solved by limiting the operation of
ijmā' to the dimly lit period of the Companions of the Prophet.
The denial of the traditional view of ijmā', especially as represented in the 'ulamā' of the age, is a denial of the dynamic aspect
of the principle of Islamic communal unity. It is also a complete
denial of the basis of the theory of ijmā' modernism and what
could be called "Islamic democracy."

The consequence of the denial of taqlīd and traditional ijmā'
must be the reopening of the gate of ijtihād.[7] It is only in this
manner that reason and individual judgment can be applied
to the Qur'ān and Sunnah. It should be marked that for the
modernist ijtihād is subordinated and closely related to ijmā' in
the sense that a consensus of individual judgments can have
legislative force. For the fundamentalists, approaching the
problem from the traditional point of view, the destruction of
ijmā' is a precondition of freeing ijtihād. Furthermore, since
the basic idea behind fundamentalism is that the original law
has been corrupted, ijtihād cannot be made free lest original law

[6] H. A. R. Gibb, *Mohammedanism* (London, 1954), pp. 170-171.
[7] See, for example, M. D. Rahbar, "Shah Wali Ullah and Ijtihad," *The
Muslim World* (Oct., 1955), pp. 356 ff.

be covered by yet newer and more insidious corruptions. The assumption is not that new laws are needed but that the original laws should be enforced. The need for ijtihād is therefore limited, and it is to be exercised only by highly qualified persons. Such persons are certainly not those who have been seduced by Western culture, nor by definition can they be the 'ulamā'.

By and large the only significant doctrinal difference between the fundamentalists and the 'ulamā' is in regard to legal theory. Boiling down all this to its essential substance, we may conclude that fundamentalists and 'ulāma' are actually defending the same laws by different arguments, the fundamentalists specifically by a more extensive use of reason. There are other frictions between these two groups. Particularly after the fundamentalist organization, the Jamā'at-i-Islāmi, was founded by Maulana Abu-l-Ala Maududi, these frictions seemed to be based on personal differences. The resultant lack of coöperation, however, arises from the most substantial disagreement of all, that is Maududi's denial of the 'ulamā''s view of themselves. In denying taqlīd and ijmā', and in blaming the 'ulamā' for the corruption of Islam, Maududi denies at once the ability, and validity of the function, of the religious institution in maintaining and personifying the historical continuity, the unity, and the divine guidance of the Muslim community. Rather than being the essential Islamic social and religious institution, the 'ulamā' do not even exist except as a problem for the Jamā'at-i-Islāmi.

THE JAMĀ'AT-I-ISLĀMI

The Jamā'at-i-Islāmi is the only significant fundamentalist organization in Pakistan, and its chief, Maulana Maududi, is its principal thinker and spokesman. Our present concern with this organization arises not merely from the interesting point of view which it presents, nor even from the considerable intellectual influence that it wields, but rather from the central part it played in the controversy over an Islamic constitution for Pakistan. The achievement of an Islamic constitution was, early after partition, made the central goal of the Jamā'at. By its prop-aganda and maneuvering it forced both the 'ulamā' and the modernist or secularist politicians to alter their positions, and it even proffered a solution that formed the basis of a short-lived agreement. The Jamā'at forced the pace of the treatment of this issue, and prevented its being worked out, if ever, by a long drawn-out process of mutual accommodation. Although many underlying questions of theory were never the subject of argu-ment, the Jamā'at forced the Constituent Assembly of Pakistan to attempt to settle these questions by the implication of con-crete law. A close examination of the Jamā'at and its founder is therefore necessary to our purpose.

On meeting officers of the Jamā'at one is struck by their devo-tion, their pride in themselves and their work, and not a little by the neatness of their dress and appearance. Their offices seem to be well organized and their accounts well kept. Jamā'at pub-lications are numerous and well printed for the most part. For an organization of such small size a surprising number of per-sons have no other occupation than Jamā'at administration, though some have other income from small landholdings. Their budgets are also fairly substantial, that of the Sindh provincial Jamā'at being in the range of a hundred thousand Pakistan rupees in 1954. Most of this sum went for the supply of free medical care to refugees in the Karachi area, for printing and paper, and for rent and salaries. The last published figures on membership show the total at 998, two having been expelled for their part in the Punjab Disturbances of 1953. These mem-bers are the select initiates who have qualified themselves for membership during a long probationary period; they were ob-served at study group meetings, in social welfare projects, and at prayer. These members subscribe part of their income to the support of the organization. They are drawn from a much wider group of adherents from which the main financial support of the organization comes, and by which much of its intelligence work and liaison with the 'ulamā' and the politicians are achieved. By and large the more prominent adherents, in either wealth or influence, are much too valuable as fellow-travelers to be brought into official affiliation, nor would some wish to be subject to such rigid discipline.[8]

On paper, at least, the organization has a fine administrative establishment divided into departments of education, propaganda, publications, finance, labor, and social services. A front group called Islāmi Jamī'at Tulabā', with its own English-language paper, works among the students. For work among peripheral adherents, the Halqa-i-Adab-i-Islāmi, Islamic Literature Circle, comprised of writers of light literature, has been organized, with one of its major purposes to combat the work of the so-called "progressive" writers of Urdu. Particularly designated individuals work among the 'ulamā'. There is apparently no department of organization, but the work of such a department seems to be handled through the appropriate section of the education department. The membership of the organization is concentrated in the cities. The headquarters are at Lahore and the most important branch at Karachi. The Jamā'at is extremely weak in East Pakistan, maintaining at Dacca a small office and a single paid official. As might be expected, Jamā'at propaganda has its greatest influence among students in the "modern" colleges—an influence that tends to continue after graduation in

---

[8] The preceding information is based on personal observation, what follows is based on a long series of interviews with officers, members, adherents, and "fellow travelers" of the Jamā'at. Some of this information may be found in Anis Ahmad, *Who is Maududi* (12 pp.), and Ali Ahmad Khan, *Jamā'at e-Islāmi* (19 pp.), Introduction Series nos. 1 and 2.

inverse proportion to the degree of success of the individual in obtaining a civil-service position.[9]

For all of this complex organization, the Jamā'at is perfectly centralized and speaks with one voice. That voice is usually the voice of Maulana Maududi. Maududi is the amir or chief of the Jamā'at, and all decisions are taken by the amir in council (i.e., the Majlis-i-Shūra). The shūra does not make decisions by majority vote, but rather by unanimous decisions. This is in accordance with the theory of the comprehensiveness of the Islamic religious and social ethic, and the explicit character of Islamic prescripts as derived from an unequivocal revealed source. The task of deciding on the proper policy for the Jamā'at is much akin to the task of legal ijtihād, which is the prerogative of the most highly qualified alone. Maududi's position is therefore extremely authoritative. The wisdom of his statements on varying occasions has never been brought into question. His subordinates refer to him in terms of unmitigated adulation. Moreover, when Maududi is unable to lead his organization, as during his two terms in prison, it is more or less inactive.

MAUDUDI

Maulana Abu-l-Ala Maududi was born in 1903 at Aurangabad in Hyderabad, Deccan, of a displaced Delhi family that claims descent from Maudud, a relater of traditions of the Prophet, who is said to have come to India with Muhammad ibn Qāsim. The family was settled near Delhi, before Mughal times, at a place called 'Arab Sarai (a short distance from Humayun's tomb). The Maududis were not 'ulamā', nor were they courtiers, though they were in imperial service. The removal of Maududi's father to Hyderabad is to be seen against the background of the

---

[9] In the single college where Urdu is the language of instruction the Jamā'at has had particular success. See the *Student's Voice* (Karachi fortnightly), Sept. 16, 1954, p. 1.

disappearance of the Mughal administrative apparatus and the emergence of the Nizām's dominion as the largest and most undefiled center of Mughal social and political tradition.[10] His father was nevertheless an advocate, and a "companion," of Sir Saiyid Ahmad Khan. The family enjoyed a modest income of about a hundred rupees a month from rented buildings in Delhi.

Maududi himself left school at Aurangabad in the tenth class to support himself after his father's death. At the age of sixteen he worked for a short time at Jabalpur as correspondent, then editor, of *Taj,* a local newspaper. In 1920 he went to Delhi where he worked as "subeditor" of *al-Jamī'at,* organ of the Jamī'at-al-'Ulamā'-i-Hind. He remained at this work until 1927, when he fell ill. Apparently his illness compelled him to return to the family home at Aurangabad where he remained for at least two years. He then returned to Delhi where he remained until 1932, when he went to Hyderabad and brought out the seventh and succeeding issues of the monthly that is most closely connected with his name, *Tarjumān al-Qur'ān.*[11] In January, 1938, he went to the Punjab at the invitation of Sir Muhammad Iqbal, and settled in the Gurdaspur district on an endowment of eighty acres containing a mosque and some four or five buildings which were to become the Dār al-Salām Islamic Academy. Iqbal died in April, and Maududi moved to Lahore in December where he served as dean of the faculty of Theology at Islamia College without payment. After one year the authorities insisted on paying him and thereby "controlling" him, so he left and returned to Dār al-Salām, where he continued writing and preaching. In 1941 he founded Jamā'at-i-Islāmi, and from there on his story and that of his organization are the same.

Two important points, arising out of this short sketch, must

[10] See W. C. Smith "Hyderabad, a Muslim Tragedy," *The Middle East Journal* (Spring, 1955).

[11] The first six issues were edited by one Abu Muslih.

be stressed; first, Maududi is not an 'alim, and second, he began his journalistic or literary career during the period of the Khilafat movement, the Montagu-Chelmsford constitutional reforms, and the Rowlatt Acts.

Maududi never attended a traditionally oriented dār-al-'ulūm in which he might have learned Islamic law along with the principles of discipleship and taqlīd. Insofar as Islamic religious studies are concerned, he is self-taught. He grew no beard until 1937, and he wore Western clothing until that time—that is, until about the time of his appointment to a religious post by Muhammad Iqbal. He did not begin the study of Arabic until the age of eighteen, and one of the first books he translated was an Egyptian work criticizing the institution of purdah; it was never published, to Maududi's present complaisance. At the age of twenty-two, Maududi began the study of English in order to read Maulana Muhammad Ali's commentary on the Qur'ān. Thus Maududi, in his twenties, presents the picture of a typical semi-Westernized, half-educated young Muslim whose personal heritage bears some imprint of the Mughal downfall, and whose adjustment to British rule and Hindu predominance was made all the more difficult by the events that gave rise to the Khilafat movement. Maududi is untypical because of his superior intelligence, his extended contact with the 'ulamā' through his work on *al-Jamī'at,* and his facility for popular writing and speaking in Urdu.

It will be remembered that the Jamī'at-al-'Ulamā'-i-Hind was organized in 1920 with the help of the Congress, and it gave its support to the Congress through the medium of the Khilafat campaign. The *Jamī'at* was, of course, pro-Khilafat, and Maududi, as its subeditor, was responsible in part for this policy. Members of the Jamā'at say that he did so only because he was paid for it, though such is strange behavior for a man who de-

manded and received a free hand regarding editorial policy.[12]
His support for the movement can be judged from the titles of
three books he is said to have translated from English to Urdu: [13]
*What Happened at Samarquand, The Condition of Christians
in Turkey,* and *Greek Atrocities in Smyrna.* It is explained that
he was not opposed to the aims of the Khilafat movement so
much as to its methods. (So was Jinnah.) He did, however, save
his lunch and movie allowances to help relieve the suffering of
Turkish refugees. It is probably fair to conclude that he was an
enthusiastic supporter of the Khilafat movement even after the
abolition of the caliphate, which fits in with his particular regard
for Maulana Muhammad Ali and his association with the
'ulamā'. Such devotion to the Khilifat movement also places
him among the considerable group of Muslims who simply refused to face reality. The end of his editorship on the *Jami'at* in
1927 corresponds more or less with the dying gasp of the Khilafat movement, and incidentally with the last prepartition appeal
of the 'ulamā' for the support of the Western educated.

One is forced to speculate about the effect of his close association with the 'ulamā' on his thinking. His position was doubtlessly extremely responsible for so young a person. It is, however, strange that among all the graduates of Deoband no one
could be found to fulfill the position of subeditor. The shortcomings of the 'ulamā' in presenting their case to educated Muslims must have been manifest to the youthful journalist. It is
also suggested that there was some friction between Maududi
and the 'ulamā' who were his superiors.

A great change is said to have taken place in Maududi's life as
the result of an incident that occurred in 1924 during the com-

---

[12] According to the same source.
[13] That is not before 1925 when he learned English, if our sources are
consistent.

munal disturbances following the failure of the "passive resistance" and Khilafat movements. A book was written by one
Dayanand Saraswati, a prominent member of the Arya Samaj
and a follower of Swami Shardanand, in which an insulting
reference was made to Muhammad the Prophet.[14] Dayanand
was murdered by a Muslim called Abd al-Rashid, and a sensa-
tional trial followed. In the ensuing discussion of it, a prominent
Hindu (said to be Gandhi, but this is hard to believe) revived
the old accusation that Islam was spread by the sword and not
by the validity of its moral teaching. Maududi answered this
accusation in a series of articles subsequently published as a
book under the title of *al-Jihād fi-l-Islām*. Jihād had already
been treated by the apologists in accordance with the dictionary
sense of the word as it appears in the Qur'ān, that is to strive
hard in devoted effort (for the good). Maududi, in close association with the 'ulamā', could not ignore the treatment of Jihād
in Islamic legal works as warfare for the defense of Islam, its
honor, and the Muslims themselves. Willingness to perform
Jihād at the risk of one's life is the test of true belief. From this
time on he is supposed to have devoted himself to the study
of Islamic theology, and his next published work *Towards
Understanding Islam* is by far his most popular one.[15] It was
translated into English in 1932 and became a required text for
senior matriculation students in various colleges throughout
India. The book has been translated into Arabic and was
circulated, along with other of Maududi's works, by the Muslim
Brotherhood of Egypt. As a result of this work Maududi sprang
into prominence as one of the leading theologians in India.

It is said that Maududi already had the idea for the forma-

[14] It is evident that these names and the incident referred to were garbled
by my informant. Such was the story, including the spelling of proper names,
that was told by a prominent member of the Jamā'at.

[15] It was originally written in Urdu, at the request of the government of
the Nizām, under the title *Risālat-Dīniyat*.

tion of the Jamā'at in 1932. There is no evidence in *Towards Understanding Islam* to support this contention; so it seems more likely that 1932 is an important date for the fact that it marks Maududi's initial success as a theologian in complete independence of the 'ulamā'. Having been founded in August, 1941, after the Muslim League's Lahore resolution was passed, the Jamā'at would seem rather to have been aimed against Pakistan, though it was undoubtedly influenced by several earlier self-differentiating and romantically oriented groups.

THE OFFICIAL HISTORY OF THE JAMĀ'AT

These considerations aside, it may be of value to summarize the Jamā'at's own view of its origin. The Jamā'at-i-Islāmi also has its interpretation of Indian history. We have already seen that the Congress interpretation of that history aimed at demonstrating the national unity of India through emphasis on the assimilative character of Hindu culture. The pro-Pakistan interpretation denied the Congress view, and stressed the distinctiveness of Islam and the exclusiveness of Hinduism. The Jamā'at-i-Islāmi interpretation sees these same events in the light of the successes and failures of the Islamic effort to convert all of India to the true faith. The Jamā'at itself represents the most recent success in this continuing effort. The following precis of a recent Jamā'at publication [16] will demonstrate this interpretation and present the Jamā'at's view of the role it played in the years before partition.

Despite the early contact of Islam with India, and the subsequent unbroken rule of Muslim kings over India for seven centuries, there were obstacles which prevented the complete conversion of the country [p. 12]. The influence of the original

[16] Mas'ūd al-Nadwi, *Nazrah Ajmāliah fi Tārīkh al-Da'wah al Islāmiah fi-l-Hind wa-l-Pākistān* (Arabic) (Cairo, 1372) (160 pp.). Page references are in parentheses throughout.

Arab Islam left but a slight trace in Sindh, which had not pene-
trated into the interior when India was overrun by Central
Asian Muslims who were themselves new in Islam [p. 15]. The
Muslim kings were tyrants, and caused the natives to become
ill-disposed toward Islam [p. 14]. The governments themselves
were not Shar'ī, but aristocratic and sought only earthly ends
[p. 16]. The credit for spreading Islam must go to the 'ulamā'
and the masha'ikh [p. 14]; but the 'ulamā' who came to India
were from Transoxiana, and they depended upon the late
Hanafi books. They were not well versed in the Qur'ān and
Hadīth. What is worse, they were imbued with the miscon-
ceptions of Greek learnings [p. 16].

The ups and downs of Islam depended thereafter on the
character of the Muslim kings. Akbar was the worst, for he took
on Hindu ways [p. 20]. In this he was assisted by venal 'ulamā'
who gave him the right to legislate as he pleased. When Akbar
decided that the new age required a new religion very few
'ulamā' stood the trial, while most bowed to the will of the king
[p. 21]. The Mujaddid Sirhindi restored Islam [p. 24], but the
emperor Jahangir failed to support him, so it again declined
[p. 25]. Aurangzeb [pp. 31 ff.] righted the wrongs of his predecessors, but his government remained hereditary and aristocratic in nature [p. 36]. Under the ensuing difficulties of the
Mughals various religious leaders arose and did their utmost
for the purification of Islam with limited success, until after
the Mutiny of 1857 the Muslims of India found themselves in
most unhappy circumstances.

Then Sir Saiyid Ahmad came forward to encourage modern
education in order to better the position of Muslims, but he
was guilty of two grave errors. He accepted British social
standards, and wrongly interpreted the Qur'ān on the basis of
Western philosophy [p. 58]. He dared to deny slavery in Islam
and polygamy, miracles, the existence of Jinn, and the virgin
birth of our lord, "al-Masiḥ." His interpretations and falsi-
fications became the sunnah of the later "deniers of the hadīth"
and the Qadianis. He did some good, but only "Allah knows

which is the heavier and which weighs down the scale of the balance of heavenly justice" [p. 59].

Deoband Academy was founded, in reaction to the modernizing movement of Sir Saiyid, in 1865 by Shaikhs, 'ulamā', and those associated with the Jihād movement.[17] They erred in another direction by maintaining the old method of interpretation which they had inherited from their Shaikhs before them. They blinded themselves to all except their own dogmas [p. 61].

The two trends struggled with one another, and the division spread throughout the community, even affecting the youth. There then arose a group of reformers who sought balance, social welfare, and reconciliation [p. 62]. These founded the Nadwat al-'Ulama' Academy in 1893. They sought to teach the Qur'ān and the Sunnah along with English and the modern sciences [p. 63]. The Nadwah stood midway between Deoband and Aligarh; it was the only school that taught Arabic as a literary language [p. 64]. It had great success in bringing the Westernized youth back to Islam.[18]

The first politico-religious mass movement in India arose out of the deepfelt reaction to the Balkan wars and the Italian conquest of Libya. After the war the movement was directed against Great Britain [p. 66]. This movement inspired the people. Nor should we forget the great contribution of the poet Iqbal, who purified the spirit of love for religion and urged the maintenance of the Islamic heritage, especially by his attacks on the Qadianis [p. 67]. Abu-l-Kalam Azad did great work in endearing religion to youth through his paper al-Hilāl, though after 1920 he changed [p. 68]. Their equal in thought, their better in deed was Maulana Muhammad Ali who devoted his life to the cause of Islam [p. 69].

The untoward events of this decade had a fortunate consequence in the change of religious atmosphere, and the reunification of the community. Westernization suffered a great blow

[17] See W. W. Hunter, *The Indian Musulmans* (Calcutta, 1945).
[18] The author is a graduate of this school as his name "Nadwi" shows.

But this religious revolution seemed to be only temporary [p. 70], because the Khilafat movement, like its predecessors, was based on a wrong ideology [p. 17].[19] With the abolition of the caliphate evil ideas once again reared their heads. Maulana Azad said that Kemal had done no harm in abolishing the caliphate, and that the Grand National Assembly was the proper form of government for an Islamic democracy [p. 72]. The worst attack on Islam came from the "deniers of hadīth" who were joined by the Westernizers in impugning some of the cardinal principles of Islam before the masses [p. 74]. This group still publishes *Tulū' Islām* right under the noses of the authorities in Karachi. Saiyid Sulaiman Nadvi led those who opposed this movement.[20]

The greatest cause of the decline in religion was the ṅeglect of duty by the 'ulamā', who wrongly involved themselves in partisan politics [p. 76]. They and many others fell for the nationalist line of the Congress, though Islam does not recognize nationalism. The nationalists sought to assimilate the Muslims into Hindu national culture.

As a result of Congress rule in seven provinces after 1937, communalism[21] grew and the Muslim League increased in power under the experienced political leadership of M. A. Jinnah. On the other hand, a group of Muslims led by the 'ulamā' grew fanatically pro-Congress [p. 80]. This was one of the most important impulsions driving the Kemalists and the *geographical Muslims* to attack the 'ulamā', and by association, religion itself. The period 1937–1940 witnessed the tri-

[19] In 1941 Maududi wrote *Tajdīd o Ihyā'al-Dīn* in Urdu, a criticism of "all reform movements from that of 'Umar ibn Abd al-Azīz to Shah Ismaīl Shahīd."

[20] Until his death, in 1953, the most prominent 'alim of Nadwat al-'Ulamā' Shibli's heir, and an important figure in the Islamic constitutional controversy in Pakistan.

[21] Qaumiyah is the word for communalism, but also serves as nationalism. Communalism became a perjorative term in India, but for the Jamā'at nationalism was worse. The present translation is justified by reference to Jamā'at emphasis upon the ideology of Islam, and denial of unrelated interests of Muslims.

umph of the geographical Muslims, and the ranks of the League grew for they imposed no condition upon membership except that a man be called a Muslim, regardless of how personally immoral he might be [p. 83].

When, in 1932, the split in the community was greatest, there appeared the movement for pure Islam. The movement was started by a pious believer, well versed in the book of God and the Sunnah, and in the problems and requirements of the age. In a monthly journal, *Tarjumān al-Qur'ān,* this ideology was explained, the ideology of the all-inclusive Islam, the content of its specifics and their beauty, the explanation of its roots and its laws so that men would accept it rationally and take it into the depths of their hearts [p. 84]. Maududi stood at the head, explaining Islam according to the laws of creation and economics and politics. He opposed the views of the avaricious 'ulamā', and the views of the Westernizers [p. 85].

The movement by which to overcome the apathy of the age was not communalism, but Islam itself. There cannot be an Islamic state in one limited territory; and an Islamic state is not merely one managed by Muslims; it must be in accordance with the principles of Islam. Islam is a perfect religion, with rules for all aspects of life, but the geographical Muslims do not take Islam for their constitution [p. 87].

The Islamic way of life must be based on the Qur'ān and Sunnah, all of which must be accepted. One may not pick and choose among the precepts of the Sharī'a. Those who hold to rigid taqlīd, which admits no ijtihād must be opposed; nor do we admit the falsehood which ascribes to ijtihād the rejection of the jointly held views of the "Salaf." [22]

The first period of the movement lasted from 1933 to 1941 [p. 89]. Success attended the efforts of Maududi in solving the religious problems of the Muslims. Then came 1937 when the Hindu threat to Islam was revealed, and Maududi felt compelled to unmask the Congress and to warn the Muslims. This

[22] That is, the ijmā' of the Companions of the Prophet.

he did in a series of articles in the *Tarjumān*. He first related
the history of the Muslims in India, debunking Congress
secularism, and showing the unsuitability of India for democratic rule. Were it not for the attacks of Maududi on the Congress the Muslim League would never have amounted to anything [p. 91]. Had the League alone been charged with maintaining Islam, there would have been no hope. It was essential
to cut off this evil before it became established [p. 92].

Finally, Maududi began to preach pure Islam as the true
way for Muslims rather than secular national democracy. The
Muslims had never come to India in large numbers yet they
ruled and prospered, developed their culture, and spread their
religion because they commanded to the good and forbade
evil.[23] They were blessed with this success because of the merit
of the 'ulamā' and the sūfis [24] who "professed the truth" in
word and deed. Had the kings employed these men in the
government *there would not now be a question of majority
and minority* [p. 95]. The Muslims are an ideological group,
and their duty is to attract Hindus to their universal ideology
as our predecessors did.

When it became clear that the majority of Muslims favored
nationalism, or "independence" [p. 97] within the logic of
majority rule, Maududi and his followers were faced with two
questions: (1) If the Muslims should fail to achieve an independent state, what shall be the method of saving Islam and
individual Muslims? (2) Should they succeed, how to preserve Islam among the minority in India, and how to defeat
the secular democratic tendencies and turn Pakistan into an
Islamic state? [25] Seeing that the future of Islam in India depended on these possibilities, and seeing that the results of their
separate efforts were slender over the past nine years, they

[23] *Qur'ān,* Surah III, verses 106 and 110, for the origin of the phrase.
[24] Mystics. For Maududi *tasawwuf* represents inner faith as opposed to outward conformity. *Towards Understanding Islam* (n.d., n.p.), p. 146.
[25] The recognition of Pakistan as a potential political framework for an
Islamic state is a much later development.

decided to join together. In August, 1941, at Lahore, seventy-five persons of all classes formed the Jamā'at-i-Islāmi, and elected Maududi the first amir [p. 99].

The second period of the movement, from 1941–1948, was devoted to organizational consolidation and character building. This proceeded in two ways, first through the select group of writers who found in the *Tarjumān* their inspiration [p. 100], and second through a great educational effort expended upon members and adherents to train them to live in accordance with Islam [p. 101]. For this purpose special study programs were organized at isolated and economically self-sufficient encampments. Character development was based on three elements. The first was the duty to proselytize among Muslims and non-Muslims, even though it incurred official hostility and often estranged close relatives [pp. 104, 105]. The second duty was to be loyal to the Jamā'at organization and its regulations because of the purpose of the organization to spread the true Islam [p. 105]. The consequence of these requirements was that for the first six years of its existence the organization numbered no more than one hundred, but there was no need of specific requirements and regulations to force the compliance of the members [p. 106]. The third duty was to freely criticize any aspect of the organization, or of the members' behavior which they might feel needed correction. The freedom of constructive criticism was a source of strength to the organization. The third period in the life of the movement followed the partition of India, and is the period of Jihād.

The publication from which the preceding was taken is a fairly recent work, so it is studded here and there with bits of penetrating hindsight. Events and ideas are nicely dovetailed so as to present a rational development, as is true of most such partisan theories of history. In other words, the Jamā'at theory is important to us mostly for its implicit judgment of events up to the time of partition. We shall, in what follows closely ex-

amine the events of the ensuing years, but first let us sum up
the ideological position of the Jamā'at on the eve of partition.[26]

MAUDUDI'S POLITICAL THEORY: PREPARTITION

Islam, according to Maududi, is the natural order by which
God wills the universe to proceed.[27] Man, like the earth, the sun,
and the moon, is perforce a Muslim in all his physical aspects,
but not necessarily in his moral attributes.[28] As a higher being
man has the freedom to choose to follow the will of God in his
social and personal behavior or not. Since God is man's creator
it follows that man ought to obey the will of God, for to do
otherwise would be to act contrary to his nature, which is the
most cruel deed of all.[29] To act in accordance with God's will,
man must know that will. To make man's task lighter God has
sent prophets to guide the human race. The last and most perfect guidance was brought by Muhammad, when the world
was ready for a universal religion. The core of Islam is the belief
that there is no God but Allah, and that Muhammad was His
last Prophet. The laws which are revealed in the Qur'ān and
through the behavior of the Prophet are then incumbent on all
Muslims.

Muhammad's mission was not merely to preach that God was
the creator of the universe, for, as the Qur'ān shows, the unbelievers accepted this fact.[30] They objected to accepting God as
their ruler and sovereign.[31] The real mission of the Prophet was
to deliver man of the injustice born of men assuming the rights

[26] The publications from which the following is taken are still circulated
by the Jamā'at.

[27] Maududi, *op. cit.,* p. 3.

[28] *Ibid.,* p. 4.

[29] *Ibid.,* p. 7.

[30] Maududi, *The Political Theory of Islam* (Pathankot, n.d.) (an address
delivered at Shah Chiragh Mosque, Lahore, October, 1939), pp. 8, 9.

[31] *Ibid.,* p. 10.

of God over other men.[32] "The basic principles (*sic*) of Islamic politics is that individually and collectively human beings should waive all rights of legislation and all power to give commands to others. The right vests in Allah alone." [33]

The Islamic state is not democratic, for democracy permits the laws to be changed by a mere majority. Majorities have been known to make foolish decisions as, for example, the Americans who repealed prohibition.[34] Theocracy is perhaps a more apt term than democracy, but since the term usually implies rule by priests whereas the whole population will run the Islamic state in accordance with the Qur'ān theodemocracy might be a better term.[35] In the Islamic state all administrative matters and other questions which are not settled by the Qur'ān and Sunnah will be decided upon by a consensus of those of sound judgment and learning in the Sharī'a.[36]

The laws of God are not so much limitations of freedom as its guarantee: for example, the laws of Sharī'a regarding the poor tax; prohibition of interest,[37] gambling and speculation; inheritance; and the rules regulating getting and spending which prevent class war, capitalist oppression, and the dictatorship of the proletariat.[38] The laws regarding purdah, man's guardian-

[32] *Ibid.*, p. 25.
[33] *Ibid.*, pp. 27, 28.
[34] *Ibid.*, pp. 34 ff.
[35] *Ibid.*, p. 31. The charge, often leveled in the Constituent Assembly, that an Islamic constitution would turn Pakistan into a theocracy run by the 'ulamā' led to a number of rebuttals. Abd al-Hamid's *Theocracy and the Islamic State* was republished by the Jamā'at in 1954 after appearing in the *Voice of Islam;* for the ijmā' modernists Khalifa Abd al-Hakim dealt with the question in *Islamic Ideology* (Lahore, 1951), pp. 201 ff.; even the 'ulamā' answered the accusation indirectly by disclaiming an institutional monopoly of interpretation, though they insisted that knowledge remained a pre-requisite. Mufti Muhammad Shafi, *Basic Principles of the Qur'ānic Constitution of the State* (Karachi) (from a lecture delivered July 12, 1953), p. 2.
[36] Maududi, *Political Theory of Islam,* p. 32.
[37] Maududi has written a book on this subject entitled *Sūd.*
[38] Maududi, *Political Theory of Islam,* p. 38.

ship of woman, the rights and duties of husband, wife, and children, conditional polygamy, the penalties for fornication and
false accusations of adultery make home life a haven of peace,
and avoid the tyranny of males over females or the "satanic flood
of female liberty." [39] The laws of retaliation, cutting off hands
for theft, prohibiting wine drinking, and the limitation placed
on uncovering the private parts ensure the preservation of human culture and civilization.[40]

The constitution of the Islamic state is enacted by God and is
unalterable. The sovereign of the state is God. All legislative
power vests in God. The government is entitled to obedience
only so long as it acts as an agent enforcing the Shari'a. The state
is universal. No distinction as to citizenship may be made on
the basis of class, caste, color, birth, social status, or profession.[41]
The right to govern rests in the whole community.[42] But the
state can be administered only by those who believe in the
Shari'a.[43] Unbelievers will not be permitted to influence the
policy of the state, though they will be accorded their Shar'i
rights as protected subjects. The object of the state is to encourage all types of virtue and eradicate evil; for which all forms of
political power, propaganda, peaceful persuasion, moral education, and social influence will be used. The amir of the state will
be elected, and "he will exercise full authority in all respects,"
and command complete obedience so long as he follows the
Shari'a. The amir may be criticized, sued in a court of law, even
deposed. The amir will consult an advisory council, which may
or may not be elected. The decisions of the council are not binding on the amir.[44] No one may announce himself as a candidate

[39] *Ibid.*, p. 39.
[40] *Ibid.*
[41] *Ibid.*, pp. 49, 50.
[42] *Ibid.*, p. 48; this is the "general caliphate" again.
[43] *Ibid.*, p. 45.
[44] *Ibid.*, p. 58.

for political office. "There can be no party divisions in the Islamic advisory council." [45] The judiciary will be independent of the executive.

The process by which the Islamic state is to come into being is determined by the nature of the state.[46] Since all authority in the state is exercised in God's own agency, the rulers have a special responsibility for which they are accountable to God in the hereafter. This responsibility lends the state a special character requiring that the army, the police, the courts, the revenue and taxation systems, the general administration, and the foreign policy differ from those of secular states.[47] Only a particular sort of individual can hold office under an Islamic government, and these individuals cannot be brought into being through the ethic of democratic nationalism. Nationalism is the antithesis of Islam, for it sets up the nation as a god. "A national state bearing the label of Islam will be bolder and more fearless in suppressing an Islamic revolution." [48] It is argued that once Pakistan is set up it could gradually be changed into an Islamic state, but that is no more true than that a lemon tree could at maturity bear mangoes.[49] A broad communal organization will not do either, for the Muslims are of varied moral character. There is no sense working for Pakistan, for it may have to be opposed afterward in any case.

"There should grow up a movement . . . which is in keeping with the fundamentals of Islam . . . [which] should produce *Muslim* scientists, *Muslim* philosophers, *Muslim* historians, *Muslim* economists and financial experts, *Muslim* jurists and politicians." [50] The technique of establishing such a movement

[45] *Ibid.,* p. 59.

[46] Maududi, *The Process of Islamic Revolution* (Pathankot, 1947) an address delivered at the Aligarh Muslim University), pp. 2–5.

[47] *Ibid.,* pp. 13 f.

[48] *Ibid.,* p. 29.

[49] *Ibid.,* pp. 17, 18.

[50] *Ibid.,* pp. 17, 18.

can be learned from the history of the success of the Prophet. Since only Muhammad's history has come down to us without falsification we must take that as our example. Muhammad concentrated first on preaching the unity of God, leaving the other problems of society for later. At first he was joined only by a few whose minds were clear, who were capable of understanding and accepting truth. Despite unspeakable hardships they stood by their beliefs until their struggle and their sufferings succeeded in making a great popular impression.[51] After a protracted struggle the first Islamic state was established at Medina with the aid of only four hundred workers. The ensuing decade was the period of the development of "a perfect sociopolitical system" from an abstract idea. Thousands were trained in the operation of an Islamic state, so that when the example of a perfect society won over the whole of Arabia by what amounts to a bloodless revolution, there were already in existence cadres of government officials.[52]

MAUDUDI AND THE CREATION OF PAKISTAN

Despite the fact that Maududi opposed the Muslim League and its goal of Pakistan, his influence over the thinking of middle-class Muslims during the years preceding partition increased. His criticism of the Congress was welcomed by the Muslim League, where as his exposition of the glories of Islam merely added to the general conviction that Muslims should have a state of their own in which to work out their destiny in accordance with their high ideals. Twice Maududi was invited to work with the League, but twice he refused.[53] The first occasion was in 1937 when he was asked to join in the work of the Muslim League research group. The second time was in 1945, when

[51] *Ibid.*, pp. 42–44.
[52] *Ibid.*, pp. 50, 51.
[53] Interview.

the Office Secretary of the Muslim League, Maulana Zafar Ahmad Ansari, was deputed to win Maududi's endorsement for the Muslim League program. Ansari was not successful with Maududi, though a close friendship grew up between the two. The fact that Maududi was felt to be useful to the Muslim League, whereas the leaders of the Ahrar and the Khaksars, for example, were not, indicates to what extent the Jamā'at was considered a religious rather than a political organization. Ansari was the same man who was entrusted at the same time with organizing the Jamī'at-al-'Ulamā'-i-Islām in support of the League.

It must be stressed that by 1945 Maududi and a great many League propagandists were generally agreed on the desirability of an Islamic state. Some even said, as did Maududi, that an Islamic state is one governed by the Sharī'a.[54] Maududi's insistence upon the sovereignty of God merely took the principle one step back, and was an outgrowth of his attempt at syllogistic theology. The real difference between Maududi and the League was over the question of whether the leadership of the League and its mass organization was suitable for carrying out the Islamic revolution that would bring a truly Islamic state into being.

The fact that Maududi denied that the League was capable of building an Islamic state by the methods it chose did not mean that he would take no cognizance of partition. In April, 1947, when the partition of India was imminent, Maududi, speaking at Madras, said that the Jamā'at would have to be split into an Indian and a Pakistani organization, each working within the political framework and under the peculiar circumstances presented by a democratic state with a Muslim minority and one with a Muslim majority.[55] After partition this, in fact, became

[54] E.g., Qureshi, *op. cit.,* p. 8.
[55] Interview.

the case; and there is now no overt connection between the two Jamā'ats.

The headquarters of the Jamā'at at Pathankot in the Gurdaspur district of Punjab fell on the Indian side of the line, so the amir and his staff moved, as refugees, to the outskirts of Lahore. At first their activity showed no deviation from the views expressed by Maududi a few years earlier. They went among the Muslim refugees from India, preaching and giving medical aid or food or clothing to those in need. As the numbers of refugees grew, and the government of Punjab increasingly revealed its inability to cope with the problem, the camps became centers of unrest. Like all groups that had opposed Pakistan, the Jamā'at was under a cloud; and the authorities suspected them of encouraging the refugees to demand more than the government could give. The Jamā'at's licenses to publish their various periodicals were not renewed by the provincial government, and their activities came under surveillance.

The difficulties from which the government of Punjab was suffering were the result of the bloody exchange of over eleven million people between India and Pakistan through the only feasible route—the one that brought the refugees first into the precincts of the provincial capital, from which they were loath to move. The Jamā'at, by its own admission, was "inactive" from August, 1947, to January, 1948.[56] The Jamā'at certainly had its own problems during this period, besides which there is no reason to believe that it should have departed from its previous methods until some external force should persuade it that another course was preferable. The first few months of 1948 witnessed significant changes both in Jamā'at policy and ideology.

[56] Interviews; Ali Ahmad Khan, *op. cit.,* p. 11; *Maududi on Islamic Law and Constitution,* ed. Chaudhri Ghulam Muhammad (typescript), introduction, p. 3.

The change in policy can be summed up by saying that the Jamā'at decided, rather suddenly, to accept the theory of the Muslim League rather than their own for the way in which an Islamic state could be created. It amounted to calling the League's bluff. Maududi now described the Islamic state and told the *politicians* how to bring it into being, despite the fact that he had already gone on record in the disbelief that a lemon tree could bear mangoes.

The changes in ideology were not only in regard to "the process of Islamic revolution" but also in regard to the constitution of the Islamic state. The most important of these changes were first an accommodation of modernist theory to the extent of permitting a limited degree of legislation by a democratically elected assembly, and secondly an elaboration of omitted details that would solve the really central question of what the Sharī'a required or permitted in regard to any specific legislative proposal.

Because of the Jamā'at's assertion that its ideology is based on the immutable law of God—and is therefore unchanging—and because of the tremendous influence of a single man in Jamā'at counsels, it is difficult to be sure of the causes of these changes. The changes themselves will be traced out presently, but first it may be worthwhile to mention certain circumstances that must have had some effect on Maududi's thinking.

The first of these circumstances was created by the fact that the Jamī'at-al-'Ulamā'-i-Islām, organized in 1945, supported the Muslim League and expected it to make of Pakistan an Islamic state. The 'Ulamā'-i-Islām did not get organized in Pakistan until December, 1947, when Maulana Shabbir Ahmad Usmani arrived in Karachi and set up an office in the home of Maulana Ihtisham al-Haqq.[57] Within a matter of days, the small house in Jacob's Lines became a center for the continuous comings

[57] *Dawn*, Jan. 1, 1948.

and goings of the Karachi 'ulamā', and their supporters.[58]
Among these supporters was Maulana Ansari, who retained his
association with the Muslim League, though Usmani was no
longer in need of a go-between. On January 13, 1948, at a meeting of the Jamī'at-al-'Ulamā'-i-Islām a resolution was passed
demanding that the government appoint a leading 'alim to the
office of Shaikh al-Islām, with appropriate ministerial and
executive powers over the qādis throughout the country.[59] At
the same time plans were being made to organize public opinion
throughout the country in "favor of a purely Islamic Constitution for Pakistan" by means of branches of the 'Ulamā'-i-Islām.
Shortly thereafter a complete table of organization of a ministry
of ecclesiastical affairs was worked out with names suggested
for each post.[60] It was proposed that this ministry be immune
to ordinary changes of government. An emissary was then
deputed to convert Maududi to this program, and he traveled
to Lahore and engaged the Amir of the Jamā'at in prolonged
conversations, but he was unable to overcome Maududi's hostility to the 'ulamā' and their methods.

The second circumstance of significance resulted from the
inability of the government of Pakistan to cope with the refugee
problem. It would be a great deal to expect of any government
to handle a sudden influx of nearly five million destitute persons, but the government of Pakistan was hardly established at
the time, nor should one forget that the flight of Hindus left
Pakistan without the facilities usually provided by the private
sector of the economy. Relations between the residents of West
Pakistan and the refugees were not good either. To alleviate at
least some of the mental anguish of the refugees, to encourage
their fraternal assimilation, and to extend their patience, the

[58] Interviews.
[59] *Dawn,* Jan. 14, 1948. What better proof of the identification of an Islamic
constitution with political recognition of their own institution.
[60] Interviews.

government offered them religious honor and made them religious promises, while exhorting the residents of West Pakistan to act as good Muslims. Refugees were called Muhajirūn, and thus associated with the first Muslims who followed Muhammad to Medina. They were told by the Prime Minister, by the Foreign Minister, by the Minister of Refugees, by the Minister of Finance, and by the Minister of Communication in public halls, in government buildings, in public parks, and in the mosques that Pakistan would be, or was, an Islamic state, that its constitution would be based on the Qur'ān, that economic equality, tolerance, and social justice would reign in Pakistan, or that Pakistan would be the laboratory of Islamic principles.[61] No wonder, then, that the refugees felt that theirs was a central problem of the Islamic state, and that the solution could somehow be achieved through the Qur'ān. Since their claims were somehow based on religion, they soon found religious leaders. On January 2, 1948, when the number of refugees filtering down from the Punjab to Karachi had become substantial, the Sindh Central Committee of Refugees was formed. Maulana Abd al-Hamid Badauni was elected its president, the same Badauni who later aided in founding the Jamī'at-al-'Ulamā'-i-Pākistān. Two days later a rival Sindh refugee committee was formed with Maulana Usmani at its head.[62] Maududi, too, had worked among the refugees and knew the depths of their misery and the elevation of their hopes.

It was not only the refugees who contrasted a wretched present with a glorious future. One might say that most of the ordinary people who supported the League expressed thereby a mild hope for a millennial solution to their problems. The leaders of the Muslim League hoped for much too, but whether through the operation of Islamic law is questionable. Many persons

---

[61] *Dawn,* Jan. 1, 3, 11, 14, 15, 24, 1948.
[62] *Dawn,* Jan. 5, 1948.

thought they saw an opposite tendency in Jinnah's words at the first meeting of the Constituent Assembly of Pakistan:

> . . . you will find that in the course of time Hindus would cease to be Hindus and Muslims would cease to be Muslims, not in the religious sense, because that is the personal faith of each individual, but in the political sense as citizens of the State.[63]

However Jinnah may have felt in August, 1947, the atmosphere had so changed that by the end of January, 1948, he felt compelled to say:

> I cannot understand why this feeling of nervousness that the future constitution of Pakistan is going to be in conflict with Sharī'at Law? There is one section of the people who keep on impressing everybody that the future constitution of Pakistan should be based on the Sharī'ah. The other section deliberately want to create mischief and agitate that the Sharī'at Law must be scrapped.[64]

On January 6, 1948, Maududi broke his long silence with the first of two speeches at the Law College in Lahore. After pointing out that neither the Westernized politicians nor the 'ulamā' could be relied upon to lead Muslims toward the goal of an Islamic revolution, he went on to say: "The case of Pakistan is not, however, the same as that of other Muslim countries, certain similarities of situation not withstanding. This is so because it has been achieved exclusively with the object of becoming the homeland of Islam." [65] By reasoning from this premise Maududi has left his own theory of Islamic revolution for that of the Muslim League. The solution to the problem thus posed

---

[63] *C.A.P. Debates,* Vol. I, no. 2 (Aug. 11, 1947), p. 20.

[64] *Dawn,* Jan. 26, 1948 (from an address before the Sindh Bar Association, on the occasion of the Prophet Day).

[65] "Islamic Law," *Maududi on Islamic Law and Constitution* (typescript and separately numbered pages), ed. Chaudhri Ghulam Muhammad, p. 4.

lies in convincing the actual government of Pakistan, and the Westernized leaders of opinion, of the validity and applicability of the Sharī'a.[66] The 'ulamā' are neglected completely.

After restating the basic theology that we have already summarized, Maududi went on to describe the Sharī'a, its sources in the books, and the prophets, its harmony with human nature,[67] its classification of required and prohibited behavior, and the *permissibility of legislation or legal adjustment in the sphere between*.[68] Permissive legislation may come into being by interpretation, analogous deduction, ijtihād where no precedents exist, and by "recommendatory legislation." [69] The practice of these four methods is strictly limited to the letter and spirit of the Sharī'a, and may be exercised only by properly qualified persons.

The rest of the talk was devoted to answering the arguments of those who object that the Sharī'a is outdated, or that it cannot be enforced because of the differences between the various schools. The first argument was disposed of by referring to the permissibility of legislation, and by the assertion that Islamic law had fallen back but one hundred years anyway. The second argument was answered by saying that the jurists had disagreed only on minor points, and though these differences would be perpetuated in regard to personal status law, for the rest and in the future *democratic ijmā'* would solve the problem.[70]

[66] *Ibid.*, p. 5.

[67] *Ibid.*, p. 11.

[68] *Ibid.*, p. 12. The classification of human acts as required or prohibited is without regard to whether the text in question is clear, or clearly applicable under the circumstances. Where it is not clear even nonpermissive parts may be altered by the first two methods mentioned in the next sentence.

[69] *Ibid.*, pp. 21, 22. All are referred to as legislation, but possibly only in the sense of replacing decisions of the same type.

[70] *Ibid.*, p. 29. The implication of the passage for democratic legislation may be wider than merely deciding which school to follow.

Wherever all the schools agreed in the past, their decision remains authoritative.

Maududi's second talk to the law students was given on February 18, 1948, but in the meantime he was touring and speaking in favor of an Islamic constitution. At about this time an eleven-year-old bill was revived in the Punjab Legislative Assembly requiring that the Shar'ī right of women to inherit agricultural land be enacted into law. Because of opposition from the landholding classes, the bill had failed to pass in 1937.[71] Now its proposal was accompanied by processions in the streets and a march of "angry amazons" on the Assembly building.[72] The bill was passed on January 29, 1948, four days after Jinnah's promise that the law of the land would be based on the Sharī'a. Thus, without the preliminaries of education, social reform, or the moral regeneration of the civil service, was one possible method of making the Sharī'a the law of Pakistan demonstrated. The law of God was enacted by an "un-Islamic" legislature, and became binding upon an "un-Islamic" judiciary.

THE FOUR DEMANDS

In his second Law College talk, Maududi still argued for a gradual change to Islamic law, referring again to the history of Muhammad's mission, and even to the gradual abrogation of Islamic law by the British. The British had completed their task nearly a century before, so Islamic law would have to be brought up to date.[73] But Maududi rejected the plea for a secular state *for the present,* arising out of the argument for gradualness. How, he asked, can an irreligious state create an Islamic atmosphere? Only if all the energies of the state are directed toward

[71] Smith, *Modern Islam in India,* p. 268.

[72] *Dawn,* Jan. 27, 1948. The intemperate language is that of the newspaper, all the women were veiled.

[73] "The Means and Method of Enforcing Islamic Law in Pakistan," *Maududi on Islamic Law* (numbered with the first lecture), p. 36.

that goal, he answered. Clearly the small band of Islamic revolutionaries had no longer the major responsibility for propagating the true Islam; this task was to be shifted to the Muslim League government! In order to achieve this goal, Maududi insisted that the goal had to be expressly declared. The Constituent Assembly must make the following unequivocal declaration:

i) that we Pakistanis believe in the supreme sovereignty of God and that the State will administer the country as His agent;

ii) that the basic law of the land is the Sharī'ah which has come to us through our Prophet Muhammad (peace be on him);

iii) that all such existing laws as are in conflict with the Sharī'ah will be gradually repealed and no such law as may be in conflict with the Sharī'ah shall be framed in the future;

iv) that the State, in exercising its powers, shall have no authority to transgress the limits imposed by Islam.[74]

It should be noted that the declaration would not have the force of law, it would merely be a statement of intentions.[75] It should similarly be noted that nothing specific is said about enacting the Sharī'a as the law of the land, only the repeal of conflicting law is desired. In a later passage, however, Maududi says the development of an Islamic state from this basis will take but ten years, "and as this change comes about gradually, the previous laws can be *amended* or repealed and Islamic laws *substituted* for them."[76] The Sharī'a itself is taken as known and undebateable.

The effect of such a declaration on the electorate would be

[74] *Ibid.*, pp. 38–39.
[75] *Ibid.*, p. 32.
[76] *Ibid.*, p. 40.

profound, according to Maududi. The people would "naturally" elect those most suited to carry out the intention of such a declaration, and the process of Islamic revolution would be begun. Subsequent events were, as we shall see, to prove Maududi greatly mistaken.

MUHAMMAD ASAD AND THE SUPREME COURT

In the weeks following his second Law College address Maududi was invited to give a series of talks over the Lahore broadcasting station. The station was owned and operated by the provincial government, but it is probable that the invitation came at the instance of Muhammad Asad, who was then the director of Islamic Reconstruction in the Punjab service. Before Asad left this position, he also managed to bring out an issue of *Arafat,* an English-language journal, in which he published an article called "Islamic Constitution Making." Asad's theological approach was more or less the same as that of Maududi's later position, though it may have been presented in terms a bit more acceptable to the Western mind. Asad's constitutional suggestions are very much like those of Maududi, except for certain additions. He expressly stated that the head of the state must be a Muslim, whereas Maududi had implied that no non-Muslim could hold any policy-making position. Asad also included a series of individual rights providing for freedom of speech so long as it does not aim at undermining the ideals of the state, freedom of religion short of the right to attempt to convert Muslims, free education for all, the right to employment, social security, and the inviolability of property. But in one other respect Asad went a great deal further than Maududi in that he provided for a means whereby disputes regarding the Shari'a provision in specific cases might be resolved:

The guardianship of the Constitution is vested in the Supreme Tribunal, the members of which shall be elected by the Majlis ash-Shūra on the advice of the Amir. This Tribunal shall have the right (a) to arbitrate, on the basis of the naṣṣ ordinances of the Qur'ān and Sunnah in all cases of disagreement between the Amir and the Majlis ash-Shūra referred to the Tribunal by either of the two parties, (b) to veto on the Tribunal's own accord, any legislative act passed by the Majlis ash-Shūra or any administrative act on the part of the Amir which, in Tribunal's considered opinion, offends against a naṣṣ ordinance of Qur'ān or Sunnah, and (c) to order the holding of a referendum on the question of the Amir's deposition from office in case the Majlis ash-Shūra prefers, by a two-thirds majority, an impeachment against him to the effect that he governs in flagrant contravention of the Sharī'ah.[77]

In the October, 1948, issue of *Chiragh-i-Rah,* a Jamā'at publication, the constitutional proposals of Asad were published along with a similarly arranged series that had been gleaned from the writings of Maududi by Na'im Siddiqi.[78] Asad was given faint praise, but his "supreme court" suggestion was criticized as not in conformity with Islam, for such was not the practice in the period of the "Rightly-Guided Caliphs." [79] Maududi's constitutional proposals are presented with enough expansion and detailing of individual and minority rights to outdo Asad, and in addition there appeared a few clauses relating to disputes between the amir or head of state and his council:

[77] Muhammad Asad (Leopold Weiss) "Islamic Constitution Making," *Arafat* (March, 1948), p. 57.

[78] Muhammad Asad and al-Saiyid Abu-l-Ala al-Maududi, *Muqtaraḥāt fi al-Dastūr al-Islāmi* (Arabic), introduction, p. 2.

[79] *Ibid.,* p. 6, n. 1. Surprisingly enough, the first reference to a body such as the Supreme Court as the proper institution for determining whether legislation contravenes the Sharī'a is contained in Qureshi, *op. cit.,* p. 15.

Clause 26   The Amir shall have full freedom in interpreting the commandments of the Sharī'a, the use of analogous reasoning, the use of ijtihād, and recommendatory legislation within the limits of the Sharī'a.[80]

Clause 35   Issues before the council will generally be settled by majority vote. . . .[81]

Clause 36   If the Amir and the Council or a majority thereof disagree . . . 1) the Amir will generally accept the opinion of the council or a majority thereof in questions connected with the administration of the State or the improvement of the government, 2) the council will generally accept the opinion of the Amir in regard to specific Shar'ī issues in which ijtihād or the interpretation of explicit laws are involved.[82]

Clause 37   When the council expresses a want of confidence in the Amir the question of which should resign will be settled by a plebiscite.[83]

Clause 38   The right of legislation is reserved to God.[84]

Clause 39   None of the laws of God may be abrogated by anyone.[85]

Clause 40   It is the duty of the Council to make definite and devise consequential laws by analogous judgment and ijtihād on any of the commands of God which are obscure or ambiguous.[86]

Clause 41   On questions which the Sharī'a leaves open, mankind have the right to legislate, but the council may not legislate on any point on which there is a provision of the Sharī'a, nor contrary to the spirit of the Sharī'a.[87]

The rights of the amir, as described in Clause 26, comprise all the methods of modifying certain aspects of the Sharī'a mentioned in Maududi's first Law College address. Despite the

[80] *Ibid.*, p. 23.
[81] *Ibid.*, p. 25.
[82] *Ibid.*, p. 26.
[83] *Ibid.*

[84] *Ibid.*
[85] *Ibid.*, p. 27.
[86] *Ibid.*
[87] *Ibid.*

"full freedom" of the amir, the same rights are granted to the council in Clause 40 and Clause 41, except for the right of "interpretation." Maududi was none too clear on this point in his Law College talks but it would seem that he was at the time willing to permit the council greater legislative powers than in his previous lectures and writings. The elimination of the power of interpretation seems to be a reconciliatory device of the compiler, in order to cover Maududi's previous statement that the amir shall not be bound by the advice of the council. The word "generally" appearing in Clause 35 and Clause 36 serves the same purpose. If in accordance with Clause 40, the amir interprets a passage in the Qur'ān in a particular manner he can prevent "democratic legislation." Ijtihād and deduction by analogy may be jointly exercised, but, according to Clause 36, the council would have to give way to the amir's opinion.

Most important of all, though, is the provision whereby the indirect authority for the decision as to what is Shar'ī may be the electorate. This decision is to be made indirectly, for the people have only the right to choose between the view of the council and that of the amir. Besides there is no indication that the issue leading to a vote of confidence will be a question of Shar'ī law; it may be simply based upon the un-Islamic behavior of the amir. Clause 37 actually provides the method by which the deposition of the amir may be accomplished, but the incumbent amir, whether newly elected or not, retains the right to decide what is or is not Shar'ī. It will be noted that both Asad's and Maududi's constitutions give no authority to the 'ulamā' whatsoever.

While Siddiqi was thus laboring to compile and reconcile Maududi's statements, the Amir of the Jamā'at was busy elsewhere. From March until May Maududi toured West Pakistan and spoke to large crowds on the question of an Islamic constitution. He did not bother much with the fine points we have here been stressing. Instead he pressed the four-point declaration that he now *demanded* of the government in increasingly unpleasant tones. From calling the government's bluff he had come to challenging the government—perhaps in order to make the great public impression that was the second phase of the process of Islamic revolution.

PART TWO

Substantiation

Introduction to Part Two

The various ideological positions described in the first part of this study are not unique to Pakistan, though the organizations that tended to support each of these views are at least in some measure different in Pakistan than they are elsewhere. The distinctive character of the organization and collective experience of the 'ulamā' of Pakistan, of the Muslim League leadership, of the military and the bureaucracy of Pakistan, and of the Jamā'at-i-Islāmi are the accidentals affecting the political and ideological interaction of these groups. Ideas themselves neither contradict one another nor blend in a bland eclecticism; it is always specific persons who attack unwelcome ideas or who compromise their views for more or less concrete reasons. Thus, it is possible to conceive of political circumstances under which contradictory ideas may never come into conflict with one another; in fact, such circumstances prevail throughout most of the Middle East today. Furthermore, where in Turkey a couple of decades ago or in Indonesia today the opposition of secularism and Islam is violent, the political interaction between the secularists and the religionists is not such as to encourage the former to make concessions nor the latter to elaborate their views in a practical manner.

Another problem of considerable difficulty centers upon the identification of really significant ideological patterns. This problem is apparent to anyone who has even cursorily examined the great variety of books and pamphlets and articles on Islam which briefly circulate in the Middle East and then are lost from view. Textual analysis of these writings may reveal the existence of a number of neat ideological categories, but one rarely finds organizations based upon the distinctive aspects of these writings, and one often finds the authors themselves coöperating with organizations having divergent goals or views.

A breakdown of contemporary ideological tendencies into a number of categories must be justified, and here our justification is neither simplification nor logical consistency but rather the concentration of political influence behind each tendency. Political events in Pakistan confirm which were the views most seriously held and which were the core ideas of each tendency. The ideological positions described in the first part are therefore to be substantiated by reference to the political interaction of the groups related to each. Our assumption that these tendencies are not unique to Pakistan is based on the fact that the tradition of the 'ulamā' of Islam is everywhere the same, though Islamic practices may vary geographically. Consequently, when other groups come to grips with Islamic tradition, they will tend to come up with the same answers.

The practical political substantiation of these views in Pakistan is the result of the special conditions prevailing in that country. However, it will be found that the political circumstances and nonreligious controversies which permitted the practical development of Islamic political thought in Pakistan are themselves unrelated to these theories. This lack of relationship further substantiates our contention that the ideological positions taken have more to do with the nature of traditional Islam than they have to do with conditions and persons in Pakistan.

Pakistan's politics are of special interest because it is almost unique among the new governments of Asia and the Middle East. Unlike most other governments of this area, independence did not find the government at the head of a vigorous national movement and in full command of either a party or a governmental administrative apparatus or both. Not only was an effective bureaucracy lacking, and the problems facing the existing bureaucracy immense, but partition resulted in the near dissolution of the Muslim League; the political institutions bequeathed by the departing British were in no sense the product of the efforts of the prepartition Muslim League.

Where strong national parties with the support of the military and the bureaucracy have inherited power from imperialist governments, and often are led by outstanding figures enjoying certain charismatic qualities, religious controversies of the kind that emerged in Pakistan never see the light of day. All groups must compromise with such a national leadership, and they must subordinate their ideologies to the benefits to be gained from the appearance of absolute support for the central goal of national independence and the leader who achieved it. The period following the achievement of independence is one of great unity and enthusiasm and often of very hard work. In Pakistan this period was a very short one, indeed.

In the second part of our study, the political problems facing Pakistan's leaders and the instruments with which they were to deal with these problems are briefly described. During the short period in which Muḥammed Ali Jinnah presided as Governor-General of Pakistan and enjoyed great political support, it is possible to discern how he intended to go about organizing the

political and administrative framework of the new state. It is
probably incorrect to assume that Jinnah had no clear notion
of how he wished to resolve the problems of the representative
formula in the federal legislature, of the future organization of
the Muslim League, and of the Islamic character of the state.
The fact of the matter is that, despite his theoretically unlimited
powers, the opposition was very great and the means at his
disposal were unequal to the task. Perhaps the best evidence of
Jinnah's policies regarding the constitution and the federal
formula is to be found in the proposed revision of the organization of the Muslim League, and it is significant to note that
the validity of this new organization was argued from an
Islamic premise which has no ideological relationship therewith. This incident is the key to understanding the whole subsequent progress of the Islamic constitutional controversy in
Pakistan.

Liaqat Ali Khan attempted to continue the centralizing and
balancing policies of Jinnah, and he made more significant
efforts to use the symbols of Islam to strengthen his own hand.
Liaqat failed in his first efforts at politically reorganizing Pakistan, and his second attempt was cut short by an assassin's bullet.
However, in this ill-fated attempt he revealed his own attitudes
toward the idea of an Islamic state and challenged the 'ulamā'
to elaborate their own. Behind the scenes of the great drama of
the Kashmir conflict and the clash of East and West Pakistan
there was enacted a smaller one among some of the 'ulamā'
and the politicians. Reports were presented and decisions taken
which made few headlines and are now matters of obscure
history. Nevertheless, in these reports and decisions and in the
comments and arguments accompanying them is the substantiation of the dominant and politically important tendencies
in Islam today.

As in the first part, an attempt has been made to maintain

a chronological framework so that the positions of each group can be discerned as they developed. The discussion now revolves about key pronouncements of the Constituent Assembly and the reaction thereto of those most concerned. These pronouncements were the Objectives Resolution, the Report of the Board of Ta'līmat-i-Islāmīa, the Interim Report of the Basic Principles Committee, and the decisions of the Suggestions Sub-Committee. It is not our purpose to elaborate a comprehensive political history of Pakistan, but each of these statements can be understood only in the context of the political circumstances of the time.

The Objectives Resolution is of such general import that its discussion requires a broad analysis of Pakistan's major problems. The debate on the resolution in the Constituent Assembly illustrates the variety of interpretations put upon this pronouncement. The Report of the Board of Ta'līmat-i-Islāmīa is a unique document illustrating in the most concrete manner both the constitutional preferences and confusions of the more traditionally oriented. The explanation of the rejection of the "Views" of the Board of Ta'līmat-i-Islāmīa leads us through a discussion of secularism and Pakistan's foreign-policy position in 1950. The Interim Report of the Basic Principles Committee ignored the Board of Ta'līmat-i-Islāmīa, but Bengali objections to the federal formula indicated in the Interim Report kept the whole constitutional issue open. The fact that the Prime Minister refused to recognize such Bengali opposition, but instead withdrew the report because it was not acceptable to religious elements compelled the reopening of discussions with the 'ulamā'. The decisions of the Suggestions Sub-Committee were made in a spirit of compromise, but they did not involve any change in the basic attachment of the politicians to the consensus theory and parliamentary supremacy.

4 The Objectives Resolution

A casual examination of the public statements of Pakistan's leaders will at once apprise the reader of the five issues that dominated the political field in the first year of Pakistan's existence. In order of importance these were the war in Kashmir, the refugee problem, "provincialism," the status of the Hindu minority, and the Islamic character of the state. The question of Kashmir's accession to India or Pakistan dominated, and to a large extent determined, the nature of all relations between the two dominions. The refugee problem was similarly an international issue of great complexity involving immigration and citizenship laws, the transfer of funds, the disposition of evacuee property, the unification of families, the payment of compensation, the maintenance of law and order, and the provision of rehabilitation facilities on a huge scale. The status of the Hindu minority was related to the refugee

problem and had international implications, but receded somewhat in importance as the Punjab was emptied of its non-
Muslims. The large Hindu minority in East Bengal was safe
and not too uncomfortable for the time being. Provincialism
was a deep-rooted attitude with powerful political and constitutional support. It was a problem because it prevented the
full mobilization of Pakistan's political and financial strength
in dealing with every other issue facing the new state. The issue
of the Islamic character of the state is the subject of the present
study, but to properly understand its resolution it must be
placed in its political context.

The same casual examination of public pronouncements
might lead to the erroneous impression that the Islamic character of the state was the central issue of Pakistani politics. Of
course, as far as the 'ulamā', Maududi, and a few others were
concerned, it was. The impression of the absolute importance
of an Islamic constitution was produced by the fact that religious slogans and exhortations were used by the politicians to
build morale in the face of unprecedented social and economic
dislocations, to unite the country behind the Kashmir war
despite divergent sectional interests, to encourage private and
provincial effort for the rehabilitation of refugees, to promote
a tolerant attitude toward the Hindu minority in accordance
with Islamic tradition, and to unite the population behind its
central government through the contraposition of "provincialism" and Islamic universalism. The proof of the merely contingent importance for the politicians of the Islamic character
of Pakistan will be demonstrated by an analysis of their deeds
rather than their words, for we have already described the
disparate views of the parties concerned, and the rest of this
study is concerned with the manner in which a working agreement was produced through the interaction of these groups and
individuals.

PROVINCIALISM

The explosive development of Islamic political theory in Pakistan is primarily owing to the failure to find an acceptable federal solution. The connection between the two lies in the simple fact that each draft of the constitution prepared by the various committees of the Constituent Assembly had not only to provide for the Islamic character of Pakistan, but had also to provide a federal formula. The inability to agree upon a federal formula kept the religious question open, and tempted the politicians to make concessions to the 'ulamā' in order to forward their own political interests.

The heritage of prepartition politics has prejudiced most Pakistanis in favor of federalism. Moreover, the peculiar distribution of the population and territory of the state all but necessitates a federal form of government. That part of India that became Pakistan included two self-governing provinces and most of two others, five princely states in various degrees of vassalage, one chief commissioner's province, and a miscellaneous collection of tribal and excluded areas. The population of these territories was over seventy-five million. Among these people at least five major languages, Urdu, Bengali, Punjabi, Sindhi, and Pushtu, are current. More striking yet is the fact that a majority of them, isolated from the rest by more than a thousand miles of Indian territory, live in East Bengal and speak Bengali. Nearly ten million, or almost a fourth of the population of East Bengal, are Hindus.[1] In the Punjab there were about four million Hindus and Sikhs, but these have now been replaced by a somewhat larger number of Muslim refugees.[2] Sindh and Karachi have also received a larger number of refugees.

---

[1] *Census of Pakistan* (1951), Census Bulletin no. 2 (table 6), p. 1.
[2] *Ibid.,* Census Bulletin no. 1 (provisional table 1), p. 1; and Kingsley Davis, *The Population of India and Pakistan* (Princeton, 1951), pp. 196, 197.

In the face of these facts the government set before itself the task of uniting the citizens of Pakistan in a national loyalty, of rationalizing the administration of the various constituent political units, and of fostering a single national language. Opposition to the government's program was labeled "Provincialist," which term has come to mean the equivalent of blackguard or traitor in Pakistan. Provincialism, however, is not without roots of considerable depth and strength.

Provincial feeling was enhanced by the fact that the British-designated provinces coincided roughly with language areas, and that the provincial populations are differentiated by noticeable racial characteristics. Provincial feeling is also sustained by certain prejudices which formed the bases of sectional Muslim majority movements: Bengal is the intellectual center of the Indian universe, Bengalis are politically more aware than others, Bengalis are unfairly excluded from the army because of their small size and narrow chests, Bengali is a beautiful literary language, Bengali Muslims have been prevented from realizing their full potentialities because of the Hindu-British conspiracy which deprived them of their rights in land and their share of government offices, and Bengali Muslims are more religious-minded than others. Punjab is the heart, the head, and the sword arm of India;[3] Punjabis make the best soldiers and civil servants; Punjab is the locus of the cultural link between the Mughal heritage of India and the rest of the Islamic Middle East. Pathans are fighting men from the hills, they are the least self-conscious about being Muslims, their primary loyalties are to the tribe, but civilization, which has restricted their economic activity (raiding), owes them a living. Sindhis are underprivileged, oppressed peasants; their language, their race, and their culture are all unappreciated. Baluchistan has been unfairly deprived of its right to provincial autonomy.

[3] *The Election Manifesto of the Punjab Muslim League* (Dec., 1950), p. 6.

Paradoxically enough the Muslim League had itself fostered provincialism through its prepartition policy of demanding greater provincial autonomy and more Muslim majority provinces. Provincial autonomy in Muslim majority areas was merely a more extreme kind of minority safeguard, whereas additional Muslim majority provinces might have increased the federal representation of the community, had a responsible government for all of India come into being. The goal of Pakistan and secession changed these considerations, but it will be remembered that the demand for provincial *sovereignty* in the Lahore Resolution of 1940 had been the price of Punjabi and Bengali support.

The tools with which the Governor-General, Muhammed Ali Jinnah, and the Prime Minister, Liaqat Ali Khan, had to work to solve this problem were the Constituent Assembly of Pakistan and the Muslim League. From the start, the Constituent Assembly was recognized as inadequately representative, and preparations were made to change its structure at an early date.[4] Still, there were limits to such alterations under the Indian Independence Act, and the solution sought through the new constitution was prejudiced by the Assembly's composition. The Muslim League, which might have been the really effective instrument of political control and direction, was strangely transformed into an entrenchment of the discontented, the ambitious, and the greedy.

THE CONSTITUENT ASSEMBLY

It is not unoften that the best laid constitutional plans of men gang agley; but, unless politics is to be classed as a mystic science it must be agreed that institutions planned for one situation will be unsuitable for another. The Constituent Assembly of Pakistan came into being as the result of the un-

[4] *C.A.P. Debates,* Vol. II, no. 1 (Feb. 24, 1948), p. 11.

reasonable extension of the principle of territorial partition to political institutions. Originally, the Constituent Assembly of (British) India was provided for in the May 16, 1946, announcement of the Cabinet Mission proposals.[5] Those proposals were meant to preserve a united India and yet provide the widest possible latitude for an autonomous, but not independent, Pakistan. Although the possibility of "Pakistan" was admitted, its probability was vitiated by permitting provinces to opt out of the various groups to which they were assigned for the first stage of constitution making. Needless to say the political unity of East Bengal and the Muslim northwest was not visualized since each fell in a separate grouping. In fact the most outstanding feature of the plan was the establishment of the all but unqualified autonomy of the provinces. The only subjects reserved for the central government were defense, foreign affairs, and communications and the power to raise the finances required therefor. In other words, controversy over federal relationships was to be sidestepped by reducing such relationships to the bare minimum. The dominant problem was the old question of the number of seats to be allotted to each community within the provincial delegations. The solution was simply to have Hindus, Muslims, and Sikhs elected in the proportion of one to a million of their actual numbers in each province by the members of their own community in the provincial legislative assemblies. It was, moreover, assumed that an interim government acceptable to all parties would rule until all the provincial, group, and union constitutions were worked out. The Constituent Assembly was elected in July, 1946.[6]

The haste with which the last viceroy decided to give effect to British promises, and the lack of a ready alternative, deter-

[5] Chanakya, *Indian Constituent Assembly* (Bombay, 1947), Part II, pp. 1–17.
[6] Lord Birdwood, *A Continent Decides* (London, 1953), p. 27.

mined that power would be delivered to *the* Constituent Assembly.[7] The League's demand for Pakistan had already become a demand for two constituent assemblies; Mountbatten's decision not only required two legally sovereign bodies, but required them immediately. The inadequate device decided upon was simply to divide the single Constituent Assembly in two.

The original plan was designed to eliminate the weightage given to minorities in order to permit Bengal and the Punjab to remain parts of subordinate Muslim federations (while maintaining their right to opt out after the first elections under the new constitution). It, therefore, permitted the provinces to bargain on terms of complete equality. The new plan destroyed this equality and determined, in the case of Pakistan, that East Bengal should provide more than half the members of the Constituent Assembly. The Indian Independence Act did not affect the relationship of the provinces to the central government; it merely provided the center with the powers that had been exercised by the Viceroy in Council.[8] Provinces were not permitted to opt out of the dominions to which they were assigned.[9] The Constituent Assembly, which was first to meet in provincial groups, was now to meet as a whole in each instance. Finally these assemblies were to serve as interim legislatures, so that constitutional issues would continually effect day-to-day policy decisions and the stability of the government.

In the Constituent Assembly of Pakistan East Bengal was represented by forty-four members, of which thirteen were Hindus and four others were non-Bengali nominees of Jinnah. Punjab had seventeen seats of which four were for minorities.

---

[7] A. Campbell-Johnson, *Mission with Mountbatten* (London, 1951), p. 99.

[8] *Indian Independence Act* (1957) (10 & 11 Geo. 6, ch. 30), Article 8 (2): ". . . each of the new Dominions . . . shall be governed as nearly as may be in accordance with the Government of India Act, 1935." (*Unrepealed Constitutional Legislation* [Government of Pakistan], p. 116.)

[9] Campbell-Johnson, *op. cit.,* p. 90.

Three of the minority seats of the Punjab were not to be filled as a consequence of the Hindu and Sikh exodus. The North-West Frontier Province had three seats. Sindh was allotted four seats, of which one was reserved for a Hindu. Baluchistan Province had one seat. The Baluchistan States, Khairpur State, Bahawalpur State, and the NWFP States and Tribal Areas, with considerably more than five million in population, were unrepresented. Over five million Muslim refugees in the Punjab and Sindh were also unrepresented. Insofar as the states were concerned, the Cabinet Mission proposals had provided that they would be given representation on the basis of agreements to be worked out with the various groups to which they were assigned. Mountbatten's plan merely urged the states to accede to one or the other of the successor states, delivering control only over defense, foreign affairs, and communications. Pakistan like India planned to bring the states into closer, more "democratic" association with the central government.

THE MUSLIM LEAGUE PARLIAMENTARY PARTY

Out of a total of sixty-nine Constituent Assembly members, the Muslim League Parliamentary Party comprised forty-nine members. The Bengal League delegation of twenty-seven thus held a permanent majority, which, together with the small group surrounding the Prime Minister, could overcome any opposition. The Prime Minister's group, excluding those from East Bengal, was about five or six strong. The Punjab delegation of fourteen Muslims was hopelessly split and unable to function as a bloc. There were some from the Punjab who acted as "Punjab firsters," but, generally speaking, the importance and influence of the province that supplied the bulk of the military and the majority of the civil service was not felt in the Assembly. The minor delegations were also divided and partly tied to the cabinet.

The Bengali majority in the Assembly Party remained the

dominant feature of parliamentary politics. It is, however, true that rarely if ever did all the members attend any particular session nor were all the seats filled at any one time. Bengal was also not without its dissidents, and the number of these grew to as many as three or four in an otherwise well-disciplined group. Some few might also prefer to follow Liaqat Ali Khan than their provincial leaders, though when the test of their loyalties came with the Interim Report of the Basic Principles Committee no more than three actually spoke up for the report in one way or another. The position of the East Bengal delegation was then one whereby it might allow the government and the faction of Liaqat Ali to put through any measure at all, or whereby, in coöperation with the perennial Hindu opposition from their own province, they might prevent any measure regardless of its origin from passing. The Bengal group did not take the initiative into its own hands.

The key to understanding the working of the Assembly is to remember the function of the Muslim League Parliamentary Party, at the private meetings of which all questions were first thrashed out. Once the majority of the League members decided upon party policy every member was expected to respond to the party whip. Discipline was by and large good, but not for the reasons one might expect. The Indian Independence Act had not provided for the dissolution of the Constituent Assembly until it had completed its task of writing the new constitution. It is true that the Federal Court of Pakistan recognized, in 1955, the limited right of the Governor-General to dissolve the Assembly, but the decision was admittedly more political than legal.[10] Even if we assume that a dissolution was possible at an earlier stage, we must remember that the indi-

[10] Federal Court of Pakistan, *Report on the Special Reference Made by H. E. The Governor-General of Pakistan,* p. 40; see also *The Pakistan Times,* March 4, 1955.

vidual MCA would not have to campaign in the villages but only among the members of his own provincial legislative assembly (unless the Constituent Assembly had itself first changed the electorate provided for in the Indian Independence Act). The various provincial legislative parties were, of course, to be bound by the choices of the Muslim League Parliamentary Board. The Parliamentary Board, however, did not at that time exist, and when it was again formed after the reorganization of the League it was not under the control of the Prime Minister.[11]

THE MUSLIM LEAGUE

Theoretically, or legally, the British delivered up Indian sovereignty to two constituent assemblies; actually it was delivered to the Congress and to the Muslim League. Mountbattan waited only for the approval of the leadership of these two groups before putting his plan into operation. The assumption on which the partition of India was executed was that the officers of the League represented the will of the Muslims of the subcontinent. Nor was Jinnah or Liaqat slow to equate the membership of the League with the Muslim "nation" itself. So it was that when the council of the Muslim League met in February, 1948, to decide upon its reorganization some rather startling "democratic" conclusions were drawn from these facile assumptions. Since the government of Pakistan ought to be responsible to the people, and since the people were the members of the League, it followed that the leaders of the League and the government ought not to be the same persons and be thus responsible to themselves. The council, therefore, accepted an amendment to the draft constitution of the League providing that no member of the Pakistan cabinet or a pro-

[11] The Central Parliamentary Board was elected by the Muslim League council at its organizing meeting on February 19, 1949. *Dawn,* Feb. 20, 1949.

vincial cabinet could hold any office in the League organization.[12] An attempt was made to exempt Jinnah from this provision, but since, in all probability, the Prime Minister was his choice as president of the League, Jinnah refused the exemption, saying that his constitutional position as governor-general made it his duty to hold the balance "evenly and fairly amongst such parties as may come into existence or be formed from time to time." [13] In other words, Jinnah's answer to those who desired the amendment was to say that the Muslim League no longer represented the nation—while he continued to do so.

The circumstances surrounding this decision of the Muslim League council are important for they reveal to some extent the constitutional intentions of the government, and the reasons why the Muslim League could not be used as an instrument of government policy. Before the council met, a subcommittee was convened to report on a draft of the new party constitution.[14] This constitution was drafted on the assumption that Liaqat Ali Khan would be the new president, and full control was centered in the Working Committee to be nominated by the president, and the Parliamentary Board on which the president would serve in an ex-officio capacity.[15] The council of the Muslim League was given the power to review all acts of the Working Committee and to pass resolutions concerning the policy of the League. The most important purpose of the draft constitution, which was unexceptional in its other aspects, was to shape the League so as to facilitate a solution to the provincial-federal problem. The composition of the council was, therefore, the crucial question. Previously the council had been

[12] *Constitution and Rules of the Pakistan Muslim League* ("Adopted by the Council of the PML at Karachi on the 23rd and 25th of February, 1948 under the presidentship of Qaide Azam M. A. Jinnah"), Article 6, p. 3.

[13] *Dawn,* Feb. 29, 1948.

[14] *Dawn,* Feb. 22, 1948.

[15] Interviews; *Constitution and Rules of the Pakistan Muslim League,* articles 33-42, pp, 10-15.

roughly representative of the dues-paying members in each province, with some weightage given to those provinces with a larger Muslim population.[16] The reason for this arrangement was to give greater weight to the more devoted members in the Muslim minority provinces. Thus the prepartition composition of the council, reflecting membership and not population, was more like that of a mere party than the representative of the "Muslim nation." In February, 1948, no one could attempt to guess at the number of League members in the various provinces; in fact the first task of the League after the meeting was to reorganize itself. The council formula was not based upon the strength of the League in the various provinces because the new League did not yet exist; it depended upon the government's idea of what was the proper distribution of power among the provinces. In other words, the postpartition composition of the council was more like that of the representative of the nation (i.e., a parliament) than that of a political party. The formula was

Punjab	150
NWFP	40
Sindh	50
Baluchistan	20
East Bengal	180
Nominated by president	10

along with the presidents and general secretaries of the provincial Muslim leagues, and the officers of the Pakistan Muslim League. The total membership would be 465.[17]

This formula for the representation of the various provinces on the council of the Muslim League is the first indication we

[16] Interview; see also Campbell-Johnson, *op. cit.,* pp. 65, 66.
[17] *Constitution and Rules of the Pakistan Muslim League,* Article 18, pp. 6, 7.

have of the probable policy of Jinnah on the all important representative formula for the federal parliament in the constitution. With this council formula accepted and with the Muslim League fully under the control of the cabinet, one might reason that it would be relatively easy to press the Constituent Assembly to accept a similar federal representative formula. However, the second premise was never fulfilled.

The draft constitution of the League had been presented, first, to a subcommittee comprised of eleven prominent Leaguers who had been advised by Jinnah himself "on the vital necessity of seeing that provincialism in all its aspects is eradicated and made secondary to the national interests of Pakistan." [18] The sessions of the subcommittee, as those of the council, were closed although press releases were published daily on their activities. The formula itself received very little attention in the press, nor is there any indication that the subcommittee recommended any changes. The lack of protest can be explained by the fact that there were only three Bengalis on the subcommittee, the council meeting was held in Karachi (which effectively prevented many Bengali councilors from attending), and at the time the government of Bengal owed its existence solely to its appointment by Jinnah. By contrast, a great deal of attention was given to the amendment regarding the eligibility of cabinet ministers. The amendment was rejected by the subcommittee, where there were six central or provincial cabinet ministers, but when moved from the floor it was passed by a large majority.[19] An explanation for this action may be found in the fact that the meeting was attended by a large number of refugee politicians who had fled to Karachi in the hope of finding jobs, homes, and political influence.

With the passage of the amendment any hope that the gov-

[18] *Dawn,* Feb. 22, 1948.
[19] *Interview.*

ernment may have had of using the League to further its
policy, or explain that policy to the public, was lost. The amendment also deprived the government of effective control of
candidacies, and it established an irresponsible source for the
emission of policy statements for the only Muslim political
party in the country. Because those in the government could
not take party office, the "outs" naturally gravitated to these
positions of influence.

Without control over candidacies there was no effective
weapon the government could wield within the party to keep
its supporters in line; it had to, and it did not hesitate to use
other methods, including the powers of the Governor-General
and the governors to appoint and dismiss ministers,[20] and to
move a tribunal to investigate a prima-facie case of corruption
and malfeasance.[21] Even the rules of the Assembly itself were
used to deprive a member of his seat.[22]

STATUTORY CONTROL VERSUS PARTY CONTROL

So long as Jinnah was alive the question of Bengali domination, or even a general provincial revolt against central authority, could not arise. This was not only owing to the
popularity of the Governor-General and the extraordinary
powers [23] he wielded with the widest consent, but also to the
initial dependence of both Punjab and East Bengal upon the
federal government. In the first place, the Governor-General
retained the power through the provincial governors of re-

[20] *Unrepealed Constitutional Legislation,* p. 15: "51 (1) The Governor's
ministers shall be chosen and summoned by him . . . and shall hold office
during his pleasure."

[21] *Public and Representative Officers (Disqualification) Act, 1949* (Government of Pakistan, Ministry of the Interior).

[22] *C.A.P. Debates,* Vol. III, no. 2, pp. 31 ff.

[23] *Unrepealed Constitutional Legislation: Act of 1935,* p. 13, chap. iv,
"Legislative Powers of the Governor-General"; *Indian Independence Act,*
Section 9, p. 117.

moving provincial ministers from office. Dr. Khan Sahib, the leader of the Congress government of NWFP was removed in this manner within a week of Pakistan's independence. Personal factionalism within the provincial assemblies increased the effectiveness of central interference. Aspiring ministers were always prepared to accept the burden of forming a new provincial government. In the second place, the task of governmental reorganization in East Bengal, which lost its capital and nearly 90 per cent of its higher civil servants, and in the Punjab then undergoing the trials of a massive exchange of population, was far greater than the administration and financial resources of the provinces could bear. In the third place, except for the central government, there was no alternative leadership capable of commanding the confidence of such diverse groups as comprised the various provincial delegations. Finally, we must note that the strongest demand for provincial autonomy came from the factions that were out of office, or were about to be removed; so that at least a part—the part in power by the grace of the center—was always willing to follow the government.

As might be expected, the tendency during Jinnah's thirteen months in office was toward centralization rather than provincial autonomy. There was no concerted plan to be found behind a few isolated acts, but they were sufficient to arouse apprehension and even violent, if limited, opposition. The financial difficulties with which the new state was faced during its first year of existence were great enough to permit a grudging delivery of certain tax powers to the center. By an amendment to the Government of India Act the center took over from the provinces the power to levy and collect the sales tax, duty on succession to property, and the estate tax.[24] By means of Mountbatten's last order, the restriction on the amount of

[24] "The Government of India (Amendment) Act 1948," *Acts of the Constituent Assembly of Pakistan,* pp. 1, 2.

the export duty on jute which the federal government might keep had been removed, so that Bengal's economic grievances were already great.[25]

The dismissal of Dr. Khan Sahib and the installation of Khan Abdul Qayyum Khan as chief minister of the NWFP raised little criticism throughout the country. Khan Sahib's brother, a member of the Constituent Assembly, was imprisoned on the suspicion of treasonable intentions,[26] but none of the Assembly members protested. Qayyum imprisoned about 250 Red-Shirts, but he had no difficulty in winning the confidence of the NWFP assembly.

Difficulties arose between the federal government and that of Sindh over the status and control of Karachi almost as soon as the central authorities took over the facilities of the Sindh government. The unwillingness of Sindh to accept refugees from the Punjab was another cause of friction. Matters came to a head in the aftermath of the communal riot of January 6, 1948, in which many refugees and civil servants were involved in the killing of local Hindus and transient Sikhs, and in the looting of a great deal of property.[27] Since "Law and Order" is, under the Act of 1935, a provincial subject, the administrative responsibility both for the riot's occurrence and for the investigation and preventive action which followed was of the Sindh government. The details are obscure, but we know that the federal government objected to the exercise of police power over its secretariat by the province. In February the Government of India Act was accordingly amended to provide for

[25] *Governor-General's Order 22, 1947.*

[26] Richard Symonds, *The Making of Pakistan* (London, 1949), p. 123.

[27] See M. S. M. Sharma, *Peeps into Pakistan* (Patna, 1954), pp. 166–173, for a Sindhi-Hindu interpretation of the riots, in which Punjabi Muslims and the Central Secretariat are blamed. Jinnah himself blamed a "conspiracy" (*Dawn,* Jan. 11, 1948), apparently of Hindus. Thereafter the Sindh government was under pressure for its poor police organization, and for the imprisonment of refugee rioters (*Dawn,* Jan. 12, 14, 15, 1948).

concurrent federal and provincial jurisdiction over "certain offenses committed in connection with matters concerning the Central and Provincial governments." [28] Mr. Khuhro, the chief minister, was dismissed by the Governor of Sindh, acting under the direction of the Governor-General, and soon after a resolution was passed by the Constituent Assembly directing the government of Pakistan to permanently establish the federal capital at Karachi and to take over the administration of the city.[29] In pursuance of the Assembly's resolution, the Governor-General established the federal capital in Karachi and ordered the central administration of the city under Section 290A of the Act of 1935.[30]

A further amendment of the Government of India Act permitted the central government to direct the manner in which the executive authority of the provinces might be exercised in an emergency whereby the economic life of a part of Pakistan was threatened by "any mass movement of population." [31] The text of the new clause was general in its application, but there was no doubt that it was directed toward the situation in the Punjab. The government of Punjab was overwhelmed by the magnitude of the refugee influx from East Punjab after partition, and it called upon the central government for aid. Both the Prime Minister, Liaqat Ali Khan, and the Refugee Minister, Mr. Ghazanfar Ali Khan, proceeded to Lahore and attempted to ease the problem by negotiations with India.[32] The vexed question of the disposal of evacuee property arose between the two dominions and incidentally became one of the reasons or excuses for the falling out between the pro-

[28] *Unrepealed Constitutional Legislation,* VIIth Schedule, p. 109.
[29] *C.A.P., Motions Moved in and Adopted by,* serial no. 17, p. 15.
[30] G.G.O. no. 15, *Gazette of Pakistan* (Extraordinary), July 23, 1948, p. 372.
[31] "The Government of India (2nd Amendment) Act 1948," *Acts of the Constituent Assembly of Pakistan,* serial no. 3, pp. 2, 3.
[32] *C.A.P. Debates,* Vol. III, no. 3, pp. 47, 52–53.

vincial Refugee Minister, Mian Iftikharuddin, the provincial Finance Minister, Mumtaz Daulatana, and the Khan of Mamdot, the chief minister. Disunity in the provincial cabinet, the constant danger of refugee disorders, and the fact that many aspects of the question were the subject of international negotiation necessitated the provision of a legal basis for overcoming the unwillingness of Mamdot to accept executive directives from the Prime Minister. Bengali members were justifiably apprehensive, though no great transfers of population had taken place in the east [33] but they overcame their fears on the assurance that the problem was strictly limited to West Pakistan, and supported the Prime Minister.

DEPENDENCE UPON THE CONSTITUENT ASSEMBLY

The death of Jinnah considerably changed the parliamentary conditions under which Prime Minister Liaqat Ali Khan worked. The bargaining power of the East Bengal delegation was immediately increased, and regardless of what might be the government's ideas on the future constitutional set-up, the Prime Minister had to come to immediate terms with that delegation. The price of full coöperation had to be some increase in Bengali influence at the center and the strengthening of the dominant faction in the provincial government of East Bengal. The requisite coöperation was achieved by appointing Khwaja Nazimuddin, the chief minister of East Bengal, to the dignified office of Governor-General of Pakistan; and by appointing in his place his nominee, Mr. Nurul Amin. Nurul Amin was subsequently confirmed in his position by the Provincial Parliamentary Party, but there were some who thought that the party election should have preceded the decision from Karachi. The prudent use of central patronage also served to smooth Nurul Amin's path, and the finances of

[33] *Ibid.,* pp. 51, 57.

the province were considerably improved in March, 1949, when East Bengal was again permitted to retain 62.5% of the export duty on jute.[34]

The strengthening of Bengali influence at the center was hardly in accord with the implied policy of the government, but it was a necessary expedient under the circumstances. The circumstances which the Prime Minister faced were difficult in the extreme, for Jinnah died without having succeeded in solving any of Pakistan's pressing problems. At the time of his death fighting was still going on in Kashmir, the Muslim League was still in the process of reorganization, the Constituent Assembly had done almost nothing toward framing a constitution,[35] the composition of the Assembly had not yet been altered,[36] factional fights raged in Sindh, the Punjab, and Baluchistan, and the refugees still pressed heavily upon Karachi, Lahore, and their hinterlands. It was, moreover, strongly feared that Jinnah's death might precipitate a "crisis in confidence." The unifying force of the Muslim League had already been sacrificed on the "altar of democracy." Before he could proceed with all the unfinished business on his desk, Liaqat had to create a new atmosphere of unity and confidence, and he had to eliminate all possible causes of serious instability.

[34] *Orders of the Governor-General* (1947–1950) (Government of Pakistan, Ministry of Law), "Government of Pakistan (Distribution of Revenue) Order, 1949," p. 135.

[35] The Committee on Fundamental Rights of Citizens of Pakistan and Matters Relating to Minorities had been set up on August 11, 1947, but had made little progress. *A Summary of Work Done,* 1st Session C.A.P.; Resolution no. 9.

[36] A committee to negotiate with the states, tribal areas, etc., was also set up during the first session. *Motions Moved in and Adopted by the C.A.P.,* p. 9. The Committee on the Addition and/or Redistribution of Seats was set up on March 2, 1948. *Ibid.,* p. 11. Neither committee had reported at the time of Jinnah's death.

KASHMIR

The two fields in which some success would lead to an enhancement of unity and stability were those that also comprehended the greatest dangers thereto. These two fields were the struggle in Kashmir and the issue of the Islamic character of Pakistan. Success in Kashmir was not so easily obtainable. Fighting had been more or less at a standstill since May, 1948, when Pakistani regulars had rushed in to stem the Indian tide.[37] The August 13 resolution of the UNCIP did not bring about an immediate cease-fire, but subsequent events brought about a greater willingness for ending hostilities. Certainly Jinnah's death was not the signal for a renewed offensive, nor does it seem that Pakistan could afford to pay for one.[38] Moreover, the position of the Indian army in Kashmir was considerably strengthened during the fall. Indian troops returned to the offensive, opening the Ladakh trade routes and relieving the besieged town of Poonch. It was during September, 1948, that Hyderabad was overrun and the superiority of India's army forcefully demonstrated. Toward the end of 1948 concentrations of Indian troops were threatening an attack in the direction of Lahore. These were sufficient reasons for Pakistan's acceptance of the UNCIP's proposals of December 11, 1948, leading to the cease-fire on January 1, 1949, but they were not all. Pakistan has always been rather confident about the outcome of a free plebiscite in Kashmir. Consequently, India's admitted readiness to consult the wishes of the inhabitants of Kashmir once hostilities ended was an important factor in Liaqat's decision to accept the cease-fire proposal. On January 5, 1949, the UNCIP added provisions for a plebiscite to its

[37] Michael Brecher, *The Struggle for Kashmir* (Canadian Institute of International Affairs, 1952), p. 98.
[38] *Ibid.*, p. 97.

August 13 resolution, and both sides accepted these resolutions as a basis for settling the dispute.

It was perhaps a foregone conclusion that a smashing success could not be achieved in Kashmir, for Pakistan's task was to withdraw gracefully from its aggressive position until it were possible to ease itself into a plebiscite. Though a fleeting optimism did result from Liaqat's successful completion of this maneuver, it was still optimism and not gratification. There were of course many who would have preferred the continuation of hostilities in Kashmir and their chagrin balanced much of the optimism which the cease-fire engendered. Several senior officers, the Azad Kashmir irregulars, and many of the rank and file of the Pakistan forces were very disappointed. Nor was it easy to change the thinking of the people who had been fed a diet of war propaganda for a year past. In particular, popular feeling had been whipped up by the cry that the struggle in Kashmir was a jihād.[39]

Not only was the jihād aspect of the Kashmir fighting used to induce greater public interest and support, but it also seems that it was hoped to direct into this profitable channel the vigorous efforts of certain zealots who were demanding that some kind of Islamic state be instituted at once. The cease-fire quite naturally permitted attention to be focused on these demands.

The most outstanding of these campaigners was Syed Abu-l-Ala Maududi whose most outstanding early work, it will be remembered, was his *al-Jihād fi l-Islām*. Perhaps it was by accident, perhaps by inspiration as members of Jamā'at-i-Islāmi claim, that Maududi came to be asked whether the fighting in Kashmir was a jihād or not; but his negative answer created a sensation. This was in May, 1948, when the Indian offensive forced Pakistani regulars into the line to save Muzaffarabad.

[39] *Dawn,* Feb. 28, 1948.

After some pressing, Maududi declared that for Kashmiris it might be a jihād, but so long as the governments of India and Pakistan were at peace there could be no jihād in Kashmir for Pakistanis.[40] Official consternation may be judged by the fact that the admission that Pakistani regulars had entered Kashmir on May 5, 1948, was not made until September.[41] Both the Kabul and Srinagar radio stations picked up and broadcasted Maududi's "fatwa" that the Kashmir war was not a jihād, and the Pakistan information services answered by denouncing him and recalling that he opposed partition.

On October 4, 1948, Maududi was detained under the Punjab Public Safety Act along with Islahi, the amir of the Punjab Jamāʻat, and Tufail Muhammad, the general secretary of the Jamāʻat. At the time, Liaqat Ali Khan was at Lahore attempting to settle the political problems of the province. Jinnah's death had taken place less than a month before. Two weeks earlier the Majlis-i-Shūra of the Jamāʻat, as a consequence of Sir Zafrullah Khan's admission to the United Nations, had declared that the war in Kashmir was a jihād.

Most of the 'ulamā' did not imitate Maududi's awkward posture. They pressed the government for an Islamic constitution, but they were not very explicit in their demands. Their support for the jihād in Kashmir was unstinting.

THE DEMAND FOR AN ISLAMIC STATE

Maulana Shabbir Ahmad Usmani was the outstanding figure among the 'ulamā' of Pakistan, and the president of Jamī'at-al-'Ulamā'-i-Islām. This was the only organization of 'ulamā' then in existence in Pakistan, and it remained true to its original purpose of supporting the Muslim League. Maulana Usmani

---

[40] Interview; see M. Hamidullah, *The Muslim Conduct of State* (3d ed.; Lahore, 1953), p. 191.

[41] Brecher, *op. cit.,* p. 91.

was himself a Muslim League member of the Constitutent Assembly of Pakistan. Second only to Usmani in importance and of even greater influence among the people was the Pir of Manki Sharif, to whom must go much of the credit for winning the NWFP over to Pakistan. In East Pakistan, Maulana Akram Khan, president of the provincial Muslim League, was a figure of some importance in religious circles, whereas the late Maulana Abd'ullah-al-Baqi was a distinguished 'alim who came over to the League from the Congress in 1946. All of these gentlemen supported the Kashmir war, and all supported the Muslim League.

Maulana Usmani was the most highly placed 'alim in. the ruling hierarchy. He had broken the Congress monopoly of the allegiances of the 'ulamā', and his requests were given a patient hearing by both Jinnah and Liaqat. As a natural consequence, Usmani became the focal point for religious pressure groups. In the second week in April, 1948, Maududi, accompanied by Islahi, Tufail, and Chaudhri Ghulam Muhammed, amir of the Jamā'at in Sindh, met Usmani to explain the "four demands." In October, Usmani is said to have protested the arrest of Maududi while reaffirming his intention of pressing the government for a positive commitment on the Islamic character of the constitution.[42]

Since Usmani had direct access to the Prime Minister it is obvious that he would not have felt the need to bring public pressure on the government had it been ready to accept his views. The struggle for Pakistan, and the Khilafat movement before it, had taught the 'ulamā' many new methods; but it must be remembered that the 'ulamā' are not revolutionaries. Usmani's public statements were merely warnings of what he might do on the one hand, and on the other they were assurances that the religious view was being represented to the

[42] Interview.

government. The second aspect of Usmani's statements was meant to lessen Maududi's influence, and to deny the urgency of his campaign. Usmani did not disapprove of Maududi's four demands, but he never publicly supported them as four, as demands, or as Maududi's. Maududi's detention did, however, come as a shock. In the first place it demonstrated that the government would not submit to unbridled public criticism. It also indicated to what degree the government feared agitation on religious issues. As disturbing as these revelations may have been they were not taken as indications of the government's determination to frame an un-Islamic constitution.

So long as the government avoided the problem of framing a constitution the religious questions remained open. So long as a federal solution was not assured the government was reluctant to approach the problem of constitution making. With Jinnah's passing, the problem became more difficult and yet it could not be put off forever. When the Indian draft constitution was reported to the Indian Assembly at the end of 1948, the pressure became persuasive. Pakistan's honor was at stake. The government decided to begin the process of constitution making, and it decided to utilize this opportunity for a dramatic and unifying statement on the Islamic character of Pakistan. With the aid of hindsight the impending official move can be discerned in the change of tone in both the English and Urdu presses by mid-January, 1949.

The preliminary statement of aims and objects was going to be Islamic, but according to which interpretation? Apparently the first intention of the government was not to the liking of the 'ulamā'. Usmani expressed his suspicions in an address to a conference of the East Pakistan Jamī'at-al-'Ulamā'-i-Islām.[43]

---

[43] Shaikh al-Islām Ḥaẓrat 'Allāma Shabīr 'Aḥmad 'Uthmāni, *Khutba-i-Ṣadārat,* Jamī'at 'Ulamā'-i-Islām Conference, Mashriqi Pākistān, Dhaka (Dacca), Feb. 9 and 10, 1949 (Urdu).

After describing the important part the 'ulamā' had played in the achievement of Pakistan, he went on to accuse the Muslim League of now desiring to be rid of them. He reiterated that Pakistan was founded in order to become an Islamic state, and he cited numerous statements of Jinnah and Liaqat Ali Khan to that effect.[44] He pointed out that the Muslims everywhere were in danger and weaker than their enemies, so that only with the help of God could they survive and prosper.[45] After listing nine basic principles of the Islamic state of Pakistan,[46] in which there is some reflection of Maududi's views but greater stress on the respect for sect and school differences so dear to the 'ulamā', he went on to answer objections to an Islamic constitution. The plea for prior preparation was rejected with characteristic realism:

> They want the Mullah to devote his attention to reforming the society while they are left free to spoil the society day in and day out. If the term "unsuitable environment" is interpreted to mean that the environment of those ruling over us is unsuitable, then the Community will have to reconsider who should govern this country . . . it is also said that the Mullah[47] wants power . . . I say when people aspire for power for worldly ends, what is the harm if the Mullah also aspires for power to set up a truly Islamic State. The Mullah does not want to rule, he only wants the rulers to be somewhat like the Mullah. . . .[48]

He minimized the disagreements of the 'ulamā' and flatly stated that they were united,[49] though he closed his remarks with a plea for unity.[50] Usmani then mentioned the various states

44 *Ibid.,* pp. 51 ff.
45 *Ibid.,* p. 26.
46 *Ibid.,* pp. 31, 32.
47 Literally "guardian" but now a derogatory term for the 'ulamā'.
48 *Ibid.,* pp. 38, 39 (translation of Yusuf Quraishi).
49 *Ibid.,* p. 42.
50 *Ibid.,* p. 67.

having constitutions based on Islam; Afghanistan, Iran, Iraq, and Saudi Arabia were all mentioned. In all of these states Islam is the established religion of the state and the ruler. Shar'ī courts, with limited jurisdiction, operate in all of them. Only the Iranian constitution provides a method for religious review of legislation, but that provision has never come into operation. Usmani denied that Islamic government was autocratic, but did not even imply that it might be democratic. Islam merely recognizes "those in authority among ye" which includes "even the District Magistrate in your District" [51]—presumably if those in authority recognize Islam as interpreted by the 'ulamā'. Perhaps the most important section of his speech was in answer to the challenge hurled at the 'ulamā' to offer an Islamic constitution. The challenge, he said, was meant to create disunity. The proper procedure was that, in accordance with his previous demand, *the Constituent Assembly "should set up a committee consisting of eminent 'ulamā' and thinkers . . . to prepare a draft . . . and present it to the Assembly."* [52]

Usmani's speech was no less than a threat. It was an attempt to bring the maximum pressure to bear on the government, and it was made in East Bengal where powerful non-League influences persisted, and where traditional Islam was strongest. The sequel to this most truculent statement of the 'ulamā' demonstrated that the government would not dare to treat the 'ulamā' as they had Maududi; but the content of the speech substantiates the contention that the 'ulamā' are not concerned with the form of government so long as that government recognizes the function of the religious institution in interpreting the law. The preoccupation of the 'ulamā' with recognition rather than the acquisition of specific administrative and legal functions is borne out by the fact that Usmani would not

[51] *Ibid.,* p. 39.
[52] *Ibid.,* p. 42 (my italics).

elaborate his own conception of an Islamic state until the Constituent Assembly itself appointed a committee to work out the application of Islamic principles in the government of Pakistan.

THE OBJECTIVES RESOLUTION

On February 25, 1949, the Muslim League Parliamentary Party met in the utmost secrecy to consider the proposed Objectives Resolution. No decision was reached, and it was not until the following week that the text of the agreed resolution was announced.[53]

To the great satisfaction of religious Muslims of all schools of thought, and perhaps to the bewilderment of the uninitiated, the newspapers announced the result in screaming headlines: "Sovereignty over the entire universe belongs to God Almighty alone." [54] On March 7, 1949, Liaqat Ali Khan moved the adoption of the Objectives Resolution "embodying the main principles on which the constitution of Pakistan is to be based":

> Whereas sovereignty over the entire universe belongs to God Almighty alone, and the authority which He has delegated to the State of Pakistan through its people for being exercised within the limits prescribed by Him is a sacred trust;
>
> This Constituent Assembly representing the people of Pakistan resolves to frame a constitution for the sovereign independent State of Pakistan;
>
> Wherein the State shall exercise its powers and authority through the chosen representatives of the people;
>
> Wherein the principles of democracy, freedom, equality, tolerance and social justice, as enunciated by Islam shall be fully observed;

[53] *Dawn,* Feb. 26, 1949.
[54] *Dawn,* March 2, 1949.

Wherein the Muslims shall be enabled to order their lives in the individual and collective spheres in accord with the teaching and requirements of Islam as set out in the Holy Quran and the Sunna;

Wherein adequate provision shall be made for the minorities freely to profess and practice their religions and develop their cultures;

Whereby the territories now included in or in accession with Pakistan and such other territories as may hereafter be included in or accede to Pakistan shall form a Federation wherein the units will be autonomous with such boundaries and limitations on their powers and authority as may be prescribed;

Wherein shall be guaranteed fundamental rights including equality of status, of opportunity and before law, social, economic and political justice, and freedom of thought, expression, belief, faith, worship and association, subject to law and public morality;

Wherein adequate provision shall be made to safeguard the legitimate interests of minorities and backward and depressed classes;

Wherein the independence of the judiciary shall be fully secured;

Wherein the integrity of the territories of the Federation, its independence and all its rights including its sovereign rights on land, sea and air shall be safeguarded;

So that the people of Pakistan may prosper and attain their rightful and honoured place amongst the nations of the World and make their full contribution towards international peace and progress and happiness of humanity.[55]

[55] *C.A.P. Debates,* Vol. V, no. 1 (March 7, 1949), pp. 1, 2.

To understand the compromise that found its way into the Objectives Resolution we must first of all keep in mind that neither the 'ulamā' nor the politicians had yet attempted to put their conception of an Islamic state into legal or even literary form. The basic differences in outlook that have been explained above were not yet made explicit, and if the Jamā'at-i-Islāmi had published a pamphlet containing collections of constitutional precepts by Maududi and Muhammed Asad these were as yet random stabs in an impenetrable darkness.

The Objectives Resolution was not the constitution; it was merely a deposit on account, to be accepted as an indication of good faith. The 'ulamā' desired to enshrine the principle of the supremacy of the Sharī'a, while the politicians, or most of them, found this principle acceptable so long as it was not clearly defined.

In this resolution the word sovereignty may be taken in its supposedly technical sense as a term of political science. It was in this sense that the first paragraph of the resolution was attacked by Mr. B. K. Datta and Mr. S. C. Chattopadhyaya of the Congress Party in the Constituent Assembly.[56] For these gentlemen the matter was simple; if sovereignty belongs to God it does not belong to the people, thus Pakistan would not be a democratic state. For those who are less ready to quibble, acknowledging the sovereignty of God was no more than a polite nod in the direction of the mosque, harmless at worst and beneficial if it appeased the "mullahs"; "in this sense however, it is patent that the entire universe is a theocracy, for is there any corner in the entire creation where His authority does not exist?"[57] Mr. I. H. Qureshi explained: "The resolution says that our polity should be based upon God-consciousnes."[58] Sardar

56 *C.A.P. Debates,* Vol. V, no. 2 (March 8, 1949), p. 13; *Ibid.,* Vol. V, no. 5 (March 12, 1949), p. 89.
57 *Ibid.,* Vol. V, no. 1 (March 7, 1949), p. 3.
58 *Ibid.,* Vol. V, no. 3 (March 9, 1949), p. 39.

Abdur Rab Nishtar pointed out that "it is a statement of fact, and whether we say it or not it is true." [59] Mian Iftikharuddin, though still a member of the Muslim League, spoke plainly:

> I see that a section of the Press gave it out as if they had scored a journalistic scoop by reporting that the authority is derived from the Higher Power. Sir, the authority, whether we say it or not, is derived from that Power. It does not lie in our power to change the law of nature or nature's God. In saying that we have not done anything very extraordinary.[60]

For the more sophisticated Westernized mind there was yet a better interpretation. Dr. Qureshi, Zafrullah Khan, and Dr. Hussain found that the preamble merely affirmed the need to keep religion as a moral force joined to politics, finding fault with Western notions of the need to separate religion and politics. Dr. Mahmud Hussain cited Bodin, blaming him for fathering the idea of absolute sovereignty, and cited Machiavelli, whom he blamed for the modern concept of "reason of State"; then he summed up stating: "The plain question is whether we propose to bring back morality to that sphere from which it has been banished, namely the political sphere." [61]

For the 'ulamā' the acceptance of what seemed to be a self-evident and therefore valueless preamble was crucial. In concert with the spirit of early Islam and the Arabic language, whence the terminology of Islamic theology, the sovereignty of God is taken in an extremely concrete sense. In all of the impassioned transcendence of the Qur'ānic conception of Allah, His over-lordship and command stand out in the immediacy of their immanence:

> Verily your Lord is God who created the Heavens and the earth in six days; then He sat upon the Throne. He covers

[59] *Ibid.*, Vol. V, no. 4 (March 10, 1949), p. 56.
[60] *Ibid.*, Vol. V, no. 4 (March 10, 1949), p. 51.
[61] *Ibid.*, Vol. V, no. 5 (March 12, 1949), pp. 84–85.

night with the day—it pursues it incessantly—and the sun and the moon and the stars are subject to His bidding. Aye!— His is the creation and the command. . . .[62]

For the 'ulamā', the logical consequence of acknowledging God's sovereignty was acceptance of His law as the law of the land. This vaguely pious pronouncement was interpreted as a commitment on the part of the politicians to recognize and give effect to the Sharī'a as known to those who spent their lives in its study.

In the approach of the 'ulamā' there is strange juxtaposition of the modern and the medieval. How many of these learned gentlemen understood the much-abused term "sovereignty" in the familiar classroom sense of Deputy Minister Mahmud Hussain, Ph.D.? Erudite references to the sins of Bodin and the excesses of Machiavelli did not stir them at all, but somehow they had come to understand that the Sovereign is the source of law, that the Sovereign's will is law. They also knew the Sovereign's will. To Maududi must go the credit for first demonstrating an understanding of the possibilities of this unhappy bit of Western terminology.

It was Maududi's fourth demand that specified the limitations upon the sovereignty, i.e., the "powers of the state." What were for the Westernized politicians moral limitations of the vaguest sort, were for the 'ulamā' the explicit duties to rule in accordance with the elaborate system of law built up about the Qur'ān and Sunnah of the Prophet. The position of the 'ulamā' was stated definitely by Maulana Shabbir Ahmad Usmani in the Constituent Assembly:

> Now if we believe that the sovereignty of the universe belongs to an Omnific [sic] and Omnipotent Being . . . we cannot admit that we are entitled to make use of a property, especially that of our Sovereign Lord, only to the extent that we are au-

[62] *Qur'ān,* Surah VII, verse 54.

thorized by Him. . . . It was to let mankind know what was sanctioned and authorized by Him that God sent prophets and gave revealed books unto them. And it is with the purpose of underlining this all-important fact that the expression 'within the limits prescribed by Him' has been used . . . and herein lies the fundamental difference between an Islamic State and a secular materialistic State.[63]

But those limits were not explicitly stated in the Objectives Resolution, to the extent that the word "Sharī'a" nowhere appears.

If sovereignty belongs to God, that did not prevent Pakistan from being a "sovereign independent State" in the second paragraph. It is apparent that agreement and compromise were purchased at the price of consistency. Orthodox political theory was no more to be denied than orthodox theology. The sovereignty of God became in the second paragraph a formality, whereas the sovereignty of the state firmly established Pakistan in the "community of nations." We note that sovereignty resides in the state of Pakistan, and not in the people of Pakistan, though the authority for its government is delegated to the state "through its people." The metaphysical heights are finally scaled in the third paragraph "wherein the State shall exercise its powers and authority through the chosen representatives of the people."

Mian Iftikharuddin mentioned during the debate that some members of the Muslim League had decided not to move amendments that would have made the people the terminal rather than the transitory recipients of God's authority.[64] Whether state sovereignty was felt to be a requirement of the modern international system or a logical corollary of the absence of popular sovereignty cannot be ascertained from the

[63] *C.A.P. Debates,* Vol. V, no. 3 (March, 1949), p. 44.
[64] *Ibid.,* Vol. V, no. 4 (March 10, 1949), p. 51.

debates, for no Muslim member attempted to bring the various parts of the resolution into accord. All the Muslim members accepted the qualification of democracy, though they did seem to feel that it would be in reality what we all mean by democracy. The Hindu members were naturally very much alarmed by what they considered (charitably?) to be the esoteric meaning of the words "as enunciated by Islam."

Liaqat Ali Khan explained that "democracy in the Islamic sense" was distinguished from both the democracy of the West and the democracy of the Soviet Union; it was in fact more democratic than both.[65] Dr. Qureshi explained to the troubled Hindus that the principles of Islam do not conflict with those of the United Nations Charter on Fundamental Rights, "only in Islam the meaning is richer and it is fuller."[66] Sardar Nishtar thought it better to avoid the much abused word *democratic,* "call a rose by any name and it will smell sweet."[67] Sir Muhammad Zafrullah Khan pointed out that "the essence of democracy is that political authority should be exercised through the representatives freely chosen by the people. . . . This is provided for clearly in the Resolution."[68] Dr. Mahmud Hussain also found that the resolution contained the "essence of modern democracy"; but he also explained that the word *state* "merely means the people" and the advantage in using that term was that it was something definite "whereas people is merely a sociological concept."[69]

The 'ulamā', represented by Maulana Usmani and Dr. O. H. Malik, were of a somewhat different opinion. They do not mention state sovereignty, for that seems to have been extorted from the 'ulamā' to balance the sovereignty of God. Usmani

---

[65] *Ibid.,* Vol. V, no. 1 (March 7, 1949), p. 3.
[66] *Ibid.,* Vol. V, no. 3 (March 9, 1949), p. 42.
[67] *Ibid.,* Vol. V, no. 4 (March 10, 1949), p. 58.
[68] *Ibid.,* Vol. V, no. 5 (March 12, 1949), p. 68.
[69] *Ibid.,* Vol. V, no. 5 (March 12, 1949), p. 86.

would be the first to admit that the people are responsible to God for the manner in which they exercised their political rights, but his idea of the limitations of Islamic democracy seem to be more concrete. "[Islam] delegates authority to the State through and by the will of the people, though the latter are not entitled to neglect the organization of the government and to lend a hand to disruption, disorder and anarchy by withholding [preventing?] the exercise of lawful authority." [70] Maulana Usmani's meaning is not entirely clear in the official translation from Urdu, but Dr. Malik's statement could not be more precise:

> . . . it will be limited democracy. The people will have some power but they will not have all the power. . . . Certain things have to be resolved by God and are in his own personal sphere. The remaining sphere has been left open to the people to deal with. The principles of Islam and the laws of Islam as laid down in the Qur'ān are binding upon the State. The people or the State cannot change these principles or these laws . . . but there is a vast field beside these principles and laws in which the people will have free play . . . it might be called by the name "theo-democracy," that is democracy limited by the word of God, but as the word "theo" is not in vogue so we call it by the name of "Islamic democracy." [71]

The Objectives Resolution, acknowledged the sovereignty of God, recognized the authority of the people derived from their creator, and vested the authority delegated by the people in the Constituent Assembly for the purpose of making a constitution for the sovereign state of Pakistan. Thus is God sovereign, the people sovereign, parliament sovereign, and the state sovereign in Pakistan. It would indeed be a narrow-minded person who was not satisfied with such a compromise.

[70] *Ibid.*, Vol. V, no. 3 (March 9, 1949), p. 46.
[71] *Ibid.*, Vol. V, no. 5 (March 12, 1949), p. 78.

Though the "enabling clause," as the fifth paragraph of the Objectives Resolution came to be known, did not create as much of a furor as the "sovereignty clause" it contains between its simple lines a similar flexibility of meaning. Within the framework of the common run of nationalist theory, the clause states the familiar case for national self-determination, and reiterates the basic claim of the Muslim League. This clause and the following one guaranteeing cultural freedom to minorities may be taken as a step to enshrine the *two-nation* theory in the future constitution of Pakistan. Though more extreme statements of Muslim nationality have included references, among other things, to a distinctive Muslim law, jurisprudence, social, and moral codes,[72] there is no strong evidence to show that the leaders of the Muslim League had in mind anything but modern democratic nationalism. The implication of this view, questionable though its application to Muslim India may be, is that in a state ruled over by a Muslim majority, in accordance with democratic principles, that majority would not be prevented from ordering their public and private lives in keeping with the cultural tendencies of the Muslim "nation."

Falling on attentive orthodox ears, the two-nation theory had a different ring. In the first place, the Muslim "way of life" was not something to be gradually developed in the future by a free democratic people working out their independent destiny. For the 'ulamā' it meant living in accordance with the Sharī'a. To the extent nationalism was at all understood—or democracy —it was rejected. In medieval theory the task of Islamic government, that is, the caliph, was to strive after achieving the welfare of Muslims in this world as well as the next. For this duty the caliph was responsible to God, not to the people, though he

[72] M. A. Jinnah, foreword to *Pakistan and Muslim India,* Home Study Circle, Malabar Hill (2d ed.; Bombay, 1946).

might be removed under certain conditions.[73] There is a certain ambiguity in early theory, but the tendency is to relieve the people of a large degree of moral responsibility. Salvation was still based on individual performance, but lacking the appropriate civic conditions, the chances for salvation of the generality of Muslims were fewer.[74] In spite of the ambiguity on this point there can be no doubt of the orthodox requirement that the caliph enforce the laws of the Sharī'a, that he prevent the dissemination of "heretical" views, that he punish backsliders, and that he encourage conformity.[75]

It was the reaction against British imperialism which permitted the politicians and the 'ulamā' to agree upon so dangerous a word as "enable." In every speech in or out of the Assembly, every Muslim member of that body heaped great praise upon the Muslim way of life and the noble principles of Islam. The modern Muslim apologetic had already established that every social virtue was contained in Islam. Should Muslims follow these principles, they asserted, every problem of organized society would be solved. "Islam is a panacea for all the world's ills." The very real shortcomings of Muslim society and individuals had to be explained, however. Nor could the British, who had not interfered in such matters, escape blame for subtly weaning the Muslims away from their higher principles by creating conditions conducive to Westernization. One of the principal features of British rule brought under attack was the education system, which trained Indians for government service in accordance with British educational goals and curricula. Merely to free Muslims to act according to their

---

[73] Abu Yūsuf, *Kitāb al-Kharāj* (Cairo, 1302), p. 3, line 10; p. 10, line 18, to p. 11, line 3.

[74] Al-Ghazzāli, *Iqtisād fi'l-I'tiqād* (Cairo, n.d.), p. 107, line 228.

[75] Al-Māwardi, *al- Aḥkām as-Sultanīya* (Cairo, 1909), p. 12, *ult.*, and p. 13, line 4.

conscience would not be any advance over the inherited situation. "The word 'enable' . . . has got a special meaning," said Sardar Nishtar.[76] Liaqat explained that "the state will create such conditions as are conducive to the building up of a truly Islamic society, which means that the State will have to play a positive part in this effort." [77] Liaqat went on to mention that divergence of opinion existed within Islam and that it was hoped that the continuation of such diversity would be a source of strength to Pakistan.

Sir Muhammad Zafrullah Khan, though not associated with the 'ulamā', was more explicit. He indicated that the Islamic laws of zakat, inheritance, prohibition of usury, and prohibition of drinking and gambling would be enforced.[78] Such statements did not save him from general condemnation as a heretic two years later for his outspoken profession of Aḥmadism. Neither Maulana Usmani nor Dr. O. H. Malik referred directly to the "enabling clause," but Usmani did refer to the key verse of the Qur'ān: "According to the Holy Qur'ān the real aim of the Islamic State is to exhort all within its sphere of authority to do good and shun evil." [79]

As it stands, the "enabling clause" would certainly give to the government more authority in religious matters than is usual in Western or Westernized states. As far as can be judged by their statements, the 'ulamā' and the politicians did not disagree in their understanding of this clause, but some doubt must remain in our minds. The 'ulamā' and the politicians, though in full agreement concerning the merits of Islam, do not all agree on what is essential and what is not. So long as these details were not spelled out, agreement was not difficult, though

[76] *C.A.P. Debates,* Vol. V, no. 4 (March 10, 1949), p. 60.
[77] *Ibid.,* Vol. V, no. 1 (March 7, 1949), p. 4.
[78] *Ibid.,* Vol. V, no. 5 (March 12, 1949), p. 67.
[79] *Ibid.,* Vol. V, no. 3 (March 9, 1949), p. 45.

one wonders about the varied thoughts coursing through the minds of the members of the Constituent Assembly during Zafrullah Khan's speech.

The wording of the Objectives Resolution is thus carefully imprecise. The principles behind the "four demands" of Maududi, and those held by most of the 'ulamā', were accepted but stretched so as not to injure the "modern" conception of Islam. The word Sharī'a was left out, and the exact meaning of "the limits prescribed," the enunciations of Islam, or the "teachings and requirements of Islam" were not ascertained. It is clear the the Westernized politicians saw nothing in Islam contrary to "liberal democracy" as known in the West. They viewed Islamic teachings merely as a set of general principles.[80] One went so far as to suggest that "some sort of a Research Institute" should be established to "elucidate . . . the principles of democracy, justice, and economy as laid down in the Holy Qur'ān and the Sunna." [81] The 'ulamā', of course, had in mind the explicit law of the Sharī'a, as well as the exclusion of all legislation (in the usual sense of the term) from certain spheres of human life. Mr. Chattopadhyaya asked the crucial question, to which there was no reply for the time being: "What are those limits, who will interpret them? Dr. Qureshi or my respected Maulana Shabbir Ahmad Usmani?" [82]

The Objectives Resolution was adopted on March 12, 1949, by a clear majority of all the Muslim members of the Constituent Assembly against the Hindu members. Immediately thereafter a committee of twenty-five, under the chairmanship of Mr. Tamizzudin Khan, president of the Assembly, was appointed to report on the basic principles of the future consti-

[80] I. H. Qureshi, *Pakistan an Islamic Democracy* (Lahore, 1951), p. 6 (address delivered at the Institute of Islamic Culture, December, 1949).

[81] *C.A.P. Debates,* Vol. V, no. 5 (March 12, 1949), p. 76.

[82] *Ibid.,* Vol. V, no. 5 (March 12, 1949), p. 90.

tution of Pakistan in accordance with that resolution. The real issue of the nature of an Islamic state was not yet joined, nor was it even clearly defined. An equivocal statement of "Aims and Objects" had been issued which had a gratifying effect at the time but failed to state clearly the purpose of the state. The 'ulamā', on the other hand, were given a tactical advantage in that at least their first premise was granted.

5 *The Views of the Board of Ta'līmat-i-Islāmīa*

THE BOARD

In mid-April, 1949, the twenty-five men of the Basic Principles Committee met and decided to split up into subcommittees whose task it would be to present detailed reports to the parent committee. Three subcommittees were set up to deal with federal and provincial constitutions, and the franchise and the judiciary. No attempt was made to coördinate the work of the various committees except insofar as the personnel of each overlapped. No doubt the Objectives Resolution, passed the month before, was their principal, if not their only term of reference; but some disagreement seems to have arisen regarding the precise relation of objectives to basic principles. Some felt that the Objectives Resolution might be embodied in special clauses, whereas others felt that the resolution should merely serve as a general guide in working out the details of the machinery of government. "After a prolonged discussion it was decided not to appoint the (ad hoc) Sub-Committee (on aims and objects) but, instead, to set up a Board of experts consisting of reputed Scholars well versed in Ta'līmat-i-Islāmīa to advise on matters arising out of the Objectives Resolution and on such other matters as may be referred to them by the various Sub-Committees." [1]

The appointment of a "Board of experts" was precisely what Usmani had demanded of the Constituent Assembly in his address to the Conference of East Pakistan 'ulamā', just prior to the passage of the Objectives Resolution. It is not surprising that this decision should have been preceded by a disagreement, nor should it be thought that the decision was in fact a capitulation on the part of the modernists and secularists. In the first place, the powers of the board were limited to *advising,* and then only on such matters as might be referred to it. As for matters arising out of the Objectives Resolution we have evidence of at least one concrete example of such a matter not being so referred: a special subcommittee was appointed to deal with the problem of implementing the "enabling clause." [2]

Opinion on the nature of an Islamic state varying as it does, membership of the Board of Ta'līmat-i-Islāmīa was a crucial issue. Consequently, the committee appointed to select those members and arrange their terms of employment was composed of the Prime Minister, the President of the Constituent Assembly, the Governor of East Bengal, the Governor of the Punjab, the Minister of Finance, Maulana Shabbir Ahmad Usmani, and a prominent Shī'ite. [3]

---

[1] *Minutes of the Meetings of the Basic Principles Committee,* April 14, 1949, p. 4 (hereafter cited as *BPC Minutes*).

[2] *Report of the Sub-Committee on Federal and Provincial Constitutions and Distribution of Powers, 1950* (hereafter cited as *Report on Constitutions*), Document no. F45-x-150-Legis., p. 75.

[3] *BPC Minutes,* April 15, 1949, p. 5.

Maulana Saiyid Sulaiman Nadvi, acknowledged to be the foremost student of Islamic history among the 'ulamā' of the subcontinent, was invited to come to Pakistan from Lucknow. Nadvi was quite old, and not in the best of health. He had inherited the position of the great Shibli at the Nadwat-al-'ulamā' Academy, and was not in the mood to start anew. His friends among the 'ulamā' urged him, and Pakistan was anxious to have him. As a non-Pakistani member, he was offered 1,500 rupees per month.[4] At last he intimated his acceptance, but he did not come until the end of 1950. Mufti Muhammad Shafi, right-hand man and successor of Usmani as the leading 'alim of Pakistan, was also appointed to the board. The late Professor Abdul Khaliq, formerly of Presidency College, Calcutta, recently professor of Arabic at Eden Girl's College, Dacca, and later independent member of the East Bengal Legislative Assembly was appointed to the board to give the necessary representation to East Pakistan.[5] Mufti Ja'far Hussain, Shī'a mujtahid, was appointed to forestall any possible complaint from that quarter. Dr. M. Hamidullah, D.Phil., Bonn, and D.Litt., Paris, author of *Muslim Conduct of State,* a treatise on Muslim international law, and at present teaching at the Sorbonne, was appointed to add the respectability of "western knowledge." Maulana Muhammad Zafar Ahmad Ansari, formerly office secretary to the All-India Muslim League, and secretary of the committee appointed to revise the constitution of the All-Pakistan Muslim League, was made secretary of the Board of Ta'līmat-i-Islāmīa.

The membership of the Board was obviously the result of further compromise, but a compromise which must have been aimed at weakening and dividing the board. In the first place,

---

[4] *Summary of the Work Done by the C.A.P. during its Sixth and Seventh Sessions,* p. 7.

[5] *Panel of Chairmen and Committees of the C.A.P.* (Government of Pakistan Press, 1953), p. 25.

Saiyid Sulaiman Nadvi was important enough to rival Usmani's position, and since the two represented somewhat different schools, the suggestion that he be appointed was as unwelcome as it was unassailable. The circumstances under which Nadvi finally came to Pakistan will be related below, but it is pertinent to note that once appointed, the members of the board were anxious for Nadvi to increase their prestige by joining them.

The appointment of a Shī'ite was perhaps unavoidable, though the vast majority of Pakistanis are Sunnis. Shī'ite political theory is based primarily on the notion of hereditary legitimacy in the line of 'Alī, the son-in-law of Muhammad, and negates completely the classical Islamic theory. Nor is it at all coincidental that these theories conflict, for the legalistic legitimization of history, which is characteristic of the Sunni theory, was primarily a contradiction of Shī'ite claims. However, since the twelfth Shī'ite Imām has remained hidden for over a millennium, and since the Shī'ites are not sure when he will reappear, some other form of government is temporarily possible, so long as certain aspects of Shī'ite personal status law are not interfered with.

What was expected of Dr. Hamidullah is hard to say, but one may surmise that this highly accomplished scholar's knowledge of Islamic law could not but reinforce the influence of classical theory. Mufti Shafi of course remained the only exponent of the traditional "ulamā' theory"; and the two (classical and traditional) theories might be reconciled through the efforts of the Secretary of the Board of Ta'līmat who had become somewhat estranged from his former Muslim League associates, and had fallen somewhat under the influence of Maududi.[6]

[6] Interview. It is suggested that the estrangement was due to Ansari's support for the amendment which barred cabinet members from holding League offices.

THE MECHANICS OF THE "VIEWS"

Meeting in September and again in November, 1949, the Sub-Committee on the Constitutions and Powers laid the foundation of the constitution of Pakistan. They decided in favor of a bicameral federal legislature, representing the provinces as well as the population; and upon a parliamentary system as much like the British as conditions allowed.[7] The most immediate influences upon their thinking were the Government of India Act of 1935 and the similarly influenced Indian Constitution Bill (passed January, 1950). The decisions of the Sub-Committee on Constitutions and Powers were then communicated to the Board of Ta'līmat-i-Islāmīa for advice.[8] Discussions then followed between the board and the Negotiating Sub-Committee, appointed for that purpose,[9] but no agreement was reached. The first batch of the board's "Views" were mimeographed on February 2, 1950. Another portion of the "Views" were prepared on April 10, 1950, for a meeting with the Negotiating Sub-Committee. At that meeting a "divergence of views" was "revealed" on nearly all points, but the board prevailed upon the unsympathetic negotiators to submit the board's opinions to the parent Sub-Committee on Constitutions and Powers. On April 11, 1950, this was done, and at its meetings on April 15 and again on June 4, 5, and 6, 1950, the parent subcommittee considered those opinions, together with certain additions, before passing them on to the full Basic Principles Committee on July 11, 1950.[10]

[7] *Report on Constitutions,* passim. Details were worked out as subsequent meetings during 1950.

[8] *Ibid.,* Document no. F-45-III/49-Legis., p. 56.

[9] *Ibid.*

[10] *Report on Constitutions,* pp. 2, 4, 56; and Appendix I containing "Views of the Board of Ta'līmat-i-Islāmīa on Certain Items Referred to Them by the Sub-Committee on Federal and Provincial Constitutions and Distribution of Powers" (pp. 57–72), p. 58 (hereafter referred to as "Views"). See Appendix A.

The first section of the board's recommendations related to the Head of the State, the second related to the executive in general, and the third to the legislature. Yet a fourth section was presented to the Sub-Committee on Constitutions and Powers during and after its July meetings, but these were in the form of rebutting the objections of the parent subcommittee.[11] The form in which these "Views" of the board were expressed, the dates on which these "Views" were presented, and their content as well, show that they were not thought through as a rational whole. Each problem was approached separately, and, wherever explicit provisions of the Sharī'a were found applicable, they were solved accordingly. The difficulty, however, did not lie with rationalizing the provisions of the Sharī'a so much as providing a workable institutional system in terms of the spirit of the Sharī'a where there was no letter. It was at this point of fixing the institutions of Islamic government that traditionalists, fundamentalists, and modernists, all except the secularists and those ijmā' modernists who were to become their apologists, became undifferentiated romantics. They became romantics in the sense of reading back institutions which are the product of their own imagination into the obscure period of the "Rightly-Guided Caliphs." Despite the romantic aspect of the "Views" of the board, the essential principle of the supremacy of the Sharī'a was not lost from view; but the fault of the "Views" lies in the fact that the word "despite" can be used, for the proposed institutional framework has no relation to this essential aspect of Islamic government. Some of the board's difficulties may be ascribed to the fact that the recommendations of the Sub-Committee on Constitutions

[11] The third and fourth sections of the board's "Views" were separately mimeographed and numbered pp. 1–10, "Constitution and powers and functions of the legislature" (hereafter "Legislature"), and pp. 1–13, "For the consideration of the Main Principles Committee" (Part Four hereafter), and pp. 1–3 (hereafter Final Section). See Appendix B.

and Powers was the basis upon which they were forced to work. On the other hand, many more of their difficulties must be ascribed to the fact that *within* the Sharī'a there is no variation in the degree of importance assigned to any one provision as opposed to another. The result has neither political nor theoretical coherence. The first section dealing with the Head of the State draws its inspiration from the classical works that were almost wholly concerned with the caliphate. The second section dealing with the executive powers is primarily aimed at restricting the autocratic powers that have been granted the Head of the State in the first; and, most importantly, providing for the 'ulamā' to perform their traditional function. The third section, on the legislature, is simply the result of the inevitable necessity of making some concession to the prejudices of the politicians, and it merely tends to restrict the powers of the legislature and to minimize its importance. In view of the fact that the BPC was determined to have a "Parliamentary" system rather than a "Presidential" one,[12] the recommendations of the board were hardly relevant and most disconcerting. The importance of the "Views" lies in the fact that it was the only statement of the traditionalist and fundamentalist notions (unreconciled) to find its way into the official committees.

THE HEAD OF THE STATE

The bulk of the questions referred to the Board of Ta'līmat-i-Islāmīa were concerned with the Head of the State. One of the main concerns of medieval Islamic theory was establishing the legitimacy of the ruling caliphs. Legitimacy was not established by means of constitutional process so much as by proving the existence of certain qualifications. The prescribed constitutional

---

[12] *Report on Constitutions,* p. 7 (decision dated 14-9-49, dissented to by Dr. O. H. Malik, p. 43).

process was so flexible as to be meaningless except as a justification of existing conditions. The members of the board do not seem to have questioned for a moment the applicability of the medieval theory of the caliphate to the requirements of Pakistan, nor did the question of equating the chief executive of Pakistan with the caliph of old give them any pause.

To begin with, they divided the questions relating to the Head of the State into seventeen separate "sub-heads," [13] the first of these being his qualifications (though this was not a specific part of their terms of reference). As if intended to exasperate, or perhaps to overwhelm, eleven general categories were listed and followed by eleven specific qualifications, each supplying the requirement of a preceding category.[14] The inclusion of such requirements as having a sound mind, not being totally blind, deaf, or dumb, being wise and sagacious, having mental poise and composure, and not being a captive of a foreign government, though they are all drawn from important works on Islamic law,[15] demonstrates their unwillingness (or incapacity) to adjust classical thought to the requirements or stylistic predilection of the time. However, the requirement of citizenship, though mentioned in passing, is not included in the list—even as it was absent from the lists given by medieval writers. One qualification was added which is not to be found in medieval sources, and that is the requirement that the Head of the State be a Muslim.[16] Certainly this was not a departure from earlier Islamic theory; it merely spelled out what was implicit. The need to specify that the Head of the

13 "Views," p. 59.

14 *Ibid.*, pp. 60, 61.

15 Nearly all the qualifications were discussed by al-Māwardi in *al-Aḥkām al-Sulṭāniya,* chap. i.

16 Because medieval writers had not discussed this obvious qualification, the board could refer only to vague Qur'ānic statements when challenged for their authority by the subcommittee. "Views" (Part Four), p. 4.

State be a Muslim could only occur where modern notions of equality and the separation of church and state exist. The condition requiring such a qualification was the desire to establish an "ideological" state, and to reëstablish the orthodox caliphate.

The "ideological" or Islamic state they conceived was to be similar to that of Soviet Russia in that only those who subscribed to the state ideology could hold policy-making positions.[17] Their assumption was, of course, the complete unification of church and state. Since nearly everything had to be done in an Islamic way, the part non-Muslims (about 14 per cent of the population of Pakistan) could play was strictly limited. Moreover, the conservative view of the social position of women is such that their political rights were limited to the franchise alone,[18] so that the second qualification of the Head of the State was that he be of male sex.[19]

The members of the board made it very clear that they contemplated the reëstablishment of the classical caliphate:

> The method adopted for performing these multifarious functions is that the Mussalmans elect the wisest and most God-fearing person from amongst themselves as their head to discharge these duties and responsibilities on their behalf and in consultation with pious and sagacious members of the Millat enjoying their confidence.[20]

This is the ideal caliph who must work for the consolidation and glory of Islam, eradicate vices, propagate virtues, procure the necessaries of life and full justice to all, diffuse knowledge, maintain internal peace, enforce the punishments prescribed by the Sharīʿa, control and disburse public funds, meet all

[17] "Views," p. 58.
[18] "Views" (Legislature), p. 5.
[19] *Ibid.*, p. 60.
[20] *Ibid.*, p. 65.

possible danger from any quarter, and protect the general well-being and prosperity of the masses.[21]

It was not only in their statements on the qualifications for the caliphate and the duties of the caliph that the members of the board indicated their adherence to traditional forms. They preferred that the Head of the State be elected for life, whereupon he should take an oath containing 5 clauses, 11 subclauses, and 302 words.[22] The oath was to be made before the federal legislature, the members of which would immediately thereafter swear allegiance individually to the Head of the State provided that he did not contravene the Sharī'a, nor the terms of his oath of office. The implication that these two might not coincide is probably owing to a logical oversight. Similar individual oaths of allegiance to the Head of the State (not the state itself) were desired of the members of the provincial legislatures, district boards, and city councils; a similar procedure was suggested for the various government departments and the military.[23] There could be no better proof of the fact that they felt that the ideal Islamic state was neither more nor less than what is presented in Sunni legal works of the Abbasid period. They equated the Islamic state with the caliph.

THE PEOPLE OF "LOOSING AND BINDING"

Happily, the traditional Sunni theory provided for a kind of selection of the caliph whenever the incumbent did not designate his own successor.[24] This provision could be and was adapted to our modern notion of election. The Head of the State would be elected not by the people, but by their learned

[21] *Ibid.*

[22] *Ibid.*, pp. 61, 70, 71.

[23] *Ibid.*, p. 71.

[24] Selection in the sense of choosing among those few who are properly qualified.

and pious representatives. That the representatives of the people might be the learned and pious among them was no more than wishful thinking, but this was a convenient formula. Sunni theory had never defined who the learned and pious or the "people of loosing and binding" entrusted with the selection of the caliph might be. Modern parliamentary theory provided for the election of the Head of the State by the legislature. Medieval and modern ideas were brought together by the obligation upon the people to elect the most learned and pious of citizens as their representatives.[25] The exact method of election did not much concern the board, but the medievalism of selection was revealed in their preference for elimination of names as the most suitable method.[26]

Among the more prominent features of medieval theory carried over by the board was the contract idea. The qualifications of the candidate, as well as those of the electors, were factors conditioning the validity of the contract, whereas the oath of office and the oaths of allegiance were in fact the formal consummation of the contract. The Head of the State might be removed if he broke the contract, or if he was no longer qualified. The conditions requiring the mandatory removal of the Head of the State were in fact the absence of any of those characteristics that qualified him for office in the first place, along with such other provisions, described as "conditions," such as acting contrary to the Shari'a, treason, personal profligacy, or contravention of the terms of his oath of office.[27] The emphasis is rather on disqualification than on removal for loss of confidence. The process by which the Head of State is removed is actually a judicial process based upon a decision as to the existence of a legal fact. It is the same with the process of election except for the discretionary aspect of selection or

[25] "Views," p. 65.   [27] *Ibid.*
[26] *Ibid.*, p. 63.

"the elimination of names." There was no place for discretion in removing the caliph according to medieval theory, but contemporary political ideas required the removal of the active executive where the confidence of the legislature is lost.

The two notions seemed to come together in the classical provision that the same body that was empowered to elect the caliph was also empowered to remove him. This brings us back to the people of "loosing and binding" or the learned and pious. Since the duties of this group are at least quasi judicial it follows that learning is the essential characteristic of these people, and piety secondary, but necessary as a guarantee that learning would be correctly used. These qualifications suit the 'ulamā' perfectly, for the 'ulamā' are the learned in the law. But the vagueness of the actual terminology permitted learning and piety to be formalized as qualifications for election to the legislature while "loosing and binding" describes the actual function of breaking or making the contract. Learning and piety, however, may qualify a man for more than merely "loosing and binding." It may qualify him for interpreting the law as well.

In point of fact, the 'ulamā' who developed the classical theory did not ascribe the exclusive power of interpreting the law to the caliph, despite the fact that the "Rightly-Guided Caliphs" did dispose of their power of making laws (as did the 'Umayyad caliphs after them). The fundamentalist approach was based on the example of the "Rightly-Guided Caliphs," but it might be reconciled with classical theory to the extent that emphasis was laid on the well-known work of al-Māwardi who suppressed any reference to the interpretative function of the learned of the community. Al-Ghazāli's theory was based upon an attempt to institutionalize this function, but the simple statement of the classical idea is contained in the work of al-Bāqillāni:

. . . [the caliph] need not be impeccable . . . having knowledge of the unseen, nor even of every aspect of the faith . . . the Imam is [only] appointed to uphold the precepts and the limitations and the commands which the Messenger promulgated. For the knowledge of the Community has precedence therein, and in everything he undertakes [the caliph] is the trustee and deputy of the Community, and the Community stand behind him guiding him and setting him right and reminding him and demanding the right from him as it is incumbent upon him, even removing and replacing him if he has committed a crime requiring his deposition.[28]

Al-Bāqillāni's meaning will be clearer if it is recalled that the collective rights and duties of the community are actually incumbent upon those competent to fulfill them. The system he has in mind is not so much representative as elitist.

In any case, it is clear that the quality of knowledge necessary for appointing or removing the caliph is not much different from that necessary for the proper discharge of the caliph's duties. The caliph differs from his electors only in skill and power; but if power is to be contingent upon, rather than external to, the constitution, and skill a matter of opinion, there is nothing to prevent the operation of these principles within a parliamentary framework. The board did not object to parliamentary institutions themselves,[29] but they resisted the attempt to invest parliament with the power to finally determine Islamic law. The board therefore wished to reduce the powers of the parliament to voting funds and electing and removing the Head of the State.[30] The legislative power, limited to fields in which the Sharī'a is silent, was given to the Head of the State to be exercised in consultation with his legislative

[28] Al-Bāqillāni, *op. cit.,* p. 184, lines 18–22.
[29] "Views" (Final Section), pp. 1–3.
[30] *Ibid.* (Legislature), p. 3.

council.[31] This is in keeping with fundamentalist theory.[32] The task of the people of "loosing and binding" in al-Bāqillāni is not legislation, but determining what is already law. This function the 'ulamā' wished to reserve to themselves. A certain inconsistency arises from the fact that the board did not also insist on the sole right to appoint the caliph—or give up the right to interpret the Sharī'a to a representative assembly in which the principle of ijmā' was institutionalized.

The board, then, divided these two powers that al-Ghazāli joined in the 'ulamā' and provided for the discretionary removal of the Head of the State:

> If his conduct of the government business generally and the measures adopted by him are considered to be detrimental to the best interests of the country of Millat and the members voting for his removal declare it on oath that in their well considered opinion the continuance of the reins of government in his hand is likely to prove a grave menace to the State or to the ideology which it stands for.[33]

Though discretionary removal was certainly to be a political act it was, particularly by the requirement of an oath, made as much like a judicial act as possible. However it may be, the parliament was required to remove the Head of the State if he should become unqualified; but they were not empowered to ascertain the judicial fact of disqualification. The parliament was not empowered to decide whether the Head of the State "promulgates and insists upon the execution of orders which militate against the Shariat or compel or positively help people to indulge in the sinful acts." [34]

---

[31] *Ibid.*, pp. 66–67.

[32] Maududi went on, however, to give the caliph, or amir, the right to interpret the texts upon which the Sharī'a was based.

[33] "Views," p. 64.

[34] *Ibid.*, p. 63.

THE COMMITTEE OF EXPERTS ON THE SHARĪ'A

The Board of Ta'līmat considered that the qualifications of the Head of the State require that he know and understand the laws of the Sharī'a from the Qur'ān and Sunnah, and that he observe the rules of the Sharī'a. The Head of the State is "the trustee of the interests of the Millat, the symbol and manifestation of its power and authority and its executive organ in all walks of the State." [35] But sovereignty belongs to God and not to the people, their representatives, nor the Head of the State, despite the requirement that they know and act in accordance with the Sharī'a. Some other institution had to decide whether or not the behavior of the legislature or the Head of the State was in accord with the Sharī'a. Some other institution was to be the immediate manifestation of the authority of the sovereignty of God in the Islamic state.

The Board of Ta'līmat-i-Islāmīa took it as a corollary of the Objectives Resolution that any "bill, law, ordinance, or administrative order" that was repugnant to the Sharī'a be declared null and void, and that "it would be up to the Committee of Experts on the Sharī'a to decide finally whether or not a particular law . . . militates against the requirements of Sharī'a." [36] The function of the expert committee would be solely negative: they could not require the passage of Islamic laws, they could only veto un-Islamic legislation. In the absence of any other specification, we must assume that the Sharī'a committee would also be able to pass upon questions regarding the legality of acts of the Head of the State, and consequently require his removal by the legislature.

The provision for a committee of experts on the Sharī'a presents the core of the traditional view. The members of the

[35] *Ibid.*, p. 66.
[36] *Ibid.*, p. 59.

committee would naturally be 'ulamā'. The members of the board indicated that they would elaborate their conception of the expert committee but for some reason, perhaps some lack of agreement among themselves, no details as to qualifications or method of appointment were ever given. As we shall see, this omission did not alter the traditionalist orientation of the board. In fact, the importance of this provision is such as to permit the board to be taken as the mouthpiece of the 'ulamā'.

THE POWERS OF THE EXECUTIVE

The members of the Board of Ta'līmat were not in the position of the medieval theorists, nor even that of the theorists of the later Ottoman period who had to prove that the Muslim community was not yet without divine guidance. The board started with the assumption that Pakistan was not divinely guided, and that their task was to attain that desired end. They realized that some things had changed, and that some new elements must be brought into the old system. The old wine must be put in new bottles. Questions regarding the salary of the Head of the State, someone to officiate for the Head of the State in his absence or in the event of an unforeseen vacancy, and the emergency powers of the Head of the State had to be answered. And another unavoidable difficulty was that caused by the modern notion of dividing the functions of government into executive, legislative, and judicial.

Classical theory was primarily concerned with the caliphate. As we have seen, the caliphate was the equivalent of Islamic government. Whenever we find any discussion of subordinate institutions, or of specific functions of government, we are invariably reading about administrative organization and not law. There was no functional or institutional differentiation at the top of Islamic government. Since the board equated the Head of the State with the caliph, it naturally made all governmental functions the responsibility of the Head of the State. The Qurʼānic exhortation to and approval of taking counsel in government [37] was used to cover both the executive cabinet and the legislative council. And to make the whole system symmetrical a judicial and propagative council were added.

> But Islamic Government being essentially . . . consultative . . . he is bound to take counsel from men of wisdom and right-eousness and to ascertain the desires . . . of the people in matters left out by the Sharīʻa as discretionary.
>
> For a big territory like Pakistan it would be advisable to have a number of councils. . . .[38]

Thus, without admitting any right to the theory of the separation of powers the members of the board attempted to meet the prejudices of the Westernized politicians. In accordance with classical theory, the board suggested that the Head of the State be empowered to appoint all executive officials, except the members of the "Executive Council" or cabinet. These could be appointed (or removed) only in consultation with the chairmen of the two houses of the legislature.[39] Though bound to consult his ministers, the Head of the State was not bound to accept their advice—unless some objections were raised "from the Sharīʻa point of view." If such an objection were raised, then the question would be referred to the Sharīʻa committee for decision.[40] The decision of the Sharīʻa committee could then prohibit an "un-Islamic" administrative act, and a recalcitrant minister who had the support of the speaker of one of the houses could continually obstruct executive action.

The board took pains to point out at length the Islamic

---

[37] *Qurʼān*, Surah III, verse 158; Surah XLII, verse 38.
[38] "Views," p. 66.
[39] *Ibid.*, pp. 67–68.
[40] *Ibid.*, p. 67.

limitations on legislation. Whatever might not be expressly
provided in the Sharī'a, or was not the subject of a consensus
of opinion "of those who are well versed in the Qur'ān and
Sunnah," would be a proper subject of the legislative prerogative of the Head of the State.[41] The Head of the State was
empowered to pass laws in this permitted category in consultation with his legislative council.

The legislative council was not the same representative body
that had been empowered to elect the Head of the State. The
nature of the duties of each group was different, too, for the
election of the Head of the State or the supervision of his
activities (the corollary of the right to remove him) was a
Shar'ī duty, whereas legislation itself was limited by the
Sharī'a, but outside of it. The legislative council was therefore
part of the executive, and presumably it would concentrate
its efforts upon purely "administrative" law. But here again
we find another functional and theoretical inconsistency. One
of the major duties of the caliph is to enforce the laws of the
Sharī'a. But since the Sharī'a is not now effective in Pakistan,
it must be enacted. One might suppose that the constitution
itself would provide for this, but as we have seen, the enabling
resolution assumed that the people of Pakistan were not yet
ready for this. Consequently the task of enforcing the Sharī'a
was transmuted to the task of enacting the Sharī'a along with
auxiliary legislation, but this was included among the tasks of
the legislative council, although it was primarily empowered
to deal with non-Shar'ī subjects. It is then possible to suggest
that the legislative council had the power to determine what
was Shar'ī by enacting it, while the Committee of Experts could
decide what was not Shar'ī by vetoing it. The issue was further
confused by the fact that the board failed to recommend a
specific provision whereby disputes between the Head of the

[41] *Ibid.*, p. 66.

State and his legislative council would be referred to the Committee of Experts on the Sharīʿa.

Despite the board's view that the limited power of legislation rested with the Head of the State, it insisted that all bills receive the assent of the legislative council as well as that of the Head of the State.[42] Should the Head of the State be unable to agree with the proposals of the council, he would be forced to resign.[43] Though the prerogative was that of the Head of the State, the wording of the board's "Views" suggests that bills might be initiated or altered by the legislative council in a manner similar to that existing in countries where the Head of the State has no legislative authority. To resolve a deadlock arising from the disagreement of the Head of the State and "his" legislative council, the board suggested all sorts of joint sessions and referenda, but they suggested no substitute for full agreement between the executive and the legislature. Although their previous suggestion is not repeated we understand that should the disagreement concern a question of Islamic law, then the Sharīʿa committee would decide the issue. In all other questions it is apparent that the legislative council was supreme, for no provision was made for a dissolution of the council, whereas the resignation of the Head of the State was mandatory in the event of permanent disagreement.

The whole of the classical basis of the "Views" of the board on the qualifications of the Head of the State was here subverted. The explicit provisions of the Sharīʿa regarding the caliphate were considered entirely separate from the powers which they assumed. The powers were, as we have seen, only nominally granted. The legislative council was given the power to force the Head of the State to resign by making every issue one of confidence or conscience; and this despite the fact

[42] *Ibid.*
[43] *Ibid.*, p. 67.

that another body, the house of representatives, might remove him from office on its own discretion.

A number of different influences brought the board to this astounding position. Perhaps the strongest prejudice under which they labored was the result of their understanding of the concept of an ideological state. They felt that all of those in policy-making positions must subscribe to the ideology of the Islamic state. That ideology they took to be a complete system. Wherever the Sharī'a was explicit, or wherever the 'ulamā' agreed, there was no discretion. Wherever a loophole in the Sharī'a existed a decision must be made in the "spirit" of the Sharī'a. As a complete and rigidly logical system there could be only one decision. If all the legislators and the executive would follow the spirit as well as the letter of the law, unanimity would naturally follow. Unanimity was not required of the legislature but it was implied in the board's rejection of any multiparty system. Even in the legal conception of consensus, despite the disagreement of a minority of the 'ulamā', unanimity is assumed. The Head of the State may have been entrusted with the legislative power in theory, but it is clear that the board took the head and his legislative council as two separate institutions. Disagreement between such separates could by no effort of casuistry be made to accord with the prejudice in favor of unanimity. That disagreement was unacceptable even in matters *not* laid down by the Sharī'a is instructive.

Islam, of course, insists that righteousness rules, and not the majority. There is not a little of the idea of the general will here, but it is complicated by the sense of the controlling verse of the Qur'ān: "Obey God, and the Prophet, and those among you who are entrusted with command; and if there is a dispute among you about something, then bring it to God and the

Messenger. . . ." [44] Once the Messenger was no longer with the Muslims, the Sharī'a had then to decide between Muslims in the event of dispute. The obvious implication of the Qur'ānic passage just quoted is that such a dispute be settled by reference to those competent to interpret the Qur'ān, but the intention of the board was to reëstablish the system as it was under the "Rightly-Guided Caliphs," when there was hardly any such group known or functioning as the 'ulamā'. In fact, at those times the caliphs were justifiably considered the best qualified to interpret the intention of the Prophet. This tendency is given added emphasis by the accepted report of those times, which has it that all decisions were in fact unanimous, with the opinion of the caliph most often prevailing. The most difficult complication arises where these principles are established within the framework of a system of legislative supremacy, nor would the 'ulamā' under contemporary circumstances be willing to grant the Head of the State a final veto. Any attempt by the legislature to override the veto of the Head of the State is tantamount to an unprecedented disagreement within the perfect state. Such an impasse is solved by the 'ulamā' by considering it to be a vote of no confidence in the Head of the State.

A similar provision is contained in the draft constitution ascribed to Maududi.[45] If the members of the board were influenced thereby, then they most certainly misunderstood Maududi's views. In his draft constitution Maududi provided that the Head of the State (amir) must follow the decision of his council in matters relating to political administration, but the council was required to accept the decision of the amir in

---

[44] *Qur'ān*, Surah IV, verse 59.
[45] Muhammad Asad and al-Saiyid Abu-l-Ala al-Maududi, *Muqtarahāt fi al-Dastūr al-Islāmi*, p. 26.

matters coming under the Sharī'a in respect of the amir's right of ijtihād and textual interpretation, i.e., "Islamic legislation." [46] Where confidence was lost, the people were to decide the issue between the amir and his council.[47]

Maududi's ideas were certainly more in keeping with the classical caliphate. He recognized the right of the amir to decide questions of Islamic law, though he made the amir responsible to the people as well as to God, but not responsible to the legislative council. The board would give the right of interpreting the Sharī'a to the Sharī'a committee, but they continued to insist that all the powers of government rested with the equivalent of the caliph. The only basis upon which their insistence upon the resignation of the Head of the State is valid is when the Head of the State and all the councilors are competent and willing to make the Sharī'a the basis of the state. Their attempt to give the 'ulamā' a final veto over all legislation could only be based upon the contrary assumption. Their stand on this question is fairly typical of the inconsistency of the thinking of the board, and it is paralleled by their stubborn insistence upon the "presidential" as opposed to the "parliamentary" system. If, they asserted, a parliamentary system was to be instituted, then no non-Muslim could be elected to the legislature by reason of the transfer of the caliphal qualifications to that body.[48] It is not mentioned whether such a system would preclude women as well, but the members of the board, in any case, insisted that a woman's place is in the home, and if women were to sit in the legislature only those over fifty years of age who observed purdah would qualify.[49]

[46] *Ibid.,* p. 26, Article 36.
[47] *Ibid.,* p. 26, Article 37.
[48] "Views" (Final Section), p. 3.
[49] *Ibid.* (Legislature), p. 7.

The same idea is behind the requirement that the Head of the State be elected by a majority of the Muslim members of the house of representatives as well as by the majority, if non-Muslims were to be permitted to sit in that body.[50]

The inconsistency of the board's recommendations becomes even more glaring when we remember that the division of the consultative council of the Head of the State into four functional groups was owing to the "size" of Pakistan rather than to any substantive difference arising out of the various functions of government. The executive council had to accept the Head of the State's decision or that of the Sharī'a committee, should a question be referred to that body. The legislative council, though flesh of the same political flesh, could go so far as to remove the Head of the State.

In their discussion of the judicial council the board made no recommendations regarding any possible disagreement.[51] The Head of the State merely controlled the judiciary with the advice and assistance of the judicial council. The propagative council was to advise and assist the Head of the State in carrying out the "most vital function of an Islamic State." [52] The Head of the State was to propagate the Islamic way of life throughout Pakistan and to organize missionary work in foreign countries.[53] Here again, though the members of this council were to be appointed in consultation with the Sharī'a committee, no provision was made for disagreement between the Head of the State and the members of the council. It is apparent that the functional differentiation in these various councils was much more than a mere convenience.

[50] *Ibid.* (Legislature), pp. 4–5.
[51] "Views," p. 68.
[52] *Ibid.*, p. 69.
[53] See discussion of the "enabling clause" of the Objectives Resolution, above.

THE ACTION OF THE SUB-COMMITTEE ON
CONSTITUTIONS AND POWERS

In submitting their recommendations to the Negotiating Sub-Committee the Board of Ta'līmat-i-Islāmīa took the opportunity of mentioning the handicaps under which they had been working.[54] The first impediment hampering their progress was the absence of Saiyid Sulaiman Nadvi, who had not yet arrived from India. The board felt that his absence rendered the whole of their work doubtful, and suggested that it might even be taken as the views of so many members rather than the official recommendations of the board. Nadvi's absence was no one's fault but his own, though the members of the board may have felt that he needed some additional official urging. By citing this difficulty they weakened their position immensely; we shall see that Nadvi's subsequent arrival did not change the board's "Views" at all. The other handicaps which they mentioned were the lack of books and research assistants. In saying that they had not referred to certain necessary sources, they impugned the integrity of their own report. They felt that they might yet have to modify some of their views "after perusal of the required books." [55] Their earlier request for research assistants had been deferred until Nadvi's arrival—apparently someone felt that the task of research might be smaller with such an accomplished scholar on the board.[56]

The membership of the Sub-Committee on Constitutions and Powers was such as to make their disinclination to accept the "Views" of the board a foregone conclusion. The doubts and difficulties enumerated by the board made this subcommittee's opposition even more determined. The special Negoti-

[54] "Views," p. 57.
[55] *Ibid.*
[56] *Ibid.*

ating Sub-Committee turned them down flat, but they did pass the board's recommendations on to the Sub-Committee on Constitutions and Powers whose report referred specifically to the "Views" of the board in only four places, and in no place did they accept the opinions of the board.[57]

At their very first meeting the Sub-Committee on Constitutions and Powers decided finally in favor of a parliamentary system of government as against the presidential system. The Head of the State was to be elected for a period of five years by the federal legislature, during which he was to act on the advice of his ministry, except in supervising elections and when acting under his emergency powers.[58] The Head of the State would not be answerable to any court for acts done in his official capacity, nor for personal acts so long as he held office.[59] The Head of the State would receive "such pay . . . as necessary to enable him to live in accordance with the dignity of the State." [60] The subcommittee felt that the acceptance of gifts by the Head of the State was not a constitutional matter.[61] The board thought that the Head of the State should "take" enough pay to allow him to live the life of an average citizen; and they forbade him to accept gifts except from close relatives.[62]

While agreeing that the Head of the State take an oath, the subcommittee completely rejected the board's notion of contract, simply suggesting that the "oath of allegiance should bear allegiance to the constitution of Pakistan and should be taken in the name of God. The Head of the State should also take the oath of office and of secrecy." [63]

[57] *Report on Constitutions*, pp. 8, 9, 10.
[58] *Ibid.*, pp. 8, 9, 10, 30.
[59] *Ibid.*, p. 11.
[60] *Ibid.*, p. 10.
[61] *Ibid.*
[62] "Views," pp. 71, 72.
[63] *Report on Constitutions*, p. 9.

The Head of the State was to appoint as Prime Minister a person who in his opinion commanded the confidence of the legislature. Other ministers were to be appointed on the advice of the Prime Minister.[64] The ministers were to be responsible to the legislature.[65] The cabinet was to furnish information to the Head of the State, but no provision was made for him to preside over cabinet meetings.[66] The Head of the State was not given the right to address the legislature, and the subcommittee preferred that he be kept entirely out of political controversy.[67]

As for the qualifications of the Head of the State, the subcommittee recommended that he be at least forty years of age, of sound mind, and with some educational qualification.[68] This was as far as they would go toward the board's views. They noted that the board had not cited any authority for the requirement that the Head of the State be a male Muslim, and they refused to accept this suggestion unless the position were "cleared."

"The Board of Ta'līmat-i-Islāmīa had not quoted any authority . . . it was necessary to know whether it was one of the fundamental principles of Islam. . . . It was absolutely essential to know the actual authorities." [69]

The subcommittee simply ignored the board's recommendation regarding the Committee of Experts on Sharī'a. They even went so far as to throw some doubt on whether they desired the nullification of all laws contrary to the Sharī'a.

> As regards the condition [suggested by the Board of Ta'līmat-i-Islāmīa] that ordinances passed by the Head of the State should not be in conflict with the Shariat, the Sub-Committee

---

64 *Ibid.,* p. 11.
65 *Ibid.*
66 *Ibid.,* p. 12.

67 *Ibid.,* p. 14.
68 *Ibid.,* p. 8.
69 *Ibid.*

thought that it should be considered by the Basic Principles Committee along with the whole field of legislation." [70]

The subcommittee did not admit any logical consequences following on acceptance of the Objectives Resolution, but the Objectives Resolution could not be simply ignored. The subcommittee suggested that the resolution be incorporated into the constitution as a directive principle of state policy.[71] The "enabling clause" was more or less repeated as a directive principle, but aside from the suggestion that there be compulsory teaching of the Qur'ān to the Muslims of Pakistan, nothing more was said.[72] The subcommittee also thought that some provision should be made in the Directive Principles of State Policy "that waqfs and mosques should be organized on proper lines." [73]

The Objectives Resolution was meant to be the basis of the constitution of Pakistan, but it was in fact only an agreed formulation which both sides interpreted in their own way. Only when this became clear to the subcommittee did they feel the need of preserving the formula in order to avoid alienating the 'ulamā' completely. Incorporating the resolution in their report was nearly the last decision of the subcommittee. When the subcommittee finished its work the 'ulamā' and the politicians were as far apart as ever, but now they realized the extent of their differences themselves. The politicians would not subordinate the authority of parliament to any other institution. The 'ulamā' would not give up their traditional function of guiding the Muslim community along the road to

---

[70] *Ibid.*, p. 9.
[71] *Ibid.*, p. 6.
[72] *Ibid.*
[73] *Ibid.* (Waqfs are endowments, usually in land or buildings, for religious purposes.)

salvation. If they thought about it the politicians would certainly insist that the Sharī'a was to be interpreted by the consensus of the representatives of the Muslims themselves. Yet the subcommittee was courteous enough to pass the "Views" of the Board of Ta'līmat on to the full Basic Principles Committee, along with their own report.

6 The Interim Report

SECULARISM

In the "Views" of the Board of Ta'līmat-i-Islāmīa, as disconnected as they were, we have found a concrete statement of the point of view of the 'ulamā'. In reality, this was their second position, for the original demand of the 'ulamā' was for a high-powered ministry of religious affairs. Their new position might be summarized in terms of an attempt to "Islamize" the whole of the government of Pakistan. Because of the association of this new position with the revived classical theory of the caliphate, it might be termed "romantic," but the emphasis on so many specific rules of the Sharī'a has led us to find the dominant external influence in the work of Maududi.

While this combination of traditional and fundamentalist points of view was being expressed in the seclusion of the committee room, the modernist points of view were being more openly expressed. The "ijmā' modernist theory" has been stressed as the most significant aspect of the modernist movement, but it has been pointed out that there was, especially among some of the Muslim League leaders, a secularist tendency in the sense that communalism itself was the extent of their Islamic politics.[1] Secularism in this limited political sense might be said to have been the Muslim League policy until some time after the Lahore Resolution was passed. In this connection it is significant to note that when the policy of the League ceased to be secular, the actual manifestation of that policy was not in the form of a concrete Islamic program, but rather in the form of achieving the endorsement of a recognized 'ulamā' organization.

Though secularism remained an important feature in the thinking of many highly placed persons in Pakistan, the suggestion that religion and politics ought to be separated (except for Jinnah's statement of August 11, 1947) could not be made once Pakistan was a fact. The new secularist position was in fact disestablishmentarian, and it pursued its goal by attempting to relegate Islam to the sphere of policy rather than law. The most indefatigable exponent of this approach was the Prime Minister, Liaqat Ali Khan, himself.

Even before the Objectives Resolution was discussed by the Constituent Assembly of Pakistan, Liaqat Ali Khan had begun to explain to the nation what was the significance of the phrase *Islamic State*. An Islamic society, he said, was one with "no inner conflicts, where a man gets just reward for his toil and where there are no parasites." [2] The foremost duty of a government based upon Islamic principles was to end all "exploitation." [3] After the resolution was passed he continued with renewed vigor to give his own interpretation of its consequences to the nation. Efforts were made to dispel the notion that Pakistan would be a theocratic state wherein the 'ulamā'

---

[1] See above, p. 67.
[2] *Pakistan News* (a government information bulletin), Jan. 30, 1949, p. 46.
[3] *Ibid.*, Feb. 20, 1949, p. 85.

would reign supreme.[4] The equality of all—Muslims and non-Muslims alike—was insisted upon, but above all the economic consequences of Islamic principles were stressed.

While others used the term Islamic democracy or theo-democracy, Liaqat spoke of Islamic socialism.[5] What he meant by this is not quite clear, for it was used more or less as a slogan. At times it seemed to mean something a bit different from the usual notions of either Islam or socialism, as when he asserted that he believed in "no other 'ism' except Islamic Socialism." [6] At other times the word "Islamic" seemed to be a superfluous addition to the word "socialism": "It shall be our endeavor to continue on these socialistic lines, for these are the same as Islam has taught us." [7] But Liaqat's own simple explanation for his meaning failed to demonstrate that his purpose was specifically Islamic or socialistic. His object was to provide the poor with "food, clothing, shelter, medical aid and education," and to benefit the common man.[8] It is hard to think of any economic *system* that does not claim this as its direct or indirect aim.

"Islamic economics" is one of the newest branches of the liberal apologetic.[9] When the liberal movement began about a century ago the one thing Western critics of Islam had not claimed was that Christianity had produced a good economic system. As apologetic gradually became polemic the weaknesses and shortcomings of uncontrolled capitalism produced an ever increasing opposition within its own fold. The Russian Revolution and the Great Depression combined with the economic grievances of Indian Muslims to produce a "self-evident"

---

[4] *Ibid.*, Oct. 16, 1949, p. 687.
[5] Richard Symonds, *The Making of Pakistan* (London, 1949), p. 178.
[6] *Pakistan News,* July 3, 1949, p. 405.
[7] *Ibid.*, Aug. 21, 1949, p. 492.
[8] *Ibid.*, July 13, Dec. 18, 1949, pp. 405, 823, 832.
[9] W. C. Smith, *Modern Islam in India* (2d ed.; London, 1946), pp. 88 ff.

argument against capitalism while adding ammunition to those who based their arguments on the superiority of ideal Islam over the evils of the real West. But socialism is as much a product of the West as capitalism, and its aims hardly suited the needs of the struggling Muslim middle classes or the feudally oriented 'ulamā'.[10] A distinctive economic system was found to be the product of the Islamic laws on alms-giving, inheritance, the denial of usury, and the protection of the rights of private property. That the Islamic state was responsible for the material welfare of all its citizens was derived from the pension scheme of Umar I in seventh-century Arabia. The resultant which Liaqat called Islamic socialism was no more than capitalism plus social security plus God.

The socialist aspect of this vague notion was lent some substance by the need for state capitalism. The almost total lack of industry in Pakistan has been well described, and it suffices for us to point out that even among underdeveloped countries Pakistan was underdeveloped.[11] At the time of partition, supplies of ordinary consumer goods had been so disrupted by the exodus of the urban Hindu population that huge profits could be made in the most ordinary of commercial transactions, and later some of these profits could be turned to light industrial projects. There was a certain reluctance, strengthened by a lack of technical skill, to move from speculation to entrepreneurship. Except for cotton textile manufacturing and food processing, for which the need was urgent and the capital requirement not very great, there was no rush to invest. It was soon apparent

[10] The "feudal" orientation of the 'ulamā' is based upon corporative social conceptions. In rural areas this involves recognition of the authority of the local landowner over "his" peasants. This orientation is also influenced by the existence of landed religious endowments in many villages for the support of the local mosque and mullah.

[11] See Walter Godfrey, *Pakistan: Economic and Commercial Conditions* (London, 1951), p. 81; Jerome B. Cohen, "Development Program of Pakistan," *Middle East Journal,* Vol. V, no. 1 (Winter, 1951), p. 99.

that the government would have to enter several fields for which there was either not enough local capital or not enough incentive to persuade local capitalists to invest.

Liaqat's statements are therefore to be understood as arising from the desire to encourage public interest and support for the government's economic program. Unctuous references to Islam became the order of the day in discussions of industrial development; and it was hoped that the general aim of the material welfare of the "common man" would overshadow the religious injunction against the giving or taking of interest. This difficulty was by no means overlooked, but it was discussed as a problem to be solved rather than a precondition necessitating anything like forced saving and state capitalism, or even the abolition of banks.[12]

Liaqat's preoccupation with economic solutions extended itself even to the much vexed problem of a postpartition ideology for the Muslim League. Chaudhri Khaliquzzaman, the League organizer, had revived the old Khilafat ideal as the goal of the new League. The restoration of the Khilafat, or the creation of an "Islamistan" was hardly a practical goal for an independent state and a member of the United Nations, whereas agrarian reform seemed, at least, a practical application of the principle of Islamic socialism. Liaqat therefore supported the Punjab dissidents who favored the abolition of zamindari privileges against the League ministry in that province.

At the first council meeting of the reorganized Muslim League on February 20, 1949, a resolution was passed asking the Working Committee

> . . . to examine the question [of land reform] in the light of Islamic Law and in consultation with the Provincial Muslim Leagues, draw up a charter of rights for the tillers of the soil

[12] Godfrey, *op. cit.,* p. 1.

in the light of the Islamic principles which may remove their existing grievances and ensure friendly relations between all classes in general.[13]

In this instance "Islamic principles" and "Islamic Law" were meant to safeguard the right of private property and hereditary privileges. Just before the Working Committee was to meet to appoint the Daultana committee to examine the Agrarian question,[14] a group of 'ulamā' were induced to make a statement to the press to the effect that the zamindari system was not un-Islamic.[15]

Speaking at Lahore on August 25, Liaqat remarked that he had received telegrams describing the proposed agricultural reforms as contrary to the Sharīʿa. He went on to assure his listeners that there would be no reforms that contravened the Sharīʿa, but "it is, of course, a different matter that we are not bound to accept the interpretation which vested interests may give to laws of the Shariat simply to serve their own selfish ends." [16] The zamindars must realize that their days are numbered. Islamic socialism entails the right of all to food, shelter, clothing, and educational and medical facilities.[17]

The government's preoccupation with the virtues of Islamic economics and the necessity for land reform was so great that these slogans were used even as a vehicle for Pakistan's foreign policy. After Liaqat's bitter disappointment with the Commonwealth Prime Ministers' Conference at London,[18] an effort was made to break Pakistan's virtual isolation by strengthening its contacts with other Muslim states. On his way home Liaqat

[13] Quoted from *Minutes of the Working Committee Meeting of the Pakistan Muslim League,* Aug. 26–29, 1949, Resolution no. 2.
[14] *Ibid.,* April 2–4, 1949, Resolution no. 10.
[15] *Dawn,* April 1, 1949.
[16] *Pakistan News,* Sept. 4, 1949.
[17] *Ibid.*
[18] Symonds, *op. cit.,* pp. 170–171.

visited Cairo, Baghdad, and Teheran, and laid the groundwork for a series of treaties of friendship, and for a conference later in the year.[19] In Cairo, Liaqat said that Pakistan had resolved to put into practice the highest Islamic principles: "Through the Constituent Assembly the people of Pakistan have shown their determination to have a system whereby the rich will not continue to get richer and the poor poorer. . . ."[20] In Teheran he said substantially the same thing in a radio broadcast; and in his broadcast to the people of Pakistan from Karachi he again repeated the same refrain.[21]

Typically, the conference scheduled for November became the International Islamic Economic Conference.

The IIEC was opened with an address by Ghulam Muhammad, finance minister of Pakistan. After referring to the supranational unity of all Muslims, and need for moving from political to economic independence, he got onto the subject of land tenure.[22] He explained that Islam prescribes no "rigid codes of land tenure." As for the modern controversy over the ownership of the means of production, Islam answered this by saying that all belonged to God—which is to say that all must be used within the limitations of the public welfare. Conversely, any system of land tenure which best serves the people is most Islamic.

Islam, he said, means "nothing other than social justice," and he went on to precise this generalization in ten "more specific" principles. Among the ten were included economic justice, the democratic republican welfare state, discouragement of feudalism through laws of inheritance, the requirement that stockholders share losses as well as gains, the right to private property and other wealth (but not too much of it),

[19] *Dawn*, May 31, 1949.
[20] *Pakistan News*, May 22, 1949, p. 300.
[21] *Ibid.*, May 29, 1949, p. 318; June 5, 1949, p. 331.
[22] *Ibid.*, Dec. 4, 1949, pp. 778 ff.

public ownership of utilities, and the condoning of coöperative farming. The problem posed by the modern banking system was too much for this worthy finance minister and he suggested that it be sent to a committee. In summing up he asserted that Islam is a middle way, with some features of the West and some of the Soviet Union.

THE MODERNIST APOLOGY FOR SECULARISM

It is obvious that "secularism" in Pakistan is not exactly the same as that which is indicated by the term in common usage. There are comparatively few people in Pakistan who will take a more extreme position, and we shall have a later occasion to discuss the only important public attack on the Islamic constitution idea. Liaqat Ali Khan, of course, did not oppose an Islamic constitution, but he suggested nothing to dispel the idea that he equated British parliamentarism and Islam so far as the constitution of Pakistan was concerned. On the other hand, he never made any statement indicating his acceptance of the consensus theory. Insofar as the consensus theory was advocated by prominent political figures, it was unofficially expounded; though there is some ground for the belief that such statements of the consensus theory were apologies for the Prime Minister's position. Since neither secularists nor "ijma modernists" favored any adventure in political institutions, they were the only ones who avoided the pitfalls of romanticism; that the consensus theory would not conflict with the institution of British parliamentarism made such an apology possible. The second point at which the secularist and "consensus" positions came together was in the view that Islam only lays down certain general principles. If Liaqat thought these principles should form the basis of policy, his apologists had to take the view that they would form the basis of legislation.

Speaking at the Political Science Conference at Lahore in

March, 1950, Dr. Qureshi, now a deputy minister, said that the important task before those making the constitution was to adjust the eternal principles of Islam to the needs of the modern age.[23] There would have been no difficulty were Islam a system of rigid laws, but Islam "requires a new interpretation at every stage of our development."[24] The "reactionary conservatives" were damned along with those who would separate politics from religion, leading to the conclusion that the Constituent Assembly was on the right track.[25] The question was now rephrased: ". . . how far can we go in discarding precedents without injuring principles?" Since the Qur'ān and Sunnah give only general principles, the answer is that all precedents could be discarded as merely "ephemeral interpretations."[26] Having rid himself at once of the claims of the "Rightly-Guided Caliphs," the consensus of the Companions of the Prophet, and "taqlīd," Dr. Qureshi proceeded to lay the basis of the modern idea of ijmā'. The Islamic state demands complete obedience so long as it adheres to the right path—but what guarantee is there that the state will not stray? "A State will remain Muslim to the extent and for the time that its people are Muslim."[27] This leads to the fundamental principle of Islamic government that the affairs of state must be settled by mutual consultation. Two consequences of this principle are that the majority view shall prevail, and the need for "an effective machinery for the dissemination of true knowledge so that the mass of the people may abide by the ideals of Islam."[28]

[23] I. H. Qureshi, *Pakistan, Islamic Democracy* (Lahore, 1951), p. 2 (an address delivered in 1949).
[24] *Ibid.*, p. 3.
[25] *Ibid.*, p. 5.
[26] *Ibid.*, p. 6.
[27] *Ibid.*, p. 8.
[28] *Ibid.*, p. 9.

On the same occasion Tamizuddin Khan, the president of the Constituent Assembly, spoke against the "closure of the gate of Ijtihād," relying on Iqbal for his authority;[29] Sardar Nishtar explained the Objectives Resolution; and Justice S. A. Rahman of the Federal Court said:

> According to the Qur'ān, change is one of the greatest signs of God. . . . We have been given immutable principles . . . but the existence of these external principles leaves a very wide field for evolutionary progress in the political and social spheres. The time has now arrived when the power of Ijtihād should be removed from the representatives of the schools to a Muslim Legislative Assembly.[30]

His Lordship added that this was Iqbal's conclusion. In fact the only discordant note at the conference was sounded by Dr. Omar Hayat Malik who said, ". . . if we adopt Islam as our guide . . . then many a controversy that have (*sic*) agitated the minds of political scientists through the ages will find a categorical solution."[31] Dr. Malik's categorical solution was not quite what was meant by ijtihād. Malik is, of course, a romantic of fundamentalist leanings, as we shall see below.

In the face of statements such as that of Dr. Malik, and the erratic pressure of the 'ulamā' and Jamā'at-i-Islāmi, the direction in which the secularists in the government and the Constituent Assembly must move was clear. As the controversy over constitutional issues proceeded, the government would have to accept the consensus theory if it wished to keep the political institutions it had inherited from the British. This alternative was not yet clear because the Prime Minister was preoccupied with other problems, and because the 'ulamā' and

[29] *Dawn,* March 6, 1950.
[30] *Ibid.,* March 8, 1950.
[31] *Ibid.,* March 7, 1950. Malik was appointed ambassador to Indonesia shortly afterward.

Jamāʿat-i-Islāmi were fairly inactive. In this regard it might be noted that the "Views" of the Board of Taʿlīmat-i-Islāmīa were not publicized and, consequently, did not arouse any public discussion.

THE INACTIVITY OF THE ʿULAMĀ

The ʿulamā', as has been pointed out, tended to work on the politicians directly rather than through the people, and when their demands were accepted they relented while awaiting further events. The unreserved acceptance that Maulana Usmani accorded the Objectives Resolution became the prevailing note for the ʿulamā'. Consequently, the period between the middle of March, 1949, and September, 1950, when the Interim Report of the Basic Principles Committee was presented, was their most inactive period since the founding of Pakistan. Of course, this is not to say that they were not called upon for, nor did they fail in, the performance of their usual political function. A group of ʿulamā' undertook a tour of Waziristan to preach against the "notorious hostile," the Faqir of Ipi.[32] Sixty-five ʿulamā' signed a "fatwa" declaring the Kashmir war a jihād, and declaring that any anti-Pakistan activity was sinful since Pakistan was an Islamic state.[33]

Islam recognizes neither priesthood nor hierarchy, but the ʿulamā' cannot do without leadership. In the Ottoman or Mughal system, which the ʿalim vaguely wished to recreate, the focal point of the institution was at the point of contact with the imperial hierarchy. Official designation of the Shaikh-al-Islām defined the leadership of the ʿulamā'. In the modern state of Pakistan this office was nonexistent except in the atavistic limbo of the Maulavi and Maulana. As the chief

[32] *Dawn,* April 1, 1949; James W. Spain, "Pakistan's North West Frontier Province," *Middle East Journal,* Vol. VIII, no. 1 (Winter, 1954).

[33] *Pakistan News,* June 12, 1949, p. 371.

recipient of official patronage Maulana Shabbir Ahmad Usmani was often known as Shaikh al-Islām, while Mufti Muhammad Shafi was honored with the unofficial title of Mufti-i-A'zām-i-Pākistān. Maulana Usmani was still president of the Jamī'at-al-'Ulamā'-i-Islām and Mufti Shafi, for the time being, the most prominent member of the Board of Ta'līmat-i-Islāmīa. The inactivity of these two organizations was in large measure responsible for the inactivity of the 'ulamā'.

The Board of Ta'līmat was not fully constituted until early in November, so that there was no occasion until after that date to define the potential disagreement with the politicians.[34] And no sooner had the board begun its work than its staunchest supporter, Maulana Shabbir Ahmad Usmani, president of the Jamī'at-al-'Ulamā'-i-Islām, died.[35]

Maulana Zafar Ahmad Usmani of Bengal became the temporary president (he claimed the permanent presidency) and promptly announced the reorganization of the Jamī'at.[36] The Pir of Manki Sharif was appointed as "organizer." The organization had not as yet undergone the formal reorganization that was the inevitable consequence of partition. The strength of the organization lay in its monopoly of government patronage in return for its services in the momentous days of the last all-India election.[37] Its weakness lay in the fact that almost all its members came to Pakistan from other parts of India, and despite the high mobility of the 'ulamā' the difficulty of individual adjustment to new conditions cannot be minimized.

Even for Jamā'at-i-Islāmi the Objectives Resolution was a turning point in the history of Pakistan. The Majlis-i-Shūra of the Jamā'at solemnly met to decide upon the future relation-

[34] *Panel of Chairmen,* p. 25.
[35] *Pakistan News,* Dec. 18, 1949. Usmani died on December 13.
[36] *Dawn,* Jan. 9, 1950.
[37] M. S. M. Sharma, *Peeps into Pakistan* (Patna, 1954), p. 125 (the interpretation is biased).

ship of the organization to the state of Pakistan. The Objectives Resolution, they felt, was a statement of good intentions on the part of the government. Pakistan was clearly on its way to becoming an Islamic state, and as such deserved the allegiance of the members of the Jamā'at. The constitution of the Jamā'at was changed accordingly.[38]

The only discordant voice was that of Maulana Abdul Hamid Badauni, of the Jamī'at-al-'Ulamā'-i-Pākistān, who demanded representation on "the Constitution making Committee . . ." and criticized the proposed appointment of a "Congress 'alim" on the committee.[39] Badauni soon found greater opportunities for advancement in directing the efforts of the miserable refugees of Karachi into disorderly pursuits, and did not press any constitutional views of his own for the time being.

Thus it was that when the BPC met to consider the report of the Sub-Committee on Constitutions and Powers, and the "Views" of the board appended thereto, Liaqat Ali Khan had no reason to suspect that whatever action he took on the religious question would evoke a strong public reaction. Apparently the Objectives Resolution maneuver had been highly successful.

FOREIGN AFFAIRS AND THE REPORT OF THE BOARD OF TA'LĪMAT-I-ISLĀMĪA

From the foregoing it is easy enough to judge that Liaqat Ali Khan and his government were almost completely out of tune with the 'ulamā'. Yet in the rejection of the suggestions of the Board of Ta'līmat-i-Islāmīa it was not these considerations that were decisive. It was rather developments in Pakistan's foreign relations which determined that expediency and conviction should run in the same channel.

[38] Interview.
[39] *Dawn*, Sept. 14, 1949.

Liaqat Ali Khan's preoccupation with external affairs left him little time to deal with internal political problems. Zafrullah Khan was an extremely able advocate of Pakistan's case on Kashmir before the United Nations Security Council, but it would seem that direct relations with other powers were largely out of his hands. It is not an infrequent occurrence that a prime minister handle a large part of the high-level work of the Foreign Affairs Ministry, but it is a rare situation in which a foreign affairs ministry spends so much time doing again and again the same task. There is of course no way of knowing to what extent Liaqat Ali Khan received or accepted the advice of his foreign minister. However, there are several circumstances that may justify the contention that, with the exception of preparing briefs for the Security Council, Zafrullah Khan had very little to do with the making of several important decisions. As examples we may mention Liaqat Ali's "don't take Pakistan for granted" speech after the Commonwealth Prime Ministers' Conference in 1949, his approach to other Muslim countries immediately thereafter, Zafrullah's absence from the International Islamic Economic Conference of November, 1949, the choice of an economic theme for the conference, Zafrullah's nonparticipation in any of the manifold direct relations of India and Pakistan and, perhaps most important of all, the manner and timing of the Prime Minister's announcement that Pakistan would support the United Nations Security Council on Korea.

The disappointment of the Prime Ministers' Conference of April, 1949, was deepened by the deadlock over Kashmir during the following summer. The Truman-Attlee appeal to both sides to accept arbitration in accordance with the UNCIP's resolution of August 30 was accepted by Pakistan but rejected by India. Pakistan was strongly of the opinion that India was being favored because of her greater potential in the cold war.[40] Three weeks later the tension between Pakistan and India increased as a result of the devaluation controversy.[41] India refused to accept the Pakistani rupee undevalued, with the result that trade broke down between the two Bengals. The loss of Pakistan's market for jute in West Bengal coincided with a decline in world demand, the British financial crisis, and the American recession. On the other side of the line, jute-mill workers were idle in Calcutta—which is a considerably more explosive city than Dacca. In February, along with the failure and the dissolution of the UNCIP, communal riots broke out in both Bengals.[42] Communication between the two prime ministers dragged on through March until Liaqat flew to Delhi on April 1, to begin the negotiations that led to the important Liaqat-Nehru Pact of April 8, 1950.[43]

The pact is significant not only because it led to a temporary *détente,* but because it provided an international guarantee that minorities in both countries should enjoy equal civil rights,[44] and because the pact was in large measure a personal achievement of Liaqat. On his return, Liaqat held a press conference at which he stressed the fact that the Objectives Resolution guaranteed fundamental rights to the minorities of Pakistan; and in a radio broadcast he reminded his people that Jinnah had said that "as citizens of Pakistan the members of the minority com-

[40] Michael Brecher, *The Struggle for Kashmir* (Canadian Institute of International Affairs, 1952), p. 101.

[41] The decision not to devalue was made at a long cabinet meeting from which the Minister of Finance was absent (in the U.S.).

[42] Brecher, *op. cit.,* p. 180.

[43] R. D. Lambert, "Religion, Economics, and Violence in Bengal," *Middle East Journal* (July, 1950), p. 307.

[44] *Pakistan News,* April 16, 1950, p. 285: "The Governments of India and Pakistan solemnly agree that each shall ensure to the minorities throughout its territory complete equality of citizenship. . . ."

munity shall enjoy equal rights with the Muslims of Pakistan." [45] So great was Liaqat's prestige that Nehru made his first trip to Karachi (after partition) for no apparent reason other than to demonstrate his own goodwill.

Triumphant in the glory of an international peacemaker, Liaqat then set out for his tour of the United States.[46] The American tour had been engineered by means of a feint in the direction of Moscow many months before, but now it was largely conditioned by the events immediately preceding it.[47] The uses to which the opportunity to address American audiences were put, were to seek American friendship through popularizing the idea of Pakistan as a progressive democratic state wed by Islam to the principle of political morality, to destroy the notion that the Objectives Resolution meant that Pakistan would be a theocratic state, to explain the Kashmir issue, and to impress upon the American people the need to industrialize underdeveloped areas in their own self-interest.[48] It was also hoped that the tour would provide the basis for substituting the United States for Britain as Pakistan's Western patron, or through such expectation drive Britain into being more "understanding." [49]

In a series of speeches across the country Liaqat pounded home his points with simplicity and monotony.[50] And in

[45] *Ibid.,* pp. 292–294.

[46] *Ibid.,* May 28, 1950, p. 258 (TV interview with Mrs. Roosevelt), and p. 361 (Walter Lippmann introduction at "Town Hall").

[47] See F. M. Innes, "The Political Outlook in Pakistan," *Pacific Affairs,* Vol. XXVI, no. 4 (Dec., 1953), esp. pp. 308, 311.

[48] Liaqat Ali Khan, *Pakistan: Heart of Asia,* speeches in the U.S. and Canada, May and June, 1950 (Cambridge, 1951); references to economic aid, pp. 9, 31, 39–40, 49, 66, *passim.*

[49] *Dawn,* May 1, 1950; references to Liaqat-Attlee meeting and meeting with Gordon-Walker en route to U.S.; *Pakistan News,* June 19, 1950, p. 392; also *Dawn,* July 11, 1950; Liaqat's BBC speech on way back to Pakistan.

[50] Liaqat Ali Khan, *op. cit.;* see also review by W. C. Smith, *Pacific Affairs,* Vol. XXIV, no. 2, p. 216.

nearly every speech he attempted to capitalize on the recently concluded Liaqat-Nehru Pact, either directly or by referring to the rights of minorities in Pakistan. He told the United States Senate: "We have solemnly pledged that our minorities shall enjoy full rights of citizenship." [51] He told the Canadian Parliament that Pakistan did not plan to become a stronghold of intolerance or medievalism: [52] ". . . our minorities shall enjoy full rights of citizenship, and shall freely profess and practice their religions." [53] At New Orleans Liaqat said:

> [Our ideals] do not spell out a sectarian mediaeval, intolerant, theocratic society. We believe in God and his supreme sovereignty because we believe that civic life must have an ethical content and a higher purpose, which we cannot but conceive of as the fulfillment of the Divine will. But democracy, social justice, equality of opportunity, equality before the law of all citizens, irrespective of race or creed, are also articles of faith with us. . . .[54]

Liaqat was anxious enough for American friendship that he committed Pakistan to the support of the Security Council resolution on Korea upon just emerging from a Boston Hospital after an operation (and apparently without consulting his foreign minister).[55]

A week after his return Liaqat reported to the people of Pakistan on the results of his tour of the United States:

> Our enemies in the United States had given currency to all sorts of wrong impressions regarding Pakistan. They had particularly presented in an ugly and ridiculous form the idea of the Islamic State . . . the people of America had been led to

[51] *Ibid.*, p. 6.
[52] *Ibid.*, p. 127.
[53] *Ibid.*, p. 119.
[54] *Ibid.*, p. 97.
[55] See F. H. Soward, "The Korean Crisis and the Commonwealth," *Pacific Affairs,* Vol. XXIV, no. 2 (June, 1951), p. 120.

believe that we are a reactionary people. . . .[56] We have made
it clear to the Americans and others in our tour that minorities
in Pakistan have the same rights as Muslims in this country. . . .[57]

The day after his radio talk Liaqat flew to Delhi to meet
Nehru and Sir Owen Dixon, the United Nations mediator, for
a discussion of the Kashmir question. The meeting ended in-
conclusively. The Kashmir problem hung like a darkened pall
over the Pakistan horizon, but the immediate difficulty was
presented by the endless stream of refugees.[58] In Bengal the
situation had much improved after the Liaqat-Nehru Pact, but
there was still a great deal of tension there as well as in Uttar
Pradesh. There were thirty-five million potential immigrants
left in India, and at any moment Nehru could send them
streaming across the border. The seed that would eventually
result in American economic aid had hardly been planted, and
Liaqat was sure that its cultivation was in some way connected
with the treatment of minorities in Pakistan. Liaqat was afraid
that accepting the recommendations of the Board of Ta'līmat
might jeopardize dollar investment, or the Liaqat-Nehru Pact
or both.[59] Thus intimidated, Liaqat "postponed" consideration
of the suggestions of the Board of Ta'līmat-i-Islāmīa at the
ensuing meetings of the BPC.[60]

THE INTERIM REPORT OF THE
BASIC PRINCIPLES COMMITTEE

The decision to call the Basic Principles Committee into
session to prepare some kind of report to present to the Constituent Assembly was occasioned by the growing criticism of

[56] *Pakistan News,* July 30, 1950, p. 439.
[57] *Dawn,* July 20, 1950.
[58] Lambert, *op. cit.,* p. 323.
[59] Interview.
[60] *BPC Minutes,* pp. 7–38, esp. pp. 10, 11, 15, 27, 34.

the Assembly's dilatoriness. Such criticism was prompted by the fact that India had completed her constitution by the end of 1949, and had promulgated it in January, 1950. In view of the rejection of the suggestions of the Board of Ta'līmat-i-Islāmīa the manner in which criticisms of constitutional delays had been parried was at least inept. These criticisms had been aimed at the Muslim League as a whole rather than at one group or another in the League. The League's answer was to lean again upon Islam as though it were their own private preserve. Thus it was that while attempts were being made to explain Islamic principles in a variety of new ways, Tamizuddin Khan could say that the delay in framing the constitution was owing to the need to consult the advisory board of 'ulamā'; [61] Nishtar could explain the delay as arising from the search for something original; [62] Tamizuddin Khan could say on the very eve of the meetings of the BPC that strenuous efforts were being made with the help of the 'ulamā' not to deviate from Islamic principles; [63] and Liaqat could say even after the decisions of the BPC that the delay was inevitable "because we want to frame our constitution on a new ideology, on Islamic principles. . . ." [64] It was somewhat disappointing to find that the Interim Report contained no more than the Government of India Act plus the Objectives Resolution as preamble, and the requirement that all Muslims must study the Qur'ān.

When the BPC met, it had before it only the Report of the Sub-Committee on Constitutions and Powers with the recommendations of the Board of Ta'līmat-i-Islāmīa attached thereto, in accordance with the request of the board. [65] Neither the

[61] *Dawn,* Dec. 13, 1949.
[62] *Ibid.,* Feb. 3, 1950.
[63] *Ibid.,* Aug. 2, 1950.
[64] *Ibid.,* Aug. 15, 1950.
[65] *BPC Minutes,* p. 8.

Franchise Committee, which was to work out the details of representation in the legislatures, nor the Judiciary Committee had completed their work as yet. It is evident that the device of an Interim Report was contrived to revive confidence in the Assembly, rather than to announce an agreement in principle. Objections to the report in committee had not been dealt with, they had merely been "postponed," like the suggestions of the Board of Ta'līmat-i-Islāmīa. Apparently no difficulties were expected in the acceptance of the report, which is an indication of how incorrect were the Prime Minister's assumptions about his own influence and the provincial loyalties of the members from East Bengal. His disillusionment was to lead Liaqat to apply himself to internal political problems with the same vigor and courage that he had displayed in external affairs; but first he had to deal with the consequences of his error.

The difficulty lay in Clause 30 and Clause 31 of the Interim Report which dealt with the constitutions, powers, and function of the central legislature. Clause 30 provided that "there should be a Central Legislature consisting of two Houses: 1) The House of Units representing the Legislatures of the Units. 2) The House of People elected by the people." [66] It was laid down in Clause 31 that each province would have representation in the Upper House, but the size of these delegations was not fixed.[67] On the other hand, the election of the members of the House of the People directly by the people did not give any assurance that provincial delegations would be in proportion to the population of each province.

At the meeting of the BPC Mr. Daultana of the Punjab had suggested that both Houses might be of about the same size— since they were to have *equal powers* according to Clause 39.[68]

[66] *C.A.P. Debates,* Vol. VIII, no. 1, Appendix I, p. 21.
[67] *Ibid.*
[68] *BPC Minutes,* p. 24.

Mr. Datta of East Bengal thought that representation in the Upper House should not be equal and the Lower House should be elected strictly on the basis of population. Maulana Akram Khan, the president of the East Bengal Muslim League, suggested that the issue be postponed until the exact composition of the Houses be reported by the Franchise Committee, and Maulana Abdullah al-Baqi, also of Bengal, thought that "equal representation in the Upper House should be subject to the condition that the position enjoyed by a Unit on the basis of population should not be adversely affected by it." [69] Later Akram Khan was willing to accept parity for East and West Pakistan insisting only that "the majority of any province in the Lower House [not] be reduced to minority in the joint Houses. . . ." [70] All of these suggested amendments were postponed.

The position of the various provinces were therefore known to the Prime Minister. The Punjabis desired to enhance the federal aspect of the central parliament, whereas the Bengalis preferred to emphasize its democratic aspect. The Punjab is the most advanced province of Pakistan, if industry, literacy, urbanization, and membership in the civil service and the military are adequate criteria. Bengal is certainly the most populous province, and if not the most politically aware, at least it may be said that Bengalis are acutely self-conscious. The smaller and more backward provinces of West Pakistan, insofar as their wishes were represented by their governments, were mostly concerned with maintaining their "independence" of the Punjab and their autonomy vis-à-vis the central government.

The Prime Minister's position on the federal question is a little more difficult to pin down. Some indication of his views

[69] *BPC Minutes*, p. 25.
[70] *Ibid.*, p. 38.

may be gathered from the composition of the Muslim League council as provided in Clause 18 of the League constitution of February, 1948. Another indication may be found in the officially inspired suggestion of January, 1949, that all West Pakistan be unified as a single province.[71] The third indication is to be found in the provisions of the Interim Report itself, even though the Prime Minister was not a member of the Sub-Committee on Constitutions and Powers.

The common element in each of these three bits of evidence is the reduction of Bengali power in the future parliament as compared with the Constituent Assembly. This tendency is doubly significant in view of the fact that the government was dependent on the Bengal League bloc in the legislature for its continued existence. There is, however, no reason to believe that Liaqat wished to transfer this dependence from East to West Pakistan. It is far more likely that he simply desired to reduce his dependence. To accomplish such a reduction he would have to increase the representation of West Pakistan to where it was equal, or nearly so, to that of Bengal, and at the same time expand his cabinet to the point where it might effectively combine now with the east and now with the west so as to permit the government to pass necessary, but locally unpopular, legislation. For this system to work, the representatives of West Pakistan would have to vote together—this was at least part of the significance of the suggestion for the political unification of West Pakistan. The suggestion evidently could not be pressed because of the opposition of the smaller provinces, so another way had to be found.

As far as we can judge, Liaqat decided to unify the provinces of West Pakistan by "political" measures since legal measures were unacceptable. That is to say, he would tie these provinces and princely states to his own support in return for certain

[71] Symonds, *op. cit.,* p. 104.

concessions. Actually, Liaqat had made some progress in this direction before the Interim Report was presented. He had increased the number of West Pakistan seats by *coöpting* five Punjabis to represent the new refugee population, and by permitting the rulers of the various states to *nominate* four representatives of their own. The cabinet bloc, mostly made up of refugee politicians like Liaqat, had also been expanded by the addition of three ministers and two deputy ministers, and possibly by the appointment of a couple of Assembly members to provincial governorships. Liaqat also made his peace with Mr. Khuhro, the most powerful politician in Sindh, and he made his choice between the two struggling for control of the Punjab.

Occasionally Liaqat was explicit in referring to the equal importance of Bengal and Punjab; more often his views were obvious from his actions. The difficulty with Liaqat's approach was that it was both short-sighted and illogical even if it held out the prospect of immediate stability. His approach was short-sighted because it did not envision the period, tragically near, wherein no unattached refugee group would hold the balance of power. It was illogical because it tended to restrict provincial autonomy while enhancing the federal aspect of the central government. In surrendering larger absolute power to the center, the largest province would logically claim a proportionately larger share—not an equal share—of central power than that of other provinces.

In point of fact, every attempt to increase the powers of the provinces at the expense of the center had been rejected by the Sub-Committee on Constitutions and Powers, and by the BPC. Under such circumstances, for the Bengal League delegation to accept a federal formula that might permit a parliamentary composition similar to that of the Muslim League council would have been sheer political insanity—particularly when they could, with the aid of the Congress Hindus, easily unseat the government.

For a while the semblance of unity was maintained in the "unanimous" decision of the Muslim League Parliamentary Party to give everyone more time to study the report.[72]

The burden of hostile comment was first carried by the press,[73] but Bengali members of the Constituent Assembly were adamant, and a meeting of the Muslim League Parliamentary Party scheduled for the first week in October, 1950, had to be postponed. It was not until November 21 that Liaqat took official note of the opposition that had arisen and moved the Constituent Assembly to postpone consideration of the report indefinitely while inviting constitutional suggestions from the public up to January 31, 1951.[74]

The comments of a few Bengali members in welcoming the motion are revealing. Mr. Shahoodul Haque said postponement was favored by all except those who wished to make political capital out of the "widespread storm of discontent that raged all over Pakistan . . . over the widely resented Interim Report."[75] Mr. Nur Ahmad told of the growing belief in Bengal that the report would "reduce the majority of East Bengal into a minority and it will turn East Bengal into a colony of Pakistan" as a result of the small measure of provincial autonomy allowed.[76] Syed Abul Basher Mahmud Husain attacked Akram Khan and al-Baqi, though not by name, and warned that no solution could be arrived at unless it was sought "on the basis of population."[77]

---

[72] *Dawn*, Sept. 28, 1950.
[73] *Dasturi Safarshat*, ed. Jamā'at-i-Islāmi (n.d.), pp. 75–144 (excerpts from the daily and weekly press dated October, 1950).
[74] *C.A.P. Debates*, Vol. VIII, no. 6, p. 181.
[75] *Ibid.*, p. 182.
[76] *Ibid.*, p. 183.
[77] *Ibid.*, p. 184.

Liaqat did not refer at all to the objections of East Bengal, concentrating on what he implied were the valid objections of those who genuinely desired to see the constitution based upon the Objectives Resolution.[78] The postponement would permit those people to tell the Assembly which provisions were not in accord with the Objectives Resolution and which additional provisions should be added to bring the report into conformity with the principles of Islam.

Liaqat's statement was, to say the least, astonishing. If his purpose was to ignore the objections of the Bengalis his accomplishment was to encourage the 'ulamā'. If he merely desired to distract attention from the division within the Muslim League Parliamentary Party, he did so at the expense of revealing a split between that party and the religious institution. Moreover he practically invited the Bengalis to join with the 'ulamā', by indicating that religious objections were the only weighty ones. From all that we have seen of his policy he was firmly committed to keeping religion, or at least the 'ulamā', out of politics. If this was so, never had a man more efficiently defeated his own purpose. Worse yet, he ventured to take the religious issue out of the committee room and into the public; for he ignored the Board of Ta'līmat-i-Islāmīa, except to imply that their suggestions had not been concrete. Thus was set the pattern for the future of the Islamic constitutional controversy in Pakistan.

[78] *Ibid.*, p. 181.

7 *The Suggestions of the 'Ulamā'*

RELIGIOUS OPPOSITION TO THE INTERIM REPORT

Two months passed between the presentation of the Interim Report and the decision to postpone its consideration. During this fairly extended period the 'ulamā' were only gradually aroused to the realization that the report was not "Islamic" and was therefore to be opposed. Those who were responsible for arousing the 'ulamā' were first the politicians, second the Board of Ta'līmat, and third the Jamā'at-i-Islāmī.

The first group of 'ulamā' to protest against the Interim Report was, significantly enough, the East Bengal branch of the Jamī'at-'Ulamā'-i-Islām, which met on October 5, 1950.[1] The burden of hostile comment in Bengal was thereafter carried on in the press, and often took the form of statements by prominent 'ulamā'. The inspiration was undoubtedly political, although the indirectness of expression was occasioned by the inability of the Bengali politicians to make public statements

[1] *Dawn,* Nov. 9, 1950.

while the report was still under discussion in the Parliamentary Party. Opposition politicians could be more outspoken, however. Electioneering was already under way for the coming provincial elections in the Punjab; and Mian Abd-al-Bari, who had been ousted from the presidency of the Provincial League, took the opportunity of his joining the opposition to proclaim that the Interim Report was neither Islamic nor democratic.[2]

The politicians associated with the government pursued somewhat different tactics. They attempted to show the 'ulamā' that they were well disposed toward Islam, though, in regard to the implementation of the Objectives Resolution, they continued to place the emphasis upon policy rather than law. On October 18 both the Governor-General and the Prime Minister ostentatiously attended the Friday service at a Karachi mosque.[3] At the opening ceremonies of the Jamī'at al-Falaḥ, a tablīgh (propagative) organization, Nazimuddin, the Governor-General, assured his audience that the Objectives Resolution, which had been included in the report as the preamble, would be fully implemented.[4] This attitude drew a statement of mild protest from the members of the Board of Ta'līmat-i-Islāmīa who were particularly disinclined to accept the Objectives Resolution as the final installment of the Islamic constitution.[5]

After the government had taken such pains to point out that the delays in presenting the report were due to the requirement of checking everything with the 'ulamā', the Interim Report put the members of the board in some difficulty. The board desired to publish their report, but they were prevented from doing so under the Assembly rule that all committee proceedings are confidential.[6] That the government intended

[2] *Ibid.,* Oct. 26, 1950.
[3] *Dawn,* Oct. 19, 1950.
[4] *Ibid.,* Oct. 14, 1950.
[5] *Ibid.,* Nov. 5, 1950.
[6] *C.A.P. Rules of Procedure,* Rule no. 41, p. 11, and Rule no. 69 (2), p. 18.

to act as though there was no such thing as a report of the Board of Ta'līmat-i-Islāmīa was evident from the statement of Dr. Mahmud Hussain on October 28, 1950:

> The main objection is that the report has not categorically declared all laws which are not strictly in accordance with the Qur'ān and the Sunnah as null and void. . . . Once we have placed the Objectives Resolution in the forefront and made it a directive principle of State policy there is no reason to apprehend that laws will be made which are not in accordance with the Qur'ān and Sunnah.[7]

The board's answer came in a statement by Mufti Shafi:

> When the reports of the Constitution Making Committee were released to the press, the people of Pakistan rightly felt perturbed to find that these reports are totally void of any provision for the positive requirement of Islam, and many of their contents are even against Islam and against the Objectives Resolution.
>
> In this context the question arose as to what are [sic] the recommendations of the Board of Ta'līmat-i-Islāmia. . . .[8]

The statement went on to deplore the misunderstanding to which the "ambiguous" statement of Dr. Hussain led; and desired that the board's report be published so that the "authorities" might take the responsibility for rejecting these recommendations.

The growing controversy soon aroused other groups and religious organizations, the most important of which was the Jamā'at-i-Islāmi. The Jamā'at quickly threw the bulk of its efforts into the campaign against the Interim Report. Of particular importance was its periodical and special publications, the most outstanding of which was a compilation of all the

[7] *Dawn,* Oct. 29, 1950.
[8] *Ibid.,* Nov. 5, 1950.

press releases of the opposition groups, all hostile editorial comment, and a detailed criticism with suggested amendments, of every clause in the report.[9] Jamā'at-i-Islāmi had been criticizing the government as un-Islamic since Maududi's release from prison at the end of May. The Jamā'at had decided to take a more friendly attitude toward the government after the passage of the Objectives Resolution, but when Maududi's sentence was extended for a second term in October, 1949, they began to see in the actions and statements of the government a sinister attempt to pervert the principles of the Islamic state. Directly upon his release, Maududi began to preach against the government, and also against the agrarian reform program which both Liaqat and Daultana had been urging.[10] The Jamā'at even decided to contest the Punjab provincial elections. It is difficult to understand why Maududi chose to support the zamindars. Perhaps he thought it best to attempt to influence the group that must decide the provincial elections; but such tactics were sure to weaken his influence among the students and the civil servants who had previously been his main targets. What is important to note here is that Maududi did not at first think it necessary to return to his earlier policy of putting pressure on the 'ulamā'. He had apparently decided to convert the Jamā'at into a full-fledged political organization, and, but for the controversy over the Interim Report, he might have continued to ignore the 'ulamā'.

THE BOARD OF TA'LĪMAT AND THE 'ULAMĀ'

Although, by November 21, Liaqat was ready to give way to the 'ulamā' (as evidenced by his speech in the Assembly) he continued to ignore the recommendations of the board. Instead he appealed over their heads to all the 'ulamā' of Pakistan, and

[9] See chap. 6, n. 73.
[10] *Dawn*, June 7, July 25, 28, 29, 30, Aug. 9, 1950.

indirectly insulted the board by insisting upon "concrete and definite" suggestions from the public.[11] On November 22 Dr. Hamidullah resigned his membership of the board.[12]

Thus publicly rebuffed, the members of the board lost for a time their leading position among the 'ulamā' on constitutional issues; and thus encouraged various groups of 'ulamā'-held meetings and announced their resolutions, or drafted Islamic constitutions by the dozen and mailed them to the secretariat of the Constituent Assembly. The Pir of Sarsina wanted the parliament to be made up of "first class" mujtahids and muftis.[13] Nine 'ulamā' wanted Pakistan declared an Islamic democratic state.[14] Seven wanted the Fundamental Rights to be subordinated to the Sharī'a.[15] One 'alīm thought the Head of the State should remain in office so long as he enjoyed the confidence of the people,[16] another thought that he should remain as long as he ruled in accordance with the Sharī'a,[17] a third was in favor of a life term, while a fourth thought his term should end with the life of the parliament.[18] Similar differences of opinion regarding qualifications of those who would elect the Head of the State and the method by which he was to be elected also appeared.[19] One 'alīm was of the opinion that all provisions regarding the Head of the State should not be amendable, while another insisted that "an Islamic Constitution does not admit of any subsequent amendment," except in those places where it is inconsistent with the

[11] *C.A.P. Debates*, Vol. VIII, no. 6, p. 181.

[12] *Panel of Chairmen*, p. 26.

[13] *Dawn*, Jan. 6, 1951.

[14] *Consolidated Statement of Suggestions Received from the Public on the BPC Report by January 31st 1951*, p. 1.

[15] *Ibid.*

[16] *Ibid.*, p. 19.

[17] *Ibid.*, p. 20.

[18] *Ibid.*, p. 21.

[19] *Ibid.*, pp. 14–18.

Sharī'a.[20] There were many more differences arising from the fact that many things were omitted in the suggestions of some, and yet stressed by others. However, when the pet notions and peculiarities of phraseology are disregarded, most of the 'ulamā' agreed that the Head of the State should be the actual executive, that he should preside over the parliament, that his cabinet should be responsible only to him, that he must be a male Muslim and a pious one, and that all acts of government must be guided and limited by the Sharī'a.

The attempts of the board, and especially Mufti Shafi, to organize suport for the board despite the board's inability to publish its views failed; and it seemed as if the government would prove correct in its contention that the 'ulamā' could never agree on any group of proposals for an Islamic constitution. The difficulties of the members of the board both in their official capacity and as the leaders of the Deobandi 'ulamā' were increased when Maulana Ihtishamal-Haqq, who headed a rival Jamī'at-al'Ulamā'-i-Islām, took the initiative in inviting some of the leading 'ulamā' of Pakistan to a meeting at which they were to agree on a series of amendments to the Interim Report.[21] Of the thirty-one 'ulamā' invited, five were members of Ihtishamal-Haqq's group, two belonged to the Bareilly group, and another, the Pir Mujaddadi,[22] was in support of the Sufi approach of the Jamī'at-al-'Ulamā'-i-Pākistān, two were Shī'ite Mujtahids, two represented Ahl-i-Hadīth, one was from the Aḥrār movement,[23] five were from East Bengal, two from Baluchistan, two from the NWFP, one from Bahawalpur, and one from Khairpur.[24] Only five were connected in some way or

---

[20] *Ibid.*, pp. 131, 133.

[21] Interview.

[22] A descendant of Mujaddid Alf-i-Thani of Sarhind.

[23] For more information on the Aḥrār, see below, chap. 9.

[24] Note the attempt at provincial distribution—a principle that the 'ulamā' are supposed to disregard.

other with the Board of Ta'līmat-i-Islāmīa; and from Jamā'at-i-Islāmī only Maulana Maududi was invited. The difficulty of getting such a group to agree on anything was obvious, and the auspices under which the meeting was convened were certainly hostile to recognizing the board's leadership.

Maulana Ihtisham al-Haqq had risen to prominence as the host of Maulana Shabbir Ahmad Usmani, but the restrictions placed upon the choice of members of the Board of Ta'līmat-i-Islāmīa by Liaqat Ali Khan determined that Mufti Shafi should be clearly preferred as Usmani's spokesman, and heir-apparent as unofficial Shaikh-al-Islam. Ihtisham al-Haqq's invitation to the 'ulamā' represented his own effort at achieving recognition, and replacing the members of the board as the exponent of an Islamic constitution. His boldness was the result of a peculiar stroke of success, for he had managed finally to persuade Saiyid Sulaiman Nadvi to come to Karachi. The 'ulamā' were quickly united behind Sulaiman Nadvi, who became the new president of the Jamī'at. The members of the board accepted him as one of their own number, though he did not join them until August, 1952. In nearly all respects Nadvi succeeded to the position of Maulana Shabbir Ahmad Usmani, and was soon referred to as Shaikh al-Islam of Pakistan. By virtue of his successorship to the great Shibli, he easily gained the support of the "modernist" groups like Ahl-i-Hadīth and the Jamā'at-i-Islāmī, while he personally tended toward the more conservative approach of the Deoband school. His first task was to travel to East Bengal to settle the problems of the Jamī'at al-'Ulamā' and to get support for Ihtisham al-Haqq's conference. He was accompanied by Ihtisham al-Haqq, but also by Maulana Zafar Ahmad Ansari who sought his support for a draft constitution, called *Nizam-i-Shariat*. The draft bore a remarkable resemblance to the recommendations of the Board of Ta'līmat-i-Islāmīa; but as an anonymous draft it had no special authority, and the effort to mobilize the 'ulamā' behind the board failed.

Nadvi was easily persuaded against joining the board in its existing straits and, inevitably, accepting the responsibility for their recommendations. The board, on the other hand, refused to compromise their official position by revealing their recommendations. Ihtisham al-Haqq, on his own part, had no constitutional suggestions to press; he was satisfied that the conference of the 'ulamā' take place under his auspices. The conference, therefore, met at Karachi with no organized agenda before it, and with Nadvi as its president.

THE JANUARY, 1951, CONFERENCE OF THE 'ULAMĀ'

Supposedly the conference was to outline an Islamic constitution in detail; and for this purpose they requested the President of the Constituent Assembly to lend them a copy of the suggestions of the Board of Ta'līmat. The January, 1951, conference wanted to see if those recommendations were in accord with Islamic principles, but since Tamizuddin Khan refused, they were content to lay down certain principles to which they hoped to add details at a later meeting—which never took place.[25]

Since there was no agenda or draft upon which it could work, the meeting adjourned for dinner during which each of the conferees was to set down his own version of the basic principles of an Islamic state. The 'ulamā' are by definition the knowers of Islamic law, and many had their pet ideas about the Islamic state, but few were prepared to put forward a complete set of principles. The members of the Board of Ta'līmat, of course, had spent a great deal of time considering

---

[25] *Fundamental Principles of an Islamic State,* pub. by Ehtishamul Haq Thanvi (Karachi, n.d.), p. 3 (hereafter *Fundamental Principles*).

such questions, while Maududi was constantly writing and talking on the subject. At this point the friendship of Ansari, the board's secretary, and Maududi laid the basis of a productive coöperative effort. Maududi read his principles first, and these were supported with some additions by the members of the board. Nadvi was agreeable, and, consequently, so was Ihtisham al-Haqq. Raghib Ahsan of East Bengal was a bit obstreperous, so most of the time of the conference was spent convincing him. The most persuasive argument was, characteristically, the need to disprove the argument that the 'ulamā' could never agree among themselves.[26]

The twenty-two principles of an Islamic state, worked out by the 'ulamā' at Karachi in January, 1951, were duly set down and sent off to the secretariat of the Constituent Assembly where they arrived late, but better than never.[27] The principles were tabulated and printed, along with the others sent in by the public, for the examination of a subcommittee appointed by the BPC.[28]

By its terms of reference the new subcommittee to examine suggestions was prevented from examining any suggestions relating to the work of committees that had not yet reported. It could only forward "suitable amendments" to the BPC, and it was specifically forbidden to "rewrite" the Interim Report.[29] The suggestions from the public were correlated with the various clauses of the Interim Report, and where there was no parallel in the report they were simply discarded. For example, only one clause of Maududi's constitution was retained for consideration. In any case, these suggestions were

[26] Interviews.

[27] *Consolidated Suggestions Received by the BPC after January 31st, 1951.*

[28] *BPC Minutes,* April 13, 1951, p. 39; *Report of the Sub-Committee to Examine Suggestions Received from the Public on the BPC Report,* June 2, 1951, appendix, p. 21 (hereafter *Suggestions Sub-Committee*).

[29] *BPC Minutes,* April 13, 1951, p. 41.

considered after the "Views" of the Board of Ta'līmat and the twenty-two principles, and all were promptly thrown out as redundant.

THE BOARD AND THE SUGGESTIONS SUB-COMMITTEE

The Suggestions Sub-Committee first took up the religious suggestions, but it did not attempt to claim final authority on their validity. Insofar as the 'ulamā' were concerned the government sought agreement and conciliation. However, the subcommittee was well aware of the fact that the Board of Ta'līmat-i-Islāmīa had not the full confidence of the 'ulamā' of Pakistan. Besides, the "Views" of the board were not generally known, whereas the twenty-two principles had been published *in English* by Ihtisham al-Haqq. The subcommittee therefore decided to coöpt Saiyid Sulaiman Nadvi to their own number, not as a member of the board but as the recognized leader of the 'ulamā'. The board was invited to present its views again, but with Nadvi's approval, all but four suggestions of the board were eliminated while fifteen of the twenty-two principles were fully considered.[30]

The board was reluctant to accept the arguments that satisfied Nadvi and subordinated their official position to his unofficial one. They thought he was being purposely confused, and they requested through him a copy of the decisions of the subcommittee, so they could prove it to him. The subcommittee, however, was satisfied with their discussions. The Board of Ta'līmat-i-Islāmīa was not again invited to the subcommittee's meetings, and the actual decisions of the subcommittee were unilateral, and unabetted by the presence of Nadvi at the meeting in question.

As far as the subcommittee was concerned Liaqat had already

---

[30] Seven of the twenty-two principles were eliminated because they referred to the work of other committees.

committed it to a sympathetic consideration of the suggestions of the 'ulamā'. That is not to say that the government's attitude had changed on the central question of parliamentary supremacy, but those conditions that had prevented the government from accepting even the most ineffective religious superstructure were substantially removed by midsummer of 1951, when the subcommittee met for the first time.

The consequences which Liaqat feared might follow on the acceptance of the suggestions of the Board of Taʻlīmat-i-Islāmīa were, by July of 1951, of merely academic interest. The Liaqat-Nehru Pact had prevented the precipitate flight of thirty-five million Muslims from India to Pakistan, but it had not prevented a continuous flow of some two thousand to four thousand refugees daily from Jodhpur into Sindh. Far worse than that were the failure of Sir Owen Dixon to arrange a plebiscite in Kashmir, the frank disagreement of Liaqat and Nehru over the joint signing of a "no war declaration" and the subsequent massing of Indian troops on the borders of the Punjab. Liaqat's hopes of winning over the Western powers to Pakistan's support were dampened by the political effects of the Korean war. It is true that Liaqat had hastily aligned himself with the United Nations, but he soon found that the United States and Britain were far more interested in keeping India's neutrality than in rewarding Pakistan's support. As for the foreign capital, which Liaqat had been so anxious about the year before, that too was now less needed as a consequence of the Korean war. The Korean conflict coincided with the end of the American recession and led to a considerable increase in the demand for Pakistan's cotton and jute. With unprecedented foreign-exchange earnings, purchases of machines for industrial development were made with almost careless abandon. Thrown back on its own burgeoning resources, disillusioned in its lukewarm friends, and threatened by a famine-ridden India, the government might sensibly decide that no harm, and perhaps some good, could come of a compromise with the 'ulamā'. Yet the government did not give way entirely.

THE DECISIONS OF THE SUGGESTIONS SUB-COMMITTEE

The Suggestions Sub-Committee was particularly stubborn regarding the four topics held over from the "Views" of the Board of Ta'līmat. It refused to require that the Head of the State resign if a bill was passed over his veto, as had been suggested by Asad, Maududi, and the Board of Ta'līmat-i-Islāmīa. They refused to limit the Head of the State's power to reprieve or pardon in the constitution. The Shar'ī requirements in that regard might be the subject of legislation.[31] The sub-committee went on to explain that the government of Pakistan had set up a committee to bring existing laws into conformity with the Objectives Resolution.[32] The board's objection to the party system, another point shared with Maududi and many romantics, was simply dropped as the private affair of the members of the legislature.[33]

The first of the twenty-two principles declared the sovereignty of God.[34] This was shown to be contained in the Objectives Resolution which would be the preamble to the constitution.[35] The third principle required that the state be based upon Islamic principles and not racial, linguistic, or geographical concepts.[36] This was shown to be contained in

[31] *Suggestions Sub-Committee,* p. 40.
[32] *Ibid.,* p. 35.
[33] *Ibid.,* pp. 35, 40; see Kemal A. Faruki, *Islamic Constitution* (Karachi, 1952), p. 71, and Abbasi, *The Structure of Islamic Polity,* Part I, "The One Party System in Islam" (Lahore, 1950), *passim.*
[34] *Fundamental Principles,* p. 3.
[35] *Suggestions Sub-Committee,* p. 40.
[36] *Fundamental Principles,* p. 4.

the fourth paragraph of the Objectives Resolution where the words "as enunciated by Islam" appear.[37]

The fourth principle made it incumbent upon the state "to uphold the right and suppress the wrong as postulated in Qur'ān and Sunnah," to revive Islam, and to provide for "Islamic education in accordance with the requirements of the various *recognized schools* of thought." [38] The subcommittee thought that the compulsory teaching of the Qur'ān to Muslims, as provided in the Interim Report,[39] covered this requirement, but they further decided that an organization be set up to make the teachings of Islam known to Muslims. On November 20 the subcommittee took a "formal decision" to the effect that the state would make the teachings of Islam known to *all* the people.[40] The change that took place in the subcommittee is unexplained, but surely to make the teachings of Islam known to the people of Pakistan, rather than only the Muslims, is to proselytize among the non-Muslims. Proselytization, or tablīgh, has been recognized as a general obligation of the Muslims, and the same attitude appears in the original Report of the Board of Ta'līmat-i-Islāmīa.[41] From the text of the 'ulamā''s principle, it is not sure whether they were referring to tablīgh or merely to a favorable attitude on the part of the government toward the 'ulamā', their educational institutions, and their view of Islam.

The fifth principle made it incumbent upon the state to strengthen the unity of Muslims throughout the world and to inhibit parochial feelings among the Muslims of Pakistan.[42]

[37] *Suggestions Sub-Committee,* p. 42.

[38] *Fundamental Principles,* p. 4 (my italics).

[39] *C.A.P. Debates,* Vol. VIII, no. 1, Annexure II, p. 16, para. 2.

[40] *Suggestions Sub-Committee,* pp. 2, 42.

[41] The obligation stems from the same source as the "enabling clause," i.e., Surah III, verse 104. See also M. A. Hobohm, "Missionary Activities in Islam," *Voice of Islam,* Vol. II, no. 11 (Aug., 1954), p. 373; "Views," p. 69.

[42] *Fundamental Principles,* p. 4.

The subcommittee readily agreed, in view of the existing international position of Pakistan, to include a provision to that effect in the chapter dealing with the Directive Principles of State Policy.[43] Significantly enough the negative part of the clause did not include nationalism as a specifically "non-Islamic" feeling.

The subcommittee also agreed to incorporate in the Directive Principles of State Policy a clause relating to the government's responsibility to provide the basic necessities of life to those of its citizens who are incapable of earning a living, as suggested in the sixth principle.[44] Principles thirteen and fourteen required that the Head of the State be personally responsible for the administration of the state, and that his "governance should be consultative."[45] The symbolic responsibility of the head of a parliamentary state sufficed for the former, and the requirement that he act on the advice of his ministry satisfied the latter.[46]

The fifteenth principle would not permit the Head of the State to suspend the constitution at all. The administration of the state must be on a consultative basis.[47] The subcommittee "agreed" to recommend that the Head of the State be empowered only to partly suspend the constitution on the advice of the cabinet. Since neither the Head of the State nor the cabinet would cease in their duties, the 'ulamā' were satisfied that the government would continue consultative.

Principle sixteen would empower the same body that elected the Head of the State to remove him by a majority of votes.[48]

[43] *Suggestions Sub-Committee*, pp. 42, 43.
[44] *Ibid.*, p. 43; *Fundamental Principles*, p. 5.
[45] *Fundamental Principles*, p. 7.
[46] *Suggestions Sub-Committee*, p. 44; *C.A.P. Debates*, Vol. VIII, no. 1, p. 17, para. 7.
[47] *Fundamental Principles*, p. 7.
[48] *Ibid.*

The subcommittee pointed out that paragraphs twenty-two and eight [49] of the Interim Report provided for the election and removal of the Head of the State by the central legislature.[50] It is worth noting here again that the 'ulamā' did not, like the romantics, equate the consultative council with a legislative assembly. Consultation of some sort was required for the administrative not the legislative part of government. Not recognizing the importance of legislation in any case, the 'ulamā' were content here to regard the legislature primarily as an electoral college.

In accordance with principle seventeen the subcommittee agreed that legal proceedings might be taken against the Head of the State for acts in his personal capacity, but refused to permit action against him for acts in his official capacity.[51] Thus the Head of the State could not be brought before a court of law on the ground that he was not fulfilling his religious duties.

The subcommittee agreed that suitable steps, including legislation, if necessary, be taken to prohibit the propagation of views contrary to the Objectives Resolution.[52] The twentieth principle had the words "basic principles and fundamentals of Islam" rather than the "Objectives Resolution." [53]

Principle twenty-one would substitute administrative areas for autonomous provinces.[54] The subcommittee insisted that the Objectives Resolution provided for a federal state, and that resolution was the basis on which they were negotiating with the 'ulamā'.[55]

[49] *C.A.P. Debates,* Vol. VIII, no. 1, pp. 20 and 18, respectively.
[50] *Suggestions Sub-Committee,* p. 46.
[51] *Ibid.*
[52] *Ibid.,* p. 47.
[53] *Fundamental Principles,* p. 8.
[54] *Ibid.*
[55] *Suggestions Sub-Committee,* pp. 31, 47.

THE GAINS OF THE 'ULAMĀ'

The main points on which the 'ulamā' made some gains were on the requirement that the Head of the State be a Muslim, and that the function of the 'ulamā' be institutionally recognized.

The Board of Ta'līmat-i-Islāmīa, in accordance with classical theory, had placed a great deal of emphasis on the qualifications of those who were to elect the Head of the State, and upon the oath to be taken by him. The opposition of the BPC and the resistance of its subsidiary subcommittees was, however, so complete as to reduce the requirements of the board to the bare minimum. The growing realization that the Head of the State would wield only symbolic power was similarly conducive to insisting only upon symbolic qualifications. There was some medieval precedent for this attitude, and it was at least a logical corollary of the institutional recognition which the 'ulamā' desired for themselves.

The twelfth of the fundamental principles, requiring that the Head of the State be a male Muslim "in whose piety, ability and soundness of judgment the people or their elected representatives have confidence," [56] was discussed before the views of the board in this regard were reconsidered.[57] Principle twelve, therefore, dealt with the qualifications of the Head of the State and its acceptance would leave only the question of the manner of his election, and the qualifications of the electors. The decisions of the Suggestions Sub-Committee were accepted for the time being and were as follows:

> *Decision.*—The Sub-Committee decided that the Head of the State after being elected and before assuming office, should, while taking oath, affirm that—

[56] *Fundamental Principles,* pp. 6, 7.
[57] *Suggestions Sub-Committee,* p. 25.

(1) In all matters regarding his personal and public life, he shall sincerely endeavor to fulfil the obligations and duties enjoined by the Holy Qur'ān and the Sunnah and (2) to perform his duties in such a manner that the requirements laid down by the Objectives Resolution and the Directive Principles of State Policy could be fulfilled in the best possible manner.

The Sub-Committee further agreed that the Members should elect such a person as the Head of the State, as in their opinion possesses ability, character, integrity and piety, and is fit to conduct the affairs of the State and fulfil [*sic*] the requirements of the Objectives Resolution.[58]

It will be recalled that the Sub-Committee on Federal and Provincial Constitutions had earlier attempted to cast some doubt upon whether the requirement that the Head of the State be a Muslim of the male sex was a fundamental principle of Islam.[59] In this case the subcommittee actually accepted the demand of the 'ulamā', but they tried to camouflage the restriction of the office of the Head of the State to Muslims by means of the oath of office. It will be remembered that the Board of Ta'līmat-i-Islāmīa had elaborated the oath of office into a complete ceremony parallel to the medieval bay'a, including the pledge of allegiance to the Head of the State by the legislature. This anachronism was now cast aside in favor of a general pledge to uphold the Sharī'a, which they were sure no non-Muslim could honestly make.

The second part of the compromise agreed upon between the board and the subcommittee also relates to the two different provisions of classical theory as propounded by al-Māwardi: the qualifications of the Head of the State and the qualifications of those who may elect the Head of the State. The Head of the

---

[58] *Suggestions Sub-Committee*, p. 44, Nov. 20, 1951.
[59] *Report of the Constitutions and Powers Sub-Committee*, June 6, 1950, p. 8.

State must indeed possess the qualifications of ability, character, integrity, and piety; but the electors must have the knowledge of who is suitable for the caliphate, as well as the ability to judge between those qualified. This provision certainly describes the basis upon which the Head of the State is to be chosen, but it does so by stating the duties of the electors.

When the "Views" of the Board of Ta'līmat-i-Islāmīa were reconsidered the manner of the election of the Head of the State was dealt with. The Subcommittee decided as follows:

> Only that person should be deemed to have been elected as Head of the State who secures the majority in the Legislature as well as a majority of the Muslim Members of the Legislature. As such a procedure might sometime result in a deadlock, it was decided that some solution should be found out for it.[60]

The board had suggested a similar formula in its statement of April 10, 1950 [61] in regard to the election and deposition of the Head of the State, but according to its final note to the "Main Principles Committee," the board reaffirmed its view that the right to depose the Head of the State was limited by "certain specific conditions." [62] The deadlock that was foreseen was not thrashed out at this time, nor is it clear how the following which appeared in the final recommendations of the Subcommittee came into being:

> 1) The Muslim Members of the Legislature should be asked to select two candidates, one at a time at elections held separately. Thereafter the legislators should be called upon to elect one of them as Head of the State. Anyone of them might with-

---

[60] *Suggestions Sub-Committee,* p. 39.
[61] "Views" (Legislature), p. 4.
[62] *Ibid.,* p. 10.

draw with the approval of the Legislature, in which case no ballot would take place.

2) A member of the Legislature, if elected Head of the State should cease to be such a member.[63]

It was to be expected in view of the purport of these decisions that the two Hindu members of the subcommittee should lodge a vigorous note of dissent which is worth quoting:

> We are against the procedure adopted by the majority of the members for the election of the Head of State. It is against all the principles of democracy. It is against the Objectives Resolution guaranteeing the fundamental rights of equality of status of the citizens of Pakistan. It directly denies the right of non-Muslims to have effective voice in the elections. . . .[64]

In view of the cumbersomeness of the resultant provision relating to the election of the Head of the State, it is understandable that in the meeting of the full BPC Mr. Fazlur Rahman's amendment explicitly requiring that the Head of the State be a Muslim was accepted.[65] At that time, Begum Shahnawaz added her dissent to that of the Hindu members of the committee.

In requiring that the Head of the State be a Muslim and in dropping the earlier provision, the committee was in fact confusing two entirely separate requirements of traditional Sunni theory: the qualifications of those who may choose the caliph, and the qualifications of the person who may be chosen as caliph. However, it may have been felt that the 'ulamā' would readily agree to what was in effect a shift of emphasis from electors to candidate. The fact that the emphasis on the ruler's profession of Islam was more important in later Sunni theory (when there was a real possibility of a non-Muslim

[63] *Suggestions Sub-Committee*, p. 4.
[64] *Ibid.*
[65] *BPC Minutes*, Aug. 5, 1952, p. 71.

ruling over Muslims) may have had something to do with this attitude.

The working draft completed in August, 1952, contains two clauses describing the qualifications of the Head of the State. The first states that the Head of the State is to be a Muslim, and the clause immediately following, providing that the Head of the State must be a citizen of Pakistan, at least thirty-five years old, and qualified for election as a member of the House of the People, was added as an afterthought upon the suggestion of the chief drafting officer, Sir Michael Drayton.[66] The provision regarding the basis on which the members should elect the Head of the State were included in the Directive Principles of State Policy. Nishtar explained that this action was taken since the subcommittee "did not want to make the qualifications . . . justiciable." [67] It is not at all clear, had they been left in the operative part of the constitution in their final form, against whom they would have been justiciable.

Of far greater consequence than the attempt to incorporate this essential feature of classical theory, was the attempt to incorporate in the constitution of Pakistan the essential feature of traditional theory. This feature was most importantly stated in the "Views" of the Board of Ta'līmat-i-Islāmīa regarding the Sharī'a committee.[68] A similar provision did not exist among the twenty-two principles, because Maududi denied both the ability of the 'ulamā' to safeguard the Sharī'a and validity of ascribing this function to the 'ulamā' in a truly Islamic state. The second of the twenty-two principles was consequently as general as Maududi's second "demand":

> *Original Suggestion of 'Ulamā'.*—The law of the land shall be based on Qur'ān and Sunnah, and no law shall be passed nor

[66] *Ibid.*
[67] *Ibid.*, p. 66.
[68] "Views," pp. 59–63.

any administrative order issued which would be in conflict
with Qur'ān and Sunnah.

Explanatory note.—If there be any laws in force in the country
which are in conflict with Qur'ān or Sunnah, it would be
necessary to lay down (in the Constitution) that such laws
shall be gradually, within a specific period, amended in conformity with Islamic law or repealed.[69]

As things fell out, the government decided to treat only with
the traditionalists, and as might be expected the 'ulamā' again
offered their own interpretation of how this principle was to
be implemented. The subcommittee was definitely conciliatory,
but it could not concede the full desire of the 'ulamā'.

The Sub-Committee agreed that (a) if not less than one-tenth
of the Muslim Members of the House raise objection that any
Bill or a part thereof is opposed to the Qur'ān and Sunnah
after the second reading is completed, the Speaker should, as
early as possible, refer the Bill or the part to which objection is
taken, to the Standing Committee of 'Ulamā', elected by the
Muslim Members of the Legislature for this purpose for their
advice. The Standing Committee of 'Ulamā', should send their
advice to the Speaker of the House concerned within seven
days of the receipt of the reference. The advice of the Committee should be placed before the House by the Speaker concerned. After considering the advice the Members of the
House should decide what to do with the Bill. Their decision
should be final.

(b) In case of difference of opinion among the members of
the Standing Committee of 'Ulamā' the House concerned
should be informed of the views of all of them.

(c) The decision of the House in this respect should be final
for all purposes so as to exclude the jurisdiction of courts.

[69] *Fundamental Principles,* pp. 3, 4.

(d) In the chapter relating to the Directive Principles of State Policy an item should be included providing that no law should be passed by the Legislature which is against the Qur'ān and the Sunnah.[70]

This provision, though it eventually appears in the final report of the BPC went through a number of changes. In the first instance,[71] a single Muslim member could raise an objection as to the conformity of the bill with the Sharī'a. In the meeting of the subcommittee of November 20, this was amended to bar any objection unless raised by a minimum of one-tenth of the Muslim membership. Initially the provision required that objection be raised after publication of the bill, but before introduction; or, in the case of a bill that is not published, at the time of introduction. At the subcommittee meeting of July 19, 1951, this was changed so that objection could be raised after completion of the second reading, "so that when a reference is made to the Standing Committee of 'Ulamā', they get the Bill in the form finally agreed to by the Legislature." [72] Certain drafting amendments were also suggested by the chief draftsman and incorporated into the working draft of the BPC.[73] These changes provided that the term of the Committee of 'ulamā' should be for the life of the House of the People, that there should be five members on this committee who might be members of the legislature, that there should be one committee for both Houses of the federal legislature to be elected at a joint sitting. In this working draft the words "advice of the Committee" were significantly changed to "views of the Committee." [74] In the working draft, under "Directive Principles of State Policy," an item was duly in-

---

[70] *Suggestions Sub-Committee,* Nov. 20, 1951, p. 41.
[71] *Ibid.,* July 18, 1951, p. 27.
[72] *Suggestions Sub-Committee,* p. 29.
[73] *BPC Minutes,* Aug. 5, 1952, p. 72.
[74] *Report of the BPC,* Aug., 1952, p. 22.

cluded prohibiting the passage of any law contrary to the
Qur'ān.[75]

The original suggestion of the board was that such a committee have final veto over all legislation, but the committee
here envisaged has no such powers. The desire to establish
such a committee and to equip it with such wide powers is a
natural corollary of the belief that the 'ulamā' are the guardians
of the Sharī'a, and that they alone have the special knowledge
necessary for the performance of such a function. The board,
which was not wholly comprised of 'ulamā', did not insist that
the membership be made up entirely of 'ulamā'. It is therefore
significant that the committee contemplated was to be made
up only of 'ulamā', and we can assume that emphasis is being
placed upon the institution itself. The fact that the entire
provision is the result of a compromise strengthens this view.
Since the 'ulamā' are not to have a final say in the matter
they might at least be able to present their views unmixed with
the loose thinking of any layman.[76]

Since this clause provides that a bill will be referred to
the committee of 'ulamā' by the Chairman of the House, the
committee is in fact treated as a special committee of the
legislature, which can of course be overruled by the whole
House. The original intention of having one committee for
each House corroborates this interpretation (and it would also
provide more jobs for the 'ulamā').

The provision for a full statement of all the differences of
opinion among the 'ulamā' surely touches upon the Achilles

[75] *Ibid.*, p. 6.

[76] It is possible that Nadvi may have hesitated at the responsibility the
'ulamā' might incur by blocking popular legislation, but it is more probable
that he was taken in by Dr. Mahmud Hussain's ingenious argument that the
fatwa of the Committee of 'ulamā' would be a direct appeal to the people,
and if a legislator voted to the contrary he would run the risk of losing his
seat at the next election.

heel of tradition. The possibility of disagreement among the 'ulamā' is considered to be great, and there is no doubt that many secularists were placing their hopes upon this subparagraph.

Clause *c* was incorporated into the working draft in the following manner: "The decision of the House in this respect should be final for all purposes and should not be questioned in any court of Law." [77] This clause obviously excludes the possibility of reference to any court of law of a petition against any act of the legislature on the ground that it is contrary to the Sharī'a. This provision is most important when we remember that a general bar to the validity of any legislation contrary to the Qur'ān was included in the chapter on the Directive Principles of State Policy.

The position resulting from a reading of all the clauses together is that the legislature is the final authority for the interpretation of the Sharī'a, and that whenever an objection is raised to a bill on this basis, the decision of the legislature becomes an authoritative statement of religious doctrine. In fact, the provision for "Special procedure with regard to certain Bills involving Islamic laws" can only be justified by reference to the consensus theory of Islamic democracy. For the 'ulamā' this position should have been intolerable, and in time they came to realize it. But for the time being they were satisfied with some recognition for their institution.

The twenty-second principle required that "no interpretation of the Constitution which is in conflict with the provisions of the Qur'ān and Sunnah shall be valid." [78] The subcommittee felt that no additional amendment was required by this principle since "every kind of legislation has been dealt with in the understanding arrived at with regard to para. 2." The

[77] *Report of the BPC*, Aug., 1952, p. 22.
[78] *Fundamental Principles*, p. 8.

board "agreed to the position." [79] Here again it is apparent that
the members of the board were not fully aware of the implications of the text of their demands, nor of the agreements
reached with the subcommittee. The 'ulamā' did not explain
what they meant by "interpretation of the Constitution," but
it is at least doubtful that interpretation might be exclusively
the function of the legislature. This is often the function of the
courts. If the 'ulamā' were thinking of the courts, then the
implication of their suggestion was that a body of 'ulamā' be
empowered to overrule decisions of the courts which might
contravene the provisions of the Sharī'a. However, when the
board accepted the contention of the subcommittee that the
agreement upon a standing committee of 'ulamā' attached to
the legislature covered this suggestion as well, they actually
made the authority of the 'ulamā' less rather than more comprehensive, since they would have no authority over the
judiciary. Moreover they lent their support to the complete
distortion of the traditional function of the 'ulamā'. The
'ulamā' were now to become no more than a committee of the
legislature, empowered to delay legislation for a maximum of
seven days. Even if we leave aside the fate of the institution
of the 'ulamā', which is, theoretically, only incidental to the
aims of the 'ulamā' themselves, we cannot conclude that the
members of the board pursued their goal efficiently. Though
they were staunch supporters of the view that the Sharī'a is
preëxisting, eternal, and immutable, they sanctioned a system
based on the completely contrary idea of the mutability of the
Sharī'a through the medium of ijmā', institutionalized in a
representative assembly.

[79] *Suggestions Sub-Committee,* July 19, 1951, p. 31.

PART THREE

Alteration

Introduction to Part Three

The third part of our study takes us beyond the theoretical statement and empirical demonstration of prevailing theories of Islamic constitutionalism in Pakistan. The early phases of the constituent process had set the stage for important changes in the positions taken by the groups identified with these theories. Their respective positions had been clarified, and the limits to which each would go in compromise had been explored. What was little expected or understood was that these limits are flexible, or, more accurately, they are a function of the political circumstances obtaining at any particular time. In what follows, it will be possible to examine the actual changes that took place within the context of the developing constitutional controversy.

The chronological framework of exposition has been retained to illustrate the central theme of the dependence of political theory upon the position and interest of particular groups in the political process. The reasons for adopting this framework are, first, that the subject matter is complex and the chronological approach is the simplest to follow, and, secondly, that these events seem, from the point of view of the development of Islamic theory, to have a logical sequence; for the secularist view was first presented in the Interim Report, the consensus theory in Nazimuddin's report, and the Supreme Court provision in the Mohammed Ali report. After the dissolution of the first Constituent Assembly in the fall of 1954, no really new proposals or ideas were forthcoming.

It will have become apparent that, throughout the whole period under discussion, the prevailing notion of the nature of constitutionalism for politicians as well as 'ulamā' was the establishment of a legal basis for the operation of specific institutions. The constituent process was similarly viewed as a law-making process. Constitutionalism as a limitation on the powers of government, as a mechanism for separating the powers or functions of government, as a means of establishing procedures for the settlement of political disputes, as the practical approximation of a social ideology, or as a process of political adjustment minimizing the use of coercion never entered into the picture at all. Logically, the constituent process must lay the basis for constitutionalism in any or all of the above senses, the assumption being that in the constituent process the political society which is to practice constitutionalism has been shaped. Changes in the structure and functioning of the political society may come about through the normal working of the political process, and constitution writing (not the same as the constituent process) is in itself usually a part of the normal political process. In Pakistan, however, the state came into being without the political structure of society having first been shaped. That is to say, the business of constitution writing coincided with the constituent process, and was confused therewith.

Strange as it may seem, the religious issue, except possibly for the Jamā'at-i-Islāmi, fell within the framework of the normal political process. For the 'ulamā', Islamic constitutional provisions were values to be sought within the existing political framework and with the coöperation of the dominant political groups, whichever they be and however constituted. For the politicians, religion was a matter of political tactics rather than one of principle. The federal problem was a matter of little or no interest to the 'ulamā', and they avoided taking a stand thereon. The politicians, however, considered the federal question in the constitution and in its relationship to provincial politics and their own careers as a matter of the utmost importance. The fact of the matter is that the politicians were all pretty much agreed that the 'ulamā' should not have much influence and that the Islamic aspects of the constitution should not hamper the working of a normal parliamentary system. The proof of this fact rests in the vague nature of the provisions of the constitution adopted in March, 1956, that is, after the federal question was in essence settled by extraconstitutional means. The mistake of the 'ulamā' was, and remains, their assumption that certain politicians supported them out of conviction.

The most complicated convergence of constitutional and religious politics, of provincial and federal issues, of personalities and social groups, of administrative and political matters, and of violence and judicial settlement occurred in the anti-Aḥmadi agitation and subsequent Punjab Disturbances. However strongly held were the opinions that impelled all the actors in this tragic sequence of events, it was nevertheless the situation and the events themselves which stand out as causes more than any personality or idea. It was in the violent participation of the 'ulamā' in the anti-Aḥmadi agitation that their faulty political estimates were most manifest.

The Punjab Disturbances have been widely discussed, and

the Report of the Court of Inquiry has become a classic of
sorts, though not an unbiased one. What have been largely
unnoticed in all of this discussion are the changes the agitation
wrought in the influence relationships of the religious groups.
No religious Muslim will admit that 'ulamā' ever feel threatened, go on the defensive, make compromises, or are influenced by political events; nevertheless this is what happened
and the resultant change in their idea of an Islamic state was
explicitly set down in the 'ulamā' 's Amendments of January,
1953. We are less surprised to learn that Maududi changed his
position as well, and accepted the Supreme Court idea of
Muhammad Asad.

The politicians changed their minds also, but the cause
is not to be sought in their relations with the religious groups.
To understand why the politicians altered their formulas for
an Islamic state one must look to the provincial elections in
East Bengal, and to another element that now became explicit
for the first time in Pakistani politics. This element was the
institutional conflict between the Governor-General, later President, of Pakistan and the legislative branch. The "Islamic
constitution" which was drawn up in 1953 and 1954 was the
resultant of the combination of all these forces.

There were other forces, too, whose views have not concerned us greatly because they deny the validity of the Islamic
state concept. These forces were the services, but their influence
on the Islamic constitutional controversy was not felt until
recently. From all the evidence at hand neither the bureaucracy
nor the military interfered in the process of drawing up the
constitution. We know that those civil servants who were
consulted did propose certain measures to safeguard the interests of the bureaucracy, but they never went on record for or
against any of the so-called Islamic provisions. They did not act
vigorously, with one or two exceptions, in the Punjab Dis-

turbances. It is widely held that the East Bengal services helped
to defeat the Muslim League in the provincial elections of 1954,
but even if true, the event is explained in terms of the animus
earned by East Bengal Muslim League politicians by their in-
terferences with and exactions upon the bureaucracy. On the
crucial federal question there is no evidence that the bureaucracy had any clear preference, though it is said to be dominated
by Punjabis. Conversations with some of the members of this
service tend to confirm the expected conclusion that like most
bureaucracies, and especially nonaristocratic ones, that of Pakistan is more interested in preserving institutional integrity and
in providing for its own security than in forwarding any substantive program. If the civil service ruled Pakistan for any
period, it did so only in the sense that it kept certain routine
operations alive.

The military, with the sole exception of the abortive Rawalpindi conspiracy, kept itself even further out of politics than
did the bureaucracy. In view of the subsequent coup of General
Ayyub Khan, it is all the more interesting to note the number
of occasions on which the military could have acted but did
not. The most outstanding instances are during the Punjab
Disturbances, at the time of Nazimuddin's dismissal, at the
time of the dissolution of the first Constituent Assembly, or
during the legal tangle that followed. A partial explanation
of this inaction may lie in the fact that Ayyub Khan was not
retired from the post of Chief of the General Staff when his
normal term was up; and we note that Pakistan's first chief of
staff was implicated in the Rawalpindi conspiracy five months
after his impending retirement was announced. It is to the
credit of General Ayyub Khan that he resisted many tempta-
tions, and that when he did act against the politicians he
recognized the President as one of those who had debauched
Pakistan's politics. Ayyub Khan must bear his full share of

the blame for preventing the holding of Pakistan's first general elections, but there are limits to anyone's ability to withstand repeated temptation.

The Islamic state controversy remained alive as long as Pakistan's politics were parliamentary and as long as there was hope for the holding of a general election. However, when the issue changed to one of efficiency versus an ill-functioning democracy, to national development versus the protection of landed interests, to discipline versus vigorous politicking, the religious controversy faded into the background. Thus the maintenance of certain features of the "Islamic constitution" in that finally adopted in March, 1956 (and suspended by Ayyub Khan in 1958), reflects the general feeling that even a minimally democratic system in Pakistan must make provision for the religious sentiments of the majority. Furthermore, the acceptance by nearly all religious groups of the watered-down version indicates another shift in their thinking, and another instance of the influence of the Jamā'at on the 'ulamā'. In the final version of the constitution, the Supreme Court provision was eliminated but the consensus theory was not inserted. Apparently the mechanism for preventing legislation contrary to the Qur'ān and Sunnah was now to be the direct participation of the 'ulamā' and the Jamā'at in the electoral and parliamentary processes of Pakistan. To this end Maududi's Jamā'at and the Nizām-i-Islām Party of Maulana Athar Ali formed an electoral coalition to contest the elections that were never held.

8 *Parity*

LIAQAT ALI KHAN: THE FINAL PHASE

The internal constitutional stalemate, and Pakistan's external isolation, combined to force the Prime Minister to devote the major part of his time to the internal affairs of Pakistan during the last year of his life. After the political crisis, occasioned by the ill-considered presentation of the Interim Report, Liaqat turned to conciliating East Pakistan as best he could, and the 'ulamā' to the extent both necessary and desirable.

Although the constitutional crisis opened many new wounds, it was the indirect cause of closing an old one. The danger that the Muslim League council meeting, scheduled to be held at Dacca, might censure the government's constitutional policy forced Liaqat to join the offices of Prime Minister and League President.[1] Some rather questionable tactics were used to ac-

---

[1] *Dawn,* Oct. 5, 1950; *Text of the Resolutions Passed by the Working Committee of the PML,* Aug. 6 and 7, 1950 (mimeographed), Resolution no. 9, p. 12; *Notice and Agenda,* published Sept. 15, 1950, by the General

complish this maneuver, but the new situation was accepted
even by the Bengalis. The necessary amendment of the League
constitution was welcomed by the provincial governments
of West Pakistan, and though the offices of Chief Minister and
Provincial League President were not joined in Bengal until
August, 1952, the value of such an arrangement was manifest.[2]

It was to be expected that the function of the party would
change in congruity with the destruction of the theory that it
was the instrument of popular control. The Working Committee and the League council would no longer criticize government policy;[3] instead the task of the League would be to
explain government policy to the people. It may be protested
that a political party ought to work in both directions, particularly a party that claimed to represent the nation, and had
a near monopoly of all the political offices in the state. The
Muslim League could not work in both directions because in
1948 it had been reorganized from the top down.[4] The reën-
rollment on which the reorganization was based never reached
the "grass roots," because such thoroughness was unnecessary
insofar as the aim of the veteran local leaders was to maintain
themselves in office.[5] The League had been consequently responsible neither to the government nor the "nation." By
making the League responsible to the government, Liaqat
achieved at least the negative benefit of preventing irresponsible criticism.

Despite the original purpose of preventing public criticism
of his constitutional policy, Liaqat readily made the fullest use

Secretary of the PML; *Text of the Resolution Passed in the PML Council
Meeting,* Oct. 8, 1950, resolutions 2 and 3, p. 1.

[2] *Council Meetings of the East Bengal Muslim League,* Secretary's Minutes,
Aug. 23, 1952; interview.

[3] *Dawn,* Oct. 9, 1950. Report of Liaqat's speech at the council meeting.

[4] *Dawn,* Feb. 21, 1949. Report of Khaliquzzaman's speech at the council
meeting.

[5] Interviews.

of the powers of the President of the Muslim League. He appointed himself as a subcommittee-of-one of the Parliamentary Board and proceeded to pass upon all applications for candidacies in the Punjab provincial election, and he was preparing to do the same in the NWFP when he was assassinated.[6] There was some precedent for this in the action of the All-India Parliamentary Board over which Liaqat had presided, before the Indian provincial elections of 1946. The purpose, then as now, was to increase the central party control by establishing the political indebtedness of successful candidates to the central rather than the provincial party leadership. It was also hoped that Liaqat could lend some of his own popularity, as the successor of Jinnah, where the provincial League label was insufficient. Since the provincial assemblies were each to elect an equal number of representatives to the House of Units, according to the Interim Report, one may also see in Liaqat's work an attempt to provide for a more unified and manageable Upper House.

As we have already seen, the unification of the voting power of West Pakistan was an essential aspect of Liaqat's constitutional policy. Since he had been unable to achieve unification through legal means he had already resolved upon various political measures. These political measures might be characterized as the establishment of a sort of personal allegiance. The powers of the president of the Muslim League considerably enhanced Liaqat's ability to pursue this second best course. As sensible as his policy may have seemed at the time, its real value to Pakistan was limited by the life span of the Prime Minister. On October 16, 1951, Liaqat Ali Khan was assassinated.

In the death of her first prime minister Pakistan sustained a loss perhaps even greater than that of the founder of the state.

[6] *Dawn*, Feb. 1 and Sept. 3, 1951.

Not only was Liaqat at the height of his power and political maturity, but the time was one of the most critical in the short history of Pakistan. In Kashmir, elections had just taken place for a constituent assembly which would attempt to legalize that state's connection with India; along the borders of the Punjab the canal waters were being diverted and the bulk of the Indian army stood massed in battle array; the war-stimulated boom in cotton and jute had begun to subside;[7] the internal political situation was, to say the least, fluid.

It may also be noted that discussions between the Suggestions Sub-Committee and the Board of Ta'līmat were still proceeding, though most of the important decisions were already indicated. It is possible then to suggest that with the unity of West Pakistan in the process of becoming, with the 'ulamā' somewhat reconciled, and perhaps separated from their Bengali supporters, and with a more "democratic" federal formula probably being worked out, Liaqat was well on his way toward producing a constitution for Pakistan. As it was, a new and far more bitter controversy arose between Bengal and the Punjab which led to the reopening of the religious question and the deeper entanglement of religion and politics. Bengal and the Punjab were already at odds with each other, but the peculiar bitterness of the new controversy was the direct result of Liaqat's legacy to his successor, that is, the presidency of the Muslim League.

NAZIMUDDIN: PAKISTAN'S SECOND PRIME MINISTER

Liaqat Ali Khan's assassination removed the only possible arbiter of interprovincial disputes, and altered the character of the federal problem. There was no longer an unattached refugee leader to speak for the balancing of provincial interests and the preservation of central power. Control of the center

[7] *Dawn*, Sept. 11, 1951.

itself now became a goal for the politicians of both the Punjab and Bengal, but the dominance of the Bengal bloc was decisive. The Governor-General, Khwaja Nazimuddin, "stepped down" to the office of Prime Minister, while the Finance Minister, Mr. Ghulam Muhammad, who was extremely unpopular with the Bengalis, was appointed Governor-General of Pakistan.

That the prime minister of Pakistan ought to be the president of the Muslim League was now so much taken for granted that Nazimuddin actually decided upon the candidacies for the NWFP elections before he was reënrolled as a member of the League.[8] The situation was hastily regularized by a poorly attended League council meeting held in Karachi a short while later.[9] No objection was raised to Nazimuddin's election as president of the League.

Nazimuddin's ministry was indeed the rule of Bengalis, but not of Bengal. The key to understanding his policy is to realize that Nazimuddin was faithfully following the line laid down by Liaqat Ali Khan. This contention may be borne out by several facts. In the first place, Bengal desired a greater devolution of power from the center, particularly in regard to communications, trade, and the manufacture of salt.[10] Nazimuddin staunchly refused even to discuss the matter.[11] In the second place, Bengal desired equal recognition for its provincial language.[12] Nazimuddin announced in the capital of East Bengal that Urdu would be *the* state language.[13] In the third place the Bengalis desired a more "democratic" and less "federal" central legislature, but six weeks after Liaqat's

[8] See *Dawn,* Oct. 25, 27, 28, 30, and Nov. 5, 1951.

[9] "Notice and Agenda" for meeting of the PML council to be held Nov. 16, 1951 (dated Oct. 27, 1951, and signed by the General Secretary, PML.)

[10] *Working Committee Meetings of the East Bengal League,* Secretary's Minutes, Oct. 29, 30, 1950; *Suggestions Sub-Committee,* pp. 55–71.

[11] *BPC Minutes,* Aug. 6, 1952, p. 78.

[12] *C.A.P. Debates,* Vol. XI, no. 3 (April 10, 1952).

[13] On February 22, 1952.

death the Franchise Sub-Committee of the BPC finally agreed "there should be parity as a whole between the two wings of Pakistan."[14]

The parity scheme, it will be remembered, was originally proposed in the BPC by Akram Khan, the president of the East Bengal League. The proposal is, on the whole, moderate; and though Liaqat "postponed" its consideration originally, it would seem to be the next most logical position for him to take after the failure of the Interim Report. At the meeting of the Franchise Sub-Committee, Mr. Nurul Amin, the chief minister of East Bengal, dissented, holding that representation in the Lower House should be on a population basis, and that the House of Units should reflect population subject to the limit that no one province should have a majority, and "weightage" should be given to smaller provinces.[15] Clearly, Mr. Nurul Amin's scheme would have provided Bengal with a majority in a joint sitting, for it implied parity in the upper House and a 55–45 division of the Lower House in Bengal's favor. The provision for weightage to the *smaller* provinces in the Upper House was meant to prevent the Punjab from benefiting from the limitation of democratic representation in the Upper House. The moderate attitude of the Franchise Sub-Committee, which had been appointed under Liaqat Ali Khan, is revealed in the compromise that was finally achieved, whereby parity in the legislature as a whole was retained, but weightage granted to the provinces of West Pakistan "other than Punjab."[16] Not only was this formula retained in the actual distribution of seats suggested in May, 1952, by the Franchise Sub-Committee, but there was some indication that it had been planned to combine Bahawalpur with the Punjab, Khairpur with Sindh, the Balu-

[14] *Report of the Sub-Committee on Franchise,* Vol. II, Appendix I, "Minutes of the Meetings," p. 34 (hereafter *Franchise Sub-Committee*).
[15] *Ibid.,* pp. 35, 36.
[16] *Ibid.,* p. 45.

chistan States with Baluchistan Province, and the Frontier
States with the North-West Frontier Province.[17] The reduction
in the number of autonomous or separately administered units
of West Pakistan was assuredly in keeping with Liaqat's constitutional policy.

It is against this background of the pursuit of his predecessor's policies that we are to understand Nazimuddin's use
of his powers as president of the League, particularly his attempt to control the distribution of candidacy tickets in the
West Pakistan provincial elections. The difficulty was that
Nazimuddin pursued the policies of Liaqat when the realization of his policy goals was a political impossibility. Liaqat
wished to unify all of West Pakistan's voting power in order
to counterbalance the more or less unified Bengalis. But Nazimuddin could not unify *all* West Pakistan because the Punjab
government and Assembly owed its electoral success to the
deceased prime minister; nor was it conceivable that Nazimuddin should desire to counterbalance Bengal, where lay his
political support. In pursuing Liaqat's policies, and in using
his political techniques, Nazimuddin was, in fact, uniting the
smaller provinces of West Pakistan with Bengal, and against
the Punjab.

DIVIDE AND RULE

What was at first the inadvertent result of a remarkable
political loyalty (which is not the least bit surprising in
Nazimuddin) became, in a short time, a conscious political
goal. The desirability of the political coöperation of Bengal
and the smaller western provinces (despite the logic of parity)
was connected with the plight of the East Bengal Muslim
League. Like all the rest of the provinces of Pakistan, East
Bengal, too, had to prepare for a provincial election. The Mus-

[17] *Ibid.*, p. 49.

lim League had, however, lost much of its popularity in East Bengal.[18] The reasons are complicated, but among them we may count that very loyalty to which we have referred, especially as exemplified in the language issue. We might also add that the reorganization of the Muslim League in East Bengal, in 1948, had been the most superficial of all. At any rate, the imminence of the elections necessitated the passage of a new electoral law to provide for universal adult suffrage and to delimit constituencies in the manner already accomplished in West Pakistan. The necessity of a new electoral law also caused the anticipation of a major constitutional issue, that is, whether there was to be a single electoral roll or separate electorates for Hindus. Although there is herein an issue of Islamic political theory regarding the rights of non-Muslim communities, the size of the Hindu minority in East Bengal made it an issue of quite autonomous political magnitude. About 25 per cent of the population of East Bengal is Hindu, of which more than half belongs to the Scheduled Castes.[19] *Since Hindus may not join the Muslim League, the institution of separate electorates must, under parity, reduce the Bengal members to a minority in the Muslim League Parliamentary Party*. On the other hand, separate electorates (and we have no information about Liaqat's views on this matter) were considered absolutely necessary by the East Bengal Muslim League. The reasons for this insistence are, to some extent, to be found in the perennial stand of the Muslim League in prepartition times in favor of separate electorates for the Muslims. However, Jinnah's repeated statements that no distinction would be made among the citizens of Pakistan, and the insistence of the Hindus, themselves, on

---

[18] For one indication see *C.A.P. Debates,* Vol. XI, no. 6 (April 17, 1952), p. 143.

[19] *Census of Pakistan, 1951,* "Population According to Religion" (table 6), Bulletin no. 2, p. 3.

joint electorates contradict the traditional League position.[20] Obviously there was something more to this perverse insistence upon safeguarding the rights of minorities against the will of the minorities themselves, particularly since the restrictions that the Board of Ta'līmat-i-Islāmīa wished to impose on the representation of minorities in the legislature did not necessarily include separate electorates, although they may have taken them for granted. What the East Bengal Muslim League feared, and with much justification, was that under joint electorates the Hindus would throw their weight behind opposition Muslim candidates. Their fears went further than this, however, to the point where they apprehended that the Congress Party might end up holding the balance between two Muslim parties in the Provincial Assembly. To avoid this possibility, and in the hope of strengthening somewhat their power in both the Provincial Assembly and the future parliament, they further divided the Hindus by providing for a separate electorate for the Scheduled Castes.[21] The Hindus reacted strongly against this attempt to divide their community but to no avail.

Once the bill for separate electorates was passed it was understood that the constitution would have to be consistent with this precedent. From this point on, that is, from the time the decision was taken, the government pursued an active policy of disuniting West Pakistan, to the extent that when the parity formula came before the Franchise Sub-Committee it was already apprehended that Bahawalpur would not be joined to the Punjab nor Khairpur to Sindh. The formula was only agreed to on the assumption of the integration of these states, failing which "the whole question would need reconsideration." [22]

[20] Muslim and Hindu members presented conflicting evidence, but the results of the 1954 elections support the Hindu contention.

[21] *Government of India (Third Amendment) Act 1952, Gazette of Pakistan* (Extraordinary), April 26, 1952.

[22] *Franchise Sub-Committee,* Vol. II, Appendix I, p. 49.

To this view the Chief Minister of East Bengal and the leader of the Congress Party in the Assembly (both members of the Franchise Sub-Committee) dissented. "They held the view that in no case the allocation of seats were [*sic*] to be changed."

The detailed recommendation of the Franchise Sub-Committee is given in table 1.

TABLE 1

RECOMMENDATION OF FRANCHISE SUB-COMMITTEE
FOR REPRESENTATION

Province	A		B		C		D	
	H/U	H/P	H/U	H/P	H/U	H/P	H/U	H/P
East Bengal	66	222	—6	—22	60	200		
Punjab and Bahawalpur	33	109	0	0	33	109		
NWFP and Tribal Areas	9	31	2	8	11	39	22	25.8
Sindh and Khairpur	8	26	2	8	10	34	25	30.8
Baluchistan and Baluch States	2	6	1	2	3	8	50	33.3
Federal Capital	2	6	1	4	3	10	50	66.6

KEY: A—seats on the basis of population; B—extra seats resulting from parity and weightage; C—total seats; D—% weightage; H/U—House of Units; H/P—House of People.

SOURCE: *Report of the Franchise Sub-Committee,* Vol. II, Appendix II, May 15, 1952, p. 88.

The first concrete move of the Bengal bloc to alter the Franchise Sub-Committee formula came in the Suggestions

Sub-Committee. This attempt was somewhat circuitous, and perhaps only symbolic, but it seems to have made a strong impression on the Chief Minister of the Punjab. It will be remembered that the Interim Report had provided that both Houses have equal powers in all matters including votes of confidence and the budget. Disagreements were to be settled by joint sittings. This provision had been opposed by Bengal, but since the Franchise Sub-Committee formula, somewhat illogically, envisaged parity in *both* Houses it was not of great moment. Nevertheless it might be argued that elections by the provincial assemblies could be far more easily controlled than popular elections, and the Upper House would be more united than the Lower as a consequence. At any rate the Suggestions Sub-Committee withdrew from the Upper House all authority in matters of confidence and the budget.[23]

THE REACTION OF THE PUNJAB

It was at this point that the government of the Punjab began to foster the anti-Aḥmadi agitation (see below, chap. 9) which had been going on in that province for some time.[24] Just as the Bengalis had attempted to use the 'ulamā' as a lever against the Interim Report, now the government of the Punjab wished to use them against the obvious intentions of Nazimuddin. By its acts of omission and commission in this regard the government of the Punjab all but nullified the painstaking efforts of the Suggestions Sub-Committee with the Board of

[23] *Suggestions Sub-Committee,* July 3, 1952, p. 77.

[24] The anti-Aḥmadi agitation will be discussed from the point of view of the religious groups and Islamic constitutional politics in chapter 9. At this point our only intention is to indicate how Daultana's response to Nazimuddin's policies took a religious form. It is also worth noting that, despite the thorough discussion of the anti-Aḥmadi affair by the Court of Inquiry, the timing of Daultana's reversal on this issue has never been correlated with the decisions of the constitution making committees.

Ta'līmat-i-Islāmīa. Moreover, it caused the 'ulamā' to be subject to great pressure from more immoderate religious groups to the point that the 'ulamā' were forced to abandon their wonted pacific role.

To the efforts of the Punjab government we must ascribe the development of the Aḥmadi question into a first-class constitutional issue. The argument of the agitators was that since the Aḥmadis deny the "finality" of the prophethood of Muhammad (i.e., that Muhammad was the last Prophet) they are not Muslims. Consequently, the Aḥmadis must be officially designated as a non-Muslim minority community, and they must be barred from all important policy making and administrative positions in the government.[25] They particularly desired the dismissal of Zafrullah Khan from the Foreign Ministry.

There is no question but what the anti-Aḥmadi agitation was a popular issue in the towns of the Punjab, and that its suppression would be difficult as well as politically unwise. Despite these risks, Daultana proceeded cautiously to suppress the agitation until the first week in July, 1952. At the end of the second week of July the government had noticeably let up on even those measures it had already taken,[26] and by the end of the month both the Punjab Muslim League and Daultana himself had gone on record favoring the demands of the anti-Aḥmadis.[27] The Chief Minister of the Punjab argued that he could do nothing about these demands, though he was sympathetic, since the status of the Aḥmadiyya was a question to be settled by the BPC.[28] Daultana requested that the central government make a declaration in this regard,[29] he urged others

[25] *Punjab Disturbances*, p. 15.
[26] *Ibid.*, p. 67.
[27] *Ibid.*, pp. 96–97, 263.
[28] *Ibid.*, pp. 97–98.
[29] *Ibid.*, pp. 74, 316 ff.

to make similar requests, and he arranged for the preparation
of newspaper articles on the Aḥmadi issue by his officials.[30]

In addition to these more or less overt acts, the Court of
Inquiry into the Punjab Disturbances of 1953 found that the
government of Punjab paid substantial sums from a secret fund
to four Lahore newspapers, which then gave much space to the
Aḥmadi issue, while urging editorially that the BPC announce
some decision thereon.[31] The Court of Inquiry concluded that
Daultana was trying to "pass the buck" to the central cabinet,
in order to avoid the unpopularity that must attend his suppression of the agitation.[32] Khwaja Nazimuddin said that
Daultana "canalized" the agitation toward Karachi because he
had not been allowed to nominate a Punjabi to the central
cabinet, and because he disagreed with Nazimuddin's federal
formula.[33] Each of these considerations probably played their
part in Daultana's decision.

Nazimuddin, though he readily agreed that the Aḥmadis
were heretics, and though he might agree that they were not
Muslims, demurred at the thought of constitutional excom-
munication.[34] Although he was convinced that the government
ought not take action on the Aḥmadi issue, Nazimuddin was
loath to permit the disaffection of the 'ulamā'. So the Prime
Minister invited prominent 'ulamā' to his home, and he discussed the issue at length with them.[35] He hoped the 'ulamā'
might accept concessions on other issues instead. He tried to
divide the 'ulamā' of Karachi and Lahore, and he also tried to
exploit the differences between the two 'ulamā' organizations,
and between the Board of Ta'līmat and the extremist 'ulamā'.
Throughout the duration of the controversy, *Dawn,* which

[30] *Ibid.,* pp. 106–107.

[31] *Ibid.,* pp. 81–87.

[32] *Ibid.,* pp. 283–284.

[33] *Ibid.,* p. 285.

[34] *Ibid.,* p. 233.

[35] *Ibid.,* p. 282.

staunchly supported Nazimuddin, heaped editorial abuse on the 'ulamā', slanted its news against them, and devoted much space to modernist "features." [36]

THE BPC REPORT

There the matter stood when the report of the Franchise Sub-Committee was taken up by the BPC on August 1, 1952. By that time the position of the government of the Punjab was well known in Karachi. The anti-Aḥmadiyya agitation and the federal controversy were certainly related, but not in such a manner that they might be settled by horse-trading. The government of the Punjab had not begun the agitation, nor, once it had succeeded in uniting all religious groups behind the idea that the status of the Aḥmadiyya was a constitutional problem, could it stop the agitation. Concessions might be made to the 'ulamā', but no good could come of concessions to the Punjab.

The most notable feature of the August 1 meeting of the BPC is the change in its personnel. Six new members appeared at that meeting.[37] Khwaja Nazimuddin had been appointed to the BPC on April 29, 1952, while six others, most of them his close associates in the government or the Muslim League, were appointed on July 12, 1952.[38] Another member, from the Punjab, was to resign immediately before the BPC made a final decision regarding the federal formula.[39]

On August 2 consideration of the clauses relating to the composition of the House of Units and the House of People, and the reallocation of seats in both Houses was postponed, while nearly all the rest were disposed of.[40] These clauses were

[36] E.g., *Dawn*, July 11–15, Aug. 24, Sept. 7, 21, 1952.
[37] *BPC Minutes*, Aug. 1, 1952, p. 58.
[38] *Panel of Chairmen and Committees of the C.A.P.*, pp. 16, 17.
[39] *Ibid.*
[40] *BPC Minutes*, pp. 61–64.

not discussed again until August 9 when the following changes were made: [41]

	House of Units	House of People
East Bengal	60	200
Punjab	27	90
Sindh	8	30
NWFP	6	25
Tribal Areas	5	17
Bahawalpur	4	13
Baluchistan	2	5
Baluchistan States	2	5
Khairpur	2	4
Karachi	4	11
Total	120	400

The main feature of the new parity formula was the separation of Bahawalpur and Khairpur from Punjab and Sindh, respectively. The princely states had not been actually joined to the provinces previously, but the integration of these states, as we have seen, conditioned the acceptability of the original formula of the Franchise Sub-Committee. The separate listing of the states merely confirmed the status quo though it was unacceptable to the Punjab. Nazimuddin went further, however, in an attempt to strengthen the representation of those parts of West Pakistan in which he had most influence. Under the original proposal Punjab and Bahawalpur were granted a number of seats in exact proportion to their combined populations as against that of West Pakistan; the weightage given the smaller provinces of West Pakistan was comprised of the twenty-two seats which Bengal "gave up." The representation of the Punjab was naturally larger in percentage terms when figured as a function of the population of West Pakistan alone.

[41] *Ibid.*, pp. 90–91.

Nazimuddin determined the representation of the Punjab not
in relation to the population of West Pakistan, nor even that of
all Pakistan, but in relation to the representation of East
Bengal under the parity reduction:

a) $\dfrac{\text{population of Punjab 19 million}}{\text{population of Bengal 42 million}} = 45\%$

b) 45% of 200 Bengali seats = 90 seats

c) total lost to Punjab (excluding Bahawalpur) = 20 seats

The main beneficiaries of the new formula were Karachi,
which would not be autonomous, and the princely states, which
would not be fully democratic. Sindh, Baluchistan, and the
Punjab, of course, lost. The decentralization of the legislative
power of West Pakistan was fixed in such a manner that
the combined powers of the prime minister and the president
of the Muslim League might be used to best advantage.

The new parity formula of the BPC was incorporated in their
(final) report,[42] and the following weeks were devoted to
minor alterations of the report in matters of details,[43] while a
powerful campaign was carried on against the Punjab, including: veiled accusations that the Punjab government was
responsible for the death of Liaqat Ali Khan,[44] the application
of the parity principle to the Muslim League council,[45] and
the threat that the central government might take over the
enforcement of law and order in the provinces.[46]

On the night of November 22 the BPC was up late discussing
some additional suggestions of the Board of Ta'līmat-i-Islāmīa.
These were the basis of the concessions which the Aḥmadi

[42] *Report of the BPC,* clauses 38, 43.

[43] *BPC Minutes,* Nov. 3–22, 1952, pp. 93–123.

[44] *The Assassination of Mr. Liaqat Ali Khan,* Report of the Commission of
Enquiry (64 pp.), esp. pp. 9, 47, 49; *Dawn,* Aug. 22, 23, 1952.

[45] *Text of the Resolutions Passed at the Meeting of the Council of the
PML,* Oct. 11–13, 1952.

[46] *Dawn,* Aug. 25, 1952 (quoting the Urdu Press).

agitation necessitated. Last-minute changes were made and the report could not be readied in time.[47] The final draft was signed on December 19 when some Punjabi members of the committee were conspicuously absent.[48] On December 22 the report was presented by Khwaja Nazimuddin, but not before a resolution regarding the Aḥmadiyya was rather summarily ruled out of order.[49]

In explaining the long delay in drafting the Basic Principles, Nazimuddin referred to the arduous task of interpreting Islam "in terms of democratic constitutional practice of the 20th Century."[50] The procedure for preventing legislation "repugnant" to Qur'ān and Sunnah was explained, and it was pointed out that once the Head of the State had refused assent to a bill on the advice of a unanimous board of 'ulamā', such a bill could be passed only if a majority of the Muslim members supported it "because the decision in such cases will involve an interpretation of the Qur'ān and Sunnah."[51] The principle of ijmā' was not referred to, but Nazimuddin referred instead to the Objectives Resolution which provided that "the state shall exercise its powers and authority through the chosen representatives of the people." The phrase "within the limits prescribed by Him" was not mentioned.

Except for a passing reference to the parity arrangement in the Assembly, this most important aspect of the report was fairly smothered in happy descriptives of the Directive Principles of State Policy. The report was not taken into consideration at that time. A few days later Daultana made a statement to the press in which he was very doubtful about "parity,"

[47] *C.A.P. Debates,* Vol. XII, no. 1, p. 1 (the changes will be discussed below).
[48] *BPC Minutes,* Dec. 19, 1952, p. 124.
[49] *C.A.P. Debates,* Vol. XII, no. 2, p. 47.
[50] *Ibid.,* p. 57.
[51] *Ibid.,* p. 59.

and he said something about a unitary state instead of a federation. The Lahore papers took it up from there, and it was soon
apparent that no agreement could be reached. Punjabi opposition was so strong and so general that a protest meeting was
held at which Muslim Leaguers spoke on the same platform
with leaders of the Azad Party, the Jinnah Awami League, the
Aḥrār, Jamā'at-i-Islāmi, and the Islam League.

9 The Aḥmadiyya Controversy and Its Consequences

THE RELIGIOUS CONSTITUTIONAL ISSUE REOPENED

In sketching the political causes of the heightening intensity of the anti-Aḥmadiyya agitation, reference has been made to the effects that the entire controversy had on the Islamic constitution issue. In brief, these effects were (*a*) to nullify much of the work of the Suggestions Sub-Committee in its discussions with the Board of Ta‘līmat-i-Islāmīa by the addition of a new subject of discussion; (*b*) to subject the ‘ulamā’ to pressure from immoderate groups by the cautious, almost respectful, attitude of the government toward such groups; and, of most importance for this study, (*c*) to weaken the status of the Board of Ta‘līmat for the second time so as to force the discussion of Islamic political ideas once more into the public, and so as to force the ‘ulamā’ into the arms of

Maududi once again. In a way, the developments that occurred in the wake of the Interim Report were repeated, but this time they resulted in concrete amendments. The 'ulamā', consequently, took up an unequivocally new position during, what is for the Islamic religious institution, an amazingly short period of time. Such a change is incomprehensible without reference to the events that brought it about.

THE AḤMADIYYA

The Aḥmadiyya [1] is the newest of Islamic sects, distinguished from the main body of Muslims by certain doctrinal peculiarities and by the social exclusiveness of its adherents. Most of the Aḥmadis are to be found in the Punjab, some on the Indian side at Qadian, and others on the Pakistan side at Rabwah and Lahore. The Aḥmadis had been the target of bitter attack ever since the founder of the sect announced his gift of prophethood. Mīrza Ghulām Aḥmad's claim was not merely heresy, but an insult to Muhammad, the last of the prophets. His claim to be a reincarnation of Jesus and Lord Krishna were not well received either. The theology of Mīrza Ghulām Aḥmad had an appeal because of its defense against the attacks of Christian missionaries; but, paradoxically, it depended upon the British-Christian regime for its freedom to proselytize among the Muslims of the Indian empire. The Aḥmadi doctrine of the rejection of jihād and their political quiescence may be derived from this situation; but partition left them in an unenviable position. The Aḥmadiyya took no position on the question of Pakistan, just as they had not favored Indian independence. The location of Qadian in the critical Gurdaspur district of partitioned Punjab further exposed the Aḥmadiyya to criticism, and the declaration of the

---

[1] See W. C. Smith, *Modern Islam in India* (2d ed.; London, 1946), pp. 298–302; *Punjab Disturbances*, pp. 187 ff.

fight in Kashmir to be a *Jihād-bi-saif* [2] must have been a source of great embarrassment. Despite their vulnerability as a small sect, despite criticism and embarrassment, the Aḥmadiyya did not slow their missionary effort among the Muslims of Pakistan —but the passage of the Objectives Resolution significantly changed the conditions under which they might continue their work.

THE AḤRĀR

An anti-Aḥmadiyya agitation was begun by the Majlis-i-Aḥrār-i-Islām shortly after the passage of the Objectives Resolution.[3] On May 1, 1949, speakers for Aḥrār made their first public demand that the Aḥmadis be declared a non-Muslim minority.[4] The doctrinal peculiarities of the Aḥmadiyya were considered enough to place them outside the pale of Islam.

The Aḥrārs were a Muslim communal offshoot of the Congress, noted for the instability of their ideology, the spellbinding power of their speakers, and their victimization of the Aḥmadiyya.[5] They had opposed the Pakistan idea with varying degrees of intensity right up to the end,[6] but after partition they announced that they would continue to function only as a religious organization. "In political matters . . . they would follow the Muslim League." [7] The Aḥrār was not listed by the Working Committee of the Muslim League among those "political" organizations in which a membership debarred a person from enrollment in the Muslim League.[8] The Aḥrārs

---

[2] That is war, not merely striving for the good.

[3] *Punjab Disturbances*, p. 11.

[4] *Ibid.*, p. 14.

[5] Smith, *op. cit.*, pp. 224–228; *Punjab Disturbances*, pp. 11, 204, 259–260, *et passim*.

[6] Smith, *op. cit.*, p. 228; *Punjab Disturbances*, p. 12.

[7] *Punjab Disturbances*, p. 13.

[8] *Text of the Resolutions Passed by the Working Committee of the PML*, Dec. 25, 27, 1949, Resolution no. 11, pp. 7, 8.

did support the Muslim League in the Punjab elections, and
their aid was gratefully accepted, even though the Aḥrārs had
consistently refused to limit their agitation against the Aḥmadi
heretics.

Having declared the Aḥmadiyya to be non-Muslim, the
Aḥrār went on to insist that Zafrullah Khan be removed from
his position in the cabinet along with all other highly placed
Aḥmadis. The method of the Aḥrār speakers was not so much
to prove theologically the consequence of the Objectives Resolution as to crudely insult and abuse Zafrullah Khan and Mīrza
Bashīr Aḥmad, the second khalīfa of the Aḥmadiyya. Aḥrār
leaders went so far as to claim that some sort of secret arrangement had been made with them by Liaqat to remove Zafrullah
from the cabinet.[9]

The agitation really achieved alarming proportions when the
'ulamā' joined forces with the Aḥrār. The immediate cause
of the 'ulamā' lending their active support to the anti-Aḥmadi
movement was Zafrullah Khan's speech before the Anjuman
Aḥmadiyya at Jahangir Park, Karachi, on May 18, 1952. More
than six months before the central government had noted with
concern the growing controversy in the Punjab, and there was
no desire to have it spread to Karachi. Khwaja Nazimuddin
disapproved of Zafrullah's intention of addressing a public
meeting of the Aḥmadiyya, but he rejected the alternative of
accepting Zafrullah's resignation.[10] Zafrullah Khan did, in
fact, resign from the BPC before making the speech.[11] The
courage of the Aḥmadiyya, and of Foreign Minister Zafrullah
Khan, was matched by the indignation of the Karachi popu-
lace. Rioting and destruction of Aḥmadi property resulted.
But of greater significance was the calling of an All-Pakistan
Muslim Parties Convention on June 2, 1952. The convention

[9] *Punjab Disturbances*, p. 16.
[10] *Ibid.*, p. 75.
[11] *BPC Minutes*, May 15, 1952, p. 54.

was presided over by Maulana Saiyid Sulaiman Nadvi, and attended by two other members of the Board of Taʻlīmat-i-Islāmīa and leading 'ulamā' of Karachi.[12] Those attending the meeting agreed to take up the demands of the Aḥrār as their own. Their acceptance of the Aḥrār program altered the whole character of the issue, which now revolved about "the unanimous demands of all the Muslims."

JAMĀʻAT-I-ISLĀMĪ

Daultana's effort at directing the Aḥmadi controversy toward Karachi was successful even with the Jamāʻat-i-Islāmi. Maulana Maududi was explicit about his opposition to the Aḥrār, and just as frank in accusing the Punjab government of fostering the agitation.[13] On the other hand, there is no question but what he agreed with the doctrinal bases of the demands.[14] Until representatives of the Jamāʻat were invited to the Muslim Parties Convention they paid little heed to the agitation.[15] Maududi called a meeting of the Majlis-i-Shūra of the Jamāʻat early in July at which it was decided that the Aḥmadi question be put off so that all efforts might be concentrated upon "getting an Islamic Constitution."[16] The Jamāʻat refused two seats on the Majlis-i-Amāl which was formed at the convention, while Maududi wrote on the Aḥmadi question "for the benefit of the Constituent Assembly" in both the daily *Tasnīm* and the monthly *Tarjumān al-Qur'ān* in July.[17] Simultaneously,

---

[12] *Punjab Disturbances*, pp. 77, 78.

[13] *Statement of Syed Abul Ala Maududi before the Punjab Disturbances Court of Inquiry*, Jamāʻat-i-Islāmi (Karachi, n.d.) (48 pp.), pp. 17, 23 (hereafter cited as *Statement*).

[14] See *The Qadiani Problem*, Jamāʻat-i-Islāmi, Karachi; "This is the pamphlet for which its author was awarded DEATH SENTENCE . . ." (48 pp.).

[15] *Punjab Disturbances*, p. 81; "The Tasneem wrote about it only rarely."

[16] *Trial of Maududi*, Jamāʻat-i-Islāmi, Karachi (27 pp.), p. 10 (hereafter cited as *Trial*).

[17] *Statement*, p. 39; *Trial*, p. 11.

with the news of the police firing on an anti-Aḥmadi mob in Multan on July 18, came the announcement that the government would withdraw its cases against the Ahrār leaders in return for their promise of good behavior. These events were followed by the resolution of the Punjab Muslim League council referring the Aḥmadi question to the Constituent Assembly. The Jamāʿat thus remained isolated in its attempt to minimize the question. Maududi then called a meeting of the Majlis-i-Shūra in the first week of August at which it was decided that the demand that the Aḥmadiyya be declared a non-Muslim minority be added to the other eight "constitutional" demands of the Jamāʿat-i-Islāmi [18] for an Islamic constitution. By their ninth demand, and by their agreement to participate in the Action Committee of the Muslim Parties Convention, the Jamāʿat linked themselves with the Aḥrār and the 'ulamā', but they did not follow either group wholeheartedly.[19] The principal differences between the Jamāʿat-i-Islāmi and the others was that, on the one hand they did not want the anti-Aḥmadi agitation to overshadow their efforts for an Islamic constitution, and on the other they were more interested in the establishment of the principle of the supremacy of Islamic law than in the establishment of the institution of the 'ulamā'. The nine demands of the Jamāʿat were essentially the same as their four demands, except for the addition of three demands relating to civil rights and the independence of the judiciary, and another relating to the responsibility of the state to provide food, clothing, shelter, medical aid, and education to all.[20]

Since Maududi's arrest in 1948 the Jamāʿat-i-Islāmi had had

[18] Maududi, *Some Constitutional Proposals for the Consideration of the C.A.P.* (first impression, Aug. 13, 1952), p. 13 (hereafter *Proposals*); Maududi, *Fundamental Principles of Islamic Constitution* (Lahore, Nov., 1952), back cover (hereafter Maududi's *Fundamental Principles*).

[19] *Statement*, p. 40.

[20] *Proposals*, passim.

several run-ins with the law, and these experiences seem to have had some effect on the Maulana's thinking. Great emphasis was now laid on the need for an independent judiciary, and for the restriction of the executive's power to order the "preventive detention" of suspected criminals or subversives. Maududi felt that the Jamāʿat was being unfairly hindered in its activities by a hostile government, for political reasons. Despite the regularity with which Maududi and his followers fell on the wrong side of the law in the courts of Pakistan, he seems to have gained some admiration for the operation of the British-Indian legal system. In any event, he changed his former views on the right of the Head of the State to interpret the Sharīʿa, and accepted those of Muhammad Asad, giving the Supreme Court sole jurisdiction in questions of the repugnancy of acts of the legislature to the Sharīʿa:

> . . . the mere insertion of the Objectives Resolution . . . will not be sufficient. Nor an article in the Directive Principles to the effect that no legislation will be made against the Qurʾān and Sunnah. . . . Nor even the formation of Committees of ʿUlamāʾ for consultative purposes (but not having final voice) . . . will do.
>
> This purpose can only be achieved if provision is made in the body of the constitution itself that no legislature, Central or Provincial, shall have the power to pass any law in conflict with the teachings of the Qurʾān and Sunnah. Moreover there should be a specific provision in the Constitution that every citizen will have the right to challenge in the Supreme Court, any law passed by a legislature on the ground of its being in conflict with the teachings of the Qurʾān and Sunnah and therefore ultra vires of the Constitution.[21]

From the foregoing, it is clear that Maududi knew almost exactly the content of the agreement between the Board of

[21] *Ibid.,* p. 5.

Ta'līmat-i-Islāmīa and the Suggestions Sub-Committee, as incorporated in the August draft of the BPC. His outright attack on what was probably communicated to him in confidence could not have endeared him to the members of the Board of Ta'līmat-i-Islāmīa. Maududi's views on the powers of the Supreme Court are said to have been first stated in May, 1952.[22] The board's request for an opportunity to reconsider the decisions of the August draft was agreed to on August 9.

In all fairness it should be pointed out that the 'ulamā' were no less concerned over the establishment of the supremacy of Islamic law than Maududi, but they insisted that the true accomplishment of this end depended upon the people entrusted to carry out the job of deciding questions of repugnancy. "The 'ulamā' were interested in practice rather than theory."[23] Others of Maududi's suggestions in support of his nine basic demands might be taken over by the 'ulamā', but, as a result of this pressure, their decision on the key issue was made for them. They had to demand that the clause prohibiting legislation "repugnant" to the Qur'ān and Sunnah be transferred to the body of the constitution, and that the Committee of 'ulamā' be given final "voice" in such cases.

THE 'ULAMĀ'

The religious groups, despite their agreement regarding the status of the Aḥmadiyya, and their common identification of the phrase "Islamic State" with the "Good," were not really unified. For our purposes the important elements of this religious coalition were the 'ulamā', the Aḥrār, and Jamā'at-i-Islāmi. There is some overlapping between these groups, that is, between the 'ulamā' and the others, but the general outlook and approach of each toward constitutional problems is very

22 Interview.
23 Interview.

different. By far the most important group is that of the traditional, nonpolitical, vaguely organized 'ulamā'.

We have already seen that it was to this group that the government turned when it sought advice or approval on constitutional matters.[24] This was in spite of the fact that there were a few people in the government with definite ideas about an Islamic constitution. In other words, it was felt that the people of Pakistan would believe that they had an Islamic constitution only if they were told so by the 'ulamā'. If a Dr. Hussain or a Dr. Qureshi were to contradict the 'ulamā' on this point he would be laughed out of court by the man on the street. This is the reason the government shifted from an attempt to establish its own kind of Islamic state to an attempt at a compromise with the 'ulamā'. This shift may be deplored by the theoretical purist, but it was successful enough; and despite some lingering doubts an agreement was reached. The emergence of the anti-Ahmadiyya agitation, and its injection into one of the more mundane political controversies, changed the position of the 'ulamā' from that of petitioners to dispensers. The Aḥrār sought their support, Mian Mumtaz Daultana sought their coöperation, Khwaja Nazimuddin pleaded for their good will, the Jamā'at-i-Islāmi sought to influence them.

The most influential of the 'ulamā' were the Karachi leaders of Jamī'at-'Ulamā'-i-Islām, with their Deoband following. Of these, Saiyid Sulaiman Nadvi[25] and Mufti Muhammad Shafi

---

[24] E.g., Maulana Usmani was consulted on the Objectives Resolution; the Board of Ta'līmat was important only as a spokesman for the 'ulamā', even though Dr. Hamidullah may have been responsible for certain "modernist" features, and the Secretary for certain fundamentalist features; subsequently the mandate of the board was the 'ulamā' 's twenty-two principles; the co-option of Nadvi to the Suggestions Sub-Committee is another example; finally Nazimuddin in his informal discussions on the Ahmadi issue dealt only with the 'ulamā'.

[25] Nadvi joined the board on August 2, 1952, according to the comptroller of the C.A.P.

were the most prominent members of the Board of Ta'līmat-i-Islāmīa. Having a fairly good channel of communication with the BPC they tended to stress the opportunities arising out of their official duties rather than the application of public pressure.

Other 'ulamā', notably Maulana Daud Ghaznavi of Lahore and Maulana Ihtishamul Haqq Thanvi of Karachi, took a much greater part in the public work of the "khatm-i-nubuwwat" [26] movement, while the leadership of the Jamī'at-'Ulamā-i-Pākistān, notably its president, Maulana Abu'l-Hasanat Qadri of Lahore and Maulana Abdul Hamid Badauni of Karachi, was also rather deeply involved. Despite the efforts of these "extremists" (and the demand of the Jamā'at-i-Islāmi for vigorous action) no further meeting of the Muslim Parties Convention was held until after the BPC report was presented —that is, until the most influential 'ulamā' thought they needed some outside help.[27]

ADDITIONAL SUGGESTIONS OF THE BOARD OF TA'LĪMAT-I-ISLĀMĪA

From their peak of prestige and influence in midsummer, 1952, the prominent 'ulamā' were to reach their nadir by the late winter of 1953, through the medium of the near-historic meeting of the 'ulamā' in January, 1953. In discussing the events leading up to that meeting and the significance of the decisions taken, we should keep three things in mind: first, that the 'ulamā' were willing to compromise with the mysterious machinery of parliamentary government as shown by the decisions of the Suggestions Sub-Committee; second, that they would not give way in a question of theology, which they naturally took as their own private province; and third, that

[26] I.e., "finality of the Prophethood" (of Muhammad).
[27] *Punjab Disturbances,* pp. 113, 130.

their traditional position as the religious leaders of Islam was being undermined.

When the BPC completed the first draft of their report in August, 1952, they agreed, in accordance with a request, to send a copy of their decisions to the Board of Taʿlīmat-i-Islāmīa.[28] Early in November the committee reconvened and, meeting nearly daily for three weeks, put the finishing touches on the report. When everything else was complete they took up the recommendations the board had made on the August draft.[29] The content of these recommendations is not known to us for certain, so we must judge by the decisions of the committee, the subsequent attitude of the board members, and a few evasive statements. It seems that the board gained a sweeping victory for its September recommendations, for with very little discussion the committee decided to include in the Directive Principles of State Policy specific requirements that the state act against drinking, gambling, and prostitution, eliminate usury as soon as possible, promote the maintenance of Islamic moral standards, set up an organization "commanding the Good and prohibiting the Evil," take steps to bring "existing laws into conformity with the Islamic principles and for the codification of such injunctions of the Holy Qur'ān and the Sunnah as can be given legislative effect," and inculcate the fundamental unity and solidarity of the Millat.[30] The subcommittee also added a paragraph promising justice in the courts free of payment.

So far the changes were only in the Directive Principles, but there were also some changes in the constitutional provisions themselves. The minimum age for the Head of the State was changed from thirty-five to forty, the person ap-

[28] *BPC Minutes,* Aug. 9, 1952, p. 93.

[29] *Ibid.,* Nov. 17, 19, 1952, pp. 115–116.

[30] *Ibid.,* Nov. 20, 1952, pp. 116–119. The following decisions were also made at the same meeting.

pointed to fill a casual vacancy in the office of the Head of
the State must be "otherwise qualified," powers of clemency
were to be circumscribed by the Sharī'a, Muslim ministers
were to affirm that they would endeavor to fulfill the obligations enjoined by the Qur'ān and Sunnah, both in private and
public life. Provincial ministers and members of the legislatures, if Muslims, were required to take a similar oath. The
reservation of seats, special constituencies, and double voting
for women were all eliminated, though their ordinary franchise remained.

On the following day the committee received a new note
from the board referring to the decisions already taken on the
'ulamā' committees to be elected by the legislatures of the
federation and the provinces.[31] As was true of the parity
formula the committee adjourned without solving the problem, to meet again the following day and to be presented with
a series of decisions arrived at by Nazimuddin and his ad-
visors in private meetings. The August draft contained a
directive principle that no law should be passed which is contrary to the Qur'ān.[32] This was now made law, and the words
"and Sunnah" were added.[33] Objection to a bill could only
be taken in the legislature, however, and not the courts. After
such a bill was passed it would be sent to the Head of the
State with the objection attached. The Head of the State would
then refer the bill to a board of 'ulamā' (not a committee)
constituted by himself. Should the board unanimously declare
that the bill, or any part of it, were contrary to the Qur'ān or
Sunnah, the Head of the State must return the bill to the legislature. The bill could then be passed by a majority of the

[31] *Ibid.,* Nov. 21, 1952, p. 120.

[32] *BPC Report,* Aug., 1952, p. 6.

[33] *BPC Minutes,* Nov. 22, 1952, p. 121. The following decisions were made
at the same meeting, and are recorded on pp. 121–123.

members present and voting including the majority of the Muslim members present and voting. Money bills were excluded from the operation of these provisions.

The 'ulamā', here, gained many things that they desired. The Directive Principles of State Policy were not justiciable provisions, and as such could serve as a catchall for inconvenient concessions to the 'ulamā'. On the other hand, there can be no doubt that most of the Directive Principles are, by their very nature, not given to legal implementation, or obviously do not belong to constitutional law. The Directive Principles, inspired by similar chapters in the Irish constitution and the new Indian constitution, were sensibly used to show the direction in which the "enabling clause" would be implemented. Specific requirements that the state act against drinking, gambling, prostitution, and usury are thus significant as an official recognition of the view that the Sharī'a contains more than a few general principles. The same idea is strengthened by the direct reference to codification of the injunctions of the Qur'ān and Sunnah. On the question of the state's responsibility for the moral well-being of its citizens there were now six separate references to the type of activity required of the government. More important, however, was the provision for the establishment of an organization for educational purposes, and for what seemed to be a task of general censorship. It is not clear whether the members of this organization would be 'ulamā'.

The provision for bringing existing laws into conformity with Islamic principles, though the term is vague, went further yet toward satisfying the explanatory note added to the second of the 'ulamā' 's twenty-two principles. The addition of a special oath for Muslim ministers and members of the legislatures was, as in the case of the Head of the State, meant to cover certain of the qualifications (e.g., piety) that the 'ulamā' felt were required of all persons holding power in trust from God. The elimination of reserved seats for women in the legislatures and all the paraphernalia of special constituencies for women, was calculated to eliminate the possibility of any female members being elected, though there was nothing to prevent a political party from supporting the candidacy of women.

Very few of the demands of the 'ulamā' remained to be satisfied. Nevertheless, at least two more demands must have come up. There is no question but what the Board of Ta'līmat-i-Islāmīa desired the declaration of the Aḥmadis as a non-Muslim minority with separate representation and separate constituencies; and we know that the board's note of November 20 referred to the 'ulamā' committees, and most probably desired that these have the final say in vetoing legislation that they felt to be "repugnant" to the Sharī'a.[34]

THE BPC AND THE AḤMADI QUESTION

The wide concessions made to the views of the 'ulamā' must be related to the failure of the Basic Principles Committee to give way to the demands of the board regarding the status of the Aḥmadiyya. It may, however, be possible to relate all the provisions for the implementation of the "enabling clause" to this problem. Was it the intention of Khwaja Nazimuddin to imply that the state would take steps to counteract Aḥmadi proselytization? The specific reference to the unity and the solidarity of the Millat and the ideology of Islam might be read with the following quotation from Muhammad Iqbal:

> . . . religiously [the solidarity of Islam] is shaken only when Muslims rebel against any of the basic beliefs and practices of

[34] Interviews.

the Faith. It is in the interest of this eternal solidarity that Islam cannot tolerate any rebellious group within its fold.[35]

Any religious society historically arising from the bosom of Islam, which claims a new Prophethood for its basis . . . must, therefore, be regarded by every Muslim as a serious danger to the solidarity of Islam. This must necessarily be so; since the integrity of Muslim Society is secured by the idea of the Finality of prophethood alone.[36]

Iqbal preferred a political solution rather than a theological counterattack, in keeping with his predominantly political, rather than theological, approach to the problem.[37] In 1952 the 'ulamā', though more interested in theology than politics, expected constitutional law to come to the aid of "Kalām" in an Islamic state.[38] Perhaps the politicians wanted to relegate the Aḥmadi controversy to the realm of theological discussion once again.

THE 'ULAMĀ' BOARDS

The changes made in the status of the 'ulamā' committees were substantial, but they still left the 'ulamā' far short of the final veto they desired. The original proposal to adjoin special committees of 'ulamā' to the legislatures has been discussed above, and it was pointed out how this arrangement did not seriously injure the ijmā' modernist's view of the function of the legislature of an Islamic state. Nor was it injurious to the modern notion of the sovereignty of the legislature, for the 'ulamā' committees could only advise. The 'ulamā' might have been satisfied with the enhancement of their prestige as a part

[35] Iqbal, *Islam and Ahmadism* (with a reply to question raised by Nehru) (republished by Anjuman Khuddam ud-Din, Lahore, n.d.), p. 45.

[36] Maududi, *The Qadianai Problem,* Appendix II (extracts from speeches and statements of Iqbal), p. 38.

[37] *Islam and Ahmadism,* p. 18.

[38] *Kalām* is the term for scholastic discussion of theological issues.

of the governmental machinery, but they were now no longer satisfied to compromise with the proponents of legislative ijtihād, neither in form nor substance.

In response to the final note of the Board of Taʿlīmat-i-Islāmīa, the BPC altered the "procedure to avoid repugnancy to the Qurʾān and Sunnah in the Federal Legislature." The final version of the "repugnancy clause" empowered the Head of the State, rather than the legislature, to appoint a board of five persons well versed in Islamic law. This ʿulamāʾ board would then advise the Head of the State regarding the "repugnancy" of bills *passed* by the legislature, if such bills had been objected to on religious grounds by a member of either House. If the board so advised, the Head of the State could return the bill to the legislature, although he was not required to do so unless the board were unanimous. If a bill were returned to the legislature it might be passed again by a "majority of the members present and voting which should include the majority of the Muslim members present and voting," whereupon the Head of the State "should" give his assent.

To discover what the Board of Taʿlīmat suggested in its final note we must look upon the final decision of the BPC as a maximum concession. The attachment of the Board of ʿulamāʾ to the office of the Head of the State is, then, an issue of substance insofar as the ʿulamāʾ are concerned. If this provision is taken along with the demand that the Board of ʿulamāʾ be given a final veto, we find that the ʿulamāʾ would remove the final authority on the Sharīʿa from any connection whatsoever with the legislature. This institutional structure destroys the very foundation of the ijmāʿ theory, and it does more besides. By attaching the function of the ʿulamāʾ to the Head of the State, they were actually reassigning to the Head of the State the classical caliphal function of safeguarding the

Sharī'a. The 'ulamā' desired that the advice of the Board of 'ulamā' be binding on the Head of the State, and to this the BPC agreed, but the committee still preserved some part of the ijmā' theory by permitting the veto of the Head of the State to be overridden by a simple majority of the legislature, if that majority included a majority of the Muslim members. The idea of parliamentary rule was still sufficiently strong to validate the votes of non-Muslims on such questions.

Although the 'ulamā' were not pleased with the limited executive veto, this does not seem to have been their major objection to the decision of the BPC. In view of the fact that the 'ulamā' had already been found willing to compromise with the working of the parliamentary system, we may suppose that they were willing to work through the sort of watered-down executive provided by that system, despite the limited legislative powers of the Head of the State. But the fear that the government might win over one of the 'ulamā' to be appointed by the Head of the State rendered the 'ulamā' incapable of accepting the new formula. The provision that the board's decision had to be unanimous to be binding upon the Head of the State was the rock upon which the whole system foundered.[39]

The fears of the 'ulamā' were not entirely unfounded. By his own admission Nazimuddin attempted to split the 'ulamā', and to exploit any difference between them reported by the CID. It was also felt by some that there were a few, perhaps only one, of the 'ulamā' who was more interested in some official position than in the "supremacy of the Sharī'a."

The new formula permitted the government full freedom in interpreting the Sharī'a any way they liked, so long as they might control at least one of the members of the board.

The day after the BPC finished its deliberations they were to

[39] Interview.

present their report to the Constituent Assembly. The committee had been working feverishly to complete its work so as to answer its critics, and perhaps to win the hearts of all those who so earnestly desired an Islamic constitution. It was thus at the last minute that Nazimuddin announced the postponement of the presentation of the report until after his return from the Commonwealth Prime Ministers' Conference in London. There were indeed many last-minute changes to be made, and Nazimuddin was scheduled to leave the following day for London; but the members of Jamā'at-i-Islāmi claim that it was they who forced the delay upon Nazimuddin, and that the changes were due to their activities.[40] As we have seen, the changes were made before the postponement, and they were due to the activity of the Board of Ta'līmat-i-Islāmīa, that is, the leading 'ulamā', and not the Jamā'at.

JAMĀ'AT ATTEMPTS AT CLOSER COÖPERATION WITH THE 'ULAMĀ'

That the position of the 'ulamā' was threatened from both the side of the Aḥrār and that of the Jamā'at should not mislead us into believing that their position had in fact become weaker at this stage. The 'ulamā' were now more influential in Pakistan than at any time before. The stronger the 'ulamā', the less inclined they were to take advice. The first move toward closer coöperation between the 'ulamā' and Maududi came from Maududi himself, though it had no great effect until it was reaffirmed in the January, 1953, meeting of the 'ulamā'.

When the word got out that the Report of the Basic Principles Committee would be presented on November 23 the Jamā'at declared that they would observe "Constitution Week"

[40] *C.A.P. Debates*, Vol. XII, no. 1 (Nov. 23, 1952), p. 1; Anis Ahmad, *op. cit.*, p. 11.

from November 14th to the 21st.[41] On November 15 a two-day conference was held in Dacca under the auspices of the Jamāʻat. On the following day a public meeting was arranged in Karachi under the presidency of Sultan Ahmad, the local amir of the Jamāʻat, while Maulana Lal Hussain Akhtar, convener of the original meeting of the Muslim Parties Convention in Karachi, Pir Illahi Bakhsh, disqualified Sindhi politician, and Maulana Quddus Bihari, president of the Karachi Traders (hawkers) Association, addressed the gathering.[42] On November 18 Maulana Maududi spoke at Lahore on the constitution and the Qadiani question.[43] On November 22, on the afternoon just preceding the final decisions of the BPC on the Board of ʻulamā' (the meeting of the BPC was held at 7:00 P.M.), a procession was taken out in Karachi, followed by a public meeting that was addressed by Maududi, Maulana Abd al-Hay Abbasi, president of the Karachi Spinners Association, Quddus Bihari, and an Awami League leader.[44] At the meeting four resolutions were passed calling for an Islamic constitution on the basis of the ʻulamā' 's twenty-two principles, the declaration of the Aḥmadis as a non-Muslim minority, and the withdrawal of the Report on Fundamental Rights, the redrafting of the BPC report in the light of the requirements of the Sharīʻa, and the publication of the "Views" of the Board of Taʻlīmat-i-Islāmīa. The procession and meeting were supposedly held under the auspices of "many" civic and religious groups.

In regard to this information, it is necessary to note that the important ʻulamā' of Karachi did not participate in these meetings, and the resolutions passed at the Karachi meeting

---

[41] *Anjam,* Nov. 13, 1952.

[42] *Ibid.,* Nov. 18, 1952.

[43] *Ibid.,* Nov. 20, 1952.

[44] *Ibid.,* Nov. 23, 1952 (this information was not carried in the English-language press).

stressed only those points on which there was common agreement between the 'ulamā' and the Jamā'at. The leaders of
Jamā'at-i-Islāmi are hardly the ones to suggest that the report
of a group of 'ulamā' would more authentically define an
Islamic state than the modern and scientifically logical work of
Maududi—and yet this is exactly what happened at the meeting.

The wooing of the 'ulamā' was carried on in Maududi's
speeches and writings. In August, the religious world of Pakistan was startled, and horrified, by the appearance in *Dawn*
of an article by A. K. Brohi, advocate general of Sindh, and
soon to become secretary of the Parliamentary Board of the
Pakistan Muslim League. The article entitled "Thoughts on
the Future Constitution of Pakistan" wished to point out that
the claim that a constitution of a country "can in any measure
either improve the character of the individual or bring about
a wholesale revolution in the outlook of several sections of the
society of which these individuals are members, is . . . an
inflated one." [45] Brohi also wrote that the constitution could
not be based on Qur'ānic law except for the general principle
of democracy. He referred to the Aḥmadi business as senseless.
A storm of protest immediately arose; and Brohi explained
that by constitutional law he meant "that branch of law which
deals with the distribution of sovereign power within the
state." [46] Bold man that he is, Brohi offered 5,000 rupees to
whoever might cite verses of the Qur'ān which fit his definition
of constitutional law. In yet a third article he mustered support
from quotations from Iqbal, Amir Ali, and Muhammad Asad,
while insisting that the Qur'ānic verses cited by "his critics"
had nothing to do with their derived conclusions.[47] Among

[45] *Dawn,* Aug. 24, 1952.
[46] *Ibid.,* Sept. 7, 1952.
[47] *Ibid.,* Sept. 21, 1952.

those who hastened to answer Brohi was no less than Maulana Maududi himself in a pamphlet entitled *Fundamental Principles of Islamic Constitution Enunciated by Qur'ān and Sunnah.* Maududi may have found more interesting verses than the others did, but he did not succeed in finding any that fit in with Brohi's definition. For our present purpose we need only note Maududi's glide toward the views of the 'ulamā' in this pamphlet as well:

> The verse (IV:59) also gives the people the right to differ with their rulers. . . . By implication there must be some institution for deciding such cases in the light of the Qur'ān and Sunnah. As the Shariat does not prescribe any one definite form for this, it may comprise a body of 'Ulamā' or it may be a supreme court. . . .[48]

The pamphlet was first published in English on November 20, 1952.

With Brohi's article still on his mind, Maududi addressed the Karachi Bar Association, or some members of it, in November, just after the presentation of the Basic Principles Report was postponed.[49] From various references in the speech we find Maududi striving to meet the views of the 'ulamā' without quite compromising his own.

The problem was described as the need to write down the already existing unwritten constitution of Islam. It was pointed out that the distinction between constitutional and ordinary law was a recent invention, and, consequently, constitutional laws were all mixed up with other laws in Islamic legal sources. In order to disentangle the constitutional laws, specially trained persons are needed. Here Maududi gave a great compliment to the 'ulamā'.

[48] Maududi's *Fundamental Principles,* p. 14.
[49] Maududi, *Islamic Constitution* (an address before the Karachi Bar Association) (typescript).

Of late a new slogan has been raised, that Islam does not recognize priesthood and therefore "Mullahs" cannot be the sole interpreters of Islam. . . . Somebody would then say there being no lawyerhood in Islam, even the most ignorant has the right to hold forth authoritatively on the law. . . .[50]

The sources that contain these constitutional laws are the Qur'ān, the Sunnah, the conventions of the "Rightly-Guided Caliphs," and the rulings of great jurists. The ingenuity with which Maududi can take traditional Islamic ideas and clothe them in the garb of Western concepts is truly remarkable. The conventions of the caliphs is no more than the ijmā' of the Companions—the idea is at once acceptable to both 'ulamā' and modernists—but ijmā' is limited to the consensus of the Companions alone in accordance with the views of the Jamā'at.[51] Rulings of the great jurists of Islam, the fourth source, though presented in the lawyer's rather than the 'alim's terminology, is in fact a concession to the notion of taqlīd. "Rulings" is not an appropriate term for the expository legal writings of the great fuqahā', who were not really jurists in our sense of the word. Maududi does not swallow taqlīd whole, however: "[The rulings] may not be eternal, yet it cannot be gainsaid that they contain fundamentals of the best guidance for understanding the spirit and letter of an Islamic Constitution." [52] The details of the constitution, he goes on to outline, are not much different from his previous writings on the subject, except so far as the special role of the Supreme Court is dealt with.

Maududi explains that there is an inherent need in the Islamic system for "an institution . . . which would undertake to adjudicate in strict accordance with the Book of God and the

---

[50] *Ibid.*, p. 6.
[51] *Ibid.*, p. 3.
[52] *Ibid.*

Sunnah." [53] Regarding judicial review of legislation objected to on the ground of repugnancy to the Sharī'a, Maududi still favored it, but with almost an apology to the 'ulamā':

> I know of no specific rulings on this question but the conventions established during the Caliphs [*sic*] go to show that the judiciary then did not enjoy or exercise such powers. . . . Even today if we could introduce some similar satisfactory arrangement in our constitution that no legislature was in a position to enact laws in contravention of the spirit of the Qur'ān and Sunnah, the judiciary need not have the authority to reject the decision of the legislature.[54]

THE MEETING OF THE 'ULAMĀ' AND THE MUSLIM PARTIES CONVENTION

At the January meeting of the Muslim Parties Convention Maududi was to go yet closer to the position of the 'ulamā', but they were also to concede a great deal themselves. Of greater immediate importance was the fact that both the 'ulamā' and the Jamā'at were to find themselves unable to withstand the pressures of the more extreme Ahrāris. These developments followed the presentation of the Basic Principles Report to the Constituent Assembly on December 22, 1952, and were part of the general deterioration in the condition of the body politic which is characteristic of the Pakistan scene during the first quarter of 1953.

When the report was published the 'ulamā' and the Jamā'at seem to have been surprised that it was quite as favorable to their views as it was. Maududi was again in Karachi on December 21 to speak on the constitution before its presentation. On December 23, at an informal meeting between Maududi and some of the 'ulamā', it was decided that none of the religious

---

[53] *Ibid.*, p. 15.
[54] *Ibid.*, p. 21.

leaders would state their individual views on the report until
the meeting of the 'ulamā' was held in January.[55] Apparently
it had already been decided to reconvene the same 'ulamā' who
had met in January, 1951, to consider the Interim Report.[56]
The 'ulamā' are also reported to have requested that the
Constituent Assembly delay consideration of the report until
they had had sufficient time to consider it and give their
opinions.[57] The 'ulamā' realized that any public difference
among them would result in the defeat of their ends; and they
were aware of the attempts to divide religious opinion.

While preparations for this conference were going on efforts
were also being made to reconvene the Muslim Parties Convention for the purpose of discussing the Aḥmadiyya issue.[58]
Since the membership of both groups largely overlapped it was
decided to hold the convention at the same time as the meeting
of the 'ulamā'. Thus, despite the success of the efforts of Mr.
Daultana and of Maulana Maududi (though assuredly for
different reasons) in joining the Aḥmadi question to that of
the constitution, that question was still deemed worthy of
separate consideration. In fact, when the time came, the 'ulamā'
decided upon a special course of "direct action" regarding
the Aḥmadi question, while they continued to pursue constitutional methods to achieve their other ends. These two meetings
signaled the weakening of the 'ulamā', the success of Maududi's
effort at compromise, and the clear victory of the tactics of the
Aḥrār.

The meetings of the 'ulamā' began on January 11, 1953, and
continued through the 18th; the Muslim Parties Convention
met on the 16th, 17th, and 18th.[59] The 'ulamā' discussed the

[55] Interviews; *Dawn,* Dec. 27, 1952.
[56] *Punjab Disturbances,* p. 130.
[57] *C.A.P. Debates* (Mr. Khuhro), Vol. XII, no. 3 (Jan. 1, 1953), p. 170.
[58] See n. 56.
[59] *Ulama's Amendments to the BPC Report,* Jamā'at-i-Islāmi, Karachi, June,
1953, p. 4 (hereafter *Ulama's Amendments*).

"entire" report of some two hundred and fifty clauses and appendixes, and "alhamd-u-Lillah" came to unanimous decisions.[60] As we shall see, the decisions were not entirely unanimous, despite the pious ostentation. The divergent views of the action taken at the Muslim Parties Convention concerning the question of the association of Jamā'at-i-Islāmi with the "direct action" decision have been discussed at length by the learned judges Munir and Kayani in their report on the Punjab Disturbances. For our purposes it is sufficient to note that Maududi's effort to disallow any special action on this single constitutional issue failed.[61] Nor did the Jamā'at have the courage to dissociate themselves from the ensuing direct action, although they realized full well that the urban mobs of the Punjab were the only groups that would respond—and that the agitation might do great harm to their goal of an Islamic constitution.[62] But before we examine how the gains of the Jamā'at were nullified let us examine what they won.

The amendments of the 'ulamā', pertaining to the chapter on the Directive Principles of State Policy, suggested that the entire educational system be changed rather than the mere provision of facilities for the study of Islamic principles within existing educational facilities.[63] This corresponds with Maududi's recommendation number 5 on the Directive Principles in the pamphlet entitled *Some Constitutional Proposals*.[64] The 'ulamā' desired that time limits be added to the clauses directing the government to prohibit drinking, gambling, and prostitution. They desired a proviso to be added to the clause on the codification of Islamic law to the effect that the differences of personal law among the various sects be respected. This was in large measure to satisfy the Shī'a, but also to keep this most

[60] *Ibid.*
[61] *Punjab Disturbances*, p. 133.
[62] *Ibid.*, pp. 133–135; *Statement*, p. 39.
[63] *Ulama's Amendments* (the following amendments are on pp. 6, 7).
[64] *Proposals*, p. 6.

sacrosanct part of the Sharī'a as untouched as it had been throughout the British raj.

The state's responsibility for the physical welfare of its unfortunate and infirm citizens would be extended to all citizens. Maududi had been satisfied with "every needy citizen" rather than "all," but that was before the report came out and was found to have included substantially the same clause as he suggested.

Other amendments were added regarding the rights of labor and the peasantry, the discouragement of linguistic and sectional feeling, the promotion of Islamic learning and culture again, the ratio of the highest and lowest government salaries, and the consideration of piety along with efficiency in promotions and appointments of civil servants.

Two new clauses were suggested which were substantially taken from Maududi's *Proposals*. These related to religious training for civil servants, and the provision of facilities whereby civil servants might observe the tenets of Islam.[65] The tendency to concentrate attention upon the educational system and the civil service is part of the general tactic of Jamā'at-i-Islāmi to convert the elite of the country. The emphasis is fully unified, since the colleges are still to a large extent training schools for the civil service.

The 'ulamā' opposed the exemption of money bills from the ban on un-Islamic legislation, but they were willing to accept a five-year transitional period during which the economic organization of the state might be brought into line with the principles of Islam.[66] They desired that the state be known as the Islamic Republic of Pakistan.[67] The provinces were to be no more than administrative units,[68] but the 'ulamā' made no

[65] *Ibid.*, and *Ulama's Amendments*, p. 9.
[66] *Ulama's Amendments*, p. 14.
[67] *Ibid.*, p. 15.
[68] *Ibid.*

suggestion to limit provincial control over extensive fields of government activity.[69] The parity proposal did not please the 'ulamā' since it definitely recognized sectional loyalties, but they declined to intervene while the politicians were trying to work out that problem.[70]

According to the report, candidates might be disqualified if convicted of an offense involving at least two years' imprisonment. A voter might be disenfranchised if similarly convicted.[71] The 'ulamā', under Maududi's direction, desired that the term "misconduct," or the nature of the offense, be limited to cases involving "moral turpitude" so that the government might not add the insult of disqualification for candidacy, or disenfranchisement, to the injury of arrest or dismissal on political grounds.[72]

Since the backbone of Maududi's proposals is the special competence he would give the courts with regard to legislation "repugnant" to Qur'ān and Sunnah one might expect that he would seek to strengthen the judiciary, extend its power, and convert its personnel.[73] Consequently the amendments suggested by the 'ulamā' provided that the piety and religiosity of the candidate be taken into consideration in making judicial appointments,[74] that neither the legislature nor the executive be empowered to appoint special tribunals, that the Supreme Court be empowered to grant leave to appeal decisions of military courts, that there be no restrictions upon the power of the court to summon witnesses or to secure the production of evidence of any kind, that nothing prevent superior courts from reversing any judgment of lower courts, and that the judiciary

[69] *Ibid.*, pp. 26–27.
[70] *Ibid.*, p. 17.
[71] *Report of the BPC*, articles 42, 48, and 49.
[72] *Ulama's Amendments*, pp. 18, 19; *Proposals*, p. 13.
[73] *Proposals*, pp. 10, 11.
[74] These amendments are on pages 20–26 of *Ulama's Amendments*.

be empowered to appoint election tribunals, while only those who served as High Court judges should be appointed as election commissioners. In keeping with Maududi's own unpleasant experiences he strongly urged the restriction of the government's power of preventive detention,[75] and the 'ulamā' agreed with him.[76]

Various other amendments were suggested relating to the oath of members of the legislature, restriction of emergency powers, prohibiting the propagation of atheism, denying the eligibility of nonmembers for any period to the cabinet, requiring religious observance for the franchise, eliminating the provincial residence requirement for candidacy for the legislature, abolishing the special privileges of certain classes of the civil service, and the reservation of one seat for the Aḥmadi "minority" in the Punjab.[77]

In many instances these amendments follow closely the suggestions of Maududi, and in all they reflect his particular approach. This is not surprising, for he was acknowledged by the 'ulamā' as an expert on constitutional questions, and they went so far as to turn the decisions of the meeting over to Maududi for redrafting (or perhaps even for adding any amendments he might like to the portions untouched at the meetings).[78] No doubt too many of the 'ulamā' did not think twice about some of the suggestions, coming as they did from an accredited expert, but the significance of these amendments, called the "'ulamā''s amendments," will become apparent farther on. We have now to consider the most important amendment of all: that relating to "Procedure for Preventing Legislation Repugnant to the Qur'ān and the Sunnah."

Maududi's success, and his importance, is largely due to his

75 *Proposals*, p. 8.
76 *Ulama's Amendments*, p. 27.
77 *Ibid.*, pp. 10, 17, 18, 23, 28.
78 *Punjab Disturbances*, p. 133.

ability to phrase and rationalize traditional ideas in accordance with the intellectual predilections of the Pakistani graduate. As long as the constitutional process remained at the stage of general discussion these tactics worked admirably, but when attention was focused upon concrete proposals, the 'ulamā' became somewhat apprehensive of Maududi's proposals. The tendency of the constitution makers to leave as little as possible to future legislation rather intensified this predicament. The inevitable result for the Jamā'at was the necessity of choosing between its principal educational goal and its immediate political purpose. As might be expected, priority was given to political success, though it may very well be questioned whether the extremely limited success that might be expected was worth the price. Official recognition of the 'ulamā' by the framers of the constitution, coupled with increasing attacks upon the civil service by the Muslim League,[79] determined the course of action for the Jamā'at.

Criticism of the civil service has been a favorite prepartition theme, for the British raj was identified with the administrative apparatus. The Pakistani "common man" still equates the civil servant with the ruling class; and a great many Muslim Leaguers think like the common man. Maududi, too, shared this view; and that is why he aimed his propaganda at this most highly educated and Westernized class of Pakistanis. Maududi's condemnation of the 'ulamā' had been, in fact, the basis of his strongest appeal to the Western-educated. But in the prevailing atmosphere of the Aḥmadiyya controversy, traditional religion had been raised to the status of patriotism, while the intriguing politicians prevented the civil service from taking its usual measures for the preservation of law and order. It was action

[79] E.g., *Text of the Resolution Passed at the Meeting of the Council of the PML,* Dacca, October 11, 12, 13, 1952, Resolution no. 9, p. 5; *Supplementary Agenda,* paragraphs 10 and 13 (3).

such as this that would eventually bring the civil service back
into power, but for the time being it certainly looked as though
Maududi had been betting on the wrong horse. Maududi's
first moves toward a reconciliation with the 'ulamā' have already been traced, but his most successful effort was made at
this meeting of the 'ulamā'.

It was but a simple matter to discredit the decision of the
BPC regarding "repugnancy" procedure. Without giving the
'ulamā' the determining voice the decision could not be defended by the Board of Taʿlīmat, whereas provision for unanimity among the members of the board was taken to impugn
the *bona fides* of the committee as well. Support by suspect
'ulamā' for a board with final say in "repugnancy" matters
presented the danger of a government-controlled board with
a certain immediacy. Consequently, Maududi was successful in
getting the 'ulamā' to oppose the device of an 'ulamā' board
altogether.

As Maududi's alternative stood, it was similarly unacceptable.
Though his suggestion rejected completely the notion of legislative institutionalization of ijmāʿ, it provided no practical
means of overcoming the difficulty of the completely secular
training of the judiciary. References to overhauling the system
of education, and to a consideration of the piety of candidates
for the services, could not overcome the prejudice of the
'ulamā' in favor of their own changeless system of training in
religious law, and the conservative spirit it imparted. For the
'ulamā' the precise nature of the institution whereby the Sharīʿa
was to be enforced was not so important as the actual persons
who would do the job. On their part the Jamāʿat was not
unaware of the fact that British-trained judges had on the
whole done a good job of upholding Islamic personal law
when such cases came before them; but it is unlikely that
Maududi used such an argument to convince the 'ulamā' whom

he understood so well.[80] The solution was to provide for a transitional arrangement whereby 'ulamā' would be appointed to the Supreme Court until such time as the right sort of judges might be produced by the ordinary law schools. The suggestion of the 'ulamā' was as follows:

> 1. To deal with constitutional objections raised under section 3 against laws enacted by a legislature or other issues concerning interpretation of constitution on this behalf there should be five Ulema in the Supreme Court who, along with some judge to be nominated for the purpose by the Head of the State in consideration of his *Tadayyun* and *Taqva* and his knowledge of Islamic law and learning, should decide whether or not the law in dispute is in conformity with Qur'ān and Sunnah.
>
> 3. Only such alim should be qualified for appointment to this office as
>   a) has worked in some religious institution as a Mufti for a minimum period of ten years; or
>   b) has been an accepted Mufti in some area for a minimum period of 10 years; or
>   c) has worked as a Qazi in some duly established Muhkama-i-Qaza; or
>   d) has been a teacher of Tafseer, Hadis, or Fiqah in some religious institution.[81]

The designation of the Supreme Court as the body charged with the preservation of Islamic principles certainly had some appeal to the educated of a religious bent. It would certainly focus attention upon Islamic law, and it would permit authoritative decisions to be made while satisfying the *sine qua non* of a "modern democratic" institution. To put 'ulamā' on the bench was almost a contradiction in terms—the entire

---

[80] Maududi, *The Qadiani Problem,* p. 48.
[81] *Ulama's Amendments,* pp. 13, 14.

advantage gained by covering the conservative interpretation of the Sharī'a with this modern superficiality was lost. On the other hand, the desired support of the 'ulamā' was won, with the exception of the representatives of Jamī'at-'Ulamā'-i-Pākistān.

Maulanas Abul Hasanat and Badauni attached a note of dissent, preferring an 'ulamā' board with final powers chosen from a list of "the names of the Ulema of Pakistan from such religious organizations of Ulema as have been working on Central and Provincial levels in a regular manner since after the establishment of Pakistan and whose organizations are intact up until now and the Head of the State should notify their names." [82] The note of dissent is an excellent example of the way in which vague differences of outlook came to be defined in the course of the constitutional process in Pakistan. The differences in the qualifications required by the majority and the minority are significant. The majority group was dominated by Deobandi 'ulamā', and about a third of the members attending the meeting were engaged in teaching, while many of the others were engaged in "tablīgh" work of a specialized type.[83] The 'Ulamā'-i-Pākistān, that is, the Bareilly group, headed by two members of the Jilani order of Sufis, were far more interested in official recognition of their group than in pursuing the usual occupations of the 'ulamā'. Under the conditions set down by the majority, these potential collaborators would be excluded. Under the conditions laid down by the minority the teachers and "tablīgh" groups would be largely excluded. The principal disagreement is between Deoband 'ulamā' and Bareilly 'ulamā', between antisufi and sufi, between "religious 'ulamā' " and "political 'ulamā'," be-

[82] *Ibid.,* p. 30.

[83] *Tablīgh* means propagation. Such preaching is usually aimed at Muslims in Pakistan. Some of these groups are Ahl-i-Hadith, Anjuman Khuddam ud-Din, etc.

tween those who sought the elevation of their institution as a means to an end and those who sought it as an end in itself. Maududi was successful only because the Deobandi group was willing to accept the enshrinement of the central principle of Islamic law at the price of their own permanent association therewith. The Bareilly group could in no circumstances give up the unofficial status of the 'ulamā'; they rather desired to make this status official by forcing the recognition of their organization in the constitution. Despite their close association in the mind of the 'ulamā', it is apparent that there was not a complete identification of the institution and its function.

Since the provision for appointing 'ulamā' to the Supreme Court was a transitional measure, it was of secondary importance from the theoretical point of view. The immediate press attacks which met the announcement of the 'ulamā''s amendments neglected the theory entirely in accusing the 'ulamā' of usurping a nonreligious institution, and in using the word "ulemocracy" to define the aims of the 'ulamā'.[84] For Maududi the theory was, however, most important and the victory his, until the Muslim Parties Convention rejected his suggestion that no special action be taken on the Aḥmadi question since a solution had been offered in the amendments of the 'ulamā'.

By this device Maududi hoped to swing the whole of the agitation behind the entire series of suggested amendments. There were enough other-minded 'ulamā' present who did not identify themselves so completely with the amendments—or who feared that the Aḥrār might now monopolize the anti-Aḥmadi agitation—or who simply said yes to every suggestion that seemed to lead to more committees, more action, and more notoriety—to leave Maududi and his amendments isolated for the time being. But this was not a complete defeat for Maududi,

[84] *Dawn*, Jan. 24, 1953.

who to this day enjoys the freely given respect of the 'ulamā'
in all questions of constitutional theory. Maududi lost ground
only because the 'ulamā' themselves became seriously weakened.

THE PUNJAB DISTURBANCES

To resist the temptation of leading a popular agitation, or of
demonstrating the vigor of their much maligned institution,
was perhaps beyond the capacity of the 'ulamā'. Moreover, not
to lead yet not to condemn the agitation would have been to
abdicate the authority they so vociferously claimed. And yet
it is a rare event in the history of Islam when the 'ulamā' have
been prominent in a violent defiance of established authority.
From the time the Murjiʿa refused to judge the merits of 'Alī
as against those of Muʾawiya, the 'ulamā' have generally preferred to let God judge their rulers, while they concentrated
upon His service and that of the community. Again and again
they have opposed rebellion on the ground of preserving that
community, and its social embodiment of the Islamic heritage.
Indeed, if there is any terrestrial value in their efforts it lies
in this direction. The 'ulamā' are practical men, and God-fearing too. Rebellion is forbidden should it divide or destroy
the Islamic community, but if it is sure to succeed, it is obligatory upon all Muslims to uphold the right and suppress the
evil. Perhaps it was with this in mind that the 'ulamā' decided
to resort to direct action should the government refuse to
accede to their demand that the Aḥmadiyya be politically
excommunicated.

By this time the anti-Aḥmadi agitation was completely out
of hand. Speeches against the Aḥmadiyya had for some time
been mere starting points for attacks on the government, and
Daultana's provincial regime came in for its share. The situation within the country certainly encouraged such criticism,

but it took on the shape of impending revolt rather than a religious agitation of limited scope. On December 15 the Deputy Inspector General of the Punjab CID wrote:

> Anti-government propaganda has been intensified of late and the food situation is being vigorously exploited. Government is being ruthlessly abused, maligned and defamed. The confidence of the public is being sedulously destroyed and confusion and panic are spreading. In all circles, business, service, etc., fierce criticism is being levelled against government. In railway trains, private gatherings and at social functions there is one topic which arouses the deepest interest and that is anti-government talk. Members of the League and Government servants are no exceptions. . . . People who return from Karachi bring a grim picture, and say that Secretariat officers and other high ups seem to have lost faith in the future and talk as if a collapse is imminent. . . .[85]

In this atmosphere Nazimuddin decided to go to Lahore to present his views to the Punjab Muslim League council. On the eve of his departure thousands of Karachi students rioted in a demand for free education and various other things such as the reopening of certain evening classes. At least ten students were killed, over eighty were injured, 261 "bad characters" were arrested, a minister was attacked and his Cadillac burned.[86] As usual the police were blamed, and sympathy was expressed for the students by prominent Leaguers and members of the Constituent Assembly, Maulana Maududi, the Karachi Bar Association, the Modern Education Society, the London Students Federation, a meeting of Karachi 'ulamā', the Pakistan Medical Association, the National Youth Federation, a meeting of Muslim League workers, and the Standard-Vacuum Employees Association.

[85] *Punjab Disturbances,* p. 116.
[86] *Dawn,* Jan. 9–12, 1953.

When Nazimuddin arrived in Lahore he was met by a protest demonstration and "black flags." The Aḥrār had done much to organize the protest, but they were encouraged by the Punjab Muslim League. Nazimuddin's efforts were doomed from the start; all he could get out of the Punjab League council was a resolution that ". . . this Council is emphatically of the view that the discussion of the Report of the Basic Principles Committee in the Constituent Assembly should be postponed for a sufficient time to enable mature deliberation. . . ." [87]

On his return from Lahore, Nazimuddin was met by a delegation from the Muslim Parties Convention demanding that the Aḥmadis be declared a non-Muslim minority, failing which the 'ulamā' would resort to direct action. Since the ultimatum gave him a month, Nazimuddin took it and spent the intervening time trying to split the 'ulamā'. *Dawn,* which was strongly pro-Nazimuddin, remained silent about the ultimatum, though it was no secret, but condemned instead the decision of a meeting of the 'ulamā' regarding the procedure for preventing legislation contrary to the Qur'ān and Sunnah, ran two articles condemning "mullahs" who support "landlordism," and prominently editorialized on a speech by the Governor of Bengal attacking those parts of the report which did not recognize the legislature's right to ijmā'. [88]

When the period of grace was over, the Council of Action of the Muslim Parties Convention decided that "volunteers would go peacefully" to the Prime Minister's house on February 27. The extremist 'ulamā' were promptly arrested, the ensuing rioting was quickly crushed, and a press communique attacking the Aḥrār was issued.

[87] Resolution moved and passed by the PML Council meeting January 15 under presidency of Mian Mumtaz Muhammad Khan Daultana (typed copy acquired from the Provincial League Secretary; original in Urdu).

[88] *Dawn,* Jan. 24, Feb. 4, 5, 13, 16, 1953.

Weak though Nazimuddin is said to have been, he was somehow brought to take firm action at the last possible moment. Not so Mr. Daultana. The flame that was snuffed out in Karachi burst forth into a blazing conflagration in Lahore. The Chief Minister, who had labored so hard to secure his popularity with the masses of the Punjab, found his own administration the object of attack. Rather than suffer any of the blame for opposing a popular demand he again pleaded with the central government for some statement on the substance of the demand. The center's answer in a secret OTP cypher telegram was far from the public statement demanded. After hampering the effectiveness of the police in dealing with the rioters, Daultana finally gave way and made an announcement that he would press the demands of the people with the central government. On orders from the central cabinet martial law was declared, the army moved in immediately. The situation was well in hand in a matter of hours, and the rest of the prominent 'ulamā', the leading Aḥrāris, and the elite of the Jamā'at were all imprisoned.

On March 10, with the military still in charge, Daultana withdrew his promise to press the demands; but a few days later he went back to his old tactics. On March 20 Daultana stated that he was in full agreement with the central government that it was the duty of the provincial government to maintain law and order, but he added that if the center had spoken up on the demands the riots might not have taken place.[89] Within a few days Nazimuddin was in Lahore, Daultana resigned, and Malik Feroz Khan Noon, the governor of Bengal, was elected leader of the Punjab Assembly by the Muslim League Parliamentary Party.

Nazimuddin then returned in triumph to Karachi to see the budget through the Assembly. In a statement on the recent

[89] *Ibid.,* March 21, 1953.

outbreaks, Nazimuddin explained the responsibility of the Aḥrār, while doing his best to absolve the 'ulamā' of all blame. The budget was passed without cut, and Nazimuddin turned his efforts to the problem of the Sindh Muslim League. On April 17, His Excellency Mr. Ghulam Muhammad, governor-general of Pakistan, acting under Section 10 of the Government of India Act, was pleased to dismiss his prime minister.

10 *Interim Constitution*

THE DISMISSAL OF KHWAJA NAZIMUDDIN

The dismissal of Khwaja Nazimuddin by the Governor-General was greeted with a feeling of great relief. Though an extreme departure from the conventions of the commonwealth system, his dismissal does not seem to have aroused any apprehensions regarding the constitutional future of the country. Nazimuddin found himself almost alone in his protest against the "undemocratic" action of the Governor-General; the country worried far less about democracy than it did about the food shortage. In a matter of a few days Nazimuddin accepted his dismissal, and a life pension of 2,000 rupees per month, provided he would stay out of public life.[1]

Of greater importance than the attitude of the public was that of the civil service. It seems that the military were not called upon to play any important part in the dismissal of the Prime Minister, though they certainly did not oppose it.

[1] *Civil and Military Gazette*, April 23, 1953; see also Government of India Act, Section 150.

The fact seems to have been accomplished by the bureaucracy and the police, not one of whom paid the least attention to Nazimuddin's protests. The civil service had several grievances though no one of them seems to have been strong enough to warrant such complete antagonism. In the eyes of this group the greatest evil is indecision. It does not matter so much what course is taken; but a good bureaucrat hates to see un-attended files pile up, and this is exactly what Nazimuddin did.[2] Though he did act with vigor on certain political issues, and on the constitution, Nazimuddin could not seem to cope with the real problems facing the country.

Perhaps it was simply Nazimuddin's misfortune to take over when the international terms of trade turned against Pakistan, and when a bad harvest coincided with a reduction of acreage planted in food grains. It may also be true that Nazimuddin inherited certain foreign-exchange commitments which the country simply could not bear after the prices of raw jute and cotton fell. Dr. Graham's failure in mediating the Kashmir dispute cannot be directly ascribed to Nazimuddin's incompetence, nor, as has already been shown, can the charge that Nazimuddin abdicated power in favor of the 'ulamā' be substantiated.[3] As for the disturbances in Dacca in February, 1952, and those in Lahore in March, 1953, his responsibility was at most indirect, though he was more to blame for those in Karachi in May, 1952, and January, 1953.

However one may apportion responsibility for the deplorable state into which the country had fallen, the day-to-day admin-

[2] Interviews.

[3] It is widely, but incorrectly, held that Nazimuddin was responsible for the decisions of the Suggestions Sub-Committee, which were altered only in detail by the BPC. Actually these decisions were the result of Liaqat's policy. E.g., C. W. Choudhury, "Constitution Making Dilemmas in Pakistan," *Western Political Quarterly* (Dec., 1955), p. 591.

istration had become more and more difficult, and the politicians made no attempt to shield the bureaucracy from bearing the brunt of public dissatisfaction. The cabinet persisted in avoiding difficult decisions and seemed to be merely allowing things to happen. Without vigorous leadership the services were gradually becoming demoralized.[4]

Khwaja Nazimuddin has pointed out, with much truth, that his policies were not greatly changed by the following ministry;[5] and he might have said with as much truth that his own policies (with the exception of the parity formula) had not deviated from the line set by Liaqat Ali Khan. In fact, it may be easily shown that many of the economic difficulties of his period had begun to appear during the last months of the previous ministry.[6] It has also been suggested that an unwise industrial development policy had depleted the country's foreign-exchange resources before Nazimuddin took over.

It is, however, certain that Nazimuddin followed his predecessor in instituting certain changes in the administrative machinery. Under Liaqat Ali Khan the government had decided (1) to institute a provincial quota system for the recruiting of civil-service officers, (2) to reduce the pay of Pakistani officers, (3) to reorganize the service on an all-Pakistan rather than a provincial basis, (4) and to reinstitute the "reversion rule" whereby senior officers after spending five years at the center or in a province would have to serve in a different province for a similar period.[7] The implementation of his program was continued under Nazimuddin. The resultant

[4] *Punjab Disturbances,* pp. 116–117.
[5] Interview.
[6] E.g., *Dawn,* Aug. 27, 1951 (middle-class budgets), Sept. 2, 1951 (poorer cotton prospects), Sept. 6, 1951 (fall in local demand), Sept. 11, 1951 (reduction of export duty on cotton), Oct. 2, 1951 (acute salt shortage in Bengal).
[7] *Dawn,* Sept. 7, 1951.

uncertainty for most of the higher ranks of the services was further enhanced by unfriendly resolutions of the Muslim League central and provincial councils.[8]

One gains the impression that the bureaucracy did more than simply permit the dismissal of the Prime Minister. The major reason for this impression is that the Governor-General and the Finance Minister were both former civil servants and, in a sense, the most outstanding exponents of the functionary class. One may speak of a "class" at least in reference to the higher officials, for they are very often the most highly educated, the most highly Westernized, and the most highly secularized group in Pakistan. Often enough the higher civil servants may be found to be more intelligent or certainly more intellectually sophisticated than the prominent politicians. These officials also have a high esprit, though it is difficult to disentangle their devotion to duty from their devotion to the civil service itself. They are at least as much devoted to their institution as the 'ulamā' are to their own. In Pakistan, where nationalism has had a difficult time taking root, it is not easy to speak of the "patriotism" of a predominantly secularist group, nevertheless the services may not be accused of indifference to the fate of Pakistan. Moreover, it is apparent that the civil service made no attempt to interfere in the government of Pakistan until a major administrative crisis had appeared—although in 1951 some of the military failed to carry out a coup which was motivated by a disagreement with Liaqat Ali's Kashmir policy. The main cause of the interference of the bureaucracy was the weakness and inefficiency of the politicians. The trouble with strength and efficiency, however, is that these alone do not solve problems. Perhaps the only problem regarding which the

[8] *Working Committee of the East Bengal Muslim League,* Secretary's Minutes, May 17, 18, June 17, and Oct. 12, 1949; *Ibid.,* Feb. 26, 1950, Feb. 22, 1952.

service elite can be demonstrably shown to have had a particular opinion is that of the proper relation of religion and politics. As a class, the higher civil servants are convinced that religion and politics ought to be separated.

Not only was the country and the civil service ill-disposed toward the former prime minister, but it is evident that his cabinet was divided as well. Six members of Nazimuddin's cabinet agreed to serve under Muhammad Ali, the new prime minister. Dismissed along with Nazimuddin were Sardar Abdur Rab Nishtar, the former minister of industries, Fazlur Rahman who had been minister of commerce, economic affairs, and education, and Abdus Sattar Pirzada who had been minister of food. Nishtar was held responsible for the Islamic features of the BPC report, Fazlur Rahman for the unhappy foreign-exchange plight of Pakistan, and Pirzada for the food shortage.

The choice of Muhammad Ali as Pakistan's third prime minister was the nearest thing to an adroit political move that may be found in all the heavy-handed political history of Pakistan. Muhammad Ali had served as parliamentary secretary to Khwaja Nazimuddin and afterward as a member of the Provincial Ministry. He is, like Khwaja Nazimuddin, related to the Nawab of Dacca, and one of the Muslim minority of Bengali landed gentry. Some friction had arisen in the East Bengal government, it is said, as a result of Ali's ambition, for which he was given the post of ambassador to Burma. From there he moved on successfully to Ottawa and Washington. At the time of his appointment Mr. Ali was on a private visit to Pakistan and, apparently, had no idea that he would soon become the prime minister. His choice was calculated to weaken any notion that Nazimuddin's dismissal was caused by the parity proposal, rather than by the poor administration of the government. Having been so long out of politics,

Muhammad Ali had very few political enemies, but he also lacked personal popularity. Nevertheless, he was able to bring a certain vigor and freshness to the office, while doing his best to avoid antagonizing those whom he had replaced.

Since vigorous action and efficiency were the goals of this "constitutional" coup, it is reasonable to assume that few important policy changes were contemplated. Nazimuddin's decision to seek an American wheat grant was successfully pursued. His plans to try to solve the Kashmir problem and other outstanding issues by direct negotiation with Nehru were also followed, though with less success. Few changes were made in commercial policy, and the budget was not changed at all. Real changes, however, seemed to be suggested in the constitutional field.

THE DOMINANCE OF SECULARISM

In mid-May, 1953, Maulana Maududi and Maulana Niazi were both sentenced to death by a military court sitting at Lahore. The severity of these sentences is an indication of the outraged view that the less restrained branch of the services took of the effects of the Aḥmadi agitation. Religious persons throughout Pakistan were, of course, shocked at this action of the military, but perhaps even more astounded at the implied generalization of guilt. Maulana Niazi had been inciting a mob in a Lahore mosque when a police official was murdered just outside its walls; [9] Maududi had merely written a pamphlet on the Aḥmadi problem which was actually published after the 'ulamā' were arrested in Karachi.[10] The military court condemned not merely lawlessness but all religious agitation. The failure to distinguish between these two forms of "evil"

[9] *Punjab Disturbances,* p. 156.
[10] *Ibid.,* pp. 250–253.

was once again evident in the commutation of both sentences, first to fourteen years and then to two years. To rationalize the attitude of the military court, one might say that Niazi was indeed guilty of inciting to murder, but the politicians were responsible for creating the situation in which he could wield such extraordinary influence. Maududi, on the other hand, was the more dangerous, for he could create a situation of unrest among more important groups than the city mob. The military and many civil servants, apparently, have been so taken in by the propaganda of the Jamā'at they actually believe that Maududi single-handedly created the whole Islamic constitution controversy. Regardless of whether this view is correct, the important thing to note is that the Islamic constitution controversy was considered the root cause of the dreadful effects of the Aḥmadi agitation.

The appointment of Mr. Brohi as minister of law and parliamentary affairs was taken as an ill-omened event by the 'ulamā' and other proponents of an Islamic constitution. This man, who had outraged the feelings of all the religious conservatives and romantics throughout Pakistan, was now suddenly charged with the major responsibility for seeing the draft constitution through the Assembly. The apprehension of the 'ulamā' was increased as a result of statements by Prime Minister Muhammad Ali advocating the abolition of the 'ulamā' boards.[11] The Prime Minister also expressed his personal opinion that any person who called himself a Muslim and recited the Kalima (creed) was in fact a Muslim. Even Chaudhri Khaliquzzaman, whom Nazimuddin had appointed to replace Malik Feroz Khan Noon as governor of East Bengal, represented the danger to Pakistan as coming from the Communists and the theologians. Khaliquzzaman agreed that the state should be

---

[11] *Civil and Military Gazette,* April 25, 1953 (editorial).

guided by Islam, but that the "church" should be subordinate
to the state.[12] Sardar Abdur Rashid, the new chief minister of
the NWFP, told a press conference that he favored a secular
rather than a theocratic state in Pakistan.[13] The retention of
Chaudhri Zafrullah Khan in the reconstituted cabinet was also
read as a significant move, whereas the views of the Governor-
General, of Malik Noon, now chief minister of the Punjab, and
of the new minister of industries, had but recently been expressed in opposition to what the 'ulamā' called an Islamic
constitution.[14]

There was no strong reaction to these statements on the part
of the 'ulamā'. They were, in the aftermath of the Punjab
Disturbances, under a cloud. Vigorous government action had
suppressed the popular agitation, while the cabinet changes
promised at least some hope of an improvement in the economic condition of the country. Nor was there any political
opposition to this policy, for Nazimuddin had himself initiated
a propaganda campaign against the 'ulamā', not only in regard
to their position on the Aḥmadi issue but also regarding their
demands for a final veto power under the new constitution.
Newspapers which habitually supported Nazimuddin favored
the anti-'ulamā' reaction with much space and editorial comment. But this was before the government's attitude toward
the new constitution became fully clear.

THE INTERIM CONSTITUTION

Late in June the government announced that it was preparing an interim constitution which would be placed before the
Constituent Assembly during its fall session.[15] The interim
constitution would avoid all the controversial issues that pre-

12 *Ibid.*, June 25, 1953.
13 *Ibid.*, July 3, 1953.
14 *Dawn*, Jan. 1 and Feb. 13, 1953.
15 *Civil and Military Gazette*, July 1, 1953 (editorial).

vented agreement in the past, but it would give the country a working constitution of its own to replace the Government of India Act. It was, of course, immediately understood that such things as the Directive Principles of State Policy, the Procedure for Preventing Legislation Contrary to the Qur'ān and Sunnah, and other similar provisions would find no place in the new constitution. The interim constitution would declare that Pakistan (like India) would be a republic, and thus perform one of the major psychological tasks required of a new constitution. More important, however, was the reported provision by which it would "make way for a new Assembly" since the existing one had lost its representative character. Rumor rather than press release determined that the existing Assembly would be dissolved by the Governor-General under the interim constitution. There was even some hint that certain safeguards would be provided against parliamentary excesses, by giving the Governor-General discretionary power to veto legislation.[16] The Assembly, or the new parliament, would not be sovereign; it would rather represent local grievances. Government had become too complicated a business to be left to inexpert politicians, so the old theory of parliamentary sovereignty had to change with the times.

To understand these proposals we must bear in mind that the Constituent Assembly considered itself a sovereign body. Not since early in 1948 had it presented any of its decisions to the Governor-General for his assent. Under Jinnah, who was also president of the Assembly, it was decided that all acts and resolutions of the Assembly would be published by authority of the president of the Assembly, and not that of the Governor-General.[17] The need for assent by the Governor-General to acts of the Assembly was at best obscure in the Indian Inde-

[16] *Ibid.*, Aug. 5, 1953.
[17] *C.A.P. Debates,* Vol. III, no. 3 (May 22, 1948), p. 45.

pendence Act, though the Federal Court has since declared that it exists.[18] Moreover no provision was made for the dissolution of the Assembly until it had framed a constitution, or until it decided to dissolve itself.[19] Similarly, there was no provision for the removal of the Governor-General, though by Commonwealth Convention the Queen accepts the advice of the cabinet concerned in that regard. Under the circumstances prevailing in Pakistan, it is most likely that the Governor-General would have to be removed in *fact,* which was at the moment unlikely, before the Queen would recognize that removal. On the other hand, it might be argued that as long as Pakistan remained a dominion the Governor-General would enjoy all the prerogatives of the Queen, and could therefore dissolve the Assembly.[20]

Just how the new Assembly would be elected and what would be its composition was not explained. It is, however, clear that these moves were aimed against Bengali domination of the existing Assembly. The constitutional conflict in Pakistan has often been described in terms of Bengal-Punjab rivalry, largely due to the controversy between Nazimuddin and Daultana. Though there is hardly any question but what the group now in power has greater sympathies with the Punjab, care must be taken to differentiate this group from the Provincial Muslim League, or any of its numerous factions. Though noting these sympathies, it would seem that the Governor-General hoped to wrest power from the provinces, and the provincial delegations, and to make it possible for the central government to make decisions and pursue a policy independent of the demands of the provincial governments.

---

[18] *The All-Pakistan Legal Decisions* (May, 1955), pp. 289, 316.

[19] *Ibid.,* March, 1955, p. 118; the Federal Court subsequently denied this contention.

[20] *Federal Court of Pakistan Report on the Special Reference Made by H. E. the Governor-General of Pakistan,* p. 31.

Generally speaking, the view of the Governor-General seems to have been that the business of the cabinet is administration, for which loyal and efficient men are needed. Popularity or political ability is not a requisite for an executive position. Politicians are under no circumstances to interfere in the administration; their job is to support the administration, to raise the morale of the people, to represent their grievances to the government, and to pass all necessary laws.[21] It goes without saying that there was no room in this system for party rule. The Muslim League was expected to be absolutely subservient to the government in power at any time. Such a view of the role of the national party was not a startling departure from the practice of Liaqat Ali and Nazimuddin, but they both maintained intact the theory of party control by means of joining the offices of Prime Minister and League President. It was, however, impossible to invest Mr. Muhammad Ali with both immediately.

THE MUSLIM LEAGUE

Nazimuddin's control over the League, both directly and through the government and Parliamentary Party in the Assembly depended primarily upon the coöperation of the Bengal League. It is true that he did not see eye to eye with the Chief Minister of Bengal on the question of provincial autonomy, but this was not allowed to disrupt the smooth functioning of the League apparatus. With Nazimuddin's removal, however, the Chief Minister of East Bengal found himself in a quandary. Should he support the former prime minister and thereby condone the poor administration he had given the country, or should he repudiate him and win the support of the central government. The coming election in Bengal overshadowed all

---

[21] *Civil and Military Gazette,* Aug. 5, 1953 (editorial attacking pro-Bengali *Dawn*).

else in the political calculations of the provincial government, and from that point of view it seemed that there was little to gain in supporting Nazimuddin, for he had never been popular with the people. Moreover, the people of Bengal had come to distrust Nazimuddin for his statement favoring Urdu as the national language, for his unwillingness to abolish the federal tax on salt, for his failure to establish a naval base in East Bengal, and for a host of other acts of omission or commission, real or fancied. The most important gain which Nazimuddin's continuation in office might attain for Bengal was the most recent parity proposal, but there were still many in the province who insisted that representation should be on the basis of population alone.

If nothing was to be gained by supporting Nazimuddin, could anything be gained by supporting the new cabinet? Muhammad Ali, the new prime minister was from Bengal, and he had been a prominent member of the League. He was not associated with any of the sins of Nazimuddin's government, but he was identified with Nazimuddin's League faction. It is, however, probable that the deciding factor was the belief, not unfounded, either, that the Muslim League could only be effective insofar as it was an instrument of the government. Besides, the central government had the power, both legal and physical, to dismiss provincial ministers. Mr. Nurul Amin's rivals were strong and not unpopular. On the basis of calculations such as these, the East Bengal Muslim League Council, meeting on May 9, 1953, under the presidency of Mr. Nurul Amin, pledged full support to Muhammad Ali.[22]

The new prime minister himself disregarded the fact that he had replaced the President of the Muslim League. The change was taken as a repudiation of the man and not the League, for Muhammad Ali immediately plunged into the Sindh cam-

[22] *Ibid.*, May 10, 1953.

paign. He toured Sindh speaking on behalf of the candidates whom had been hand-picked by the Central League executive. The success of these candidates became in part the success of the new prime minister, and the League's monopoly on patriotism was extended.

Nazimuddin still retained the presidency of the League, but on May 26 the General Secretary of the Muslim League announced that a meeting had been requisitioned to consider a motion of no confidence against the President. Two weeks later Nazimuddin announced the names of the thirteen members of his Working Committee. Malik Noon, Qayyum Khan, and Nurul Amin promptly refused to serve on the Working Committee, and within a few days the Prime Minister's probable candidacy for the presidency of the League was discussed in the press.[23] Muhammad Ali was not elected president until the October meeting of the council,[24] but it was a foregone conclusion that the League presidency and the Prime ministership must go together. That is to say that even in acting against the highest officer of the League, it was the government, in this regard the Governor-General, who determined League disputes.

THE RETREAT TO PARITY

The Bengal Provincial League was primarily interested in strengthening their position in the forthcoming elections. Their support of the new prime minister was calculated to help toward that end. To support the new interim constitution was much more of a problem. The influence of Bengal in national affairs was at this point almost solely owing to their large delegation in the Assembly. Had the East Bengal League ac-

[23] *Ibid.*, May 26, 27, June 13, 16, 25, 1953 (for the whole development).
[24] *Text of the Resolutions Passed at the Meeting of the Council of the PML*, Oct. 17, 18, 19, 1953, Karachi, Resolution no. 4 (the vote was 258 to 36), p. 1.

cepted the interim constitution it seemed as though this advantage might also be lost. Nurul Amin would have been accused of selling out to West Pakistan to save his own position.

Moreover, it is unlikely, had he the desire to do so, that Nurul Amin could have given full support to the central government. The interim constitution threatened to unseat all the members of the Assembly; not merely to unseat them, but to accuse them of being unrepresentative. The voters of East Bengal would, in fact, be invited to elect others who would be more representative of their interests.

The political opposition emanating from East Bengal brought an announcement from the Prime Minister that, though the government was determined to go ahead with the interim constitution, it had no intention of giving one man the power to dissolve the Constituent Assembly.[25] The government did not propose to tamper with the "sovereign character" of the Assembly. Opposition continued to develop during September until, just prior to the meeting of the Assembly, the council of the East Pakistan League resolved to oppose the interim constitution.[26]

When the Parliamentary Party met on September 22, it was decided to adjourn the Assembly for two weeks to allow the various leaders to iron out their differences on the Basic Principles Report. There followed a series of meetings between the Prime Minister and the provincial chief ministers. Three suggestions came from the Punjab for settling the key question of the composition of the future parliament, at least two of which were based on parity of representation between East and West Pakistan. One of these contemplated merging all the states and provinces of West Pakistan into a single unit, but

[25] *Civil and Military Gazette,* Aug. 16, 1953.
[26] *Ibid.,* Sept. 17, 1953 (all of the following developments were reported in the press).

this was opposed by the Chief Minister of Sindh and the Chief Minister of Bahawalpur. Nurul Amin was willing to accept the second, which provided for a "Zonal Federation" in West Pakistan, with indirect elections to parliament from a "Zonal Assembly," because it implied an increase in provincial power. On October 3 an agreement was reached and the interim constitution plan was forgotten.

The new formula was presented to the Assembly on October 7 by Muhammad Ali in opening discussion on a motion to consider the Report of the Basic Principles Committee. The "Muhammad Ali formula" provided for parity in the combined chambers, each of which would have equal powers. Bengal would have a majority of seats in the House of People while the country would be divided into five areas which would be equally represented in the House of Units. The breakdown was as follows:

Section	Upper House	Lower House	Total
East Bengal	10	165	175
Punjab	10	75	85
NWFP, Frontier States, Tribal Areas	10	24	34
Sind and Khairpur	10	19	29
Baluchistan, BSU, Bahawalpur, Karachi	10	17	27
Total	50	300	350

Representation from the smaller units of West Pakistan within the bloc quotas of ten each was to be on the basis of population, and nothing was said about merging them. In fact it would hardly be possible to merge Bahawalpur, Karachi, and Baluchistan, which are not contiguous. Additional safeguards were to be provided by requiring the concurrence of at least 30 per cent of the members from each wing in votes of confidence and other important measures, and by requiring that the Governor-General and the Prime Minister come from opposite wings.[27]

The plan was accepted unanimously by the Muslim League Parliamentary Party and by the provincial chief ministers. The principal merit of the formula, insofar as the Punjab was concerned, was a slightly larger share of seats. Beyond the six or seven seats which this entailed, its benefits for the Punjab were few indeed except, of course, equal status for the Upper House wherein there would be numerically equal provincial delegations. The 30 per cent rule meant little, except as an additional safeguard for East Pakistan, since about one-fourth of the East Pakistan seats would be filled by Hindus under separate electorates. Under such circumstances the Bengal delegation would have to win over at least that many seats from West Pakistan. The provisions regarding the Governor-General and the Prime Minister were soon found to be too unwieldy, and were dropped from the formula or suggested as a possible voluntary convention.

It is significant that the Chief Minister of the Punjab did not deem it necessary to speak on the merits of the new formula at the time of the introductory motion. When the formula was actually brought before the Assembly as an amendment to the BPC report it was accepted without any discussion. The formula was openly opposed by only Mr. Fazl al-Haqq of East Bengal and Mian Iftikharuddin of the Punjab, both of whom preferred greater provincial autonomy.[28]

THE RETURN TO PARLIAMENTARY SUPREMACY

At the time the defeat of the interim constitution seemed much more than a temporary set-back for the Governor-General. In fact the entire political complexion of the country

[27] *C.A.P. Debates,* Vol. XV, no. 2 (Oct. 7, 1953), pp. 12–17.
[28] *Ibid.,* Vol. XV, no. 2 (Oct. 7, 1953), p. 19; Vol. XV, no. 13, pp. 397 ff.

seemed to be changed. The power of political decision once again rested with the Assembly. The cabinet, which had been looked upon as an instrument of the Governor-General, became the servant of the Assembly, in which the Bengal delegation now reëmerged as the dominant group. The former ministerial group of Nazimuddin with its West Pakistan allies continued to coöperate with the provincially oriented bloc of Nurul Amin, and it retained a great deal of initiative in matters relating to the constitution.

The stability and strength of the new cabinet depended at least as much upon the Assembly as it did upon the Governor-General, while the achievement of such an important agreement as the Muhammad Ali formula greatly increased public confidence in the Assembly. Shortly after the agreement, the Prime Minister was elected president of the Pakistan Muslim League and it looked as though the rather unconventional constitutional arrangement had been regularized by the restoration of party government. From this point on the Prime Minister treaded a narrow path between the party caucus room and Government House, without endearing himself at either place, but maintaining the required link between the actual and the theoretical sources of power in the state. His policies underwent severe criticism in the legislature, and in the Assembly he was almost powerless to prevent the substantial approval of the BPC report.

Amendments to the report, which attempted more and more to restrict the power of the Governor-General, were gradually adopted—while the attitude of the Prime Minister shifted from hostility to ambivalence, and thence to support tempered by a certain amount of prudent apprehension. To the extent that the power of the Governor-General was restricted, the position of the Prime Minister might be more secure, provided he could really command the confidence of the House. On the other hand, to the extent that far-reaching changes of this sort were brought into the future constitution there was a greater likelihood of the Governor-General exerting his demonstrated power of changing the ministry. The problem of the Governor-General was not so much that he failed to control his prime minister. It was rather that he had failed to change the Assembly.

The Islamic constitution issue was considerably affected by the rather remarkable shift in the distribution of political power that was occasioned by these events. The Bengali-dominated Assembly was now forced to establish its popularity against the Governor-General's claim to responsibility. Where Western politicians might indulge in national flag-waving, the Bengalis and their allies from the smaller provinces of West Pakistan took up the banner of Islam. Such political tactics were all the more pointed because of the temporary ascendancy of an unabashed secularism. The immediate result was the drafting of a constitution that satisfied the religious groups in almost every way, but the combination of extremes brought about a combination of failures.

11 *Islamic Constitution*

RENEWED ACTIVITY OF THE 'ULAMĀ'

Religious opposition to the interim constitution, though ineffective during the early summer, was not entirely negligible. Nearly all religious groups participated, including both 'ulamā' organizations and Jamā'at-i-Islāmi; but the most notable thing about this opposition was the fact that it neither stressed the agreed amendments of the 'ulamā' 's convention of January, 1953, nor the recommendations of the Board of Ta'līmat-i-Islāmīa. The reasons for this rather surprising attitude may be ascribed to the fact that both the "Amendments" and the "Views" were tied to the proposals of the Basic Principles Committee. Politically unfeasible as the BPC report seemed to be at the time it was wise to dissociate the two. Furthermore, the government's attitude bespoke an intention to withdraw all the concessions thus far made to those who pressed for an Islamic constitution. The anti-Aḥmadi agitation, and the interim constitution plan which resulted from it, had set the Islamic constitution movement back to where it was five years before. The issue was no longer the nature of an Islamic constitution, but the necessity and value of one.

The approach followed by Mufti Muhammad Shafi of the Board of Ta'līmat-i-Islāmīa in a couple of public lectures was reminiscent of the arguments of the 1948–1950 period.[1] One important change was not added and one omission was made. Mr. Brohi's presence in the cabinet determined that the issue as to whether the Qur'ān supplied the basis for a constitution would be reopened. Happily enough Mufti Shafi did not choose to flog the half-dead horse of "Islamic theocracy"— this was left to become the special field of Jamā'at-i-Islāmi.[2] Shafi reasserted the special right of the 'ulamā' to interpret the Qur'ān in an argument borrowed from Maududi's Bar Association address.[3] Continuing to echo Maududi he asserted that the Qur'ān "deals with the problems of the Constitution" but that the "constitutional principles it has enunciated are found scattered in different chapters."[4] In one of those chapters he found the basis for the following Qur'ānic constitutional principle:

> If, in connection with any law, a difference of opinion arises between the rulers and the ruled as to whether that particular law is in conformity with the Shariah or not, decision will ultimately and invariably rest with the Quran and the Sunnah, which in its practical form, will take the shape of the *decision of experts of the Quran and Sunnah*.[5]

He went on to cite the most famous of the "political" verses of the Qur'ān (IV:59) interpreting the term "ul al-amr" (those

[1] Hazrat Maulana Mufti Muhammad Shafi, *Basic Principles of the Quranic Constitution of the State* (Karachi, 1953), 32 pp.

[2] E.g., Abdul Hameed, "Theocracy versus the Islamic State," *The Voice of Islam* (July, 1953), pp. 357–366 (afterward separately published by Jamā'at-i-Islāmi).

[3] See p. 279, above.

[4] Shafi, *op. cit.*, p. 3.

[5] *Ibid.*, p. 6.

in authority) to include "both the 'ulamā' and the men in governmental authority in the State." [6]

There are few clearer statements of the conservative position than that of Mufti Shafi, and few better illustrations of the sources from which the 'ulamā' of Pakistan may draw their inspiration. Mufti Shafi delivered his lecture and added his analysis on and after July 12, 1953. It was afterward published in two English biweeklies [7] during that summer and again in pamphlet form in September. During October it was quoted in the Assembly.[8] It was apparently the most important religious pamphlet of the period. It was published in English for the particular benefit of "the Constituent Assembly and the Ministers of our State," [9] but no reference to the interim constitution was made at all.

When political opposition to the interim constitution gained some strength it turned almost automatically to the antireligious implications of the still unknown document.[10] Nazimuddin, Sardar Nishtar, and Fazlur Rahman made no great effort to justify their own administration; they sought rather to justify themselves in terms of their efforts to give the country an Islamic constitution. It is pertinent to note that they did not differentiate between the diverse recommendations of the BPC; all were Islamic, including, no doubt, the Nazimuddin parity formula. For most of the members of the Assembly, justification of the BPC report meant the justification of their comparatively long tenancy of the chamber. It was, then, the only logical answer to the interim constitution.

The voters of Bengal had long ago been convinced that their prosperity and welfare depended far more upon the central than upon the provincial government. It was to change this

---

[6] *Ibid.*, p. 7.
[7] *Yaqeen* and *al-Islam.*
[8] *C.A.P. Debates,* Vol. XV, no. 9 (Oct. 20, 1953), pp. 240–243.
[9] Shafi, *op. cit.,* p. ii.
[10] *Civil and Military Gazette,* Sept. 18, 1953.

that the demand for provincial autonomy was pressed by Bengal. Be that as it may, the Bengal elections would be fought to a great extent upon the achievements of the Bengal delegation in the Assembly. There was little in the way of legislation that could be pointed to with advantage by the Bengal Muslim League; the BPC report was their only achievement. Since parity was not popular in East Bengal the East Bengal League would appear before their constituents as the upholders and defenders of Islam, as the framers of an Islamic constitution.

The Jamī'at-al-'Ulamā'-i-Pākistān (Bareilly) are one of the most accurate political weathervanes in Pakistan. A week before the Assembly was to meet, the General Secretary of that organization demanded that the BPC report, *as amended by the 'ulamā' in their meetings in January, 1953,* be adopted. He admitted that the provision for distribution of seats might be changed but urged against the interim constitution.[11] It was only later that the Jamī'at-al-'Ulamā'-i-Islām met to condemn the interim constitution plan and to demand an Islamic constitution.[12]

The 'ulamā' therefore permitted themselves to be dragged along in support of the Bengali bloc. Their purpose was to salvage as much as they could of their past efforts, but they also tied the fate of the Islamic constitution to that of the Bengal Muslim League and the BPC report.

THE SELECT COMMITTEE OF THE PARLIAMENTARY PARTY

As the preliminary discussion of the BPC report got under way, its controversial aspects were discussed by the Parliamentary Party, whence the religious issue was further referred to a select committee composed of Nazimuddin, three of his

[11] *Ibid.,* Sept. 15, 1953; the divergence from Shafi's approach is significant.
[12] *Ibid.,* Sept. 29, 1953.

supporters, and Mr. Brohi.[13] This group struggled for weeks with such questions as whether the Head of the State must be a Muslim, whether Pakistan should be called an Islamic state, whether Islam should be declared the state religion, and whether issues concerning the "repugnancy" of certain laws to the Qur'ān and Sunnah should be referred to the Supreme Court.

During this period the 'ulamā' were extremely active, as were members of Jamā'at-i-Islāmi. Even Saiyid Sulaiman Nadvi, then on his deathbed, made a last effort. He issued a widely publicized statement in which he urged that Pakistan be declared an Islamic republic, that Islam be the state religion, that the Objectives Resolution be made an "integral part" of the constitution, that the amendments of the 'ulamā' to the BPC report (of January, 1953) and any others that might be made be incorporated, and "sixthly that the Head of the State should not be vested with autocratic and dictatorial Powers for dismissing ministeries [*sic*] and dissolving Parliament arbitrarily, without the advice of the popularly elected Council of Ministers enjoying the confidence of the popularly elected Legislature and the people." [14]

Nazimuddin once again became the focal point of religious pressure, but others too, including Brohi, were visited, and had the 'ulamā' 's amendments explained to them. So determined was Nazimuddin to justify his own work that he was disinclined to support the 'ulamā' on their Supreme Court amendment to the "repugnancy clause." He argued that the 'ulamā' did not realize what was best for them, and spoke ominously of the potential effects of the report on the Punjab Disturbances.[15]

[13] *Dawn,* Oct. 11, 1953.
[14] *Yaqeen,* Nov. 7; *Dawn,* Oct. 19, 1953.
[15] See p. 342, below.

The debate which had already begun in the Assembly was turned immediately to religious issues by the Hindus, who did their utmost to show the dangers and follies of an Islamic constitution. Mr. Bhupendra Kumar Datta repeated the charge that the state would be theocratic and cited Professor Sherwani as his authority.[16] He referred to the 'ulamā' boards as the "Third House" of the legislature, and asserted, on the basis of the same authority, that Islamic and parliamentary government were incompatible. He disregarded the provision by which the Legislature might overrule the decision of the 'ulamā' board, accusing the BPC of being unable to rely upon "the good sense of the collective body of the elected Muslim representatives of the people." [17] Then, arguing the other side, Datta proceeded to show how the report was not consistently Islamic since it provided for preventive detention, party government, and handsome pay and allowances to the Head of the State. From there the attack was directed against the 'ulamā':

> If four or five Ulemas re-shape the existing laws so as to make them conform to the Shariat according to their light, where is the guarantee that four hundred or five hundred other Maulanas, Maulvis and Mullahs will not declare the favoured four or five as infidels.[18]

He thought that the provisions regarding the qualifications and related oath of the Head of the State would lead to hereditary kingship in a slur at the unpleasant facts of Muslim history. He called Turkey a "great Islamic State," and he quoted the praise of Turkey's "laicism" from the handbook on world constitutions prepared for the Constituent Assembly by its secretary.[19] Separate electorates for Hindus were at-

---

[16] *C.A.P. Debates,* Vol. XV, no. 2 (Oct. 7, 1953), p. 23. Professor Sherwani is the author of *Muslim Political Thought and Administration.*

[17] *Ibid.,* p. 25.

[18] *Ibid.,* p. 28.

[19] *Ibid.,* p. 31.

tacked vigorously, and he compared their position with that of the Christians of Najran, the Jews of Khaibar, and the Zoroastrians of Tabaristan. Datta ended with an impassioned plea on behalf of "maximum decentralization of political power." [20]

The eight Hindus of the Congress Party who spoke on the motion followed B. K. Datta's lead. Seth Sukhdev objected to any suggestion of a derogation from the power of the legislature. [21] Dhirendra Nath Datta objected that the report was being considered in "Parda," that is, in the Select Committee of the Muslim League Parliamentary Party, implying that speeches in the Assembly could do no good. [22] He urged against the "Mulla Board," opposing it with the "ijmā' " argument that "most of the Members would belong to the Muslim Community. They will know what is repugnant to the principles of the Holy Quran." [23] Professor Chakravarty wanted the "whole world" to know that separate electorates were being forced upon the minority community. [24] He suggested that the "repugnancy clause" might endanger the personal law of the non-Muslims, but then he went on to quote an editorial from a back issue of the *Morning News* which argued the difficulties of instituting the Sharī'a in Pakistan. [25] For his pains he was reported by the *Morning News* on the following day as "assailing Islam." [26] Kamini Kumar Datta requested that the explicit "principles and rules" of the Sharī'a relating to the state be brought forward in place of vague generalizations. [27] Babesh Chandra Nandy thought that Board of 'ulamā' was only a political device, whereby the support of the conserva-

[20] *Ibid.*, p. 45.
[21] *Ibid.*, p. 51.
[22] *Ibid.*, p. 53.
[23] *Ibid.*, no. 3 (Oct. 8, 1953), p. 59.
[24] *Ibid.*, no. 4 (Oct. 9, 1953), p. 76.
[25] *Ibid.*, p. 78.
[26] *Ibid.*, no. 5 (Oct. 10, 1953), p. 91.
[27] *Ibid.*, p. 108.

tive religious forces was to be acquired. On the subject of the Head of the State he cited Liaqat Ali Khan's explicit declaration in the Assembly that "a non-Muslim can be the Head of the Administration under a constitutional Government with limited authority. . . ." [28] Sris Chandra Chattopadhyaya, a signatory of the report, favored its consideration, but he wanted to make it clear that the report was the result of a majority decision. He further stated that certain decisions to which he had agreed had been changed, and so to defend his own position he requested that the minutes of the meetings of the Suggestions Sub-Committee be made available.[29] The Hindus, he said, were not being associated with the real task of constitution making, for he daily read in the newspapers of some substantive decision regarding the amendment or acceptance of various provisions by the Muslim League Parliamentary Party. Even Bhandara, the representative of the Parsis, who favored an Islamic state and separate electorates, opposed the Board of 'ulamā' and the requirement that the Head of the State be a Muslim on the ground that they were unnecessary though harmless.[30]

Mian Iftikharuddin and Shaukat Hayat Khan, who were opposed to the Muhammad Ali formula, were joined by two other Muslims in opposing the whole idea of an Islamic state, or each of the major "Islamic" provisions then under discussion.[31] Thirty-two other Muslims, all members of the Muslim League, favored the new parity proposals and the Islamic state notion; though the members from Khairpur, Baluchistan, and Karachi were all more concerned with the fate of their own units in the federation.[32]

Despite the general unity on the issue of whether Pakistan

[28] *Ibid.*, no. 8 (Oct. 19, 1953), p. 204.
[29] *Ibid.*, no. 13 (Oct. 24, 1953), p. 425.
[30] *Ibid.*. no. 2 (Oct. 7, 1953), p. 47.
[31] *Ibid.*, nos. 3, 6, 9, 11, pp. 59, 127, 244, 292.
[32] *Ibid.*, nos. 6 and 8, pp. 113, 122, 219.

was to be an Islamic state, there seems to have been some hesitation to speak out clearly in favor of provisions that were still under discussion in the Parliamentary Party. Most of the members from Bengal used up a large part of their time in excusing the long delay in constitution making, in recalling the struggle for Pakistan, in thanking God that an agreed formula had been worked out, in hailing the millennium when all the ideals of Islam would be realized through an Islamic constitution, and in praising the virtues of Islam. But when all this was said only six members specifically demanded that the Head of the State be a Muslim, only two specifically demanded that Islam be declared the state religion, and only eight specifically demanded that Pakistan be declared an Islamic republic.[33]

With regard to the Head of the State, some thought it was necessary since there were certain duties incumbent upon the head of an Islamic state which could only be performed by a Muslim.[34] Others used the "ideological state" argument of Maulana Shabbir Ahmad Usmani.[35] Perhaps the most enlightening of all was the explanation presented by Abdulla al-Mahmood:

> The other day, I met Maulana Ehtasham-ul-Haque and discussed the whole matter with him. Some of my friends think it is only a symbol. But it is not so; it is fundamental like a power house generating electricity. The cables and wirings have been fitted. I am a Muslim. I believe in Allah. My religion is Islam. I want that proper bulb should be fitted so that the electricity, that is generated, should give proper light. Therefore . . . we must have a Muslim as the Head of the State.[36]

[33] *Ibid.,* nos. 4, 5, 6, 8, 10, 11, 13, 14, pp. 95, 136, 140, 153, 259, 311; 95, 209, 210; 87, 155, 267, 316, 391, 436, 452, 461.
[34] This is in the classical tradition.
[35] See p. 385, Appendix A.
[36] *C.A.P. Debates,* Vol. XV, no. 11 (Oct. 22, 1953), p. 313.

The significance of this statement, coming as it does (by report) from one of the orthodox 'ulamā' should not be overlooked. It represents the classical association of the caliphate with the divine guidance of the community.

The 'ulamā' boards were opposed by fourteen Muslim members, five of whom argued that the Muslim members of the legislature were themselves competent to decide whether or not a bill was "repugnant" to the Qur'ān or Sunnah. They argued against Mufti Shafi and Abu'l-Ala Maududi that interpretation is not the special monopoly of any one group. Though some admitted that they were not well versed in Islamic learning,[37] they insisted that all Muslims enjoyed the right to determine the law themselves.[38] One suggested that the provision for the board was a political trick, another that the 'ulamā' should stand for election if they wanted to influence legislation, while others simply announced their opposition to the "mullahs." [39]

Shaukat Hayat noticed early in the debate a tendency to avoid discussing the 'ulamā' boards, and in fact thirteen members from Bengal did not mention the boards though they all praised the "repugnancy clause" which the boards were to implement.[40] The existing clause of the BPC report did receive a form of support from six members.[41] These pointed out that according to the exact text the words 'ulamā' or mullahs were nowhere mentioned. All that it said was persons well versed in Islamic laws would be appointed to a board by the Head of the State.

Only five members argued in favor of referring all questions of "repugnancy" to the Qur'ān and Sunnah to the Supreme Court. One said that the Federal Court (Supreme Court) had

[37] *Ibid.*, nos. 6 and 11, pp. 128, 291.
[38] *Ibid.*, nos. 5, 6, 14, pp. 95, 129, 142, 450–451; 117.
[39] *Ibid.*, nos. 2, 6, 10, pp. 117, 130, 256; 50.
[40] *Ibid.*, nos. 6, 8, 9, 11, 13, pp. 120, 124, 129, 140, 152, 153, 208, 210, 223, 283, 288, 409, 433, 436.
[41] *Ibid.*, nos. 6 and 7, pp. 129, 147, 166, 177.

the "right" to decide such questions. Another pointed out the
fact that foreign judges had given some "very brilliant and
illuminating judgments" regarding cases on Muslim personal
laws. He suggested that the court might even request advice of
the 'ulamā' on some questions.[42] Mr. Fazlur Rahman thought
that the Supreme Court should specifically be given jurisdiction in cases under the "repugnancy clause" which they
would not otherwise enjoy. He thought that provision to this
effect would bring about a revolution in Islamic law. It would
reopen the gate of ijtihād which, he said, had been closed as
a remedy to "anarchism in ijtihād." He asserted that ijtihād,
qiyās, and ijmā' were the guarantee of the dynamic character of
Islamic law, but he made no attempt to explain how ijmā'
might work in Pakistan.[43] Dr. Omar Hayat Malik tried to
answer objections that had been raised against extending the
jurisdiction of the Supreme Court to "repugnancy" questions.
(These objections had not been raised in the Assembly, nor in
the press; perhaps they had been raised in the select committee
still discussing the issue.) Ambassador Malik agreed that there
might be some difficulties, but these could be eliminated or
minimized if the government would seek "legal" advice before
proposing a bill and if the Supreme Court would grant leave to
raise such an objection only if a prima-facie case existed.[44] He
felt that as cases are dealt with, and the law codified, the number of such cases would gradually diminish. The major advantage to be gained would be the reopening of the gate of
ijtihād. He condemned the "mullahs" who thought ijtihād
sinful, and insisted that Islam could adapt itself to modern
conditions only through "a continuous process of interpretation
and re-interpretation."

The proposition that reference of "repugnancy" questions to

[42] *Ibid.,* no. 4 (Oct. 9, 1953), p. 88.
[43] *Ibid.,* no. 10 (Oct. 21, 1953), p. 260.
[44] *Ibid.,* pp. 268, 269.

the Supreme Court would reopen the gate of ijtihād was hardly compatible with the further suggestions of the 'ulamā' that five of their number be associated with the court for such cases. If the judges themselves should be adherents of *taqlīd* there would be no ijtihād. On the other hand, there was no denying the dearth of competent judges who were also well trained in Islamic jurisprudence. The solution suggested by Dr. Malik is reminiscent of a passage in Maududi's Law College lecture of 1948.[45]

It would be imperfect in the beginning, but as time goes on, if we so desire, we can create and develop a type of person that will suit in a matter like this. We can make a provision in Law Colleges, as Mr. Brohi proposed, so that this type of persons or this type of Muslims is generated, who have the capacity to understand what is given in the Qur'ān and the Sunnah and also have the capacity of understanding the conditions as they obtain in the modern world and are applying the laws of Islam to modern conditions.[46]

On the day after Mr. Fazlur Rahman and Dr. Malik spoke of ijtihād, the Select Committee made its decision, and on October 23, 1953, that decision was announced to the Assembly by Mr. Brohi in the course of a marathon address covering more than fifty pages in the official report. Mr. Brohi related the limitations upon the powers of the legislature in the "repugnancy clause" to those expressed in the Objectives Resolution: "The competence of the legislature to enact a law is subject

[45] Maududi, *The Means and Methods of Inforcing Islamic Law in Pakistan* (Second Law College Lecture): "The third important measure will be to change the prevailing method of education in our Law Colleges and replace it by such reformed curriculum and mode of imparting education as may prepare the students both academically and morally for the enforcement of Islamic Law in the country" (p. 46).

[46] *C.A.P. Debates,* Vol. XV, p. 270.

to limitations and barriers prescribed by God and every legislature must know that its authority is not unlimited but limited,
restricted and not unrestricted." [47]

The method of implementing this clause as suggested by the
report was improper, he thought, for "no class of persons is
competent to arrogate to himself the position of being the sole
interpreter of the law of God." This is, of course, the old argument against the Islamic state based on the epithet theocracy.
The argument was repeated many times in the House both
by those who wanted the legislature to decide "repugnancy"
questions and those who wanted them referred to the Supreme
Court. It is difficult to understand why, if this argument is to
be the basis of the decision, the judges of the Supreme Court
should by constitutional law be made "competent to arrogate
to themselves the position of the sole interpreters of the law of
God; but the Minister of Law went on

> to announce that we shall be moving an amendment on the
> floor of the House so that the Honourable Members may con-
> sider the whole position when we go on to discuss the Report
> clause by clause that the ultimate adjudication power of this
> repugnancy clause be vested in the Supreme Court of Pak-
> istan. It will be for our Judges in the Supreme Court, con-
> stituted with the authority of law, to interpret for all practical
> purposes what that law is. If the argument be once again that
> they are human and that they can err, the answer to that
> would be that there is no other authority available to us at all.
> Even the Law of God, as it stands revealed, has to be under-
> stood by man.[48]

This decision of the Muslim League Parliamentary Party
was shortly followed by others confirming the BPC's recom-

[47] *Ibid.*, no. 12 (Oct. 23, 1953), p. 340.
[48] *Ibid.*

mendation that the Head of the State be a Muslim and accepting the amendment of the 'ulamā' that the name of the state
be the "Islamic Republic of Pakistan."

THE CONSIDERATION OF THE REPORT

After the Select Committee concluded its deliberations the
motion for consideration of the report was passed and the BPC
report was taken up clause by clause. The first change suggested by Maulana Akram Khan was that the word "God"
be changed to "Allah" wherever it occurred in the report.[49]
This amendment passed with little opposition from the Hindus, but from here on the members of the Congress Party
fought tooth and nail against nearly every Islamic provision
of the report. Mr. B. K. Datta went so far as to suggest that
teaching of the Qur'ān and Sunnah to the *Muslims* should be
made "attractive" rather than "compulsory."[50] His attempt
failed, and in fact the Hindus accomplished little more than
the harassment of the Muslim members. On every opportunity
they stressed their rights as a minority and their fear of forcible
conversion or second-class citizenship in an Islamic state. At
other times they might quote hadīth or Qur'ān or the "Views"
of the Board of Ta'līmat-i-Islāmīa if such sources could support
their position. They managed, in all, to win a clause safeguarding the personal law of non-Muslims in the event of the
codification of certain injunctions of the Qur'ān and Sunnah
and one exempting the Hindus from payment of taxes to
support a governmental organization for propagating Islam
and urging or enforcing its practices.[51] On the whole they
were, understandably, unsympathetic to the idea of an Islamic

[49] *Ibid.,* no. 16 (Oct. 28, 1953), p. 485.
[50] *Ibid.,* p. 501.
[51] *Ibid.,* no. 20 (Nov. 2, 1953), p. 656.

state. Their arguments were not always cogent (though more often than was true of the Muslims), and at times they resorted to some rather spiteful obstructionism.[52]

An interesting discussion took place concerning the safeguarding of non-Muslim personal law. Both Mr. B. C. Nandy and Professor Chakravarty had asked for such safeguards when the Minister of Law suggested that the following clause be added: ". . . duly safeguarding the personal laws of the non-Muslims as has been enjoined by the Holy Qur'ān and Sunnah." Fearing that this phrasing might in some way qualify even the general term "safeguarding" the Hindus refused to accept it. The Muslims for their part insisted that even in this matter they were following the dictates of Islam, and they went on to cite the fact that no such safeguards could be expected under a secular democratic government.[53] A compromise was worked out by the President of the Assembly who suggested the following wording and punctuation: ". . . duly safeguarding, has been enjoined by the Holy Qur'ān and Sunnah, the personal laws of Non-Muslims." [54]

Only slight changes were made in the Directive Principles of State Policy. Riba (usury) was to be eliminated "as and when" possible rather than "as soon as." [55] The 'ulamā' had been satisfied with this provision as it stood. Indeed the new wording was doubtlessly an unwelcome change. Mr. Abdulla al-Mahmud explained that "some means have to be devised *as to when* we can eliminate Riba." The emphasis was really on the word "as" rather than "when." Mr. Brohi went on to suggest that part of the procedure for eliminating "riba" would probably involve a new definition of the term.

[52] *Ibid.*, nos. 18 and 19 (Oct. 30, 31, 1953), pp. 620, 626, 627.
[53] *Ibid.*, no. 16 (Oct. 28, 1953), pp. 521 ff.
[54] *Ibid.*, p. 526.
[55] *Ibid.*, p. 503.

The essential thing to be noted about riba is that although the word appears in Quran, its actual practice, as discoverable from the case law in relation to the historical development of this doctrine of Riba is of a kind and character that we are entitled to adjust it to suit the given conditions and it has in fact been so adjusted down the ages.[56]

As understood by the 'ulamā' and Maulana Maududi, "riba" means *interest,* whether large or small; that too is the way the Governor of the State Bank understood the term in 1949.[57]

When the state had been directed to discourage un-Islamic, parochial tendencies, the 'ulamā' suggested that linguistic prejudices be similarly proscribed.[58] Instead, "sectarian and provincial" feelings were added to this directive.[59] "Sectarian" may have been a reference to the recent anti-Aḥmadi agitation, and "provincialism" could have referred to any group in the Assembly, though it most probably referred to all those who opposed the Muhammad Ali formula. The interest of the 'ulamā' in discouraging "linguistic feelings," whatever that may mean, was related to the state language controversy. Urdu is, of course, the language of religious groups in Pakistan, but the people of Bengal are more religiously orthodox and somewhat more politically aware than those in the West. This is the sort of problem that led several Bengali members to suggest *Arabic* as the state language. In any case, language was one of the elements of provincialism which Mr. Brohi, as opposed to the 'ulamā', thought worth preserving. Only un-Islamic provincialism would not be countenanced.[60]

[56] *Ibid.,* p. 511.

[57] Maududi, *The Economic Problem of Man and Its Islamic Solution,* p. 46; Walter Godfrey, *Pakistan: Economic and Commercial Conditions* (London, 1951), p. 1.

[58] *Ulama's Amendments,* p. 8.

[59] *C.A.P. Debates,* Vol. XV, no. 16, p. 548.

[60] *Ibid.,* p. 547.

It will be remembered that the provision regarding the qualifications of the head of an Islamic state, which so engrossed the attention of the Board of Ta'līmat-i-Islāmīa, had been relegated to the section on the Directive Principles of State Policy. At the time the intention was to satisfy the 'ulamā' without making such things as the religious behavior of the Head of the State a justiciable issue under the constitution. In so doing no particular attention was paid, as well it might not while all the conventions of dominion parliamentary government were observed, to the phrasing that was actually based on the medieval theory of the qualifications of the caliph. This directive principle provided that the Head of the State must have ability, character, integrity, and piety, and be fit to conduct the affairs of state in accordance with the Objectives Resolution.[61] On the other hand, just as the Head of the State was not really to conduct the affairs of state, so he was not really to have all these qualifications. The board's view that these qualifications would become applicable to members of the cabinet in a parliamentary system was disregarded. Now even the fiction of the Pakistan caliphate was done away with in the searching effort of the Assembly to restrict the powers of the Head of the State under the future constitution. Mr. Brohi moved, and the Assembly adopted, an amendment to this directive requiring that the Head of the State merely be "fit to perform his duties and obligations in accordance with the Objectives Resolution." [62]

The directive principle by which the state was to ensure justice in the courts to all free of payment was deleted.[63] Mr. Chattopadhyaya of the Congress strongly objected to this action and he cited the views of the Board of Ta'limat-i-

---

[61] *Ibid.*, Vol. XII, no. 2, Appendix I, p. 85.
[62] *Ibid.*, Vol. XV, no. 16, p. 548.
[63] *Ibid.*, pp. 561 ff.

Islāmīa in his own support. He contended that the exorbitant court fees in East Pakistan constituted a denial of justice, and he went on to taunt the Muslim League for not living up to their declared intention of establishing an Islamic government. In answer, Brohi admitted that the court fee was anti-Islamic, but he differentiated between the ideal that was to be achieved and that which was possible under existing conditions.[64]

A slight gain was registered by the 'ulamā' when a directive principle was added instructing the state to revise the pay structure of the civil service so as to reduce the existing disparities to a minimum.[65] The 'ulamā' had suggested a similar amendment, but they had avoided referring to that mysterious 1 to 40 ratio for the maximum pay disparity that seems to have fixed itself in the mind of many reformers.[66] Failing any specific ratio or even a common criterion for such readjustment the clause has little meaning, and certainly little meaning as an "Islamic provision." Nevertheless it may be taken as a victory for the 'ulamā'.

On the whole there was little for the 'ulamā' to be pleased about in the Directive Principles as adopted by the Assembly. Only one of the eleven amendments they proposed was accepted, and even that was a somewhat clouded issue. Moreover, other changes were made which considerably weakened the influence of both the Objectives Resolution and the Directive Principles themselves. From the first directive, in the sentence "the state shall be guided in all its activities by . . . the Objectives Resolution," the word "all" was omitted.[67] At the end of the chapter a new clause was added limiting the scope of the directives as follows: "The provisions contained in this chapter are intended for the general guidance of the

[64] *Ibid.*, p. 565.
[65] *Ibid.*, no. 17 (Oct. 29, 1953), p. 588.
[66] *Ulama's Amendments*, p. 9.
[67] *C.A.P. Debates*, Vol. XV, no. 16, p. 498.

State. The application . . . shall be the duty of the State but shall not be enforceable in any court of Law.[68]

The requirement that the Head of the State be a Muslim was retained in accordance with the decision of the Select Committee of the League Parliamentary Party.[69] The provision that the pay and allowances of the Head of the State would be according to the "status and dignity" of that office was removed in accordance with the requirement of the Board of Ta'līmat-i-Islāmīa, though the 'ulamā' said nothing about it in their amendments.[70] In accordance with the 'ulamā' 's amendments, disqualification for voting or holding office on account of conviction for some offense was restricted by providing that such offense be one involving "moral turpitude." [71] However, there was a reversal of the decision not to set aside a certain number of seats for women. Two seats were reserved for women in the House of Units. Fourteen seats were so reserved in the House of People. Similarly, seats were to be reserved for women in the provincial legislatures.[72]

The Hindus objected strenuously to the provision that no legislature could enact any law "repugnant" to the Qur'ān or Sunnah. If it were passed, they insisted, safeguards should be provided for the personal laws of the non-Muslims. Mr. Brohi did his best to convince the members of the Congress Party that it was improper to add such a proviso to a *negative* clause.[73] There was a possibility that, if the amendments suggested had been adopted, a law, though "repugnant" to the Qur'ān for abridging the rights of non-Muslims in an Islamic state, could not have been challenged in the courts on that ground. At any rate, the Hindus were extremely dissatisfied,

[68] *Ibid.,* no. 17, p. 588.
[69] *Ibid.,* no. 23 (Nov. 5, 1953), p. 680.
[70] *Ibid.,* no. 22 (Nov. 4, 1953), p. 672.
[71] *Ibid.,* nos. 23 and 24, pp. 688, 696, 697; *Ulama's Amendments,* p. 18.
[72] *Ibid.,* nos. 23 and 28, pp. 684, 688, 743.
[73] *Ibid.,* no. 18 (Oct. 30, 1953), p. 620.

so much so that they opposed the amendment of Mr. Kizilbash, the chief minister of Khairpur, and a Shīʿite, who proposed that "the Holy Qurʾān and the Sunnah . . . shall mean, when applied to any sect, such interpretation thereof as is . . . accepted by that particular sect." [74] The scope of this amendment went far beyond the suggestion of the 'ulamā'. The 'ulamā' had merely proposed, regarding the directive principle on codification of the Sharīʿa, that the *personal* law and *ritual* of each school be safeguarded.[75] What possible legislative confusion this amendment might have produced is a subject upon which it is now useless to speculate, but it might have been great indeed.

The exclusion of money bills from the "repugnancy clause" was made much more comprehensive, but a sort of time limit, much longer than the five years of the 'ulamā' 's amendments, was added.[76] The mere fact that a time limit was set, was, however, gratifying to the 'ulamā'. The exact text is relevant.

> 10. (1) The provisions of paragraph 4 should not apply to fiscal and monetary measures, laws relating to banking, insurance, provident funds, loans and other matters affecting the existing economic, financial and credit system, except after the time and in the manner prescribed in sub-paragraph (2).
>
> (2) After a period of 25 years a Commission should be appointed to report on the steps and stages by which sub-paragraph (1) can be amended so as to make paragraph 4 applicable to the matters mentioned in sub-paragraph (1).
>
> (3) The terms and conditions of contracts and commitments made before the implementation of the recommendation of the Commission should not be affected.[77]

[74] *Ibid.*, no. 19 (Oct. 31, 1953), p. 628.

[75] *Ulama's Amendments*, p. 7.

[76] *C.A.P. Debates*, Vol. XV, no. 21 (Nov. 3, 1953), p. 669; *Ulama's Amendments*, pp. 14–15.

[77] *Report of the BPC* (as adopted by the C.A.P. on September 21, 1954), p. 4.

A more important concession to the conservative religious groups was the provision for setting up an organization for propagating the teachings of Islam to the *people,* and for commanding the right and forbidding the wrong. The exact meaning of the last phrase was left indefinite, but it did not excite as much apprehension among the Hindus as did the clear implication of the word "people." This provision had been in the chapter on "Directive Principles of State Policy" in the BPC report, but now it was incorporated in the chapter on "Procedure for Preventing Legislation Repugnant to the Qur'ān and Sunnah." [78] In this manner by its position in the operative part of the draft, and by its proximity to the "repugnancy clause" it was given double importance.

We can only speculate on the method by which the government would have carried out this obligation, and the precise purposes for which the organization might have been used. Two possibilities present themselves: the organization might have become an organization for the propagation of the views of the government on certain questions of Sharī'a law, or it might simply have been a handy means for placating difficult 'ulamā' by employing them in positions affording good pay and high prestige.

Whatever the clause meant to the government, to the 'ulamā' it meant the implementation of the "enabling clause." It went farther than the demand of the 'ulamā' since the obligation upon the government was made justiciable, but it did not include all the details which the 'ulamā' had stressed.

The Hindu members made their strongest speeches against this clause,[79] but all they could achieve was an exemption from the payment of taxes to support the organization. When they objected that they did not want to be the subject of proselytization they were told by Shahoodul Haque that

---

[78] *Ibid.,* p. 5.
[79] *C.A.P. Debates,* Vol. XV, no. 19, pp. 631, 638, 639, 642, 644–651.

this amendment comes in as a logical sequence to the amendment which we have just adopted that "every citizen" of Pakistan instead of "every Muslim citizen" of Pakistan should have a right to challenge the validity of the legislation on the ground of repugnancy to Qur'ān and Sunnah in the Federal Court of Pakistan.[80]

On the following day Mr. S. C. Chattopadhyaya, leader of the Congress Party, announced that his group would no longer participate in the work of drafting the constitution. After listing the Islamic provisions that had been passed, he said: "The frequent references about Islamic constitution and undue emphasis on it is creating such an atmosphere as makes our presence in the House useless." [81]

THE "REPUGNANCY CLAUSE"

The new procedure for preventing legislation contrary to the Qur'ān and Sunnah was adopted without any discussion.[82] The transitional provision whereby the 'ulamā' desired that some of their own number be associated with the Supreme Court for this purpose was disregarded. Every citizen, Muslim and non-Muslim alike, could challenge the validity of legislation on the ground of its "repugnancy" to the Qur'ān and Sunnah. An application in this regard had to be filed within three months from the date of assent by the Head of the State. Decision would be by the majority of a full bench of five judges.

The 'ulamā' objected to the limitation of three months which they felt might be used in some way to obstruct, or might eventuate in the omission of, action against a "repugnant" law. They also continued to press for a transitional arrangement, but

[80] *Ibid.*, p. 655.
[81] *Ibid.*, no. 20 (Nov. 2, 1953), p. 658.
[82] *Ibid.*, no. 19, p. 629,

on the whole they accepted the new clause, and felt it to be a great victory. In view of the fact that they would not be associated with the court, and they knew this, it would be unfair to deny that they were here more interested in the principle of the supremacy of the Sharī'a than the practice of their own monopoly of interpretation. We have already traced by what political vicissitudes and tricks of fortune the 'ulamā' came to be faced with this difficult choice, and it must be said that by their own action they have proved that the Islamic legal system, if not Islamic law, is still capable of adaptation to changing circumstances. Much of the credit or blame must go to Maududi, but had he not convinced the 'ulamā' he might not have convinced anyone else. We should, at the same time, remember that the 'ulamā' continued to hold to their transitional provision, and thereby established a basis upon which they would be able to reject the decisions of the court on their own authority. Be this as it may, they admitted that Pakistan would, in theory at least, be an Islamic state, and that the *BPC report as amended was an Islamic constitution.*

Under the "repugnancy clause" the task of the Supreme Court would simply be to determine what were the prescriptions of the Qur'ān and Sunnah in regard to legislation passed by the future parliament of Pakistan. In other words, the court would succeed to the traditional function of the 'ulamā'. It would, indeed, supplant the classical ijmā' of the 'ulamā' and the Ottoman Shaikh al-Islam. As Fazlur Rahman and Dr. O. H. Malik pointed out, the gate of ijtihād would, in fact, be reopened; but only in respect of individual judgments, and only to the extent that the judges would reject the doctrine of taqlīd. The use of the words Qur'ān and Sunnah rather than Sharī'a went far toward reopening the "gate" and rejecting taqlīd. The actual personnel of the court further assured these possibilities, though the probable necessity of winning over the 'ulamā' to whatever decision would be made must restrict the court's freedom of interpretation.

The court had no power to enforce Islamic law as the law of the land. In fact, a rather anomalous situation was created whereby the legislature would have to "reënact" Sharī'a law, until which time such law would be effective in Pakistan only in the negative sense that nothing "repugnant" thereto might be enacted. The possibility of a conflict between the interpretation of the Supreme Court and the enactments of the legislature acting under the directive principle instructing the state to codify such of the Sharī'a laws as might conveniently be given legal effect did not seem to disturb anyone. It is, however, clear that the legislature might, under the BPC report, enact laws suggested by the Sharī'a Law Commission, only to have them rejected by the Supreme Court as "repugnant" to the Qur'ān and Sunnah. Under this system the legislature would, in fact, have no power to determine what was or was not Sharī'a law. They might best leave such legislation until a related case had been passed on by the Supreme Court.

Brohi's emphasis on the limitations upon the power of the legislature in an Islamic state is, therefore, well taken. These limitations are set forth in a general manner in the Objectives Resolution, but no attempt was made to define how they might be implemented. The implication there was that the "state" would voluntarily keep from overstepping Islamic limits, but since the power and authority of the state was to be exercised by the representatives of the people under that resolution, we must so construe the word "state" as to exclude the Supreme Court. We must further understand the Supreme Court as being above the state, and, to the extent that God's authority is to be exerted negatively, to be the immediate exponent of that authority in the state of Pakistan.

What has now become of the theory of ijmā' institutionalized in an elected legislative body? It would seem that the consensus theory was rejected by the Constituent Assembly when they adopted these amendments.

Maududi and the Board of Ta'līmat-i-Islāmīa have assured us that there is scope for a legislature in an Islamic state. It may deal with subjects that have not been covered by the Sharī'a. Though some 'ulamā' do not seem to agree with this view, there are numerous examples in Islamic history and in the history of Islamic legal theory which go to prove that customary or "noncanonical" law found an important place in every Muslim country. The validity of Maududi's opinion in this matter is therefore solidly based in Islamic tradition, but the important thing to note is that such customary or administrative law, known alternatively as *'adah, 'urf,* or *qanūn* was clearly differentiated from Sharī'a law. In regard to the sphere of customary law, the caliph or the sultan did wield legislative power, and it is from this that the legislative power of the parliament of an Islamic state may be derived.

Islamic legal theory cannot permit the innovation *ex nihilo* of Sharī'a law. Ijmā' was a process by which existing law was discovered or applied to a specific case. It is impossible, even incredible, to give the sanction of ijmā' to a law, for example, establishing a port authority in the city of Karachi and thereafter to consider such to be a part of the Sharī'a. Moreover, the enactment by parliament of a clear injunction of the Qur'ān as, for example, instituting the punishment of severing the hand of a thief (with whatever qualifications may be deemed necessary in accordance with conditions obtaining in Pakistan) cannot have any validity in Islamic legal theory. The law already exists; to say that it is enacted in an Islamic state by a process of ijmā' when it already exists in the Qur'ān is to turn the system upside down.

The specific application of the Qur'ānic injunction to the

conditions of Pakistan might well be performed by ijmā'; but let us suppose that the parliament of Pakistan passed such a law, but limited its operation to the punishment of persons with an income of 500 rupees per month and upward who were found guilty of stealing. We might further suppose, and not without some grounds, that the Supreme Court would, if questioned within three months of the matter, declare that law "repugnant" to the Qur'ān. Had the legislature the authority of ijmā' behind its decisions, the court could not so declare the law invalid. Only if the court validated the act of the legislature would it *appear* that the legislature had institutionalized the process of ijmā'. If the court so chose, and *adhered* to a policy of accepting the decisions of the legislature as ijmā', then only would the ijmā' theory of legislation in an Islamic state be valid.

Long after these amendments to the BPC report were added (in August, 1954) Sardar Nishtar, after referring to the Supreme Court's right to interpret the constitution in "some respects," went on to say that

> a body like a legislature has been one of the basic sources of Islamic Law—Ijmā' (consensus of opinion)—which means a decision taken by the learned representatives of the people collected together, is one of the sources of Islamic Law. As you know, Sir, there are four sources of Islamic Law (1) The Holy Qur'ān (2) the traditions of the Holy Prophet (3) this Ijmā,' and (4) Qijās, the opinion of jurists and judges.[83]

If Sardar Nishtar meant that the judgments of the Supreme Court were to be in the nature of qiyās opinions (really analogical judgments derived from parallel cases), then they ought not have been given the force of abrogating the ijmā' which he found in the decisions of legislature. On the other

[83] *Ibid.*, Vol. XVI, no. 24, pp. 327-328.

hand, if he referred to the seldom doubted but oft repeated dictum that ijmā' cannot repeal the Qur'ān, then we may assume that he felt that the legislature was the exponent of the authority of ijmā' only to the extent that such decisions did not in the opinion of the Supreme Court abrogate clear injunctions of the Qur'ān.[84] The difficulty with this view is that nothing was set down in the constitution whereby we might differentiate between Shar'ī and noncanonical legislation. That is, according to Nishtar's theory, if such it may be called, a port authority in an Islamic state must be an "Islamic Institution."

Furthermore, by institutionalizing ijmā' and regulating the procedure whereby it is defined, and at the same time limiting its validity, an inescapable difficulty arises. By definition an ijmā' cannot be erroneous, and in accordance with Sardar Nishtar's views, by constitutional definition anything passed in a certain manner by the future parliament of Pakistan assented to by the Head of the State, and promulgated in *Gazette of Pakistan* would be ijmā'. But such an ijmā' might be found in error by the Supreme Court.[85]

The importance of the decision of the Constituent Assembly to refer questions of "repugnancy" to the Supreme Court lies in the fact that it would compel judges, legislators, lawyers, students, and interested laymen, as well as 'ulamā', to apply their minds to the adaptation of Islamic law to the conditions prevailing in Pakistan. Call it what you will, this is in fact a reopening of ijtihād. If the curriculum of the law schools would change as a consequence of this compulsion, there would probably be an even more revolutionary change in the cur-

[84] S. A. Q. Hussaini, *The Constitution of the Arab Empire* (Lahore, 1954), p. 51; Muhammad Iqbal, *The Reconstruction of Religious Thought in Islam* (London, 1934), p. 174.

[85] Sardar Nishtar's confusion has been stressed in order to emphasize the implied rejection of ijmā', but it also represents the peculiar nature of romantic thought.

riculum of the traditional religious educational institutions. The principle of movement which Iqbal saw in the structure of Islam might then be visible to all. But it would not come about by the institutionalization of ijmā'. It would be the result of the interaction of the power of parliament to enact laws purporting to be adaptations of the Sharī'a, of the authority of the Supreme Court to reject any law passed by the Assembly on the ground of "repugnancy" to the Qur'ān (and therewith to state its views on what is or is not Sharī'a), of the arguments of lawyers and experts on the Sharī'a, of academic research done in the law schools and theological academies, and the result of the use made by the 'ulamā' of their reserved opinion. Eventually one might suppose that a legal modus vivendi might be worked out between all, and even if achieved long after any particular issue was imperative, an agreement might be reached. Should this be the eventual result of such a clause, ijmā' might again become a living principle of movement in Islamic law, but it would not—could not—be institutionalized.

OPPOSITION

The Hindu objection to an Islamic constitution had little effect, as well it might with an election in East Bengal in the offing and the most recent failure to negotiate a settlement in Kashmir still with the Muslim members of the Assembly. In any case, Muslims could hardly be expected to accept the advice of unbelievers as to the benefits and practicability of an Islamic constitution. As for those Muslims who opposed the idea, they were for the most part silent. The only effective argument against an Islamic constitution came in the form of tangential discussion in the report on the Punjab Disturbances of 1953. That report contained a short section on the purport of an Islamic state (as part of the background discussion of the anti-Aḥmadi agitation) which is a catalogue of all the anti-traditionalist arguments.[86] The report suggested that Muslim political leaders were confusing the Islamic state idea with Islamic dogma, personal law, and ethics. It cited Iqbal, who, in his famous Muslim League presidential address of 1930, reassured the Hindus that an autonomous Muslim state would not introduce religious government. The report also remembered that Maududi had said that Pakistan could not and would not be an Islamic state. Jinnah's various statements that Pakistan would be a modern democratic state were also recalled. The ambiguities of the Objectives Resolution were mentioned along with the opinion of some 'ulamā' that it was a hoax, and therefore did not provide the basis of an Islamic state. The disagreements of the 'ulamā' were stressed, while ijmā' was limited to their agreements. Ijmā' could not be institutionalized in a legislative assembly because it is not a democratic process, nor could non-Muslims participate in ijmā'. The report concluded on the basis of the answers it received from various 'ulamā' that Islam does not permit legislation in its proper sense. The consequences of making Pakistan an Islamic state were described with the gravest foreboding. Non-Muslims could not be given equal rights. The penalty for apostasy would be death, and, since the Sunnis and Shī'is sometimes call each other unbelievers, a Muslim who changed his sect might be killed. The propagation of other religions would be banned. Because of the law of Jihād the Islamic state would have to be perpetually at war with India. If prisoners of war should be taken they could only be ransomed or exchanged or sold into slavery—in contravention of international law. All sculpture, card playing, portrait painting, photography of human beings, music, dancing, motion pictures, and dramas would have to be prohibited. The dissection of the bodies of dead Muslims would be banned. Moreover, the military and

[86] *Punjab Disturbances,* pp. 200–232.

police might disobey their officers if so advised by an 'alim on an issue of Islamic conscience. The learned judges concluded their digression with the comment:

> The sublime faith called Islam will live even if our leaders are not there to enforce it. It lives in the individual, in his soul and outlook, in all his relations with God and men . . . and our politicians, should understand that if Divine commands cannot make or keep a man a Musalman, their statutes will not.[87]

This part of the report was, in effect, the answer of the man who shortly became chief justice of Pakistan to the unwelcome suggestion that his court have jurisdiction in all cases where legislation is challenged on the ground of its "repugnancy" to the Qur'ān and Sunnah.

[87] *Ibid.*, p. 232.

12 *Defeat and Dissolution*

THE EAST BENGAL PROVINCIAL ELECTIONS

The term "Islamic Constitution" may be used for the amended draft of the Basic Principles Committee report only in the sense that it conceded, in principle at any rate, all of the demands of the 'ulamā' and the Jamā'at-i-Islāmi; and, as we shall see, both the 'ulamā' and the Jamā'at called this draft "Islamic" when they feared that it might not be passed. The defeat of the interim constitution plan and the preparation of an Islamic constitution was the result of a return to parliamentary government. The reason for these sweeping concessions, despite the contradictory convictions of nearly all the leading members of the Nazimuddin group was the need to acquire popular support against the Governor-General's accusation that the Assembly no longer represented the will of the people.

Concessions to the 'ulamā' were not the only accomplishment of the Assembly in the period preceding the Bengal elections. The most important of the other amendments altered the parity structure of the future parliament and restricted the powers of the Governor-General. As we have seen, the parity formula was altered somewhat in favor of the Punjab, but specifically rejected were both the proposal for the unification of West Pakistan and the alternative of its reorganization in a "Zonal Federation." The opposition to these two schemes was based on the desire of the Nazimuddin group to preserve the basis of a parliamentary structure which would permit them once again to control the government. The basis of such control would have to be the disunity of West Pakistan. It is, therefore, significant to note that Mr. Nurul Amin, the chief minister of East Bengal, was willing to consider the "Zonal Federation" plan. The benefit that East Bengal might hope to gain from some degree of unification in West Pakistan was the provision of a rational basis for the devolution of certain federal powers to *both zones*. It was understood that East Bengal would not be permitted to wield greater powers than its sister provinces in the west. The point of view of the government of East Bengal and of the Bengali group in the central government were, consequently, opposed to one another. The "Zonal Federation" plan was favored by the Punjab government because it would extend their political sphere both territorially and functionally. The "One Unit" plan was favored by the central government and the Governor-General because it would reduce their parliamentary dependence on East Bengal, and because it would greatly rationalize the administration of West Pakistan. The latter argument naturally had a strong appeal among the bureaucracy.

When the elections did take place in East Bengal, the opposition parties argued that parity would reduce the Bengali majority to a minority in the parliament, that the limitation of provincial autonomy would permit the exploitation of East Bengal as a source of raw materials only, and that the dismissal of Nazimuddin proved the lack of courage and strength of the Bengal Muslim League. The program of these parties included new elections to the Constituent Assembly, the rejection of the Basic Principles Report, provision for a purely democratic parliament, the limitation of central authority to defense, foreign affairs and currency, and the establishment of Bengali as a state language.

Opposition politicians were aided in their campaigning by two important groups, the students and the bureaucrats, especially the district magistrates.[1] Bengali students are, even in Pakistan, outstanding for their engagement in political controversy; and, in this instance, they devoted themselves to ousting the Muslim League for a combination of "patriotic" and personal reasons. The combination was based on the language issue, for if Bengali were not recognized as a state language the students feared they might have to learn Urdu in order to get the civil-service positions most of them desired.

The civil servants opposed not the Muslim League but the Bengal Muslim League. Their grievances were based upon the pressures they had been subjected to by the individual members of the provincial legislative assembly for favors of various sorts, and the abuse they had suffered at the hands of the Provincial League Working Committee. It is also pertinent that most of these officials were not Bengalis, since it was the policy of the government to place officials for at least five years in a province other than the one of their origin. Under the circumstances the district magistrates and others could more easily identify their interests with those of the opposition United Front.

The Muslim League fought its electoral battle on the ground that the League had achieved Pakistan. Muslim Leaguers also warned Bengalis that the Hindus would hold the balance of

[1] Interviews.

power if the Muslim vote were split. These arguments actually avoided the real political issues, just as did the argument that the draft constitution was an Islamic constitution and could be passed only by the Bengal group. The Islamic argument failed: first, because it could be borrowed by the opposition; second, because the religion of predominantly rural Bengal is traditional and more impressed by general statements, such as the Objectives Resolution, than the complicated procedure for preventing legislation "repugnant" to the Qur'ān and Sunnah; third, because the Western dress and manner of the Muslim Leaguers, in contradistinction to the colloquial speech and country costume of Fazl al-Haqq, the leader of the United Front, seemed to belie their claims; fourth, because the 'ulamā' of Karachi, still very much interested in attaching some of their group to the Supreme Court, did not warmly support the Bengal Muslim League; and finally, because Maulana Athar Ali, the president of the Jamī'at-al-'Ulamā'-i-Islām of East Bengal, and some of his close associates, ran for office as independents on the theory that Pakistan would be an Islamic state only if the "people of loosing and binding" became members of parliament.

The East Bengal Muslim League was overwhelmingly defeated. The United Front parties took over the administration and promptly pressed their demands on the central government. The United Front was made up of three major groups, the Awami League, the Krishak Sromik Party, and the Ganatantri Dal. They were, however, soon joined by a group of thirty independent members, who subsequently formed the Nizām-i-Islām (Islamic Administration) Party under the patronage of the Jamī'at-al-'Ulamā'-i-Islām of East Bengal.[2] The Congress Party won among the Hindus, and it had the

---

[2] *Resolutions Passed at the Provincial Nezam-e-Islam Conference, 21st April and 1st May, 1954,* Nezam-e-Islam Party, Dacca.

complete support of the Scheduled Castes. The Congress Party also agreed with the views of the United Front on most constitutional issues.

THE REJECTION OF "ZONAL FEDERATION"

With East Bengal almost unanimous in its repudiation of the Muslim League, and in its demand for greater provincial autonomy, the question of the unification of West Pakistan again arose. For a time it was impossible for any agreement to be reached in the Muslim League Parliamentary Party in the Constituent Assembly, and all progress on the draft constitution ceased.

Instead of taking up the controversial issue of the "relation between the Federation and the Units," the Constituent Assembly concentrated upon the chapter on the judiciary. From April 13 until May 7 the Assembly met twice, only to adjourn immediately each time since the Muslim League Parliamentary Party had been unable to arrive at any agreement.[3] All manner of other issues were taken up thereafter including the language question which was settled by accepting both Urdu and Bengali as the official languages.[4] In fact, the controversial chapters which faced the Assembly before its November adjournment were not taken up until mid-September, one week before the adoption of the amended report.[5]

When the debate on the distribution of powers between the federation and the units opened, Malik Noon, the chief minister of the Punjab, revealed his version of some of the discussions that had taken place in the Muslim League Parliamentary Party. He said that as a result of the victory of the United Front, and their demand that only foreign affairs,

[3] *C.A.P. Debates,* Vol. XVI, nos. 7 and 8.
[4] *Ibid.,* no. 9, May 7, 1954, p. 93.
[5] *Ibid.,* no. 27 (Sept. 15, 1954), p. 353.

defense, and currency go to the center, Noon, Pirzada, and Nurul Amin met and drew up a list of subjects they thought might be added to the provincial list for East Bengal, and be similarly placed on a "Zonal Federation" list for West Pakistan in anticipation of the establishment of such a federation.[6] He said that originally "a committee" appointed to decide upon the distribution of powers had been unanimously in favor of merging all the provinces and states of West Pakistan into a single unit, but now they would accept "Zonal Federation" as second best.

Noon's statement was refuted at once by Khwaja Nazimuddin who said that there had never been any intention of meeting the demands of the United Front, and Mr. Pirzada, the chief minister of Sindh, who said that hardly anyone in West Pakistan besides Mr. Noon favored the idea of "Zonal Federation."[7] Pirzada insisted that the "One Unit" or "Zonal Federation" proposals came up before the party for the first time only three days before. In fact, only Malik Shaukat Ali of Punjab supported Chief Minister Noon.[8] The Prime Minister, Mr. Muhammad Ali, did not oppose the idea of a "Zonal Federation," he merely said that consideration of the proposal at this juncture would delay completion of the draft. He hoped that the draft would be completed before his projected visit to the United States one week hence, after which the "Zonal Federation" might be included in the actual constitution bill.[9] From the debate it is clear that nearly the whole Bengal delegation opposed "One Unit" for West Pakistan, as did the West Pakistanis who were part of Nazimuddin's group, including one cabinet minister, while the representatives of the states remained for the most part silently unsympathetic. Other mem-

[6] *Ibid.,* p. 357.
[7] *Ibid.,* pp. 354 ff.; see p. 372 also.
[8] *Ibid.,* p. 365.
[9] *Ibid.,* p. 354.

bers of the cabinet did not speak in the Assembly, though it was stated in the press a few days later that Mr. Gurmani, minister of the interior, was pressing for the merger of the states with adjoining provinces "here and now." [10]

THE DISMISSAL OF THE UNITED FRONT GOVERNMENT

The failure of the "Zonal Federation" plan must be related to the events in Bengal. Shortly after the elections Mr. Fazl al-Haqq, stopping over in Calcutta, made some unfortunate statements about reuniting Bengal. These were interpreted as treasonous in Karachi, and when followed by the Adamji Jute Mills riot in Narayanganj, where nearly five hundred persons were killed, it was felt that some action must be taken. Khaliquzzaman, then governor of East Bengal suggested patience until the leaders of the United Front might fall out among themselves and a new ministry might be formed— something he was using his powers as governor to achieve.[11] In Karachi, the cabinet decided that the government of East Bengal had been dangerously derelict in its duty in not using armed police soon enough to stop the rioting. The political goal of breaking the Front was subordinated to the need of a powerful and efficient administration in a province that was isolated, poorly defended, subject to Communist propaganda and infiltration from Calcutta and Burma, and in which secessionist elements were gaining strength. Major General Iskandar Mirza was sent out to Dacca to rule the Eastern Province under Section 92A of the Government of India Act, while the Ministry was dismissed and the Assembly prorogued.[12]

---

[10] *Dawn,* Sept. 21, 1954.

[11] Interview.

[12] Some additional troops were also dispatched, but their numbers are not known. In any case, no important disorders occurred. Bengalis themselves are swift to admit that the central government was seriously provoked.

The dismissal of the Fazl al-Haqq ministry and its designation as secessionist removed the pressure from the Bengal bloc in the Assembly. It was now argued that the demand for greater provincial autonomy was part of the same secessionist policy. The central cabinet had strengthened the position of Nazimuddin's group immeasurably by repudiating the choices of the people of Bengal.

The political situation in Pakistan was now anomalous in the extreme. The bureaucracy ruled East Bengal directly under the orders of the Governor-General. The Punjab was governed by a group that was allied to the Governor-General. The Chief Minister of the NWFP (formerly in the police service) was similarly allied, while the government of Baluchistan and the Tribal Areas was also controlled by the bureaucracy. Only the Chief Minister of Sindh supported the Bengali group which dominated the Constituent Assembly. The central cabinet itself was wholly comprised of nominees of the Governor-General.

The Bengal Muslim League group in the Assembly had the authority to pass all manner of constitutional legislation without, it was thought, the necessity of obtaining the Governor-General's assent. But the Bengal group had no political power. They, therefore, proceeded to use their legislative authority to gain political power. The main object of the Bengalis was the reduction of the powers of the Governor-General, and they may also have desired to prolong the life of the seven-year-old Assembly indefinitely.

THE RESTRICTION OF THE GOVERNOR-GENERAL'S POWERS

The vendetta against the constitutional counterpart of the Governor-General had begun the previous fall with a slight alteration of the description of the head of an Islamic state in the Directive Principles. In addition to that, the discretionary power of the Head of the State to admit the accession of new territories was deleted, his discretionary powers in general restricted, the Governor-General's power to frame rules for the election of the future Head of the State until the new legislature was able to do so was transferred to the Constituent Assembly, the choice by the Head of the State of a prime minister was restricted to a member of the legislature who would seek a vote of confidence in two months, and the "status and dignity" of the office of the Head of the State was no longer to be a criterion of the pay and allowances of the incumbent.[13]

After the Bengal elections the same tendency persisted. The Head of the State in appointing puisne judges of the Supreme Court was required to accept the advice of the Chief Justice. A similar restriction was made in regard to the appointment of judges of the Provincial High Court, and temporary judges of the Supreme Court. The qualification that such appointees be, in the opinion of the Head of the State, distinguished jurists was also removed. The power of the Head of the State to transfer judges with the concurrence of the Chief Justice was altered to require him to act on the recommendation of the Chief Justice. The treaty-making power of the Head of the State was restricted by the addition of a proviso that "treaties dealing with political alliances" be ratified by the federal legislature. The Head of the State retained the power to appoint members of the Public Service Commission, but was unable to remove them. They could be removed only on the grounds of misbehavior and infirmity of body or mind. Reference in this regard had to be made by the Head of the State to the Supreme Court, which would then decide if the member of the commission should be removed. The advice of the Public Service

[13] *C.A.P. Debates,* Vol. XV, nos. 20 and 22, pp. 665, 666, 672, 673.

Commission was made binding upon the Head of the State.[14]

These changes all related to the future constitution of Pakistan, and in many instances really restricted the power of the Prime Minister rather than of the Head of the State, who had to act on advice in nearly all matters. On the other hand, no one knew for sure how much power the Governor-General was actually wielding at the time, and some were apprehensive about the future. Regardless of these considerations it is probably justified to consider these changes as symbolic moves against an individual. The real issues were the composition of the House which had already been settled (though that settlement was now being disturbed) and the distribution of powers which remained to be worked out. In anticipation of the settlement of those issues the procedure for amending the constitution (that is, before all its provisions were known) was made somewhat more difficult.[15]

Then the assembly turned its attention to three amendments of the Government of India Act, for which there was no apparent pressing need. The first gave the High Court of Pakistan the power to issue writs of habeas corpus, mandamus, quo warranto, and certiorari.[16] In setting out the reasons for the amendment of Section 223, Mr. Brohi explained,

> It is the essence of good government that the executive should, within the limits imposed by law, exercise properly the powers that have been conferred upon it by the legislature. Sometimes it so happens that out of undue zeal to serve the State or on account of the imperfection which is inherent in both mankind and in all human institutions, executive officers in utter

[14] These changes are recorded in the order mentioned in *C.A.P. Debates,* Vol. XVI, no. 2, pp. 13, 39; no. 4, p. 62; no. 5, p. 67; no. 10, p. 117; no. 14, p. 165; no. 15, p. 179.

[15] *Ibid.,* no. 13 (May 27, 1954), pp. 147 ff.

[16] *Ibid.,* no. 17 (July 6, 1954), p. 188.

disregard of all the limits imposed by law . . . act in excess of their authority to the prejudice of the citizens of a country.[17]

The second amendment of the existing constitution, that is, of Section 290 of the Government of India Act, took from the Governor-General the power to create a new province, to increase or decrease the area of a province, or to alter the boundaries of a province by order, and delivered that power to the Constituent Assembly.[18] The third amendment withdrew the power of the Governor-General to legislate for Karachi under Section 290A of the India Act.[19]

Following these changes in the Government of India Act, the Assembly took up the transitional provisions that would operate in the crucial period until the new constitution would come into effect. These new provisions, passed before the end of July, 1954, seem to reveal the pattern of political development desired by the Nazimuddin group. They may also show the precise basis upon which the tenuous coöperation between the Prime Minister and that group was based. These new clauses provided that the Constituent Assembly should not be dissolved until just prior to the first meeting of the first parliament elected under the constitution. In Pakistan, where it takes a long time to hold an election, this is an important provision. The President and Deputy President would continue to fill the same offices in the provisional parliament. The Governor-General would not serve automatically as the first president of Pakistan. The provisional president would be elected by the Constituent Assembly, and so often as a vacancy occurred a new election would be held. This was an open threat on the one hand to remove the Governor-General, and on the other

---

[17] *Ibid.*, p. 189.
[18] *Ibid.*, no. 18 (July 13, 1954), p. 211.
[19] *Ibid.*, p. 216.

to extend the transitional period. The central and provincial ministers would all continue in office as before, as would judges, members of the Public Service Commission, the Auditor General, provincial governors; everyone, in fact, except His Excellency Mr. Ghulam Muhammad was assured of staying on under the new regime.[20]

Following the adoption of the Report of the Committee on Fundamental Rights, the Assembly moved on to the chapter on "Relation between the Federation and the Units and that on Tribal Areas." By the decisions taken on the first of these two chapters the designation of a special list of subjects for East Bengal and for a future "Zonal Federation" in West Pakistan was ruled out.[21] In place of the chapter on "Tribal Areas," a chapter on "Bahawalpur and Khairpur" was inserted granting these states the status of provinces, and thus ruling out for the time being their merger with Punjab and Sindh, respectively.[22] The position of the Tribal Areas of the NWFP and of the Baluchistan States Union remained substantially unchanged, and each was guaranteed a share of representation in the central legislature proportionate to its population.[23] Baluchistan itself was given the status of a governor's province with the reservation of certain powers for "prevention of any threat to the peace of the province." [24] On the following day the Constituent Assembly adopted the Report of the Basic Principles Committee, and turned it over to the Drafting Committee.[25]

Before this long-awaited step had been taken two more constitutional changes were made. The Public and Representative Officers (Disqualification) Act, 1949, was rescinded and the

[20] *Ibid.,* no. 20 (July 27, 1954), pp. 235–237.
[21] *Ibid.,* nos. 27, 28.
[22] *Ibid.,* no. 30 (Sept. 20, 1954), p. 466.
[23] *Ibid.,* pp. 477–479.
[24] *Ibid.,* p. 486.
[25] *Ibid.,* no. 31, p. 571.

Government of India Act amended so as to bind the Governor-General to accept the advice of the Council of Ministers, and to require him to appoint as prime minister a member of the Assembly who enjoyed the confidence of the majority of its members.[26] The ministers were to be responsible to the legislature and to cease to hold office on expression of want of confidence in any one of them by the federal legislature. The then prime minister was to be deemed to have been appointed in the prescribed manner.[27]

The motivation behind these last-minute acts is fairly obvious. Mr. K. K. Datta told the Assembly of certain reports that several PRODA petitions against members were pending before the Governor-General. Rumors were then current that the Governor-General was actually considering twenty-two PRODA petitions, most of them against members from Bengal. The bill was unanimously repealed.

The bill to restrict the Governor-General's powers was ostensibly meant to bring the existing situation into conformity with what had been set down in the amended Report of the Basic Principles Committee. On the other hand, the report had been adopted and the final draft was to be considered in one month, on the Prime Minister's return from the United States. The Prime Minister had promised the people of Pakistan that the new constitution would be promulgated by December 25, 1954, the birthday of Muhammad Ali Jinnah.[28] Had there been no danger that the Governor-General might use his wide powers again to dismiss the Prime Minister, and somehow prevent the adoption of the draft constitution, there would have been no need to pass this legislation in such haste, and with such little regard for usual procedure in the House.

[26] *Ibid.*, no. 30, p. 451.
[27] *Gazette of Pakistan* (Extraordinary) (Karachi), Sept. 21, 1954, pp. 1771–1772.
[28] *Dawn*, Oct. 2, 1954.

From this summary of the events, which took place between the Bengal elections and the adoption of the amended Report of the Basic Principles Committee, we find that the most aggressive action of the Bengal group came during the last week or so of the Assembly's meetings. During the entire intervening period there was no indication of the reaction of the Governor-General to the "symbolic" restrictions of the power of the future Head of the State. It was rumored that he had requested the support of the military in dispersing the Assembly, and that the military refused. It seems more likely, however, that until its final meeting the Assembly had not yet provoked such drastic action, particularly since the absence of parliamentary government in East Bengal would have complicated the task of electing a new Assembly.

THE LAST EFFORT OF THE 'ULAMĀ'

Not only was the Governor-General silent during this period but so were the 'ulamā'. The 'ulamā' were, of course, pleased with the concessions made to their "Amendments," but they still insisted upon transitional provisions that would permit some 'ulamā' to participate in the work of the Supreme Court. The 'ulamā' were, however, not unaware of the precarious position of the Assembly; and so they were determined to say nothing that might further weaken it. The 'ulamā' were dissuaded from their silence by the growing realization in Karachi that the Governor-General, at least part of the cabinet, and their bureaucratic support would not permit political control to be wrested from their grasp. Once again the Bengalis were able to enlist the support of the 'ulamā' who now proclaimed with less and less reserve that the amended report was, indeed, the draft of an Islamic constitution.

The 'ulamā' were not motivated by any love for Khwaja Nazimuddin or his political supporters.[29] They were driven to

[29] Interviews.

support Nazimuddin's group out of the fear of losing all that they had gained. The interim constitution plan was taken as an indication of the Governor-General's secularist views. Though the details of that plan had never been revealed the 'ulamā' thought that its sentiments were revealed in the report on the Punjab Disturbances, of which Nazimuddin had warned them.

It must be said in defense of the 'ulamā' that they never went back on their "Supreme Court Amendment" to the "repugnancy clause," despite this blistering attack. On the other hand, the publication of the report must have increased their determination to have some 'ulamā' assist the Chief Justice in his decisions on "repugnancy" cases; but Nazimuddin had given them a choice of the 'ulamā' boards or the Supreme Court. Under the circumstances the hesitancy of the 'ulamā' in supporting the Bengal Muslim League was understandable, but so is their eventual support of the amended Basic Principles Report. The value of the Supreme Court's provision depended upon the personnel of the court, and the personnel of the court depended, at that time, on the Governor-General. The 'ulamā', therefore, lent their support to the group that intended the removal of the Governor-General.

When it was openly rumored in Karachi that the Governor-General intended to dissolve the Assembly, the 'ulamā' began a vigorous campaign to prevent that possibility. Once again the Bareilly 'ulamā' demonstrated their accuracy as political weathervanes. They were the first to urge the passage of the draft constitution bill; but, despite this "political" move, we find them still echoing the traditional religious position of 1948! On October 9, at the convention of the Jamī'at-al-'Ulamā'-i-Pākistān, Shah Murid Husain Hashmi "expressed his satisfaction over the progress in framing the Constitution and hoped that it would bring into practice the principles of the Qur'ān and Sunnah in Pakistan. He stressed the need of the opening of an ecclesiastical department to help implement the Islamic

Principles in matters of divorce, inheritance, religious education and maintenance of Mosques." [30]

On October 12 the central executive of Jamā'at-i-Islāmi declared that "the proposed Constitution of Pakistan was to a very great extent Islamic in character and demanded its adoption forthwith." Dissolution of the Assembly was opposed.[31] Like the executive of Jamā'at-i-Islāmi, the President of the Holy Qur'ān Society deplored the fact that money bills had been exempted from the operation of the "repugnancy clause" for twenty-five years, but he warned that the prospects of maintaining the present Islamic character of the draft would be less if the Assembly were dissolved.[32] Mufti Shafi told the press that the agitation for dissolution of the Assembly was "an ingenious design to destroy the Islamic character of the proposed constitution to whatever extent it is." [33]

Mufti Shafi's next statement to the press called upon the citizens of Pakistan to celebrate Islamic Constitution Day on October 22, and to demand the enforcement of the draft constitution without delay. The demand for dissolution, he said, was designed to destroy the Islamic character of the constitution.[34] Maulana Ihtishamul Haqq also joined in the religious chorus against dissolution.[35] Jamā'at-i-Islāmi supported Mufti Shafi's call to observe October 22 as Islamic Constitution Day and urged that the new constitution be enforced on December 25 by the Assembly, after duly amending it in accordance with the amendments of the 'ulamā'.[36] At the October 22 meeting held under the auspices of the Jamī'at-al-'ulamā'-i-Islām resolutions were passed demanding the enforcement of the constitution by December 25.[37] The Jamā'at-i-Islāmi announced that similar resolutions had been passed in seventy-seven mosques

[30] *Dawn,* Oct. 10, 1954.
[31] *Ibid.,* Oct. 15, 1954.
[32] *Ibid.,* Oct. 16, 1954.
[33] *Ibid.,* Oct. 15, 1954.

[34] *Ibid.,* Oct. 19, 1954.
[35] *Ibid.,* Oct. 20, 1954.
[36] *Ibid.,* Oct. 21, 1954.
[37] *Ibid.,* Oct. 23, 1954.

in Karachi at Friday prayers. Meetings were also held in Hyderabad, Larkana, and Quetta. On October 23, posters containing the press release of Jamā'at-i-Islāmi appeared on walls throughout Karachi.

On the evening of October 24, three days before the Assembly was to reconvene, the Governor-General announced that the "Constituent Assembly as at present constituted has lost the confidence of the people and can no longer function." A state of emergency was declared and early elections promised.

Maulana Abdul Hamid Badauni sent the Governor-General a congratulatory telegram, thus the ranks of the 'ulamā' were split hours after dissolution of the Assembly.[38] No public protest was raised, no procession was taken out against the Governor-General's action, and no further agitation went on in the mosques. The man in the street was unconcerned—completely indifferent.

On October 30 Major General Iskander Mirza, newly appointed minister of the interior, told reporters that Pakistan needed "controlled democracy for some time to come."[39] He added that in his personal view religion and politics could be, and should be, separated. On the first of December, in his monthly talk to the nation, the Prime Minister announced the government's plan to unify all West Pakistan into a single unit.[40] The word "Islam" was used only once in this speech, and then only in a quotation from another statement made several months before.

[38] *Ibid.*, Oct. 25, 1954.
[39] *Ibid.*, Oct. 31, 1954.
[40] *Ibid.*, Dec. 1, 1954.

13 *Aftermath*

At the end of 1954 it seemed that the struggle for an Islamic constitution had ended in a defeat for the religious interests, as had the struggle for a parliamentary government by the politicians. The situation was similar to that prevailing after Nazimuddin's dismissal and to that existing at the present writing when General Ayyub Khan has taken over the reins of government and has suspended the constitution of 1956. On all these occasions, the sources of the power by which the executive took over authority and maintained it were never clearly in evidence. What is obvious is that Pakistan's parliament, its political parties, its cabinet ministers, its religious groups, and even the general public of its major urban centers did not immediately or effectively challenge the actions of the Head of the State. It is also clear that the civil service and the police obeyed the Governor-General, while the military did not openly involve themselves until called in by President Iskander Mirza in the last of these three antiparliamentary actions. The military, however, were always there, and it is reasonable to suppose that they acquiesced in all that went before.

After each of the first two occasions when executive action confounded the constitutional operation of parliamentary government, the expectations of the services were disappointed. The continuation of the Constituent Assembly after Nazimuddin's dismissal and its replacement after the dissolution meant a gradual return to the same brand of parliamentary politics, intensified on the one hand by the open conflict of Governor-General and Assembly after Nazimuddin, and on the other by the reduction of the Muslim League and the emergence of new parties in the elections for the second Constituent Assembly.[1] The disunity that prevailed among the members of the Assembly, and the constant difficulties of succeeding prime ministers in maintaining their positions against both President and Assembly, opened the way for a renewal of the Islamic constitution issue. Just as the interim constitution proposal was stillborn, so were General Iskander Mirza's secular state and controlled democracy ruled out by the renewal of parliament. Above all, the prospect of a general election to be held soon after the passage of a constitution bill required all ambitious politicians to hold fast to the idea of an Islamic constitution. Nor should anyone suppose that the romantic notions of the politicians were not a serious motivation in the insertion of something in the constitution of Pakistan that would distinguish it from that of India or from the Government of India Act of 1935. Finally, as we have seen, in the struggle between Governor-General and Assembly, that executive's preference for a secular constitution was the easiest point from which to mount an attack and upon which to justify a restriction of his powers. Thus it was after Nazimuddin's dismissal that the

[1] See K. Callard, *Pakistan: A Political Study* (New York, 1957), pp. 64 f., 118 f., *et passim*.

"Islamic Constitution" was passed, and again after the dissolution of the first Constituent Assembly that a similar constitution bill was adopted. In the eyes of the members of the services, neither the constitution nor its Islamic provisions were so
much wrong as was the return to parliamentary politics and
the inability of a succession of cabinets, each lasting about one
year, to solve Pakistan's domestic and foreign problems. Once
again, the idea of an Islamic constitution flourished or waned
as a by-product of the more usual kind of political struggle,
and the religious groups were unable to lift this single issue out
of the rest of the political complex. Not only were they unable
to place the Islamic constitution idea above politics, but they
gradually allowed themselves to be drawn more deeply into
parliamentary and electoral politics.

It is still too early to judge whether this latest interference
with constitutional processes in Pakistan will end as did the
others, and therefore impossible to say in what form the religious
controversy will reëmerge. Nevertheless, at some point in the
future, we may surmise, the present regime will seek some
sort of popular approval for its stewardship. At that time we
may expect to see some of the old pattern repeated. General
Ayyub Khan did not declare that the "mullahs" were the
source of Pakistan's troubles, nor has he avoided appealing to
Islam in his attacks on corruption and inefficiency. Even if the
suppression of Islamic constitutional provisions was not one of
his major aims, as was true with Ghulam Muhammad, Ayyub
Khan's action has made one point clear: the impossibility of
instituting the laws of Islam in any but a government of laws.
Another point that may or may not be obvious to religious
groups in Pakistan is that their bargaining position was very
largely dependent upon the democratic aspiration of Pakistan's
politics at a time when so few fundamental questions were
settled as to give every group a more than generous hearing.

Islam has coexisted with autocracy and bureaucracy in the past as it will in the future, but never have the leading men of Islam demonstrated their ability to move along at the intellectual pace required in the twentieth century as they had in democratic Pakistan—as poor as that democracy may have been.

Logically our study ends with the dissolution of the first Constituent Assembly, for at that time the religious groups openly declared that the draft constitution was an Islamic constitution. In that Islamic constitution we have found the essence of traditional Islam reasonably adapted to the institutions of a modern parliamentary state, and at the same time we have seen that all the groups participating in the religious controversy had retained their freedom of action. The passage of an Islamic constitution did not require that any group relinquish its principles entirely, it merely established an accepted procedure for dealing with each problem as it arose. Above all it did not exclude the 'ulamā' and other religious groups from regular participation in those aspects of the political process which interested it, and therefore might have gone far toward preventing the growth of religious fanaticism or (as is evident in some other parts of the Muslim world) despair and pessimism.

The logic of this conclusion is, of course, a highly synthetic one. It may be justified only in terms of a restricted hypothesis concerning the relationship between the development of political ideology and real political groups and situations. But the whole of our study must find its place in a wider conceptual framework where problems are never "solved" but merely change, and where case studies have sequels that are equally good case studies of the same or similar social processes. Within this framework neither groups nor interests nor institutions are constant, and the authoritative decisions that flow from these institutions are either implemented differently from the manner in which originally conceived or have some unexpected effect because of the new group and/or institutional structure situation. When, as in the case of the "Islamic Constitution," a decision has been produced by means of the authorized and legitimate political process but then rescinded through some exceptional authority, whether the Governor-General of Pakistan or the Supreme Court of the United States, the issue will be rejoined, if at all, in a dynamically different situation. The issue then resolved will be differently understood and will be dealt with by different individuals, and that resolution will be a new one also.

To the dissolution of the first Constituent Assembly, no final decision was made, and we had, in effect, a continuous, if not constant, political struggle between the politicians and the religious groups. The constantly changing situation and the changing distribution of influence among both protagonists prejudiced the legitimization of any agreement not made immediately public nor brought before the Constituent Assembly. The absence of such a final decision permitted a repeated reworking of ideas from the same series of reports and tentative agreements, and we have seen that the religious groups continually revised their position. However, up to the dissolution of the first Constituent Assembly, these changes illustrated the deepening understanding of constitutional government by the religious groups (if not by the politicians) and their gradually improving adaptation of their own ideas thereto. In the changes that came after the first dissolution and were included in the constitution of 1956, this kind of development is not in evidence. The religious groups did not, apparently, change their ideological position, but the altered situation brought with it a change in emphasis, strategy, and tactics.

The last episode of constitution making in Pakistan, lasting from December, 1954, to March, 1956, was perhaps the most eventful and complicated of all, but bearing only obliquely upon our study we shall but briefly review the most significant political changes, the new position of the religious groups, and the resultant Islamic provisions of the constitution.

The only attempt to set aside the Governor-General's action in dissolving the Constituent Assembly was the case brought by Maulvi Tamizuddin Khan (with the backing of Nazimuddin and Fazlur Rahman) against a government order requesting him to vacate the house granted him as president of the Constituent Assembly. Though Tamizuddin's contention that the Governor-General had acted beyond his powers was upheld by the High Court of Sindh,[2] the Federal Court at Lahore, under Chief Justice Muhammad Munir, ruled in favor of the Governor-General and his new cabinet. During the hearing of the case, the Chief Justice indicated his belief that the matter was a political one and should have been settled outside of the courts; after which there followed rumors that a new Constituent Assembly might be called into session in a manner agreeable to both parties. However, the Muslim League of East Bengal, that is, the group opposed to the Governor-General, had lost all justification for participation in the federal legislature as a result of the 1954 provincial elections, so that no compromise was politically acceptable to both sides.

The point on which the Federal Court ruled in favor of the government was the requirement that all laws passed by the Assembly must be assented to by the Governor-General and not merely be issued in the name of the president of the Assembly.[3] This decision invalidated the 1954 revision of the Government of India Act which provided for the issue of writs of quo warranto by the courts. It also invalidated all acts of the Constituent Assembly passed after the death of Jinnah, released the Rawalpindi conspirators from prison, and placed the coun-

---

[2] *The All-Pakistan Legal Decisions,* VII/3, March, 1955, Sind 96–178.
[3] *Ibid.,* VII/5, May, 1955, Federal Court 240–378.

try in a legal turmoil. When the Governor-General tried to validate certain laws by emergency decree,[4] the Federal Court refused to admit the constitutionality of this procedure.[5] Finally, the government referred a number of questions to the Federal Court to find out how to proceed with the calling of a new Constituent Assembly and how to validate some of the post-1948 constitutional legislation. The court also required the government to submit a further question on the validity of the dissolution itself, a point not considered in Tamizuddin Khan's case.[6]

The Federal Court found that the Governor-General had the authority in this special case to dissolve the Constituent Assembly, that he must designate the electorate and not the membership of the new Assembly, and that the laws could be temporarily validated until the meeting of the new Assembly.[7] It is clear that the Chief Justice felt that there was no choice but to permit the Governor-General to proceed under some sort of constitutional cover lest "Pakistan hurtle into the chasm beyond any hope of rescue." [8] Whether by this chasm he meant unconstitutional government is not so clear. Nevertheless, the court rejected the alternative of reconvening the old Constituent Assembly.

Though the court did not expressly require that the existing provincial legislative assemblies be the electorate of the new Constituent Assembly, this was the only feasible measure.

[4] *Gazette of Pakistan* (Extraordinary) (Karachi), March 27, 1955, Ordinance No. IX of 1955, pp. 661 f.

[5] *The All-Pakistan Legal Decisions,* VII/5, May, 1955, Federal Court 387–401, "Usif Patel Case."

[6] *The Federal Court of Pakistan: Report on the Special Reference Made by H. E. the Governor-General of Pakistan* (Lahore, 1955), p. 8.

[7] *Ibid.,* pp. 111, 113; see also confirmation in *Civil Appeal No. 14 of 1953,* Federal Court in Appellate Jurisdiction (mimeographed by the Ministry of Law).

[8] *Report on Special Reference . . . ,* p. 2.

Most importantly, this meant the replacement of the representatives of the East Bengal Muslim League by those of the United Front. The Assembly met first during the summer and then was adjourned to September, 1955. At this time the Muslim League Parliamentary Party rejected Muhammad Ali (Bogra) and elected Chaudhri Muhammad Ali as party leader. The United Front split, and Chaudhri Muhammad Ali was able to form a government having a more or less stable support comprised of the predominantly West Pakistan Muslim League group, the rump United Front of Fazlul Haq, and some others. The first task of the newly elected Assembly was to approve the formation of a single province of all the political areas comprising West Pakistan. The government's proposal having been duly passed, the stage was set for completing the work of writing the constitution. The federal formula was no longer an issue, for the second Constituent Assembly was itself composed on the basis of parity for both sides, while the unification of West Pakistan provided the essential prerequisite for increasing the powers of the provinces. A draft constitution was now prepared by the government, no new Basic Principles Committee having been appointed; and this draft was presented to the Assembly on January 8, 1956.[9] With few important amendments, this draft was adopted by the Assembly on February 29, 1956, and promulgated on March 23, 1956.

There were five sections of the draft which may be taken to represent the gains of the 'ulamā' and other religious groups: the preamble, the Directive Principles of State Policy, the name of the state, the qualifications of the Head of the State, and the Islamic provisions. In none of these five sections was any substantial change made in the finally adopted version. It seems, therefore, that insofar as any influence was exerted upon

[9] The full text of the draft is presented in K. J. Newman, *Essays on the Constitution of Pakistan* (Dacca, 1956), pp. 1–114.

the government by religious groups, this was done in private before the publication of the draft, and thereafter pressures were maintained against the possible elimination of agreed provisions.

The preamble was still the Objectives Resolution with the addition of a clause referring to Jinnah's desire that Pakistan be a democratic state based upon Islamic principles.[10] The issue of whether democracy and Islamic principles accord was sidestepped in keeping with the ambiguity of the rest of the Objectives Resolution. Pakistan was declared a federal republic to be known as the Islamic Republic of Pakistan.[11] The question of whether federalism and Islam are compatible was thus similarly sidestepped. The president of Pakistan must be a Muslim, at least forty years of age, and qualified to be elected a member of the legislature.[12] The Directive Principles of State Policy were somewhat rearranged but remained essentially the same as in the Report of the Basic Principles Committee. The "bonds of unity" among Muslim states were to be strengthened, the Muslims of Pakistan (not *all* the people) would be provided with facilities for understanding the Islamic way of life, the Qur'ān would be taught them compulsorily, the observance of Islamic moral standards would be promoted, zakat, waqfs, and mosques would be properly organized, parochial, racial, tribal, sectarian, and provincial prejudices would be discouraged, prostitution, gambling, and the taking of drugs would be prohibited, the drinking of alcoholic beverages would be prohibited except for medicinal purposes or in the religious ceremonies of non-Muslims, and usury would be eliminated as early as possible. The Directive Principles, as before, were not to be justiciable.

[10] *The Constitution of the Islamic Republic of Pakistan* (Government of Pakistan, Ministry of Law, March, 1956), preamble, p. 1.
[11] *Ibid.*, Part I, Article 1, p. 5.
[12] *Ibid.*, Part IV, Article 32, p. 21.

The Islamic provisions were only two.[13] The first instructing the president to establish an Islamic instruction and research organization to assist in the "reconstruction of Muslim society on a truly Islamic basis." This organization would be supported by a special tax on Muslims. The second was the revised "repugnancy clause," and it contained an important change from previous versions. It provided that no law should be enacted contrary to the Qur'ān and Sunnah and that existing law be brought into conformity with these injunctions of Islam. However, the implementation of this clause was now to be accomplished by means of a commission to be appointed by the president which would make recommendations:

(1) as to the measures for bringing existing law into conformity with the injunction of Islam, and

(2) as to the stages by which such measures should be brought into effect; and

(3) to compile in a suitable form, for the guidance of the National and Provincial Assemblies, such injunctions of Islam as can be given legislative effect.

The commission would present its final report within five years to the National Assembly, which would then "enact laws in respect thereof." The personal-status laws and citizenship rights of non-Muslims, and the provisions of the constitution were specifically exempted from the operation of this clause, and the personal-status laws of all Muslim sects were similarly safeguarded.

The new "repugnancy clause" seems to go back to the consensus theory in that the National Assembly has the final authority for enacting or confirming what is Islamic law. The implementive provisions really have nothing to do with the emphatic negative of the main part of the "repugnancy

[13] *Ibid.,* Part XII, chap. 1, articles 197–198, pp. 143–145.

clause," they really seek to implement the second part of the clause providing for bringing existing law into conformity with the injunctions of Islam. Paragraph (b) of the implementive provisions shifts from the negative of the "repugnancy clause" to positive enactment of whichever of the injunctions of Islam that can be made the law of the land. Presumably, if paragraph (b) were faithfully implemented there might result a series of conflicts of ordinary and constitutional law. The constitution could not be affected, but the resolution of other conflicts would have to be met by the National Assembly acting on the report of the Islamic Law Commission—if the conflict arose within the five years that the commission was to exist. Even then, the membership of the commission (which was not in any way restricted) and the views of the majority of the Assembly (including non-Muslim members) would be crucial. The single test we have had on this type of matter was the report of a commission on the marriage law, which is, of course, a part of the personal-status law that was all but excluded from the operation of these provisions; and its consequences have been not at all to the liking of religious groups.

The strangest thing about the new "repugnancy clause" was its acceptance by the religious groups including the Jamā'at-i-Islāmi. According to some reports, the major influences in achieving the retention of any Islamic provisions whatsoever were Maulana Athar Ali, who was connected with the Nizām-i-Islām Party of East Bengal, and the then Prime Minister, Chaudhri Muhammad Ali, of whom it is said that he holds strong religious convictions. It might also be pointed out that the United Front of East Bengal was, along with the Muslim League, committed to the enactment of an Islamic constitution. The center of opposition to these provisions had always been in certain quarters of the services, but no practicing politician hoping to stand for election had ever openly opposed the Islamic constitution idea.

These facts help explain why the constitution contained such Islamic provisions as it did, but they do not explain why the religious groups parted so easily with Supreme Court implementation of the "repugnancy clause." The explanation for this lies first in the fact that the Supreme Court proposal emanated almost exclusively from West Pakistan 'ulamā' who had coöperated with Nazimuddin's discredited East Bengal Muslim League. Athar Ali and the Nizām-i-Islām Party were active in the support of the United Front and were unwilling to accept the leadership of the West Pakistan 'ulamā'. Furthermore, the bargaining power of the 'ulamā' was considerably reduced with the resolution of the federal representative controversy, while the opposition under Mr. Suhrawardy tended to be less receptive to their views than the Prime Minister. In general, we may say that the position of nearly all the politicians ranges from a vague romanticism to ijmā' modernism, and it was the latter view that they sought to legitimize while accepting certain minimal demands of the religious groups: that the Head of the State be a Muslim, that Pakistan be declared an Islamic state, and that no law be enacted contrary to the Qur'ān and Sunnah. The solution is reminiscent of the ambiguities of the Objectives Resolution and really settles little. It represents no advance in Islamic constitutional thought.

The Supreme Court proposal was in fact easily released by the religious groups. It was understood even before the dissolution of the first Constituent Assembly that 'ulamā' would not be appointed to the court. The 'ulamā' were willing to go along with this handicap as we have seen, but with the publication of the report on the Punjab Disturbances they began to have some doubts. When Muhammad Munir was appointed chief justice of the Federal Court, then the highest court in Pakistan, after his service on the Court of Inquiry, and when they saw his judgment in the Tamizuddin Khan case and in the Special Reference of the Governor-General, these doubts were confirmed.

There was, however, no alternative to the Supreme Court proposal that would be acceptable to the politicians. Consequently, the religious groups involved did not change their views, but circumstances apparently compelled a change in emphasis upon goals, in strategy, and in tactics. The emphasis now appears to be on the positive enactment of Islamic law, on what Islam commands rather than on what it forbids. The new strategy was to enter into the political arena directly through attempting to elect some of their own adherents to the National Assembly, rather than to try to work through the executive or judicial branches. The new tactics involved operating in the mode of a political party, joining forces with those willing to coöperate, and even openly opposing the government of the day. With these changes the religious groups were attempting to challenge the politicians on their own ground, and to implement the Islamic provisions of the constitution directly. In this regard it is significant to note that the Jamā'at-i-Islāmi and the Nizām-i-Islām Party formed an electoral coalition to fight the general elections of 1959. Such a coalition was possible despite the fact that the Nizām-i-Islām tends to be traditional rather than fundamentalist because the Jamā'at never took root in East Pakistan. Developments along these lines, however, were not to be realized, for in October, 1958, the constitution was suspended and the elections further postponed by the coup that eventually placed General Ayyub Khan in power.

In the tribulations of Pakistan from March, 1956, to October, 1958, and in the coup that followed, neither Islam nor the religious groups are to be blamed for the national failures; nor are they to be praised for mitigating their bitterness. The claims and the ideals of Islam remained largely irrelevant to the difficult problems that dogged Pakistan's progress. However, if the influence and the activity of religious groups were inconsequential in these events, they have suffered no particular loss of prestige or influence.

As yet it does not seem that the 'ulamā' have come to the realization that constitutional government is essential for the application of Islamic law to modern political conditions. The organized religious parties, however, did understand that they could have no real influence except under constitutional conditions, and further, that constitutional provisions alone will be meaningless without organized and efficient social support. Nevertheless, the religious groups have preferred to dissociate themselves from the sins of the politicians rather than to strongly identify with the principle of democratic constitutionalism. Perhaps the reason for this hesitancy rests with the fact that thus far the religious parties have not been overwhelmingly successful at the polls, while the traditional 'ulamā' have had moderate success in direct negotiations with the government. Still, there has not yet been a real test of the electoral strength of the religious parties on a nationwide basis, and even the Nizām-i-Islām Party was formed after its members were elected to the East Bengal Assembly.

The opportunity for development along the lines of direct participation in the electoral and legislative processes has not been totally lost. On Pakistan Day, 1959, coinciding with the anniversary of the suspended constitution, General Ayyub Khan made a speech reported on Radio Pakistan in which he declared his intention of reëstablishing representative institutions; and on other occasions he has reiterated the Islamic character of Pakistan. Obviously, the religious controversy will continue in Pakistan, and religious groups may have the opportunity of trying their new strategy.

The consequences of this new strategy are not easy to foresee, but speculation leads us along three lines. First, to be at all successful, the religious parties must broaden the scope of their political interests and they must somehow relate the resulting policies to the principles of Islam. These parties must preëmpt the use of the symbols of Islam and prevent their use by other parties. They must win the support of the traditionally oriented 'ulamā' and prevent them from lending spiritual support to the government in power in return for nominal recognition and specious prestige. Should these lines of action be followed, a situation akin to that in Indonesia might arise, wherein Islam is an issue dividing rather than uniting the body politic.

Secondly, this strategy may bring about a strong reaction from both the politicians and the traditional 'ulamā' which will cause it to fail. Even a representative government is capable of suppressing religious parties. The traditionally oriented 'ulamā', despite occasional lapses into direct political action, prefer private lobbying techniques; and they may be encouraged in these by the politicians themselves. There are also significant geographical, school, and personality differences among the 'ulamā' which are not well understood by the general public, which may prevent this institution from operating in any but the traditional manner.

The third possibility is the most likely of all, whereby the emphasis upon the practical implementation of particular Islamic objectives will be paramount, while the political tactics pursued will remain diffuse. Thus on any particular issue, such as the Aḥmadi controversy or the "repugnancy clause," the 'ulamā' in organizations and as individuals, religious parties old and new, *ad hoc* groups, and various ambitious politicians and publicists will be temporarily mobilized and succeed or fail as the particular political conditions of the time may determine.

At the present writing, the constitution of 1956 is suspended, and we cannot yet know if it will be reinstituted or if another will be prepared, and if so by what means. It is more than likely that the constitution of 1956 is definitive insofar as its Islamic provisions are concerned. If, however, a new constitution is to be prepared we may witness a recurrence of the events following the presentation of the Interim Report, the Report of the Basic Principles Committee, and the passage of the "Islamic Constitution."

Regardless of the circumstances under which the issue may be rejoined, it is most probable that the attitudes and broad political behavioral patterns of the various contending parties will remain more or less constant in the foreseeable future. It may therefore be of some use to sum up certain conclusions regarding these attitudes and political behavior tendencies for the light they may shed on future developments. Since these conclusions should have at least a minimum of predictive value, they will here be set down as originally derived in the spring of 1956.

1. The views of the 'ulamā' are not rigid. They have changed and they do change. The 'ulamā' are practical and willing to compromise. They are not opposed to modern democratic institutions, nor even to the existence of a secular legal system. Under ordinary circumstances the 'ulamā' are both reasonable and pacific. It would be entirely incorrect to despair of any aid from the traditionalists in the process of adjustment.

2. The 'ulamā' still provide an important link between the government and the people. A political appeal to Islam remains

a political appeal to the 'ulamā'. The leading 'ulamā' are alert and well aware of political developments. Unfortunately they have a very incomplete notion of foreign affairs.

3. The 'ulamā' are not solidly united, in fact there are many issues upon which they may easily divide. On political issues, as opposed to doctrinal questions, they tend to fall in only a few groupings. Divisions among them are more easily encouraged by the distribution of official patronage. Generally speaking, the less principled, the more obscurantist, and less educated 'ulamā' put up the least opposition to modernization. All 'ulamā' desire, in some way or other, that their institution be recognized.

4. Fundamentalist views have a special attraction for both the 'ulamā' and the romantics. Given economic development and ease of communication, it is possible that all intermediate positions between the fundamentalist and the modernist may be eliminated.

5. The fundamentalists at no time made direct contact with the politicians. Their influence over the decisions of the politicians was solely due to their influence over the 'ulamā'. Should the traditional point of view (though not the 'ulamā') be eliminated, deep hostility might be the result.

6. The fundamentalist movement is a lower middle-class movement, whose social outlook is oriented to the institutions of a former and now passing age. It is quite possible, as economic development progresses, that such groups will become the support of reactionary landed interests.

7. Fundamentalist ideology is far less rigid than that of the 'ulamā', though more precise at any one time. The tactics of the fundamentalists are primarily opportunistic.

8. The discipline and self-righteousness of the fundamentalists may permit grave political excesses, but the movement need not be violent, as it was in Egypt, for instance.

9. Fundamentalism, because of its attempt to reconcile modernism and traditionalism, remains the most fruitful source of Islamic intellectual innovation. Fundamentalist ideas, if separated from the fundamentalists themselves, may considerably facilitate the transition of Islam.

10. Although all groups in Pakistan tend to follow the "devil" theory of history, the fundamentalists are more addicted to this view than others. Personal rivalries and motivations are the rule among the politicians of Pakistan, but such explanations when used regarding religious issues disregard conscientious differences by the suggestion of mere impiety.

11. Most of the politicians are romantics, the intellectuals among them tend to be ijmā' modernists, while the practical and more efficient among them tend to be secularists. The secularist group is the smallest of all, and tends to merge with the ijmā' modernist group under religious pressure. Ijmā' modernism is not expressly described in the draft constitution, so the action of the parliament itself will be the basis on which a possible split between modernism and secularism may occur.

12. Political parties remain for the most part cliques. Popular participation has not proceeded apace with urbanization, and certainly not with the democratization of the franchise. The intellectual and cultural gulf between the politician and the average voter is so great as to compel the politician to appeal to the 'ulamā' for aid when he wants popular support. However, since political success is only occasionally based on popular support, such appeals are signs of weakness.

13. The people of Pakistan find it difficult to identify their religion and their government. A politician cannot be a religious leader, for the present at any rate.

14. The original enthusiasm of the people of Pakistan for an Islamic state has been largely dissipated. The length of the controversy, the political intrigue built around it, and the

complex detail into which it has gone has discouraged the interest of the public. For the urban lower classes the Islamic state meant economic satisfaction as much as spiritual uplift. Grinding poverty and social deterioration have instead been the lot of the average refugee city dweller. The people of Pakistan are skeptical at present.

15. One can perhaps discern among the lower middle classes, and some of the more highly educated, a tendency toward the development of a secular Pakistani nationalism. It is, however, too early to judge whether there will be any tangible results to this tendency. Nationalism is not encouraged by the politicians, who stress provincialism when they do not talk of Islam.

16. To the extent that Pakistan will remain prematurely democratic (in the sense that economic development and literacy may be the proper bases of democratic government), to that extent will Islam be stressed rather than actual political issues. To the extent that economic development and literacy increase, to that extent will Islam become more of a real issue in itself.

Appendixes

Appendix A

The Board of Talimmat-e-Islamia have been asked to tender their opinion on the following points coming up for consideration before the Sub-Committee on Federal and Provincial Constitutions and Distribution of Powers.

(1) Special and ordinary powers of the Head of the State and of the Heads of the Units.

(2) Head of the State—Procedure for selection, etc.

(3) Constitutional powers and functions of the Legislature.

(4) Emergency laws.

(5) How to enable the Muslims to order their lives in accordance with the tenets of the Holy Quran and *Sunna* as laid down in the 'Objectives Resolution.'

(6) Note by Malik Firoz Khan Noon regarding creation of a National Council.

At the outset, the Board deem it necessary to make a mention of the handicaps under which they have been working and the impediments which have so far hampered their progress of work.

The first to be mentioned is the fact that the Board is yet incomplete due to the nonarrival of so important a figure as its Chairman. This has not only deprived the Board of the valued opinion of, and guidance from, a person of the erudition and learning of Allama Syed Sulaiman Nadvi, but has also made the position of the present members rather doubtful whether they, without the Chairman, at all form the required Board and whether the views put forth by them would amount to the views of the Board or whether they be taken as the view of so many individual Members.

The second difficulty which the Board have been facing is that no effective arrangement has so far been made for the procurement of necessary books with the result that even the present Members feel that they may possibly have to amend or modify some of their views after perusal of the required books, and obviously, they could not, in the absence of necessary books, be so sure of their position as they could be after perusal of the required references.

The third thing to be mentioned is that the present Members at the very outset felt the necessity of obtaining the services of a few assistants capable of rendering them effective help in the work of researches. They raised this question in the very beginning, but it was postponed to be taken up after the arrival of the Chairman of the Board.

The sooner these impediments are removed the earlier shall the Board be able to prosecute their work with the required satisfaction, confidence and speed.

It may not be out of place to reiterate, at this place, the request made by the Board on the occasion of their first meeting with the Negotiating Committee to the effect that should any Sub-Committee or the Main Principles Committee, after free and full discussion with the Board, find it impossible to agree with any opinion put forth by the Board and the Board find themselves unable to modify their views so as to come in line with those taken by the Sub-Committee or the Main Principles Committee, both the views, i.e.

those of the Committee concerned and those of the Board should be brought before the highest body authorized finally to accept or reject a particular view.

The Board also deem it desirable to make the following pre-liminary observations which, they hope, would facilitate a correct appreciation of their views on the subject.

The decisions taken by the Constituent Assembly in the form of the 'Objectives Resolution' go to give Pakistan the character of an Islamic State, i.e., an ideological State as distinct from a National State; and this character of the State has got its own implications.

Islamic State means a State ruled in accordance with the tenets of Islam or, more correctly, a State where the Divine Order, as con-tained in the Holy Quran and *Sunna,* reigns supreme and the entire Government business in its various spheres is conducted with a view to executing the will of Allah as laid down in *Shariat.* The next significant implication of an Islamic and, for the matter of that, of any ideological State is that all the places wherefrom the policies of the Government emanate must necessarily be in the charge of such persons only as not only believe in the fundamental principles under-lying that particular ideology but also conform to the minimum standard of conduct necessary to ensure sincere execution of the code promulgated under that particular ideology. This is so in the case of any ideological State whatsoever. For instance, it would look patently absurd if someone were to suggest that the keyposts of a Soviet should be open to those who repudiate the very fundamental principles underlying that ideology.

This implication was very aptly brought out in the following passage by the late Shaikhul Islam Allama Shabbir Ahmad Sahib Usmani (may Allah bless his soul) while delivering his speech on the 'Objectives Resolution' in the Constituent Assembly on March 9, 1949. He said:—

"The Islamic State means a State which is run on the exalted and excellent principles of Islam. It is evident that a State which is founded on some principles, be it religious or secular (like the U.S.S.R.), can be run only by those who believe in those principles. The services of such persons as do not subscribe to those ideas may be utilized in the administrative machinery of the State but they cannot be entrusted with the responsibility of framing the general policy of the State or dealing with matters vital to its safety and integrity."

It will also be relevant to mention that the Constitution of an Islamic State is a unified whole wherein various provisions are correlated and interdependent; and a certain provision may be acceptable to the Board only on the presumption that its correlated provision exists at some other place in the Constitution. Therefore, until a full picture of the Constitution comes up before the Board their views on any particular aspect of the Constitution should be treated as tentative and open to modification and amendment by them at any stage.

The Board also take it as a corollary of the 'Objectives Resolution' that necessary provision would be made at some proper place in the Constitution to ensure that any bill, law, ordinance or administrative order that militates against the requirements of *Shariat* and of the Objectives Resolution shall be deemed as null and void and that it would be up to the Committee of Experts on *Shariat* (details whereof shall be recorded later on) to decide finally whether or not a particular law or bill or ordinance or a section thereof militates against the requirements of Shariat. With this presumption, the Board proceed to record as seriatim their tentative opinion on the points mentioned on page 57.

The first two items regarding (1) the special and ordinary powers of the Head of the State and of the Heads of Units, and (2) Head of the State—Procedure of selection, etc. (to the exclusion of matters relating to the Heads of Units which should be dealt with altogether separately at a later stage) and item No. (4) regarding Emergency Laws may conveniently be treated as one item, viz. matters relating to the Head of the State and divided and discussed under the following 17 sub-heads:—

1. The qualifications of the Head of the State.
2. Election of the Head of the State—for life or for a prescribed period.

3. If for a prescribed period, what period should be prescribed and whether or not the Head of the State should be eligible for re-election?
4. Who should elect the Head of the State?
5. The method of election.
6. Who can remove the Head of the State from office?
7. On what grounds he *must* be removed from office?
8. On what grounds he *may* be removed from office?
9. During his temporary absence or on similar occasions, who should officiate for him?
10. Whether or not the Head of the State can be prosecuted for any offence.
11. If prosecution is permissible, the conditions and details thereof, if any.
12. The normal duties and powers of the Head of the State.
13. The duties and powers of the Head of the State in a state of emergency.
14. Oath of office of the Head of the State.
15. Emoluments and allowances during the term of office and thereafter.
16. Limitations to be imposed on the Head of the State regarding acceptance of gifts and presents, etc.
17. Demonstration of allegiance to the Head of the State.

Under the above sub-heads the Members of the Board have the following preliminary and tentative views to offer:—

1. *Qualifications of the Head of the State:*
The Islamic Shariat prescribes the following qualities as necessary for the Head of an Islamic State:

(a) Islam.
(b) Manhood.
(c) Soundness of mind.
(d) Soundness of the three senses of sight, speech and hearing.
(e) Puberty of age.
(f) Maturity of mind.

(g) Erudition and learning.

(h) Nobility and virtue of character.

(i) Wisdom and sagacity.

(j) Mental poise and composure.

(k) Freedom.

We can fulfil the above requirements in the following or some similar terms.

For the Office of the Head of the State of Pakistan, the name of any citizen of Pakistan can be proposed provided that he:—

(a) is a Muslim;

(b) is of male sex;

(c) is of sound mind;

(d) is not blind or dumb or totally deaf;

(e) & (f) has completed 40 lunar years of age;

(g) is a man of erudition and learning in the terms of Shariat, i.e. has got sufficient knowledge of the limits prescribed by Allah and the tenets and requirements of Islam and is capable of understanding the laws of Shariat from Quran and Hadith;

(h) is virtuous in the terms of Shariat, i.e. observes the limits prescribed by Allah and the principles laid down by Shariat, is not guilty of major sins, is not habitually indulgent in the commitment of minor sins and is not openly profligate in the observance of the Rules of Shariat;

(i) is wise and sagacious and is capable of assessing, understanding, and forming an opinion about, the present day needs and requirements of the country and Millat;

(j) has got mental poise and composure and is able to control his humours; and

(k) is not a captive in the hands of a foreign Government.

EXPLANATION

(i) Conditions (e) and (f) have been combined into one because even though the age of less than 20 years is sufficient for puberty, to ensure maturity of mind the minimum age for the office of the Head of the State should be fixed at 40 which has been described by

Quran as the age of maturity of mind and is also the age at which Prophethood was bestowed on our Holy Prophet (peace be on Him).

(ii) Should there be any controversy regarding the connotation and interpretation of the technical terms of Shariat used above, the matter shall be referred to the Federal Committee of Experts in Shariat, and their decision shall be final.

2. *Election of the Head of the State for life time or for a prescribed period.*

In this behalf, the practice in the early days of Islam, as well as later on, has invariably been to elect the Head for life-time, of course with the provision that he could be removed, at any time in accordance with the principles of Shariat prescribed under this head. However, there is nothing in the Holy Quran or *Sunna* declaring prescription of time limit as expressly illegal should it be considered indispensable in the interest of the country and Millat. If it be so, even then with a view to keep possible semblance with the precedents and practices of early Islam and to maintain the dignity of the Head of the State, who is the symbol and embodiment of the dignity of an Islamic State, the Board deem it advisable that some provision on the principles narrated below should be made in this respect. They hope that if any of the following procedures is adopted the dangers of one man becoming too powerful for an indefinite period could easily be warded off; although the removal of a Head of the State elected in accordance with the criteria laid down in Islam and by persons considered to be qualified on Islamic standards would, in the opinion of the Board, seldom prove beneficial to the Millat except in the conditions provided for by Islam.

They suggest that no term be fixed for H/S but following procedure

(a) The Head of the State be elected without any specification of the term of his office, but on every fresh terminal elections, the new Legislature (both Houses sitting together) should in their inaugural session, decide by majority of

votes whether a fresh election for the office of the Head
of the State should be held or not. And a fresh election
should be held only if a majority of the Members of the
two Houses, sitting together, so decides.

(b) The Head of the State should address the joint inaugural
session of the Houses, and after presenting a report of the
working of the Government during the outgoing term and
an analysis of the problems facing the Government in the
near future and the broad outlines of the policy desirable
for the solution he should request the two Houses to confide
to some more suitable person the responsibilities of the
office in order that the country and Millat may have occasion to progress under the guidance of the best talent
available. The two Houses should re-assemble sometime
within a week after this inaugural meeting and consider
the request of the Head of the State. If a majority of those
present accept the request, announcement for fresh election
should be made.

(c) The Head of the State should, as a matter of convention,
submit his resignation to every newly elected Federal Legislature and, if it is accepted, fresh elections should be held.
This need not be provided in the Constitution but should
only be taken as a convention or an unwritten law.

(d) There should be no mention of any time limit in the
Constitution, but in the Oath of Office the elected President should be required to undertake that he will, of his
own accord, relinquish his office on the termination of a
period of, say, five years, with effect from the date of the
resumption of office to enable the Millat to avail of a better
talent available for this high office.

In this connection, it may also be worth consideration whether it
would not be advisable if in the first election to be held under
the new Constitution, the Head of the State is elected for a fixed
period of, say, five years, but after this transitory period every
subsequent election of the Head of the State should be for life-
time. However, in view both of the traditions of Muslim polity

and of the stability of Government, the Board prefer life election in the case of the Head of the State.

3. *If the election is for any specified period, what period should be prescribed and whether or not the Head of the State should be eligible for re-election.*

Should it be considered necessary to prescribe a limited period for the term of office of the Head of the State it may, in the opinion of the Board, be fixed at any period of four to seven years. Probably the period of five lunar years would be appropriate.

An opinion on the eligibility or otherwise for re-election will depend on the decision taken in regard to the devices mentioned in the preceding section and shall be given as soon as that decision is known.

4. *Who should elect the Head of the State?*

Under the law of Shariat, the power to elect the Head of the State vests in the learned and pious representatives of the people. In the present circumstances we can designate collectively the Members of the proposed Federal Houses including the Federal Committee of Experts on Shariat (who should be ex-officio Members of the Upper House) as the body required by Shariat for the purpose of the election of the Head of the State. The two Houses sitting together along with the Committee of Experts on Shariat should elect the Head of the State by majority of votes. Further, to ensure representation and confidence of a still wider circle the Legislatures of the Units, or a fixed number out of them, say one-third of the total strength of the respective Houses, elected for the purpose on the basis of proportional representation, together with the Members of the Provincial Committees on Experts on Shariat may be invited to participate in the election session of the Federal Houses.

5. *The method of election of the Head of the State.*

In the opinion of the Board, the process of election by elimination of names would be most suited. The Board can give their opinion on any alternative methods that may be suggested in this connection.

Voting may be held openly or even by secret ballots; both are permissible according to Shariat. In case of a single candidate also votes should be taken and a positive majority of the votes of the electors should be prescribed as necessary for the election of the Head of the State.

6. *Who can remove the Head of the State?*

The very body which is entitled to elect the Head of the State is also entitled to remove him from office, provided the conditions prescribed in the Constitution exist.

7. *Under what conditions the Head of the State must be removed?*

In the Law of Shariat the persons of learning and piety representing the people *must* remove the Head of the State under the following conditions:—

(a) If the Head of the State becomes apostate.

(b) If he has fallen a captive into the hands of an enemy country and there is no hope of his early liberation.

(c) If he becomes dumb, deaf (totally bereft of the sense of hearing) or blind.

(d) If he becomes mentally deranged.

(e) If he openly indulges in dissoluteness and profligacy against, and disregard of the provisions of Shariat.

(f) If he is convicted of treason, or of being in conspiracy with some enemy of the State.

(g) If he contravenes the terms of his oath of office.

(h) If he promulgates and insists on the execution of orders which militate against the Shariat or compel or positively help people to indulge in sinful acts.

(i) If he is physically disabled or incapacitated due to some illness or accident in such a manner as to be permanently unable to perform his official duties.

8. *Under what conditions removal of the Head of the State is discretionary?*

An absolute majority of the total number of members of the body eligible to elect the Head of the State may under the following conditions remove him from office:—

(a) If the Head of the State is considered to be incapacitated to perform his duties on account of old age.

(b) If his conduct of Government business generally and the measures adopted by him are considered to be detremental to the best interests of the country of Millat and the Members voting for his removal declare it on oath that in their well considered opinion the continuance of the reins of Government in his hand is likely to prove a grave menace to the State or to the ideology which it stands for.

9. *Who should officiate for the Head of the State?*

If the office of the Head of the State falls vacant temporarily due to his death, resignation, removal from office, falling a captive into the hands of an enemy country and journey outside the State, or due to other similar causes, it would, in the opinion of the Board, be desirable that a Council of Regency, consisting of the following members, performs his duties pending his resumption of work or fresh election as the case may be.

They suggest a Council of Regency consisting of:

(a) The Head of the Supreme Court;

(b) The Head of the Federal Committee of Experts on Shariat.

(c) The President of the Upper House or/and the President of the Lower House.

The Chief Secretary to the Federal Government shall also act as Secretary of the Council of Regency.

Members of the Council should preside by rotation and the President should exercise two votes in case the Council is constituted of four members.

10. *Whether or not the Head of the State can be prosecuted for any offence.*

The Head of an Islamic State is as much bound by the Law of the country as any ordinary citizen, and any aggrieved person has, or his heirs have, a right to seek redress from the court against any wrong done to him by the Head of the State in his personal capacity.

11. *If prosecution is permissible, the conditions and details thereof, if any.*

Should it be considered necessary in the interest of the Millat and country to make some provision for safeguarding the dignity of the Head of the State against such elements as may for mere personal or group ends be out to injure his position unnecessarily, the Board would be only too willing to consider and give their opinion on any appropriate measures that may be suggested in this behalf.

12. *The ordinary powers and duties of the Head of the State.*

Mussalmans residing in a territory over which Allah has given them control and supremacy are in duty bound to set up and run the government as His vice-gerents agents working for the implementation of whatever He has ordained and in the manner He has ordained.

Such a State is required to work for the consolidation and glory of Islam, implementation of its scheme of life in all its fulness, eradication of vices, propagation of virtues, creation and maintenance of healthy moral atmosphere, ensuring procurement of necessaries of life and dispensation of full justice to all the people inhabiting the territory irrespective of their religion, race or colour, etc., preservation of human dignity as enunciated by Islam, diffusion of knowledge and learning, maintenance of peace and order inside the territory, enforcement of punishments and penalties prescribed by Shariat, control and disbursement of public money in an equitable manner as laid down by Islam, maintenance and consolidation of armed forces to avoid and meet all possible danger from any quarter whatsoever, protection, as a Divine trust, of the legitimate interests of Non-Muslims living within the territory and the general well-being and prosperity of the masses.

The method adopted for performing these multifarious functions is that the Mussalmans elect the wisest and most God-fearing person from amongst themselves as their head to discharge these duties and responsibilities on their behalf and in consultation with pious and sagacious members of the Millat enjoying their confidence. The Head of the State undertakes to discharge his duties in a sincere and God-fearing manner according to the laws prescribed by Quran and *Sunnah* and the people in their turn undertake to follow him in all circumstances as long as he performs his duties in the manner ordained by Shariat. It is their right, rather their positive duty, to watch his actions, give him sincere advices, correct him whenever necessary and even to depose him should they honestly feel convinced that his behaviour is openly against Shariat or positively detremental to the interests of the State or of the ideology whereupon the State is based or for which it stands.

The people exercise and discharge these rights and duties through accredited representatives of theirs in whose selflessness, integrity, piety and wisdom they have full confidence.

The above analysis brings out three constituent elements, namely, the people, the councillors and the head, each with its own scope of rights and obligations.

The people are responsible for electing their head and giving him full allegiance, co-operation and support and keeping an eye over his activities, the councillors for giving wise and sincere advices and such assistance in the discharge of his duties as may be required of them, and the head for the functioning of the entire machinery of the Government within the framework of Shariat and with a view to accomplishing the aforementioned objects.

The head of the State may have a single advisory council for the performance of his multifarious functions—legislative, propagative, executive and judicial—or, if exigencies of times and climes so require, a number of councils with well-defined scopes. He is the trustee of the interests of the Millat, the symbol and manifestation of its power and authority and its executive organ in all walks of the State. But Islamic Government being essentially a consultative Government, he is bound to take counsel from men of wisdom and righteousness and to ascertain the desires and wishes of the people in matters left out by Shariat as discretionary.

For a big territory like Pakistan, it would be advisable to have a number of Councils,—Legislative Council, Executive Council, Propagative or Cultural Council and Judicial Council.

Details about the respective functions of these Councils shall come at their proper places, suffice it here to make a cursory mention of their scopes of work and the role of the Head of the State vis-a-vis these Councils.

(A) *Legislative.*

Legislation in an Islamic State is a limited activity in so far as the function of an Islamic State, based as it is on the idea of the sovereignty of Allah, is primarily to execute whatever has been ordained by Allah.

However, there is a wide range of affairs left out by Shariat as discretionary which call for a legislative machinery to cater to the day-to-day requirements of the Millat and country. But this machinery is to function in such a manner that the laws promulgated thereby are not only not in conflict with the requirements of Shariat but are also devised in the light of its broad and basic principles, go well with the spirit of Islam and are conducive to the accomplishment of the aims and objects of an Islamic State mentioned in the foregoing paragraphs.

The commands and injunctions of Allah are either to be found *expressly* laid down in Quran and *Sunnah* or are determined by a consensus of opinion of those who are well versed in Quran and *Sunnah*. In regard to these two categories, there is little to be done by the Head or by the Councillors or by the people. In matters falling outside these categories, the Head of the State can pass laws in consultation with the accredited representatives of Millat constituting the Legislative Council.

There is nothing against having a bicameral legislature as has been proposed by the Sub-Committee concerned.

The two Houses can have their own respective Chairmen, but whenever the Head attends a House he himself should preside.

The joint session should be presided over by the Head of the State or in his absence, by the Chairman of either of the Houses.

No Bill should become an Act unless it has received the approval of the Head of the State.

The Head of the State may address or send his recommendations to any House in regard to any Bill at any stage he likes.

He may also return a Bill for reconsideration by the House or Houses concerned.

Should the House or Houses disagree with the recommendations or views of the Head, the Head may convoke a joint session of the two Houses and explain to them his point of view. If there is still a difference of opinion between the joint session on one side and the Head on the other, the Head may convoke a special session of all the Federal and Provincial Houses and his respective Advisory Councils. If the majority of even this large body gives its verdict against the view taken by the Head and he conscientiously feels that he should not give his assent to the measure proposed, he should resign and hand over charge to the Council of Regency. This Council may, if it approves the Bill, give its assent or else the matter should be postponed till the election of a new Head of the State.

Another procedure in the event of a disagreement between the Head of the State and the Federal Houses sitting jointly is that the matter may be referred to the people for decision by means of a referendum and if the Head of the State cannot reconcile himself with the result of the referendum he should resign and hand over charge to the Council of Regency.

The Head of the State alone shall have the power to convoke or prorogue the meetings of the two Houses sitting separately or jointly or of the special session of the Federal and Provincial Houses and the various Advisory Councils.

Government Bills for the consideration of the Houses should be initiated at the direction and on behalf of the Head by the Members of his Executive Council.

(B) *Executive*.

(i) The executive powers of the Pakistan State should vest in the Head of the State to be exercised by him, subject to the requirements of the Constitution, with the advice and assistance of his Executive Council.

(ii) The Head of the State should select the Members of the Executive Council, in consultation with the Chairman of the two Federal Houses of Parliament. Such members should hold office during the pleasure of the Head of the State, provided that he should consult the Chairmen of the two Houses if he desires to remove from office any Member of his Executive Council.

(iii) The Head of the State may allocate to the Executive Councillors such executive departments as he may deem proper, but he himself would be responsible to the Millat for the work of their respective departments.

(iv) Should there be a difference of opinion between the Head of the State and the Executive Council, it should be permissible for the former to enforce his decision, except, in case some Member of that Council challenges the validity of the view of the Head of the State from the Shariat point of view. In case of such controversy, the matter should be referred to the Committee of Experts on Shariat. Should this Committee decide that the view taken by the Head of the State is in conflict with tenets and requirements of Shariat, the Head of the State should not enforce his decision.

(v) The Executive Councillors should be held responsible for their work to the Head of the State.

(vi) All the executive functions of the State should be conducted on behalf and in the name of the Head of the State.

(vii) The Head of the State should preside over the meetings of the Executive Council. In his absence, the members should preside by rotation, provided that the decisions arrived at in meetings not presided over by the Head, should not be enforced unless they have received his assent.

(viii) The Head of the State should have the power to appoint and accredit the high officials of the State, for instance, Heads of the Units, Judges of the Federal and Provincial

Courts, Members of the Executive Council, Auditor-General and Ambassadors, etc.

(ix) The Supreme Command of all the armed forces of the State should vest in the Head of the State.

(x) The Head of the State should lead Friday and *Idain* congregational services in the capital and should also nominate someone as his deputy in his behalf to officiate for him during his absence or in cases of his inability due to some legal excuse.

(C) *Judicial*

One of the main aims and objects of an Islamic State is the administration of justice in conformity with the requirements of Shariat Law. The Head of the State is responsible for the freedom and proper functioning of the Judiciary. It is, therefore, desirable that the Head of the State should set up a Judicial Council with whose advice and assistance to control and ensure the proper functioning of the judicial machinery of the State. This Council should consist of a number of reliable, experienced, aged and God-fearing jurists of special ability and integrity. A detailed account of such Council shall be given separately under the discussion regarding Judiciary.

At this stage, it is sufficient to mention the power of the Head of the State in respect of such Council.

(a) The Judicial Council should have the Head of the State as its President. In his absence some Member nominated by the Head should preside.

(b) No death sentence should be executed unless it has been confirmed by the Head of the State.

The Head of the State should have the power to pardon, commute or reprieve, with the consent of the aggrieved person or persons or of his or her or their legal heirs, sentences in cases of (1) murder and (2) criminal offences not falling in the category of *Hudud;* provided the offender shows his repentance as required by Shariat.

In cases of an offence against the State or Millat, the Head of the State being the most trusted representative of the State and Millat, may give his consent on their behalf and then pardon, commute or reprieve the punishment in consultation with the Judicial Council.

(D) *Propagative*

As the most vital function of an Islamic State is to propagate the tenets and ideals of Islam and to enforce the Divine commands and injunctions, it is highly desirable that the Head of the State should, with the help and advice of a Propagative or Cultural Council, arrange for the propagation throughout the country of the Islamic way of life in all its fulness and should also organize missionary work in foreign countries as far as circumstances may allow. The Head of the State should be the President of this Council and in his absence such member as may be nominated by him should preside over its meetings. The members of the proposed Council should be nominated by the Head of the State in consultation with the Committee of Experts on Shariat.

13. *The Special Powers of the Head of the State.*

(1) In the opinion of the Board, the Head of the State must have special powers to be exercised by him, of course within the limitations laid down by Shariat, in order to enable him to meet emergent conditions.

(2) It should be up to the Head of the State to declare, in consultation with the Council of Regency, that a State of emergency has arisen calling for the exercise of special powers vested in him; provided that such declaration should be brought before the Federal Houses at their first session to be held after this declaration for their information and comments in case it has been withdrawn and is not to operate any longer and for consideration as a Government sponsored Bill if the intention is that it should continue to operate further.

(3) So far as the Central Executive is concerned, the Head of the State has got enough powers to change his Executive Councillors whenever he deems proper. Therefore nothing more is required in this behalf. As regards provincial administration, the Head of the State should have the power to assume to himself, in consultation

with the Members of the Council of Regency, the executive functions of the provincial machinery and make such special arrangements as may be deemed expedient in view of the emergency.

(4) In the legislative sphere the Head of the State may, in consultation with the Members of the Council of Regency, promulgate, during the recess of the Federal Houses, such Ordinances *not* in conflict with the requirements of Shariat as come under the domain of the Legislature and in his discretion are necessary to meet the emergency. The Head of the State may also suspend the Provincial Legislative Councils and, in consultation with the Council of Regency, assume to himself the powers of the Legislature of any or some or all the units during the period of emergency.

(5) In the judicial sphere he should have no special powers and the judicial machinery of the State must be allowed to function independently and freely in its normal manner. In the propagative or cultural sphere the Head of the State may, in consultation with the Committee of Experts on Shariat, suspend its activities temporarily if circumstances so require or change its normal course in such directions as may be deemed proper to meet the emergency.

14 & 17. *Oath of Office of the Head of the State and Demonstration of Allegiance.*

A joint session of the Federal Houses or, if so desired, of the Federal and Provincial Houses should be arranged to be held within three days of the announcement of the election result for the performance of oath of office and oath of allegiance ceremony. It should be presided over by the outgoing Head of the State, if any, or, in case there is none, by the Chief Justice of the Federal Court or by the Chairman of the Federal Committee of Experts on Shariat. The person elected as Head of the State should, in his oath of office, undertake:

(a) to live up to the precepts of Islam both in his private as well as public affairs, and work wholeheartedly for the glory of Islam and for the prosperity and progress of Pakistan on the lines laid down by Islam;

(b) to abide by the provisions of the Constitution of Pakistan and always to use his discretion wherever required, in a selfless and God-fearing manner;

(c) to do his utmost to ensure that the entire machinery of the State is run in accordance with the rules and requirements of Shariat, as required under the Constitution, and in a manner effectively conducive to—

(i) the consolidation and glory of Islam,

(ii) the implementation, in all its fullness, of the scheme of life promulgated by Islam.

(iii) the creation and maintenance of healthy moral atmosphere,

(iv) the procurement of necessaries of life and dispensation of full justice, to all the people inhabiting Pakistan irrespective of their religion, race or colour, etc.

(v) the preservation of human dignity as required by Islam,

(vi) the diffusion of knowledge on the widest possible scale,

(vii) the maintenance of peace and order throughout the country,

(viii) the protection, as a Divine trust, of all the legitimate interests of Non-Muslims living in Pakistan.

(ix) the maintenance and consolidation of armed forces to ensure the integrity and security of Pakistan.

(x) the control and disbursement of public money in an equitable manner as desired by Islam, and

(xi) the general prosperity and well-being of the masses in all walks of life;

(d) to discharge honestly and to the best of his capabilities the duties and responsibilities incidental to his office, with the advice and assistance of the wisest and most God-fearing persons available to him;

(e) to keep in touch with the masses as far as practicable in order to keep himself well informed of their conditions and desires.

As soon as oath of office has been taken by the Head, the Members of the House should, in a pre-arranged order, take oath of allegiance thereby undertaking to follow him and to give him their fullest support and co-operation in all circumstances as long as he performs his duties in accordance with provisions of Shariat and does not contravene the terms of his oath of office.

It would also be desirable if Provincial Houses and local boards of districts and cities are made to hold their respective sessions within a reasonable period of the announcement of election result to perform oath of allegiance ceremony. Governors of provinces and persons nominated by them for the various cities and districts should take oath of allegiance from these Houses on behalf of the Head. Similar procedure can be adopted in various Government Departments and the Army, etc.

15. *Allowances, etc. of the Head of the State.*

The office of the Head of an Islamic State is intended in no case to be taken as a job of high salaries and privileges. It is a Divine trust fraught with immense responsibilities for which one is doubly accountable before the people as well as before Allah. Thus the idea of any remuneration or salary is repugnant to the dignity and sanctity of this high office. All that is permissible is that the Head of the State, who has obviously to devote all his time and energy to the performance of his duties leaving no time for him to earn his livelihood, may if he so needs, take such maintenance allowance as may enable him and his dependants to lead satisfactorily the life of an average citizen.

It is, therefore, recommended that it may be left to the discretion of the Head of the State to take such amount as may be required by him for him and his dependants' maintenance provided that it should in no case exceed 40 times the emoluments of the lowest-paid Government servant.

It may, however, be mentioned that legitimate expenses incurred by him in connection with his State duties should go to the State account.

The Head of the State may also be given a house in the Capital, conveyance and such other amenities as may be deemed necessary to facilitate efficient performance of his duties.

The maintenance allowance taken by the Head of the State should continue for life even in case he vacates his office so that during his term of office he may have no reasonable cause to worry for his future means of livelihood. Provided that a Head of the State who has been removed from office after impeachment for treason or bribery, etc. he should not be held entitled to such allowances after his removal.

16. *Limitations regarding acceptance of gifts and presents, etc.*

Acceptance of gifts and presents by State officials or by their dependants is not only a corrupt practice according to Islam but has been called "Khayanat" or breach of trust.

However, in the case of near relations and close friends it is permissible, although not desirable, that such terms as may have existed in this behalf before acceptance of office may, on the same level, be maintained during the term of office also. Therefore it is highly essential that all Government officials, and particularly the Head of the State should be stopped from or made to observe limitations in regard to the acceptance of gifts and presents.

In the light of the above principles the Board recommend that the following limitations should be imposed upon the Head of the State in this behalf.

The Head of the State should not accept, nor should he let his dependants accept any gifts or presents except that—

(1) in the case of close friends and near relations it should be permissible that such terms as may have existed in this behalf before acceptance of office may, on the same level, be maintained during the term of office also; and

(2) gifts and presents, acceptance whereof may be considered necessary or desirable for strengthening international bonds for the good of the State, may be accepted by the Head but all such gifts and presents should be treated as belonging to the State.

If the articles received as gifts and presents from foreign countries are preservable they should be preserved in Government museum or some other suitable place and if perishable they should be distributed among the needy.

Opinion of the Board of Talimaat-e-Islamia on the question whether "Religious Societies" should form a Federal subject or a Provincial subject.

The Board of Talimaat-e-Islamia have been required to give their opinion as to whether 'Religious Societies' should form a Federal subject or a Provincial subject.

The precedents and practices since the very days of Holy Prophet (peace be on Him) indicate that while the units were free to exercise full powers in this behalf the Central authority always deemed it to be its duty and privilege to keep a general watch and to interfere whenever necessary for desisting a unit from adopting a wrong course or for forging necessary uniformity in the procedures followed by the various units. No doubt such interference came very rarely and in cases where and when it was deemed to be very necessary.

Therefore, the Board are of opinion that 'Religious Societies' should be included in the Concurrent List.

Appendix B

VIEWS OF THE BOARD OF
TALIMAT-E-ISLAMIA

(*In continuation of Board's report dated 10-4-50*)

III *Constitution powers and functions of the legislature.*

As has already been elucidated in the previous report the main function of an Islamic State is to execute the commands and the will of Allah. Here it would be desirable to keep in view the fundamental difference between an absolute democratic state and an Islamic state. In an Islamic state the implementation of the commands of Allah is the basic consideration and the will of the people occupies a comparatively subservient position; while, on the contrary, an absolutely democratic state aims at the unconditional implementation of the will of the people. Hence it follows that in an Islamic state, the real function of any properly constituted legislature is to enact and enforce the commands and injunctions of Allah and His Prophet insofar as they are enforceable through legislation whether of a positive nature or of a negative character. Should there be any difference of opinion regarding the interpretation of a command or requirement of Islam, the matter should be referred to and decided upon by men of wisdom and character who have deep insight into, and a comprehensive knowledge of Islam in its various aspects and are conversant with the needs and requirements of the age. Apart from this should there arise any necessity, which in modern conditions is sure to arise off and on, of framing such other laws, for the wellbeing and prosperity of the people, as admit of various forms equally acceptable from the point of view of Shariat, or about which Shariat has made no express pronouncement, these laws should be made in the light of the fundamental requirements of Shariat so as to ensure maximum conformity with the nature and spirit of Islam and to help promote the aims and objects of an Islamic State. In other words, we may even say that any legislation which does not militate against the injunctions and requirements of Islam and is not detrimental or prejudicial to the aims and objects of an Islamic State is permissible. In short, this is the nature of the functions which any properly constituted legislature in an Islamic State must needs perform.

The legislatures in vogue at present in various countries are generally the most powerful and the most representative bodies. It is these bodies that make laws and set up ministries. They also perform other functions which are more of an administrative and judicial rather than of legislative nature, e.g., consideration of the Budget, ratification of treaties and hearing of cases against the Head of the State. It is these bodies again which are empowered to elect and throw out the Head of the State.

Although there is nothing from the Shariat point of view against our delegating similar powers to our legislature also, yet if we do not deem it necessary or very commendable to follow the traditions of the British Parliament or to imitate the Bharati Constitution, and may aspire to adopt a slightly different course, there are other alternatives possible which would not only be in closer semblance with our traditions and serve our purposes in a better manner but may also prove to be technically more sound, may enable us to exonerate ourselves from the charges of servile imitation betraying the mental bankruptcy of the Millat and country and may also be more befitting the oft-repeated claims and declarations of our leaders to the effect that our future constitution would not be a copy of the constitution of any contemporary Western or Eastern democratic state.

In the reports of certain committees received by the board in the very beginning a strong tendency towards imitating the traditions of the British Parliament or the Indian Constitution was quite evident. The Board, however, thought and hoped that it was in regard to certain items only that this attitude had been adopted and that it would not be so in respect of other items and, therefore, they did not deem it desirable to make any reference about it in their report. The Board themselves tried to adjust the requirements of Islam within the proposed framework as far as possible. But now that numerous reports have been received and without any exception whatsoever all the reports betray the same tendency the Board feel it necessary to invite the attention of the Committees concerned in order that they may consciously realise their approach and attitude of mind which is forming the very basis of all our constitution making work. It is, however, a side issue and even though it may appear a little beyond our province, it is felt essential to invite the attention of the Committees concerned towards this vital point.

Now if the Committee concerned considers it desirable to divide among various bodies the multifarious functions at present considered to belong to the legislature, the following functions may be entrusted to a larger representative body which may be called the Supreme House (Majlis-i-Hall-o-aqd) or the General House or the House of Representatives or the House of the People or may be given some other suitable denomination:—

1. Election and deposition of the Head of the State.
2. Taking stock of the activities of the Executive.
3. Problems held in dispute between the Head of the State and the Federal Legislature.
4. Peace treaties and declaration of war.
5. Budget.

The power to form ministries, as has already been suggested, should vest in the Head of the State which he should exercise in consultation with the Chairmen of the proposed Federal Legislative Houses.

Besides these matters, the residuary functions performed by the present legislatures come purely under the head of legislation and may be entrusted to the legislative council whose actual duties have been mentioned on page 1.

The very nature of these functions also determines the qualifications and characteristics required of the members of our legislature, i.e., this body must consist of such persons as are thoroughly conversant with the injunctions and requirements of Islam, as also with the requirements of the country and of the modern age and in whose God-fearing nature, erudition, sagacity and integrity people have full confidence, and who are acquainted with the desires and likings as well as the troubles and sufferings of the masses.

At this stage, the question whether or not non-Muslims should be held eligible for the membership of the legislature or of the proposed larger representative body is also very significant. The spirit and the traditions of Islam give no express indication in support of the idea that any consultative body in an Islamic State should be composed of Muslims and non-Muslims both or that the people discarding the very basis on which an Islamic State is founded can as a matter of right demand that they should be included in the consultative machinery to frame the policy of such a State. Of course, as loyal inhabitants of the State they are free to form their own organisations to safeguard their interests by apprising the Government of their point of view.

However, the Board after full consideration of the numerous aspects of this problem, the exigencies of time and clime and other relevant factors have come to the conclusion that if proper provision is made to ensure that the injunctions and requirements of Islam shall not be affected or allowed to suffer in any manner (for which certain devices have already been suggested in the previous note) and circumstances so require, non-Muslims can be taken into the legislature not only to put forth and represent the interests and the feelings of their community but also to give their opinion in regard to the problems of general interest to the country. The same holds good in respect of the proposed larger representative body as well.

The guarantee against the injunctions and requirements of Islamic Shariat being adversely affected should be provided for on the following lines.

It should be expressly laid down in the Constitution that:

1. A Bill which militates against the Shariat law can in no case become an act,

2. No law passed by the legislature shall be promulgated unless it has received the sanction of the Head of the State,

3. Should the legislature be entrusted with the power to elect and throw out the Head of the State, the majority alone should not be deemed sufficient in this behalf, but the majority of the Muslim members and the majority of the House as a whole should both be essentially required for such decisions.

Another question which arises at this stage is whether or not women should be held eligible for the membership of the Legislatures or of the proposed larger representative body.

The view point adopted by Islam in regard to women, the position determined for them in the society and the functions they are required to perform in the establishment and development of Islamic social order are all based on a thorough consideration of the innate capabilities, natural tendencies and special characteristics of women-folk. Here it is neither the occasion nor the necessity to dilate at length upon this subject, yet it would be proper to refer to two basic principles regarding the position etc., of women. According to Islam, it is inevitable for the progress and prosperity of mankind that men and women do perform their own respective functions prescribed by Islam rather by nature herself according to their respective natural faculties and aptitudes.

The pivot of the activities of women is her home and her real function is to manage the domestic affairs efficiently, bring up children with such physical, mental and spiritual training that they should fear none but Allah and obey none but Allah and come forward equipped with best moral virtues, as promoters of human welfare and prosperity. They are responsible for creating such atmosphere within the four walls of the house as can help men perform their social functions prescribed by Islam, with happiness and tranquility of mind. No burden of any other social duty has been placed on the shoulders of women so that their main functions may not be hampered and the collective progress of mankind may not thereby be allowed eventually to suffer.

The association of women even in the most laudable form of congregational service, i.e., Namaz has at no time been considered as desirable. It has, on the other hand, been laid down that it is better for women to say their prayers inside their houses. Similarly men have been enjoined, in view of their natural capabilities and aptitudes to perform some other specific functions. The society can enjoy poise and equilibrium and make progress only so long as men and women perform their specified duties in their respective spheres for the furtherance and development of society. Whenever men or women attempt to step beyond their own respective spheres, except of course in emergent conditions, the society as a whole is bound to face severe disorder and disruption.

Secondly, Islam has vigorously condemned the free mixing of men and women, has regarded it to be the greatest cause of social disorder and has devised various means to ward off this evil. Despite all these limitations and restrictions the scope for permission in cases of emergency is so wide that it can meet any and every real need.

As has already been mentioned the real abode of woman is her home and the orbit of her activities is her household which in itself is of immense importance to the real development of social life. However, under unavoidable circumstances, women are allowed to take part in outdoor activities but in such a manner that all possible vices may be warded off to the utmost and at the same time there may be no difficulty in meeting the emergent needs. For instance, while on outdoor errands they are required not to adorn themselves ostentatiously, not to apply strong scent, not to walk in such manner as to make the tinkling of their ornaments audible, to walk on a side of the road, to take care to cover themselves, to talk only as much as necessary and not to adopt an attractive tone etc., etc.

The underlying idea under these principles is that women folk should not be made to bear the burden of social activities, except in conditions of urgent necessity and even then care should be taken to see that as far as possible their real functions are not interfered with or hampered, and that the evils that crop up through the free association of the two sexes are avoidable to the utmost.

Hence in the opinion of the Board, it would be preferable if women are not brought into the legislature or into the proposed larger representative body. Should it, however, be deemed indispensible in the modern circumstances, they may be made eligible for membership subject to the following two conditions:—

1. Only such women may be elected as have attained the age of fifty years; and

2. they should observe Purdah as required by Shariat.

It is also absolutely essential, according to Islam, that the following principles are fully observed:—

1. The Legislature activities should be immune from all sorts of external interventions and influences through party politics, and every Muslim after being elected as a member of the Legislature should be required to undertake in his oath of membership that he would always give his independent opinion on any matter, as a well-wisher of Islam and Pakistan and shall not be bound by any party's decision. As for non-Muslim members, they should also be required solemnly to declare that keeping in view the general interest of Pakistan and for safeguarding the legitimate interests of their community they shall always express their own independent views. It may not be out of place to mention that such provisions are to be found in the Weimar constitution also.

2. In view of the established principle of Islam that office-seekers should not be entrusted with any office, some suitable legislative measure must be adopted through legislation at the centre, to stop this malpractice and to restrain people from launching a campaign of canvassing the support of the people for their own candidature. This is necessary to minimise the chances of office-seekers getting into the legislature.

3. While there should be universal suffrage, the names of only such persons (Muslims) should be allowed to be put forth for the

membership of the legislative as possess the following qualifications;—

1. Should have adequate knowledge of the laws and requirements of Islam.
2. Should have Islamic character, i.e., should be observant of the tenets of Islam, should not be guilty of major sins and should not be openly indulgent in profligacy and dissoluteness.
3. Should not have been convicted of any moral crime.
4. Should be sound of mind and should have attained puberty. There is no fixed age limit but if any age limit, for instance 25 years is prescribed there is nothing objectionable. However, in the case of women the minimum age must be 50 years.
5. Should be a citizen of Pakistan.
6. Should be literate.

There should also be universal suffrage in the case of non-Muslims, but a non-Muslim candidate for the legislature must fulfill the following conditions:—

1. Should not have openly repudiated through writings or speeches the constitutional basis of the Pakistan State i.e. the idea of the sovereignty of Allah. This, however, has no concern with religious beliefs or forms of worship.
2. Should be of sound mind and should have attained puberty. Any age limit may also be fixed if desired. In the case of women candidates the minimum age must be 50 years.
3. Should be a citizen of Pakistan.
4. Should not have been convicted of any moral crime.
5. Should not have been indulgent in admitted forms of obscenities and vices, for instance public drunkenness, gambling and other sorts of moral etc. [*sic*] By the way, it may be worth mentioning here that similar rules and restrictions are also to be found in the constitutions of some of the Western countries. Not only this, but the commitment of such offences, in certain cases, even results in the right of citizenship being suspended.

Besides regional or territorial representation, it would also be desirable to provide for vocational representation in the Legislatures, e.g., the representation of businessmen, industrialists, agriculturists, writers, etc., etc. The inclusion of some experts as ex-officio members would also not be undesirable, but their number should not be such as to subdue the voice of the members elected by the people.

The proposed legislative council may be bicameral as has been suggested by the Sub-Committee concerned, and there is nothing in Shariat against having the members of one of the two Houses elected by direct election and of the other by indirect election. The two Houses should, however, be entrusted with the day-to-day legislation business only. There seems to be no need to have a very large body for this purpose. The present proportion of one member for every one million seems to be quite sufficient for the proposed Lower House. As for the Upper House, the number may be still less, e.g., it may be sufficient to have 40 members. However, as has been mentioned above, it seems to be essential to have a larger representative body to elect and depose the Head of the State to ask necessary questions from the Head of the State regarding the governance and administration of the country, to elect the members of the legislature and to take up the consideration of, and to represent and express public opinion regarding, such problems as are held in dispute between the Head of the State and the Federal Legislature, and also to deal with matters relating to peace treaties and declaration of war. This larger representative body can be brought into existence by two methods. For instance, any number of the members of this body may be fixed before hand and the people may elect them directly. There is nothing against taking some ex-officio members also. This very body should then take up the election of the Members of the legislature under rules to be prescribed in this behalf. Another method for the constitution of this body is that this large assembly may be composed of the members of the Central Councils (Legislative, executive, judicial and propagative and the Committee of Experts on Shariat), a suitable proportional number of the members of the legislatures of the units (in such manner as may not affect the requisite proportion of the various units at the Centre), the Committees of Experts on Shariat in the Units, the members of the Executive, judiciary and propagative Councils in the Units and also the members of the main bodies in the States which have acceded to Pakistan. Whichever of the two methods is considered more suitable may be adopted for the constitution of this larger representative body. Under the rules of the Shariat both are permissible. This body would be the largest representative Assembly of the country, something resembling the Majlis-i-Hall-o-'Aqd of the early days of Islam and would perform all such functions as have been mentioned above. In accordance with the proportion of the population, non-Muslims may also be included in this body provided that the above mentioned guarantees are duly provided for in the constitution.

This larger body must meet once in a year under the presidentship of the Head of the State. The same qualifications that have been mentioned in connection with the legislature should also be required for the membership of this body, except that the first qualification regarding knowledge may be relaxed. The remaining qualifications, especially those regarding character, should be held as equally essential for the membership of this larger assembly also.

(FOR THE CONSIDERATION OF THE MAIN PRINCIPLES COMMITTEE)

The Board have not yet received a consolidated report of the Sub-Committee on 'Federal and Provincial Constitutions and Distribution of Powers' so that they could tender their opinion clause-wise wheresoever necessary. However, an analysis of the proceedings of the meetings held at Nathiagali from June 4 to 8, 1950, brings forth the following points:

1. The Board have been asked to elucidate the basis, from the Shariat point of view, of their recommendation that the Head of the State must necessarily be a Muslim.

2. The Board have been asked to elucidate the basis, from the Shariat point of view, of their recommendation that the Head of the State must necessarily be of male sex.

3. As regards the system of Government, it has been remarked that the Board, while recommending the Presidential form of Government, have not advanced any reason, from the Shariat point of view, to prove that the Presidential form is the only right form ac-

cording to Shariat or that the Parliamentary system is against the Shariat.

4. It has been remarked that the function of the Head of the State to lead Juma and Idain congregational services is a subject which has nothing to do with the constitution.

5. The qualifications in regard to education and character, recommended by the Board as essential for the Head of the State, have been ignored.

6. The list given by the Board to show the functions of the Head of the State has almost totally been ignored.

7. The principles recommended by the Board regarding the fixation of the allowance of the Head of the State and its proportion (to the emoluments of others) have also been ignored.

8. The recommendations of the Board regarding the acceptance of gifts and presents by the Head of the State have been held as a matter of the Legislative domain and as having nothing to do with the constitution.

9. The recommendations of the Special Committee in regard to the Enabling clause and the confirmation thereof by the Sub-Committee, have rendered the 'Objectives Resolution' quite ineffective rather null and void.

10. In regard to the removal of the Head of the State, the Board recommended that it should be held permissible in cases of certain specific conditions only. This item has also been ignored.

11. The Board recommended that the Head of the State or the Head of a Unit should have the power to grant pardon, in cases of murder or of crimes not falling in the category of Hudud, subject to a certain limitations and that in cases of Hudud, none should have the power to grant pardon. All these points have altogether been ignored.

12. With regard to the constitution, powers and functions etc. of the Legislature, the recommendations of the Board have been almost totally ignored.

13. Certain special items recommended by the Board, e.g., propatative Council etc., have been altogether ignored.

The Board have been asked, expressly in regard to items 1 and 2 and in an implied manner in regard to item No. 3, to elucidate the grounds, from the Shariat point of view, on which their recommendations are based.

The procedure so far adopted by the Board has been thoroughly to examine and consider from the Shariat point of view, the material relevant to a particular matter and then to apprise the Sub-Committee concerned of the conclusions and the substance of the inquiry instead of burdening the Sub-Committee of the Constituent Assembly with all the lengthy details of the considerations and arguments leading to that conclusion.

However, as has now been specifically desired the grounds on which the Board's recommendations in regard to these items are based, are hereby elucidated.

As for the rest of the items, which in themselves are quite important from the Shariat point of view, the Board would tender their opinion as soon as the consolidated report of the Sub-Commitee has been received.

As has already been explained in the very first report of the Board, an ideological State which is founded on a definite ideology and a particular system of thought and action and has got some specific objective in view and which does not stand for 'Government for the sake of Government' but, on the contrary, which aims at the implementation of a particular system of life, cannot, obviously enough, afford to give the reins of its government in the hands of such persons as have neither any faith in, nor a knowledge of, those specific principles and that particular system of life but, on the other hand, repudiate them through their professions and practices. It is quite obvious that such a State can be run only by those who are conversant with these basic principles and who can confidently be considered to have the promotion and implementation of that ideology as the very aim of their life. To question why the duty and function of implementing and promoting the Quranic order of life cannot be assigned to persons who not only do not believe in, but rather openly repudiate, the Quranic order is, to common sense, just like asking why a capitalist, whose beliefs and actions go to repudiate the Communist ideology, cannot be entrusted with the task of running a Communist Government.

This problem does not, therefore, require any external proof whatsoever; and even if there had been no express provision in the Quran in this behalf the conclusion would have been just this and nothing else as is self-evident. For the last thirteen and a half centuries, it has been held as an accepted tenet and the Ummat have throughout been acting accordingly. However, Quran itself lays down in very clear terms as to whom the Mussalmans should obey and whom they should not, and also as to whom they should choose as their friends, associates and confidees and whom they should not. A number of verses, some expressly describing the tenet and some leading to this inference, are to be found in the Holy Quran. A few out of these are quoted below:—

1. Verses of the Quran enjoining upon the Muslims not to obey the non-Muslims, hypocrites and transgressors.

---

a) And obey not of them the transgressor or the disbeliever. (76/24)

b) And obey not the disbelievers and the hypocrites. (33/48)

c) And obey not him whose heart We have made heedless of Our rememberance, who followeth his own desire and whose case hath been abandoned. (18/28)

d) Therefore obey not thou the repudiators. (68/8)

e) And obey not thou the command of the prodigal. (26/151)

f) Oh ye who believe! If ye obey those who disbelieve, they will make you turn back on your heels, and ye turn back as losers. (3/149)

2. Verses of the Quran wherein it has been prohibited to choose non-Muslims as friends, charge-holders or confidees.

---

a) Let not the believers take disbelievers for their friends in preference to believers. (3/28)

b) Oh ye who believe! take not the Jews and the Christians for friends. They are friends to one another. He among you who taketh them for friends is (one) of them. Allah guideth not wrong-doing folk. (5/51)

c) Oh ye who believe! choose not My enemy and your enemy for friends. (60/1)

d) Be not friendly with a folk with whom Allah is wroth. (60/13)

e) Whoso taketh him for friends, he verily will mislead him and will guide him to the punishment of the Flame. (22/4)

f) Allah forbiddeth you only those who warred against you on account of religion and have driven you out from your homes and helped to drive you out, that ye make friends of them. Whosoever maketh friends of them (All) such are wrong-doers.

g) Oh ye who believe! choose not your fathers not your brethren for friends if they take pleasure in disbelief rather than faith. Who so of you taketh them for friends, such are wrong-doers. (9/23)

h) Oh ye who believe! choose not for friends such of those who received the Scripture before you, and of the disbelievers, as make a jest and sport of your religion. But keep your duty to Allah if ye are true believers. (5/57)

i) Oh ye believe! take not for confidees others than your own folk who would spare no pains to ruin you. (3/118)

The prohibition enjoined in the above verses about taking non-Muslims as friends or making them charge-holders or confidees undoubtedly implies prohibition at least regarding entrusting to a non-Muslim the charge of our affairs or making him the ultimate referee in our matters or the Head of our State, while if we actually ponder over the broad implications of the literal meaning of the word used, many a relation of even lesser significance would also be covered.

3. The verses of the Quran stating as to who should be obeyed.

a) *Oh ye who believe!* obey Allah and obey the messenger *and those from amongst you* who are in authority.

b) And if any tidings, whether of safety or fear, come unto them, they noise it abroad, whereas if they had referred it to the messenger and to such *from amongst them* as are in authority those among them who are able to find out the matter would have known it. (4/83)

4. That verse of the Quran from which all the leading Muslim Jurists and Mujtahids have unanimously reached the same conclusion (i.e. non-Muslims cannot be appointed to hold charge of affairs of Muslims and allegiance cannot be owed to them), but, it may be noted here that to infer a Shariat law requires a good deal of technical knowledge and learning.

a) And Allah will not give the disbelievers any way (of success) against the believers. (4/141)

Although the above-quoted verse is not as clear in expression as the other verses quoted under item 1, 2, and 3, and it also requires technical knowledge and learning to deduce as to what it actually signifies, it is worth noting that all the leading Muslim jurists and Mujtahids, irrespective of whatever school of thought they may belong to, have, since the very advent of Islam, always interpreted this verse to mean that in an Islamic State such offices as carry with them the final authority can not be entrusted to non-Muslims. There has never been any difference of opinion among Muslim savants (ulema) on this point. Even amongst the later ulema, a person like Allama Jamalu-ddin Afghani, notwithstanding his so-called liberal-mindedness, held this same view.

There are other verses also which lead to the same conclusion. There are also genuine sayings of the Prophet (peace be on him) in this behalf; and then there is an unbroken record of thirteen and a half centuries during which period the Ummat have always acted up to this principle.

The specific requirements of an Islamic State also make it inevitable that the Head of the State should be none else than a Muslim. From the Shariat view point a free Mussalman can recognize an individual, or a body empowered to make final decisions and issue final orders, as the final authority or symbol of allegiance, only in case that individual or body is 'Muslim.' No Muslim can be required to owe allegiance to an individual or a body that is not 'Muslim.' Rather it is not permissible for any Muslim not under any compulsion to agree to owe allegiance to such individual or body out of his own free will. In view of certain purely religious and devotional duties too it is indispensible that the Head of the State be a Muslim. For instance, according to Sunni sect, Jumma and Idain prayers must necessarily be led by the Head of the State, personally in his headquarters and through deputies (appointed by him) in other towns of the realm, and this is a condition for the validity of these congregational services. Similarly a non-Muslim Head of the State cannot collect and expend the Zakat. There are other similar functions too which a non-Muslim is incapable of performing.

Some countries adopt a hypocritical attitude by leading the world, through planned utterances and writings, to understand that any and every person residing inside the territory of the State, regardless of the fact as to which group or class or cult he belongs, is equally eligible for election to the office of the Head of the State; while as a matter of fact they neither really mean it nor does it ever become practically possible. Islam does not believe in hypocritic ways and it condemns hypocrisy with greater vehemence than even disbelief. The Muslims of Pakistan have quite a natural and legitimate desire that the Head of the State be a Muslim. This is also an express requirement of Islam and there is no room for adopting any hypocritical attitude in stating the same.

If we only just examine the attitude of other countries in this behalf it may give some satisfaction to know that this step of ours would not at all be a matter of surprise or something quite unique for the world abroad. Even if it had been so, there was no alternative for us but to adopt, in the face of the entire world, whatever is required of us by Islam, provided we wish to live as Muslims.

The stipulation that the Head of the State must be the follower of a particular religion or creed is to be found not in the constitutions of most of the Muslim countries only but also in those of England, Norway, Denmark, Sweden, Spain, Belgium and Greece. And if the actual traditions practices were to be taken into account it would become quite evident that in the countries where there are no such constitutional provisions, the real position is that the underlying intents have purposely been concealed under the veil words—a device which Islam of course would never like to be adopted—and in effect it has been practically impossible for persons belonging to a religion or creed different from that of the dominant community of the country, to get hold of the reins of government.

In England the King must be a Christian: not only that, but he should also belong to a particular sect of Christianity; and furthermore to one particular Church of that sect. The same is the case in Norway, Denmark, Sweden and Spain etc., as would be borne out from sections 4, 5, 2 and 9 respectively of the constitutions of these countries. Similar is the case in regard to Belgium and Greece. The restrictions in the Constitution of Sweden are still harder, so much so that none except those belonging to, and following the official Church can be appointed as Ministers. In Norway it is stipulated that 'more than half the number of the ministers shall profess the official religion of the State' and that whenever any problem relating to the official religion is to be discussed, the ministers not professing the official religion shall be required to leave the House.

In the Iranian Constitution it is to be found specifically stipulated that the Head of the State must be a Muslim and that he must belong to the Ithna Ashari sect. According to section 2 of the present constitution of Syria the President of the Republic must be a Muslim. Under section 58 of the Supplementary Fundamental law of Iran and under section 75 of the Constitution of Afghanistan, none except a Muslim can hold the post of a minister in these countries. As for Russia, it is common knowledge that even in the elections to the Parliament only the party consisting of the followers of the Communist creed can nominate the candidates and none but a follower of Communism can achieve the office of the Head of the State or that of a Minister.

It is also worth consideration that in different cultural and social units the factors forming the basis of discrimination are different. For instance, in America none but those born in America are eligible for the Presidentship with the result that persons permanently domiciled in America and even having acquired full rights of citizenship can never aspire for this particular office, simply because of their being born somewhere outside America. Thus they are permanently deprived of this privilege despite all other necessary qualifications. In certain other countries, e.g. Australia, South Africa, Canada, the States of South America and even in the United States of America, discriminations are maintained on the basis of colour and race (vide amendment 14, sec. 2 of the Constitution of U.S.A.; section 127 of the Constitution of Australia; section 26, 34 and 35-44 of the Constitution of South Africa).

In an Islamic Society or State such considerations as race, colour or place of birth, which are just incidental and are not of one's choice, are not recognized as significant enough to form a basis of discrimination in regard to such offices. It is rather the ideal of life adopted by an individual out of his own choice which is considered by Islam to be a factor significant enough to provide a basis for discrimination.

In this connection, it may also be profitable to examine how certain particular creeds and their adherents are being meted out special treatment in other countries, including such countries as proclaim themselves to be secular and do not profess to stand for some specific ideology.

England is populated by adherents of various religious orders, but the special patronage and the privileged position the Anglican Church enjoys as against others is a matter of common knowledge. The Archbishop of Canterbury enjoys the status of a minister.

In the Parliament, the Archbishops of Canterbury and York and other 24 bishops are taken as ex-officio members of the House of Lords and they all belong to the Anglican Church. Not to say of the Religious heads of non-Christian Englishmen, even the Catholics have no access to this House.

In undivided India, the Britishers who were Christians by faith, patronised only Christianity in spite of their proclamations of equality etc. and had set up an Ecclesiastical Department for this purpose, wherefrom the Bishops were paid their salaries officially. On the contrary, it was never deemed necessary to appoint Mufties, Imams, Shastries and Pandits for the two great major communities i.e. Hindus and Muslims inhabiting India. This was the condition in

British India. In the Indian States e.g. Kashmir, Mysore Cochin, Travancore, Bhopal, Hyderabad etc., where either a Hindu or a Muslim chief ruled the official religion was always meted out special treatment on the governmental plane. The same is the case even today in the States which have acceded to Bharat, notwithstanding the professed secular character of the Bharati Constitution.

According to article 21 of the Constitution of Burma, Buddhism enjoys a privileged position in that country.

In the Constitution of Italian Republic, under article 7, the Catholic Church enjoys sovereignty in her own domain.

Article 44 of the Constitution of Ireland lays down that 'the State recognizes the special position of the Holy Catholic Apostolic and Roman Church as the guardian of the faith professed by the great majority of the citizens.'

Article 29, 30 and 87 of the Constitution of Sweden provide that the King shall appoint the archbishops and bishops in the manner provided by the Church Law, and the Church Council in Sweden has got a special position.

Provisions to the same effect are also to be found in the Constitution of Norway (vide article 2 of the Constitution of Norway).

In accordance with article (73) (30) of the Constitution of Denmark, there is an official religion of the State which, as such, is subsidised by the State.

Under article 87 of the New Constitution of Japan, the Government helps the State religion only.

Article 6 of the Constitution of Spain provides that Catholic Religion shall enjoy official protection and that external manifestations and ceremonies of the Catholic religion alone to the exclusion of those of every other religion shall be permitted in public.

The Constitution of Argentine lays down that the Government is responsible to protect and establish the Catholic Apostolic Roman Church.

Many other similar instances could be quoted to bear out the fact that in spite of all claims of secularism, in most of the countries, rather in almost all the countries, some creed or other enjoys a specially privileged position and necessary steps are taken to meet the requirements of that particular creed.

An Islamic State, too, which is also an ideological State and which has blended religion and politics into a comprehensive order, has got its own specific requirements which needs be fulfilled. The very nature of an Islamic State and the specific requirements of the Muslim social order make it imperative that the charge of affairs should be entrusted to such persons only as may consider it to be the very aim of their life to implement the Islamic order.

Islamic Shariat does not at all mean to deprive a particular class or community of its legitimate rights or to be in any way unjust to them. But, if, in spite of all the tolerance and generous treatment stipulated by Islam in regard to non-Muslims, some class of people were to try to make us violate an express command of Allah, we simply cannot do that to appease them. Allah enjoins on us: "Beware of them lest they seduce thee from some part which Allah hath revealed into thee." (5/47)

THE HEAD OF STATE MUST BE OF MALE SEX

The Board have been asked to furnish the reasons and authorities, from the Shariat point of view, whereupon they have based their recommendation that the Head of the State must be of male sex.

The following two verses will suffice to enable one to understand the Quranic view point in regard to men and women and the superiority of the one over the other notwithstanding their equality in certain respects:—

a) "Men are in charge of women, because Allah hath made the one of them to excel the other." (4/34)

b) "And they (women) have rights similar to those (of men) over them in kindness, and men are a degree above them." (2/228)

Evidently when it has not been allowed that women folk should lead, dominate and wield ultimate authority in the domestic affairs, how can it be considered permissible in respect of the much wider domain of state politics. To ignore it is basic view point and to make a woman the final authority and thereby to reverse the relation of the obeyer and the obeyed is tantamount to a flagrant contravention of the Quranic view.

Furthermore, as it is one of the duties and functions of the Head of an Islamic State to lead Juma and Idain prayers which it is impossible for a woman to perform, the question of the charge of this office being held by a woman is out of consideration.

The provisions of Quran in regard to the evidence of women furnish a further proof of the superiority of men in such matters and this provides another reason as to why a woman cannot be entrusted with the office of the Head of the State.

"And call to witness, from among your men, two witnesses. And if two men be not (at hand) then a man and two women." (2/282)

According to *Ahadith* it is the most unfortunate day for a nation when the reins of authority go into the hands of a woman.

a) "A nation that appoints a woman as its ruler shall never prosper." (Bukhari)

b) "When the best from amongst you are your rulers, the rich from amongst you are liberal and the affairs of your State are decided upon by consultation among yourselves, then the surface of the earth is better for you than its inside. And when worst among you are your rulers, the rich among you are miserly and the affairs of your State are entrusted to women, then the inside of the earth is better for you than its surface." (Tirmidhi)

3. A perusal of pages 5 and 6 of the Board's report dated June 1, 1950 may also be of some use in this context wherein it has been clarified that such discriminatory provisions in no way imply any sort of degradation of women folk. As a matter of fact, according to Islam, it is quite inevitable for the progress and prosperity of mankind that men and women do perform their own respective functions prescribed by Islam, rather by nature herself, according to their respective faculties and aptitudes given to them by nature.

III PARLIAMENTARY OR PRESIDENTIAL FORM OF GOVERNMENT

A note on this item is being put up separately (in continuation of Board's note dated the 27th July, 1950)

Presidential or Parliamentary System of Government

The system of Government recommended by the Board is somewhat similar to the Presidential form of Government as understood in the modern terminology. The Sub-Committee concerned, on the other hand, has accordingly recommended that form of Government. It has also remarked that the Board, while recommending the Presidential form have not elucidated the relevant grounds and reasons, from the Shariat point of view, to show that the Presidential form is the only form which is conformable to Shariat or that the Parliamentary system of Government is against the rules of Shariat.

Obviously, such terms as 'Parliamentary' or 'Presidential' are not the technical terms of Shariat. Therefore, any verdict on these, given from the Islamic point of view, must be based on an examination of their imports, implications and corollaries.

As regards the Parliamentary system of Government, the following points deserve special consideration:—

1. The ultimate responsibility and accountability and the charge of affairs is entrusted to a body of persons instead of one individual.

2. The Head of the State becomes an almost entirely powerless and titular figure.

3. For the fulfillment of the specific requirements of an Islamic State or society this would be an altogether new and untried form. The Millat have never so far made any experiment of implementing the Islamic scheme of life by means of such a structure.

Throughout the thirteen and a half centuries long history of Islam it has always been an individual and not a group of persons who has held the reins of ultimate authority and has been considered as accountable before the Millat and such individual has always enjoyed effective power. Therefore no constitution purporting to be based on the fundamentals of Islam can afford to ignore the significance of this feature of our history and traditions: particularly the traditions and practices of the golden age of Islam have got a special weight and importance. It would never be advisable on our part to deviate from them and to follow the practice of those whose aims and objects of State-management are different from those of Islam, unless of course it is absolutely imperative for some unavoidable reasons.

However, if, at any time, some inevitable circumstances affecting the country or Millat necessitate the adoption of the Parliamentary system as against the proposed Presidential form, there is no express injunction laid down in the Shariat to denounce this form as such a contravention of Shariat rules.

It was due to this reason that the Board urged upon the Negotiating Committee to elucidate the reasons why the Parliamentary form of Government was considered to be necessary or preferable in the case of Pakistan. After full consideration of all the arguments put forth by the Negotiating Committee in this behalf, the Board could not feel convinced that our present needs of the country or of the Millat were really such as to make it indispensible or even preferable to adopt the Parliamentary system and thus ignore our past traditions, give up our well-tried system and to accept a form which not only militates against the practices and traditions of our classical authorities, rather of the entire Ummat, but is also quite a new and untried a method for purposes of the achievement of the aims and objects of an Islamic State and society. The Board are rather of the opinion that even our present circumstances demand that we do adopt the Presidential system of Government.

However, it is possible that opinions may differ in regard to the real requirements of the exigencies of the present day and if our Constituent Assembly feels that in the interest of the Country or Millat, it is indispensible to adopt the Parliamentary system and that if they do otherwise the country or the Millat will be involved into some unsurmountable difficulties or complications, the Board would not hold the Parliamentary system as such, as being something altogether unacceptable from Shariat point of view provided that due provision is made for certain basic principles of Islam which must be preserved at any cost.

As has already been elucidated in detail in the Board's Report dated 27-3-50 with necessary arguments and references from the point of view of the Shariat, which need not be reiterated, it is a fundamental principle of Islam that whosoever holds the reins of authority and is held as accountable to the Millat or to whom allegiance is to be owed and who wields ultimate authority must necessarily be a Muslim possessing the qualifications prescribed for the Head of the State. Therefore should it be held necessary to assign such position to a body of men and not to an individual all the members of such body without single exception must necessarily be Muslims possessing the requisite qualifications.

In view of all these considerations, if under the present conditions it is still considered inevitable in the interest of the country or the Millat to adopt the Parliamentary form, it would not, in the opinion of the Board, amount to a violation of Shariat provided the condition specified above is fulfilled, viz. that every member of the executive Council must be a Muslim possessing the requisite qualifications although the Board would not consider it desirable in view of the fact that it involves an unwarranted deviation from our classical practices and traditions and is an altogether untried form (for purposes of the fulfillment of the requirements of an Islamic State).

August 7, 1950

Index

Muslim names are listed under the most distinctive part of the name, following common usage in Pakistani newspapers and documents. For names beginning *al-*, see the second element.